THE INVENTION
OF THE SELF

Also available from Bloomsbury

Simulated Selves: The Undoing of Personal Identity in the Modern World
Andrew Spira

Aesthetics of Ugliness: A Critical Edition
Karl Rosenkranz

Art as Human Practice: An Aesthetics
Georg W. Bertram

THE INVENTION OF THE SELF

PERSONAL IDENTITY IN THE AGE OF ART

Andrew Spira

BLOOMSBURY ACADEMIC
LONDON • NEW YORK • OXFORD • NEW DELHI • SYDNEY

BLOOMSBURY ACADEMIC
Bloomsbury Publishing Plc
50 Bedford Square, London, WC1B 3DP, UK
1385 Broadway, New York, NY 10018, USA
29 Earlsfort Terrace, Dublin 2, Ireland

BLOOMSBURY, BLOOMSBURY ACADEMIC and the Diana logo are trademarks of
Bloomsbury Publishing Plc

First published in Great Britain 2020
Paperback edition published 2022

Copyright © Andrew Spira, 2020, 2022

Andrew Spira has asserted his right under the Copyright, Designs and Patents Act, 1988,
to be identified as Author of this work.

For legal purposes the Preface and Acknowledgements on p. vii constitute an extension of
this copyright page.

Cover design by Maria Rajka
Cover image: *Girl Reading a Letter by an Open Window* by Johannes Vermeer
© Archivart / Alamy Stock Photo

All rights reserved. No part of this publication may be reproduced or transmitted
in any form or by any means, electronic or mechanical, including photocopying,
recording, or any information storage or retrieval system, without prior
permission in writing from the publishers.

Bloomsbury Publishing Plc does not have any control over, or responsibility for, any
third-party websites referred to or in this book. All internet addresses given in this
book were correct at the time of going to press. The author and publisher regret
any inconvenience caused if addresses have changed or sites have ceased to exist,
but can accept no responsibility for any such changes.

A catalogue record for this book is available from the British Library.

A catalog record for this book is available from the Library of Congress.

ISBN: HB: 978-1-3500-9105-4
       PB: 978-1-3502-9817-0
       ePDF: 978-1-3500-9104-7
       eBook: 978-1-3500-9106-1

Typeset by RefineCatch Ltd, Bungay, Suffolk

To find out more about our authors and books visit www.bloomsbury.com
and sign up for our newsletters.

CONTENTS

	Preface and Acknowledgements	vii
1	The Concept of the Self	1
2	The Emergence of the Self: the Structure of the Medieval Church and Popular, Heretical and Visionary Dissensions from it	10
3	The Resurrection of the Self: Imaginative Empathy with the Suffering and Death of Christ	35
4	The Localisation of the Self: the Origins of Perspective and the Accommodation of the Self in Pictorial Space	57
5	The Necessitation of the Self: the Ennoblement of the Artist and the Invention of an Archetype	69
6	The Abstraction of the Self: the Secularisation of Subject-Matter and the Commodification of Art	88
7	The Imaginary Environments of the Self: its Physical and Intellectual Frames of Mind	109
8	The Privatisation of the Self: Fireplaces, Beds and Mirrors	142
9	The Automation of the Self: the Material Culture of Time-keeping	161
10	The Sensibilities of the Self: Courtesy, Conversation, Letter-writing and Novel-reading	172
11	The Behaviour of the Self: the Codification of Sensibility in Domestic Life	207
12	The Portrayal of the Self: Facial Expression and the Language of Personal Emotion	226
13	The Enjoyment of the Self: Sexuality and the Valorisation of Meaningless Pleasure	252
14	The Embodiment of the Self: the Awakening to Sensation	281
15	The Autonomy of the Self: the Invention of Taste and Aesthetics	298

16 The Naturalness of the Self: the Picturesque Transformation of
Nature into a Mirror of Personal Sublimity 311

17 The Consummation of the Self: the Sanctification of Art 336

18 The Seamless Garment of the Self 360

NOTES 366
BIBLIOGRAPHY 381
INDEX 392

PREFACE AND ACKNOWLEDGEMENTS

In 1968 a woman walked into a psychiatrist's sitting room complaining of nightmares during which she experienced burning. She was not alone. In the following weeks, a number of other patients appeared, reporting the same phenomenon. After long and fantastical deliberation, the psychiatrist concluded that this group of individuals, brought together by their shared experience, were reincarnations of Cathar heretics who had been burnt at the stake in the thirteenth century. It soon transpired that he was also a reincarnated Cathar, which is why they manifested to him.[1] This story intrigued me when I was a teenager – to such an extent in fact that I made a pilgrimage to the ruined site of Montségur in the south of France, where the final mass burning of Cathars took place in 1244. Outlandish though the story may be, it sparked an interest in medieval heresy in me and I began to read about the subject assiduously. The Cathars had been dualists who believed that there were two divine principles in the universe – one good, one evil – and that the evil one had jealously stolen the pure light of divinity from the good one and thrust it into matter and flesh (thereby creating the world) where he could control it; he created gender difference and lust to ensure that it would be splintered into ever smaller, more irretrievable particles. The motive of a good human being was to liberate the light of divinity from matter and to return it to the good god, aided by angels. I found the idea that angels invade the earth in raindrops especially beguiling.

At the same time, the story awakened in me an interest in the movement of history. Are historical events distant and defunct, like faded photographs that represent the unknowable dead, worthy only of curiosity and nostalgia? Or are they somehow latent in the present moment, telescoped into it as a kind of momentum – linking it to its source like the stem of a plant which transmits nutrients to the plant's fruit and flowers from the soil beneath it, while also tracing the trajectory of its growth? To address these questions, I began reading philosophers of history – from Joachim of Fiore and Hegel to Rudolf Steiner and Teilhard de Chardin – who proclaimed that history is the evolutionary medium through which the purposes of God are unfolded into, and as, the world. From their perspective, a human life was not simply a temporal circumstance in which experiences of a 'spiritual' nature may or may not happen; it was itself a spiritual experience, a vision of the divine order, extended in time. The timeless truth about reality – whatever it might be – invaded the world not merely in raindrops but in every atom and act. Such passionate thoughts I had, and I began making notes.

However, while the vision of historical time as a kind of 'sacrament of eternity' was compelling, it had fatal flaws. Firstly, it had nothing convincing to say about the origin of time and so was 100 per cent speculative (and could never be otherwise).

And secondly, it clearly remembered, selected and organised the data of history in keeping with its own agenda. Moreover, it made no allowance for the notion that history might not be a grand line with an overarching purpose advancing from beginning to end; it might equally well be like a stretch of felt, made of innumerable multidirectional linear fibres, all stopping and starting, compacted together into an inchoate mass. So the allure of the visionary theory and an awareness of its fundamental inadequacy sat side by side, unmixed, like oil and water. I put my notes in a drawer.

Twenty years later, I was attending my first meeting in a new teaching post, at which colleagues were discussing who would give which lecture in the coming term. When the subject of French Rococo Furniture came up, there was ghastly silence. Eventually, when the silence became unbearable – and partly to show willing – I volunteered to give the lecture myself. All the dogs in my soul howled in protest. I had avoided the rococo period for years because I perceived it to be superficial and elitist, and it bored me. But this was an ignorant prejudice and the encounter turned out to be revelatory; indeed it was the agent that made it possible for what had hitherto seemed like oil and water to merge. For by shifting the focus of attention away from abstract ideas that seemed to exist on their own, towards the primacy of sensation without which it is impossible to develop the language with which we understand ideas, the rococo style and its contexts revealed the extent to which our ideas are a reflection of our capacity to develop ideas and indeed of our capacity to be selves. Exploring these issues by studying Condillac's treatises on the status of sensation and the origins of language, before reading his later commentators, was like eating off Sèvres porcelain. A penny dropped. The perceived coherence of history was not so much a characteristic of the evidence of which it was made as a projection of the self-sense that processed it. Any pretensions to determinism that seemed to link history to a higher principle or rationale were suddenly seen to be rooted in the solipsistic logic of self-reference. The element of autonomy and necessity that is perceived to be characteristic of the notion of objectivity was no longer as incompatible with the palpable impossibility of objective history as it had seemed to be. Making allowance for the hidden role of the self-sense in the construction of history, it became clear that it was *as if* history was objective. Out came my notes from their drawer; this project could continue its journey. This book – on the historical emergence of the self-sense – is the first of its two parts. The second part – on the demise of the self-sense – is published in a separate, complimentary volume, *Simulated Selves: The Undoing of Personal Identity in the Modern World*.

Needless to say, many people have helped me along the way in numerous different capacities. Carlotta Berger and William Anderson were instrumental in the earliest stages, as were Jinty Nelson and Diana Webb at King's College London. Joy Law made many constructive suggestions. Helen Brunner, Malgorzata Sady, Antony Buxton, Carl Gombrich, John Milner, David King, Patrick Walsh, Stuart Proffitt, Sally Holbrook and Tim Hyman all provided help in various ways, from engaging in heated conversation to providing new references. Conversations with students over many years have also provided a highly fertile soil and I thank them all for tilling it with me. Petra Cramsie devoted many long hours to reading, and writing all over, early drafts of the 'lytel bok', and I am immensely grateful to her. The abundant use of reproductions was always intended to be an integral part of the project, partly to make the book more accessible but also to demonstrate the primary role of images, objects and environments in the development of human values (one of the book's key arguments). But the sourcing of images is a laborious and expensive process and their ample provision here would have been impossible without the generous contributions of Jaime and Connie Gonzales, Jeremy Walsh and the Duke of Buccleuch (KT, KBE). Warm thanks to you all. I would also like to express my gratitude to picture librarians all over the world for their patience and cooperation. The production process is also a painstaking one and I would like to thank Liza Thompson, Frankie Mace, Lucy Russell and others at Bloomsbury for helping the book emerge into the light of day. Finally, huge thanks are due to my friends and family, for their unflagging patience, support and belief in the project over many years.

CHAPTER ONE

The Concept of the Self

The Invention of the Self is about the way in which personal identity – the sense of 'I' or 'me' – is culturally constructed in our lives. It proposes that the sense of self that currently prevails in the westernised world does not exist as an absolute phenomenon in its own right but that it is created and supported by cultural conventions. By highlighting the extent to which those conventions are subject to historical conditions, the book suggests that the formation of personal identity is itself subject to historical conditions, and it charts its rise.

An awareness of the provisional nature of personal identity is often expressed on abstract theoretical grounds, and the concept is sometimes relativised in relation to other 'denominations' of identity – religious, national, social and sexual. Nevertheless, despite such theorising, it is frequently overlooked that the very fabric of daily life – the way we experience the world in every moment – is radically programmed around the presumption of a *personal* self – the notion of 'I', *prior* to the attribution of 'qualities' (British, atheist, female etc.). Indeed, despite intellectual acknowledgement of the instability of personal identity, it is arguable that belief in its existence has become so deeply naturalised in our lives that it has become unnoticeable to us. Even when our *ideas* suggest an awareness of its expedience, it is rarely observed how, at a practical level, a sense of personal self pervades (or seems to pervade) our lives at a subliminal, sub-conscious level, radically informing and structuring the ways in which we sleep, eat, speak, travel, work, dress, socialise, entertain ourselves, think and feel.

Moreover, it is not only the material circumstances of personal identity that are culturally constructed – as if the self exists independently of them; it is also the frames of mind that these circumstances facilitate and support. That is to say, our subjective capacity to experience the world is also subject to the psychological infrastructures that are available to us at any given time. Thus although we may feel free to experience 'meaning', 'pleasure' and 'beauty' whenever they seem to present themselves to us – this freedom is surely one of the most definitive properties of selfhood – it is arguable that even our capacity to have these experiences is determined by cultural conditions. For how would it be possible to experience these phenomena if the discourses that accommodate and propagate them (linguistically and psychologically) did not exist? Of course, this is not to say that, prior to the evolution of the notion of the self, people did not 'have experiences'. It is simply to suggest that those experiences did not arise and cohere in consciousness as expressions or functions of a personal *self* – as personal experiences of 'meaning', 'pleasure' and 'beauty'; they appear to have been identified as functions of some other frame of reference, in relation to extraneous criteria – for instance, as demonic temptation, divine grace or the influence of the stars. Nor does the notion that 'our capacity to experience is conditioned' necessarily suggest that *consciousness* is subject to conditions. Indeed, it is conceivable that although *experience* presupposes a subject – the 'I' that experiences – *consciousness* does not, and that consciousness *as such* is not 'experienced' – at least not by a 'self'.

The fact that the parameters of personal identity (and the possibilities of experience that are implicit in them) are conditioned is not necessarily limiting; there is no reason why they should be – just as there is no reason why a wealthy multi-linguist should be more free and happy than an impoverished mono-linguist, even though the possibilities of experience (and, therefore, of self-definition) that are afforded to him by his circumstances appear to be greater. In some senses, conditions simply form part of the circumstances of life – like the colour of one's eyes, or the fact that we blink, or that our blood flows through our veins at a certain speed – and it would be absurd to seek to be 'free' from such conditions; indeed, at that level, one could argue that a rich man is not 'free' – while he is rich – to experience poverty. Moreover, with regard to health, personal distinctiveness – as a sign of 'freedom from conventions' – is positively undesirable, as the more one departs from the norm the more unhealthy one is likely to be. Nor does the conditioning of personal identity always have to have negative connotations, as the words 'selfish' and 'egotism' suggest. On the contrary, in itself it is neutral. It can certainly lead to unhappiness and disillusionment – if its agendas are frustrated – but it can also give rise to the most sublime products of human civilisation. Moreover, it plays a key role in the 'theatre of human relationships' and, in several areas – for instance with regard to laws and customs – it is surely necessary for social cohesion. Even so, whatever the outcome of cultural conventions and conditioning may be, if we take the sense of self that is implicit in them to be an absolute and immortal truth, oblivious to the cultural contexts that give it substance and significance, we are likely to become as confused as we would be if we aspired to meet a fictional character from a film in the real world.

Each of us knows, in a conventional sense, who we think we are. For instance, if someone sticks a pin into my hand, I notice that it hurts *me*, whereas if they stick it into a chair I feel nothing. Similarly, I can remember experiences that *I* have had in the past but I cannot remember experiences that *other people* have had. Broadly speaking, we identify with our bodies and our minds: we are born, we experience, we think, we feel, we die. But, if I actually analyse the experience of 'pain' or 'memory' in the moment in which it happens, the manner in which I know it to be happening to *me* is by no means clear; however much I may pursue it with my mind, that to which the words 'I' and 'me' refer remains ever-elusive. In a social and practical context, it is understandable that an individual should trace the instinctive impulses of his or her body to survive and prosper to a principle of self-determination. But, if one goes beyond expediency and investigates the evidence on its own terms, the existence of a 'self' becomes much harder to ascertain.

This is something that we can explore on the basis of our own experience. For instance, most people talk to themselves. Some of these verbalised thoughts are consciously applied to the circumstances of life in a practical and purposeful way but others are random and inconsequential. Regarding the latter type, people say such things to themselves as: 'I think I'll have a cup of tea' or, more self-critically, 'now look what you've done!' etc. This habit may seem innocuous, but it raises significant questions about the notion of personal identity and its relationship to language. Nominally, the purpose of language is to communicate, and this is obviously the way that it is used between people; but observations of *conversations with oneself* suggest that communication is not always its function. It is often the case, for instance, that when we speak to ourselves, we are highly repetitive. This is especially noticeable when we are being critical of ourselves. We do not simply say: 'now look what you've done!'; we say: 'now look what you've done, why did you do that?! I knew that would happen! I'm so fed up with you, you're such an idiot!' and so on. The implication here is that the words are not spoken purely for the sake of their content, which could be communicated by expressing the sentence only once. The grammatical coherence, conversational tone and apparently meaningful content of such internal statements may give them a superficial resemblance to ordinary external communication between people and make them seem social in some sense; but the fact that they are often so banal, repetitive and semi-unconscious – and, therefore, not very effective as communication – suggests that they also serve some other purpose. Moreover, it is especially significant that we cannot *stop* talking to ourselves even if we want to, or be in full control of the contents of our thoughts. The unstoppability and uncontrollability of our thinking indicates not only that it is as much (if not more) the *activity* of mentation as the *content* of mentation that preoccupies us, but also that we may not be as free to operate as independent selves as we like to think. Thus, although our internal dialogues may seem to serve as sincere expressions of our thoughts and desires, they also seem to arise in spite of us. We do not always choose to have them and, if their content is anything to go by, they do not seem to serve an important practical purpose. Furthermore, considering that these conversations seem to take place within a single person, the question inevitably arises: when I talk to myself, who exactly is the 'I' that speaks – referring to him- or herself as 'I' – and who is the 'you' that is being addressed? A dialogue of a kind is implicitly taking place, but *who* is talking to *whom*? The verbal form of the thought, implying communication, suggests that at least two 'people' are present – a speaker and a listener – but surely these 'people' cannot be the same person . . . for is it not illogical to ask or tell oneself things that, being oneself, one already knows? If I am aware that I would like a cup of tea, do I need to inform myself of the fact? Do I not already know it? Could I not simply take the necessary action without endlessly talking to myself about it? Thus, despite believing myself to be an integrated self, I talk to myself as if I am composed of several 'people'. These reflections are basic but they expose a fundamental inconsistency in the way we construct our 'selves': on the one hand, thoughts are expressed on behalf of an integrated nameable self and, therefore, seem to be 'my' thoughts; on the other hand, the fact that they are spoken in words, which are designed to communicate between people, suggests a degree of internal fragmentation.

Moreover, if one explores the question of personal identity directly, using one's own present experience as evidence (instead of logical deduction), and actually allows one's attention, in a purely practical way, to gravitate towards that which seems to refer to itself as 'I' (when speaking *as* itself) or 'you' (when speaking *to* itself), the results are no more conclusive. Even if it was possible to trace the source of the 'I' that thinks thoughts, what would be the source of the 'I' that is motivated to pursue such an enquiry? Ironically the very form of the enquiry – the thinking process itself – mitigates against the possibility of finding an answer to this question for the simple reason that, regardless of its content, the thinking process presupposes the identity of the thinker, and thereby imposes the parameters of selfhood on whatever it addresses. Indeed, it is arguable that it is for this very reason – to *avoid* realising that which precedes the self-sense, and therefore to avoid rendering the self redundant – that we engage in chronic internal dialogues. Although such dialogues may seem to function as sincere expressions of our thoughts and desires, it is also plausible that their more hidden purpose is simply to realise and articulate a sense of personal identity, perpetually seeking to prove its existence by presenting it to itself in every moment. For without the medium of language, how else can the sense of a 'self' be known? and how else does it exist? Moreover, because verbal language is inherently informed by a dualistic structure (the subject and object of communication), there is a case for suggesting that the self engages in it, regardless of its content, in order to appropriate the dualism that informs it, and thereby to perpetuate both itself, as a subject, and the objects that necessarily seem to complement it. By projecting the narrative of subject and object on to the spontaneous process of mentation, we also seem (despite the contradictions) to appropriate responsibility for thinking, further identifying and empowering our 'selves' – as the authors of our thoughts. That is to say, by engaging in language, we activate the semantic associations of selfhood – 'in the beginning was the word' – and 'reverberate' throughout our world.

Thus, although language is primarily considered to be a means of communication and appears to have evolved for that purpose, it is also engaged as a means of self-affirmation and self-understanding, albeit in the guise of self-communication – that is to say, as a continuous attempt to process the experience of life and integrate it into a unified sense of self. The sense of a personal self, therefore, is instituted in the structure of language; it can find itself inherently present in that structure precisely because the logic of language is its own logic, evolving directly from itself in keeping with its needs and capacities. Language is the medium of the personal self because it provides it with a unique means of self-reference. By subscribing to language, therefore, we subscribe to the structures and logic of personal identity. Conversely, to the extent that we are identified as a 'self', we are merely a performance of the possibilities latent in language. The fact that 'I talk to myself' does not, therefore, presuppose that there *is* an 'I' and an 'other', as the communicative function of words would suggest (and as Descartes concluded with his 'I think therefore I am'), but simply that thinking is happening – as it were, impersonally, like blinking. From this perspective, the 'I-thought' arises because the activity of thinking subscribes to the principles and characteristics of the medium in which it occurs or through which it is filtered (verbal language) and the object/subject polarisation that is implicit in that medium.

The symbiotic relationship between personal identity and language is especially clear in relation to words for the simple reason that the only referents that are specifically intended to refer to personal identity *are* words: 'self' and 'identity'; the personal pronouns ('I', 'me', 'you', 'he', 'she' etc.) and the possessive adjectives ('mine', 'yours', 'his', 'hers' etc.). In fact, all words, whether they make specific reference to personal identity or not, tacitly presume the existence and legitimacy of the notion of selfhood because, as we have seen, they imply communication between a subject and object. This principle could be extended to all language – not just verbal language, but all forms of communication. And it is in this all-inclusive capacity that language will be understood in the present context; that is, as *any medium that communicates*. Language, in this broad sense, appears in a multitude of different forms. Some forms of language, such as words and signs, have no innate meaning but are specifically *created* to communicate. Some, such as symbolic images, are *adapted* to communicate; doves, for instance, are not *created* to communicate peace but they can be *adapted* for use in this way. And others are merely *understood* to communicate, without having been either created or adapted for this purpose. The latter case covers all objects that have acquired *associations* – for instance, the sound of rain which, besides unintentionally communicating that 'it is raining', can also communicate a range of moods, by association. This non-deliberate form of communication also includes all identifiable objects *per se*, as the characteristics of a physical object that enable us to identify it as an object – and not merely to experience it as an undifferentiated mass of perceptions – appear to be *communicated* to us. At this level, all forms of experience and cognition – from abstract thoughts and feelings, to perceptions and sensations of objects – could be seen to involve the mediation of language to the extent that they are invested with meaning and are seen to be communicative of that meaning. A phenomenon's status as an element of language, therefore, arises not so much from its innate characteristics as from its *capacity to be invested with communicable meaning* – its capacity to be *used* as language.

Language, in this broad sense, is the medium through which the indeterminacy of experience is made meaningful or significant. While its applications are of course infinite, its unifying principle – that which brings unity to all its communications – is singular; it is its *user* or *subject* – a self-sense. Having said this, the self is not simply the detached *user* of language – existing independently of it, and prior to it – it is itself a *product* of language, only existing to the extent that it communicates itself to itself in any given moment; it is *formed* by the language which it uses to identify itself, and by the phenomena which it identifies (with the help of language) as objects. It is arguable that this subtle process of 'looping' self-communication is latent in all its cognitions, and therefore seems to be continuous – simply because all moments of cognition presuppose differentiation, which in its turn presupposes interpretation and language. Of course, these cognitions are too infinitesimal and subliminal to be observed individually, and, therefore, the sense of self that they support is too subliminal to be identified as such. But many of the components of verbal and cultural languages are at least visible and it is, therefore, possible for us to probe the sense of self that they seem to accommodate.

Verbal language is especially well equipped to communicate aspects of personal identity because it is itself a direct product of the self-sense and is, therefore, perfectly calibrated to mediate the self, and vice versa. But while words are better suited than any other medium to the representation of abstract ideas, the fact that they are directly produced by the human mind ensures that they are innately subjected to its capacity for self-awareness, and are, therefore, liable to represent it in keeping with its own self-image – that is, as it is inclined, or able, to see itself. Verbal analyses cannot, therefore, be trusted as definitive accounts of the state of the self at any given period any more than a man's description of himself – whether of his character or his state of health – can be taken to be an authoritative account of himself. In fact, just as a man's random comments and habits may be more revealing of his nature than his self-conscious autobiography, so the accidental material culture of a period may say more about contemporary notions of selfhood than its self-conscious attempts to describe those notions. It is for this reason that *The Invention of the Self* focuses on personal identity and its relationship to cultural language as a whole rather than to verbal language alone. Moreover, the book makes little reference to recent theoretical discourse. This is partly due to the fact that theoretical perspectives on the self have already been analysed very extensively elsewhere over many years; but also, more pointedly, it is because the book presents the self-sense as being contingent on cultural processes (both material and mental) rather than as a philosophical object. Indeed, besides *describing* the historical emergence of the self-sense, the book also attempts to represent it, or *demonstrate* it, by presenting the story in such a way that the 'self-agenda' implicit in it is elicited or made apparent – *without* having to theorise it. Thus although it does take verbal analyses of personal identity into consideration, it prioritises the conventions of material culture – including ordinary utilitarian objects, environments and behaviour – precisely because they are less self-conscious and subject to censure than words, and therefore, arguably, more revealing.

Chief among these conventions is 'art'. The book's approach to the notion of 'art' is radical. It is usually taken for granted that 'art' has an undoubtable, and even absolute, cultural value that can be traced back to the origins of human civilisation; it is in support of this assumption that it seems natural for us to talk about 'prehistoric art', 'ancient Egyptian art' and 'medieval art' – regardless of the fact that these phenomena pre-date the evolution of the concept of 'art'. Despite this inconsistency, *The Invention of the Self* acknowledges that what we currently call 'art' functions for us as an expression of the impulse to explore, understand, celebrate and communicate the 'experience of life' in some way. Especially since the rehabilitation of highly stylised imagery in the late nineteenth and early twentieth centuries – after four hundred years of illusionistic 'naturalism' – even ancient images can be made to function as the most exquisite and profound expressions of that 'artistic' impulse, regardless of their very different original purposes; indeed the aesthetic effect, apparent self-expressivity and proto-modernism of such images are among the reasons that they now appeal to us. But to seek (and find) such qualities in them is anachronistic, sometimes to the point of misunderstanding and falsification. So why do we do it? What are we doing when we reconfigure objects in such a way that we can relate to them as 'art'? This book suggests that such 'pre-artistic' images and objects are often seen and made to function as 'art', or at least as 'aesthetic culture', not on their own account but in order to feature in, and perpetrate, the 'theatre of personal identity' – that is to say, for *our* sakes, in order to enable *us* to dramatise *our* own self-narratives through them retrospectively. Indeed it argues that the concept of art co-evolved with the sense of personal self in the fifteenth and sixteenth centuries, enabling the self-sense to realise itself through it – initially through patronising, making and appreciating it but eventually (from the nineteenth century) by applying the *concept* of art to any cultural material, from any time or place, that it felt inclined to use in this way. What we call 'art' therefore functions at two levels. On the one hand, it is a *conscious expression* of the creative impulses of mankind – both on the part of its makers and on the part of its viewers and users (both original and later); this is the reason we seek to engage with it. But on the other hand, it is an *unconscious manifestation* of a self-sense that is individuated and separate, existing prior to the felt need to express itself. Indeed it is arguably *on account of this tacit and more fundamental sense of separation* that the uniquely human need to 'explore, understand, celebrate and communicate the experience of life' arose – and arises – in the first place. It is the way that artistic culture unconsciously manifests a separate and self-referential sense of self – *reflecting its independent existence* – rather than the way it consciously expresses the longing of the separate self to redress that apparent separation, that this book aims to expose.

With regard to its historical and geographical scope, *The Invention of the Self* focuses on western European culture from the Middle Ages (approximately the twelfth century) until the end of the eighteenth century, as this is the culture and period – or so it is suggested here – in which the discourse of personal identity, in its present form, first evolved and acquired currency. In taking this position, it does not mean to suggest that notions of identity did not exist in other places and at other times – that would be absurd. Some incipient sense of personal identity is surely innate in the conceptual mind and language altogether; indeed – to the extent that such things can be known – it presumably co-evolved with them. Moreover, it is arguable that all forms of monotheistic religion – from the ancient veneration of a transcendental deity to the incarnation of God as an individual human being – reflect and objectify a degree of personal selfhood. Nevertheless the *concept* of the self took many centuries, and even millennia, to evolve.

Although the earliest Greek philosophers – the pre-Socratics – articulated a concept of the *soul*, they did not associate it with a sense of *self*. They considered it to be a function of physical nature, made up of the elemental materials of which the universe itself was made – for instance, air, yielded from the body for the last time at the moment of *expiry*; or fire, which kept the breath and body warm until the moment of death. Despite some suggestive precedents, it is Plato who is usually credited with the notion that the soul is immaterial, paving the way for its immortality, and – by virtue of its equivalence with ideas (which were also thought to be immortal) – that it is the seat of mental functions. Having said this, although Plato articulated a sense of the moral and rational nature of the soul, he did not discuss his *own* soul (thereby *practising* self-reflexivity); he put his words into the mouth of his teacher and alter ego, Socrates. It was St Augustine who first institutionalised the practice of self-examination – in his *Confessions* of AD 397/8 in which he scrutinised his *own* soul and gave direct voice to his *own* experience. It was arguably the discourse of Christianity that enabled him to do this, for by seeming to incarnate himself in human form, the God of the Christians implicitly invited each individual to engage with him *personally*, and in an embodied capacity, thereby quickening the 'soul' into a personal 'self'. Indeed it is arguable that it was precisely this valorisation of the body, and its possibilities of action and volition, that enabled Augustine to identify himself as a personal 'self' to the extent that he did. Having said this, Augustine did not view the self-sense as a wholesome and independent entity; on the contrary it was fundamentally flawed on account of original sin, and therefore thoroughly dependent on grace. While it was the seat of rationality in man, it was also a problematic and incomplete phenomenon, the sign and cause of man's separation from God. Arguably it was not until the late Middle Ages that the notion of the autonomous self began to establish itself on its own terms.

The book covers the notion of the personal self from its inception until its consummation at the end of the eighteenth century. It proposes that the self-sense emerged among the elite between the thirteenth and fifteenth centuries, as reflected in the personalisation of Christian devotion, the development of naturalism in painting, the emergence of the notion of 'art', the secularisation of subject-matter in painting and the 'civilising' of personal behaviour. In the seventeenth century, the self-sense became explicit and consciously self-referential, informing an ever-changing sequence of cultural conventions as it did so, especially in relation to the commodification of domestic space, and the expression of personal feeling. It was not, however, until the end of the eighteenth century that it reached its apogee, as reflected in the formation of the archetype of the independent artist (no longer subject to the agendas of elite patrons), the legitimisation of the experiences of pleasure and sensation, the development of the discourses of taste and aesthetics, and the naturalisation of personal emotion. It was at this point that a sense of personal self became infused into the consciousness of society as a whole, and mechanisms of self-reference became embedded in the fabric of the culture. Although the self-sense could be experienced openly, if vicariously, through the practice of art appreciation (made newly possible for members of the 'public' through the establishment of public institutions, such as museums), it also infiltrated everyday conventions to the point at which it was no longer noticed. Like food that is consciously tasted and savoured before being absorbed beyond awareness into the metabolism of the body, so the fresh *taste* of the new concept was eventually superseded by its imperceptible but pervasive *effect*.

The reach of the book also has geographical limitations. It focuses on European culture, not because notions of identity did not exist beyond the confines of Europe but because the self-sense is innately self-referential and, to the extent that it was conceived within the parameters of medieval Catholic Christendom – where our story begins – it sought the sources of its legitimacy within that tradition; that is to say, it reinforced itself by developing and perpetuating mechanisms of self-reference and naturalising them as cultural conventions. St Augustine, for instance, had considered the tri-partite activity of mental self-reference that, he believed, constituted the mind – in which the 'object of perception', 'act of perception' and 'will to perceive' are *one* – to be an image of the Christian Trinity. The self-sense subsequently perpetrated itself within this frame of reference – firstly as Christian/European and then as European – remaining ignorant, and dismissive, of other traditions for several centuries.

Furthermore, it is arguable that the technological ambitiousness and precociousness of Europe reflected a unique belief in the possible autonomy of the 'objective' world that subtly corroborated a corresponding belief in the possibility of autonomous 'subjectivity', which thrived in Europe accordingly. Conversely it has been argued that it was the latent impulse towards autonomous subjectivity in Europe that drove its societies to objectify their world by automating it industrially, thereby enabling that subjectivity to find itself more effectively realised in it. As early as the eighteenth century, adherents to this view believed that it was the absence of this inner impulse in China that caused that empire to stagnate technologically (in favour of political stability), after centuries of inventiveness. Either way, the innate vitality of the 'subjective' world and the apparently automatic functionality of the 'objective' world can be seen to have evolved in Europe in conjunction with each other.

Thus, while the book acknowledges the diverse modes of identity-formation that have existed throughout human history, it does not presuppose that a concept that evolved and became universally taken for granted in a particular culture at a particular time – like that of the modern self-authenticating 'self' – can be applied abstractly to all cultures at all periods; nor can its vocabulary and associations. On the contrary, to do this would already be to ignore the way in which cultural values and concepts are organically determined, validated and invested with meaning by the circumstances that generate and sustain them. As a result, the book focuses not on the personal self as 'a reality in itself', but on the way in which it became established as a psychological convention, and acquired cultural and social value. It addresses the notion of identity precisely as it is reflected in the cultural forms that are coterminous with it, and not as an abstraction that is presumed to exist independently of, and prior to, those forms. It contends that cultural forms both reflect the dynamics of identity in its various states of formation and serve as agents for its further evolution, thereby facilitating and determining new experiences of selfhood. As such, cultural forms and personal identity are two sides of the same coin; to the extent that it is possible to discuss them as independent phenomena at all, the former (forms that are invested with cultural value and communicative potential) are a direct living embodiment and realisation of the latter (the sense of personal identity) which does not, and cannot, exist without them. On this basis, it will be suggested that the possibilities of experience are determined by the capacity of the cultural forms of any given period to realise and accommodate them, and, therefore, that personal identity is as much a performance of the possibilities latent in the 'language' of culture as it is a free expression of independent 'selves'. What precedes the formation of personal identity cannot be known – at least not by personal identity.

CHAPTER TWO

The Emergence of the Self: the Structure of the Medieval Church and Popular, Heretical and Visionary Dissensions from it

While the dynamics of personal identity can be seen to have developed in different social contexts at different times, it is broadly arguable that the *origins* of personal identity can be traced back to as early as the twelfth or thirteenth century when the first signs of the valorisation of personal experience began to appear, albeit among an elite minority. Prior to this shift, the notion of identity tended to be communalised and invested in the Church, in the sense that it was through participation in the life of the Christian community, which revolved around the Church, that the wholeness of individuals, only fully realised in their salvation after death, was possible. It was commonly accepted that, without the grace of God, salvation simply could not happen; damnation was inevitable. On the one hand, the Fall of Adam had tainted mankind with original sin; on the other, the suffering and death of Christ on the cross had initiated the redemption of mankind, in which human beings could participate by leading a life of Christian virtue, as prescribed by the Church.

There were many ways in which the faithful could receive the unique and necessary blessings of the Church. The most important was to partake of the sacraments – especially the Eucharist, the sacrament of communion, believed to have been instituted by Christ at the Last Supper. During the course of this historic meal Christ had instructed his apostles to 'eat his body' and 'drink his blood', in the form of consecrated bread and wine, in remembrance of him. To participate in communion was to ingest the transformative reality of God. It was also believed that Christ had instituted the Church and priesthood through which the sacraments were to be administered. The significance of communion – and the power of the Church that administered it – reached its apogee, and became absolute, in the theory of transubstantiation. This theory – which became formal doctrine at the Fourth Lateran Council in 1215 – stated that the sacramental bread and wine were not mere symbols of God but that they were actually transformed into the physical body and blood of Christ at the moment of consecration; they actually *became* God, a unique and miraculous physical embodiment of his sanctity. To partake of the Eucharist therefore was to partake directly of the substance of God. Although personal experiences of God were becoming increasingly acceptable to the Church at this period, any attempts to achieve a direct link with Christ that was independent of its sacramental mediation were regarded as heresy.

The Church's monopoly of divine communion was consolidated by the doctrine of papal infallibility, which developed in the fourteenth century. This doctrine taught that, by virtue of his holy office (which descended directly from St Peter), the pope was constitutionally incapable of making incorrect pronouncements on matters of faith. Through the sacrament of ordination (the initiation of priests), the unique authority and efficacy of 'sacred office' was extended to the entire priesthood. The theory decreed that it was the blessed status of their role, rather than their personal virtue, that gave priests the power of transmission, enabling them to administer the sacraments. Moreover, in the twelfth century, the practice of daily communion 'in two kinds' (i.e. using both bread *and* wine) had been withdrawn from the laity (partly on the grounds that they were unworthy of it) and reserved for the celebrating priest or 'vicar' who subsequently communed on their behalf, requiring them to commune 'vicariously' through him. The laity received the Eucharist (often 'in one kind', i.e. just the bread) between one and three times a year – at Easter, Pentecost and Christmas. Although the Eucharist was increasingly being theorised as absolutely necessary for salvation, it was also being withdrawn from the congregation.

The outcome of these developments was that the Church came to monopolise access to salvation, and the priesthood became exclusively empowered to mediate it. This newly formulated authority was further enshrined in the first significant attempt to synthesise the legal precepts of the early medieval Church into a coherent and consistent corpus of canon (church) law. The result was a legal textbook, the *Concord of Discordant Canons* or *Decretals*, which consisted of a rationalised compilation of texts drawn from a wide range of authorities, including Roman law, the Bible, the teachings of the Church Fathers, decrees from ecclesiastical councils and papal decrees. It was produced by a Bolognese jurist called Gratian in around 1150 and it superseded the thoroughly inconsistent and often contradictory legal practices that had hitherto prevailed throughout the Church. Above all, it systematised and objectified the authority of the Church, establishing it on a legal basis that served to put it beyond the realm of human subjectivity. The absolute autonomy of its power was finally realised in relation to the paradoxical problem of popes who were perceived to have sinned. In response to this awkward possibility, canon lawyers developed the notion, bristling with legal complexities and qualifications, that because popes were infallible and, therefore, 'unable to sin', popes that *had* actually sinned were deposed, not by human agency, but 'by the law itself'. In this way, jurists managed to abstract the authority of the Church and to autonomise it, investing it in an unassailable principle with its own power to judge and act.

The process through which the Church strove to refine and perfect the principle of its own identity was continuous. When unforeseen problems arose out of the implications of its solutions to other questions – such as the possibility of a sinful pope – it preferred to 'clarify' the meanings of its traditional theological sources in order to 'reveal' answers that were 'implicit' in them, than to invent new answers. Especially following the formulation of the doctrine of transubstantiation, all manner of challenging questions arose. For instance, what should one do if a sick person vomits after taking the sacrament, or if a mouse eats a consecrated host (Fig. 2.1)? Regarding the mouse, St Bonaventure (1221–74) stated that the creature's spiritual unreceptivity would spontaneously prevent the consecrated bread from remaining 'as Christ' in its stomach – it would simply become physical bread – and, therefore, that it was impossible for a mouse to defile the sacrament. The trouble with this theory was that

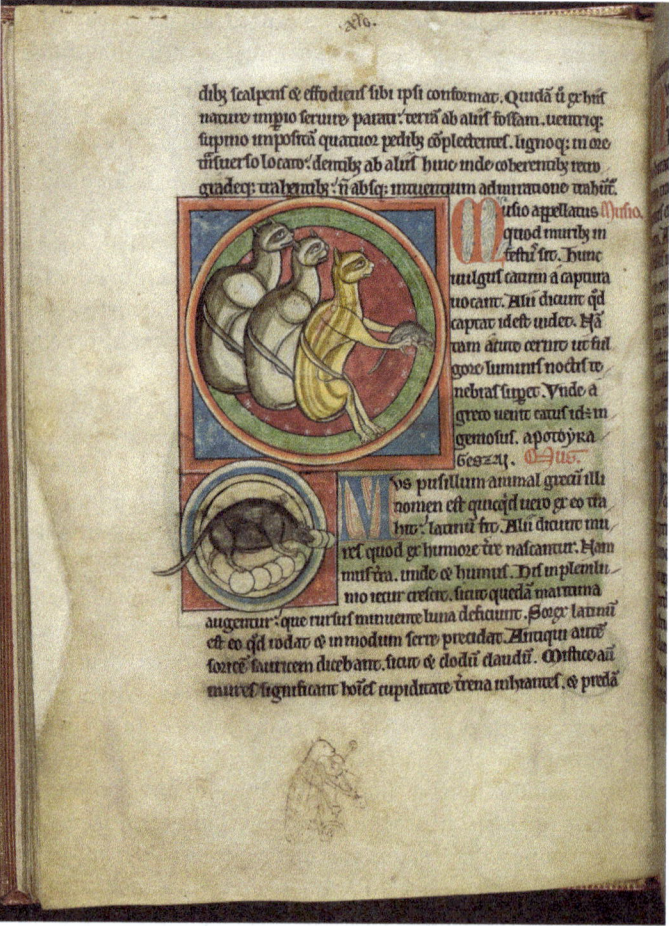

FIGURE 2.1: Three cats capturing a mouse and a mouse eating eucharistic wafers. From a medieval bestiary. England (Salisbury), 2nd quarter of the 13th century. Harley MS 4751, f. 30v. British Library, London.

it also suggested that the priest's consecration of the sacrament was conditional, and that the efficacy of the sacraments depended, to some extent, on the moral disposition of the recipient, thus undermining the absolute power of the priesthood, the Church and the sacrament itself. This implication was unacceptable. An alternative solution – that offending mice should be caught and burned and that their ashes should be washed down the *piscina* (a basin near the altar used for washing the communion vessels) – protected belief in the absolute sanctity of the sacrament and the priesthood but raised its own practical problems: what if one could not catch the mouse?

Theologians worked hard to adapt their descriptions of the Eucharist to accommodate these new subtleties. Above all, their priorities were 1) to express their belief in the sanctity of the sacrament and 2) to be consistent within themselves – in order not to contradict or relativise the principle of authority that constituted the identity of the Church. In a modern context, some of their arguments seem absurd. But, to judge them according to their philosophical value is to miss the point. Whether they are absurd or not, their importance lies in the common belief that underpins them: that the sacrament is absolutely holy and that its dignity must be preserved at all costs. This process of continuously refining the theology of the sacrament was a kind of extended ritual meditation on the sanctity of the sacrament itself. The differences between theologians were secondary; their primary purpose was simply to serve as a pretext for the ongoing affirmation of belief. Thus, although the two solutions to the problem of the host-eating mouse appear to contradict each other, their greater significance lies in the fact that they both tacitly articulate a belief in transubstantiation – and it is as expressions of this belief, rather than as solutions to some tangential problem arising from its rationalisation, that they contributed to the consolidation of Church power.

These developments – the attribution of total sanctity to the Eucharistic elements, the evolution of the concept of papal infallibility and the enshrinement of ecclesiastical authority in a self-authenticating system of religious law that transcended the vicissitudes of human subjectivity – resulted in a situation in which the power of the Church was absolute and self-legitimising. The withdrawal of the sacraments from the laity reinforced the autonomy of the Church, not only by isolating the sacramental process within the Church itself but also by ensuring that it became an object of popular *belief* and *need* among the faithful. Because people believed themselves to be naturally damned on account of 'original sin', they needed the Church to be what it said it was – the unique gateway to their salvation. They became dependent on it to the extent that they sacrificed themselves into it, partaking of its identity through its beliefs, rituals and places, and validating themselves by doing so. As such, they were 'selfless', for their sense of identity was divested from themselves and projected into that of the Church, following the example of Christ: 'I seek not mine own will but the will of the Father which hath sent me'.[1] Only in this way could they appear in the 'Book of Life' in which the names of the saved were written. Reflecting the extent to which an individual's life and identity depended on the Church and the Church's monopoly on access to salvation by means of the Eucharist, one fourteenth-century priest who withheld the sacrament from a member of the faithful was compared to a murderer.[2]

The power of the Church was transmitted to the faithful by means of ritual activities. First among these was the Eucharist service itself, a ritual re-enactment of

FIGURE 2.2: Ivory panel showing the consecration of the eucharistic bread and wine, from the cover of a liturgical book. Ivory and painted wood, around 900. MS. Barth 181, Ausst. 67, Univeritatsbibliothek Johann Christian Senckenberg, Frankfurt am Main.

the Last Supper, which involved a complex structure of inter-related objects, words, actions and places. The communion itself revolved around the altar. In the early Middle Ages, when the consecrated bread and wine were still regularly offered to the laity, the celebrating priest stood behind the altar facing the congregation (Fig. 2.2), like Christ in many images of the Last Supper. The front of the altar, visible from the nave, was decorated with images (Fig. 2.3); chalices and patens, from which the sacraments were served, were large enough to hold wine and bread for everyone present. In the thirteenth century, when communion was withdrawn from the laity and reserved for the priesthood, chalices and patens became much smaller and the priest came to stand in front of the altar, with his back to the congregation. As a direct result of this change, the back of the priest's chasuble – a large ceremonial mantle – came to be decorated with Christian iconography, visible to the faithful. As the priest's body now concealed the consecration of the host, the practice of 'elevating' the host evolved, enabling the congregation to see it above his head. At the same time, because the front of the altar was partly obscured, the imagery that previously decorated it was raised and moved to the back of the altar where it could be seen more easily from the nave. In this position, it could also expand in size and serve as a theatrical backdrop for the liturgical drama taking place in front of it. The moment is captured in detail in a representation of *The Mass of St Giles*, in the National Gallery, London, painted in around 1500. Significantly, the gold panel used as a 'retable' behind the altar in this picture is known to have been made originally – in the ninth century – as an altar frontal (Fig. 2.4).

FIGURE 2.3: Altar Frontal showing Christ in Majesty and the twelve apostles. From a church in La Seu d'Urgell, Catalonia, 1125–50, tempera on panel, 102.5 × 151 cm. National Museum of Catalan Art, Barcelona.

FIGURE 2.4: *The Mass of St Giles*, by the Master of St Giles, Paris, oil on oak, around 1500, 62.3 × 46 cm. National Gallery, London.

Apart from attending mass and taking communion, an immensely complex web of secondary conventions evolved to involve the faithful in the practices and identity of the Church. Firstly, there were the accessories of the mass which became ever more elaborate during the Middle Ages. These 'sacramentals' took the form both of objects (bells and candles, 'corporals' to catch crumbs from the broken host, tongs with which to administer the sacrament to the infectious sick, and many others), and of actions and utterances (gestures, processions, hymns, prayers etc.). Numerous texts were written to explain how these objects and rituals should be used and performed. Secondly, the reverberations of the sacraments extended far beyond the mass itself, substantiating a context in which every aspect of daily life – from conception, birth and education to work, marriage and death – acquired sacred significance and became a medium of grace. The times of day were punctuated by the ringing of church bells; the times of year were measured by saints' days. While these conventions played an integral role in maintaining the fabric of social life in the Middle Ages, they also reflected how a sense of identity was only considered meaningful and 'redeemable' when it was translated into the currency of Christian value.

Although the medieval Church managed to evolve a self-image that was internally coherent and deeply suffused throughout the material culture of the time, the fact remains that it was fundamentally solipsistic and, by slow degrees, its limitations became apparent. While the Church did its best to accommodate inconsistencies by developing new interpretations of its right to authority, new cultural forms, offering new means of Christian communion, also began to evolve. Despite theological justifications of the withdrawal of the bread and wine from the laity, the popular desire to participate actively in ritual communion led to the generation of new forms of communion that the Church was not always able to control.[3] These developments are of immense importance because they reflect the first stirrings of a sense of *personal* identity that was independent of Church authority.

Although secondary forms of communion were considered inferior to the Eucharist, they were nevertheless believed to be effective, as they evolved directly out of the communion service, extending its grace rather than competing with it. One of these new forms was 'optical' or 'spiritual' communion, which consisted of communing with the sacrament by gazing at it contemplatively. This practice originated in the twelfth century, when regular 'edible' communion was withdrawn from the laity and the elevation of the host became the focal point of the Mass, but it was not until 1215, when the Fourth Lateran Council imposed conditions on receiving annual communion (prior confession, tithe-paying and a period of sexual abstinence) that the practice became widespread. It gathered further momentum in 1264 when Pope Urban IV instituted the Feast of Corpus Christi, dedicated to the celebration of the Body of Christ in the form of the sacrament. This feast was an elaboration of the veneration paid to the host at its elevation; its high point was a grand procession around the cathedral, parish or town during which the consecrated host was paraded before the faithful in a monstrance (Fig. 2.5). The monstrance (from the Latin *monstrare*, to show) was a new form of liturgical vessel in which the host, previously kept in a closed ciborium, was displayed behind mounted crystal so that it could be seen and contemplated by all.

Significantly, as soon as the host was reconceived as an object of absolute value, its opposite or shadow – the possibility of its destruction – also evolved, as an inverted expression of belief in it. As a means of 'alienating' this traumatising possibility, a contingent of Christian zealots projected their fantasy of the desecrated host on to the Jewish community. Soon after the theory of transubstantiation became doctrine in 1215, evidence was 'found' to suggest that various Jewish communities were using their guile to obtain hosts in order to torture them – as if to re-enact the Crucifixion – in satanic rituals (Fig. 2.6). By elaborating this fantasy, these Christians were further substantiating their belief in the absolute sanctity of the host; by polarising the host against the possibility of its non-existence, they were attempting to necessitate it.

A second area in which new forms of communion evolved was the veneration of relics – the physical parts of saints, holy objects and places that were 'relinquished' or left behind by a holy person at their death (Fig. 2.7). In contrast to pictures and images which were considered by Latin theologians to be primarily narrative, educational or commemorative, relics were believed to be physically sanctified, and, therefore, capable of sacred transmission and healing. In this respect, they resembled

FIGURE 2.5: Corpus Christi Procession from the De Gros-Carondelet Book of Hours, Flanders, c.1500. Picture by courtesy of Ketterer Kunst, Hamburg.

the Eucharist and attracted the same kind of sacramental attention. Indeed, originating in the early Christian tradition of saying masses over the graves of martyrs, it was an ancient requirement that consecrated altars contain relics. Although relics had been venerated since the origins of Christianity, the practice only crystallised into a cult in the fourth century when Helen, the mother of the emperor Constantine, miraculously discovered the relics of the 'True Cross' on which Christ had been crucified, thereby initiating a long tradition of pilgrimage to the Christian holy sites. Fuelled by the Crusades to the Holy Land, the cult of pilgrimages came to a head between the eleventh and thirteenth centuries, when numerous new churches were built or expanded to accommodate the needs of their increasing visitors. One of the major attractions of these sites (and, therefore, a

FIGURE 2.6: The Desecration of the Host. Detail of a page from the Lovell Lectionary, around 1400–10. British Library, Harley 7026, f.13.

major source of income for the Church) was their relics and the blessings they promised. The proliferation of side chapels in pilgrimage churches, each with its own relic-powered altar, reflects this trend.

The increased appeal of relic veneration was also reflected in changes to the design of reliquaries. Until the twelfth century, reliquaries had tended to be closed vessels, like ciboria; but, from the thirteenth century onwards, they began to reveal a part of the relic they contained (e.g. a piece of bone or fabric) through a small window of rock crystal, like a monstrance. This enabled the faithful to gaze at the relic, in optical communion. One of the commonest forms of reliquary at this period was architectural. Some examples of this type resemble miniature churches, with enamels and ivories in place of stained-glass windows and portal sculpture; others, from around 1400, were based on a cross-section of the nave of a church. Especially in these latter cases, the opening up of the interior of the reliquary was paralleled by the glazing and dematerialisation that characterised contemporary Gothic cathedral architecture. Indeed, some of the most ambitious reliquaries are light-pervaded

FIGURE 2.7: Arm reliquary of St. Valentine, 14th century, Switzerland. Metropolitan Museum of Art, New York.

configurations of buttresses, piers and pinnacles – exactly like their monumental counterparts – in which their relics are entirely exposed to view (Fig. 2.8). One of the most celebrated relics of the period was the Crown of Thorns, worn by Christ at the Crucifixion. This treasure was one of a huge number of relics that were brought to Europe following the crusaders' sack of Constantinople in 1204. It was purchased by King Louis IX of France who – reversing the metaphor of reliquary-as-church – had *La Sainte Chapelle* in Paris especially built for it, in the form of an entirely glazed reliquary on a monumental scale (Fig. 2.9). Consecrated in 1248, this remarkable building suggests that, in High Gothic architecture as in High Gothic reliquaries and monstrances, light was a medium of blessings and that grace could be received through seeing.

Significantly, it was precisely during these years that the philosopher and theologian Robert Grosseteste hypothesised that the universe itself was made of light. In his treatise *De Luce* (*On Light*, 1215–20), Grosseteste unfolded his theory that the 'corporeity' of matter – that which gives matter its form and enables it to be extended in space – is light. He proposed that unlike matter, which in itself 'lacks dimensions', light is naturally extended in all directions towards infinity; it was, therefore, the element of 'light in matter' that enabled matter to become extended in space. Moreover, the causal priority of light over matter linked it to other immaterial forms, such as intelligence. On this basis, Grosseteste also subscribed to

FIGURE 2.8: Reliquary, Barcelona, around 1500–20, silver, 46.2 × 21.3 cm. Victoria and Albert Museum, London.

FIGURE 2.9: La Sainte Chapelle, Paris, 1238–48.

an 'illuminationist' theory of knowledge which proposed that knowledge was acquired in the same way that objects are seen. By drawing a parallel between the invisible light that makes objects visible and the unknowable intelligence that makes knowledge possible, this theory was consistent with the contemporary belief, practised through optical communion, that grace is transmitted by light.

The medieval belief in the metaphysical nature of light – in Christ as 'light of the world' – was clearly demonstrated in its architecture. While the power of the Church was manifest in its monopoly of access to salvation via the Eucharist, it was also dramatically celebrated by the High Gothic cathedrals which were flooded by light, reflecting the glorious vision of salvation that it promised the faithful. This tradition reached its peak at the beginning of the thirteenth century, precisely when optical communion was becoming common and when Grosseteste was developing his philosophy of light.

The perfectly translucent Gothic cathedral had taken several centuries to evolve. Over a period of three hundred years, the Church had substantiated and systematised its identity through its architecture, just as it had with the structures of its theology, canon law and liturgy. Broadly speaking, this development was achieved, firstly, by expressing the structural functions of the component parts of a building in visual features and, secondly, by manifesting those structural functions at ever greater levels of precision, while at every stage ensuring that the various relationships between them remained logical and internally coherent – exactly like their theological and legal counterparts. While each region developed its own highly distinctive characteristics and style, there was an overall trend that is reflected in buildings all over Europe.

At the beginning of this development – in the Romanesque period (tenth and eleventh centuries) – the stone walls of many churches were solid and undifferentiated. Some of the smaller churches were single spaces with simple pierced openings that allowed relatively little light to penetrate their interiors.[4] Their purpose was to support the wooden roof and, no doubt, protect the inhabitants of the town or village against marauders. When the church was divided into a nave with two side-aisles, the lower supportive part of the nave wall was transformed into an arcade; an unadorned example survives in the eleventh-century church of San Michele, Oleggio, Italy (Fig. 2.10). The masonry between the openings was usually identified as a series of rudimentary piers or columns, sometimes punctuated with capitals and bases to express the classical idea that the upper part of the wall is supported by the lower part (though, at this level of simplicity, any given part of the wall supports what is above it and is supported by what is below it, whether the function of support is expressed by a feature or not). In some cases, a 'string course' – a horizontal moulding, dividing the wall into two levels to emphasise the difference between these two areas – was also introduced (Fig. 2.11). In due course (and with innumerable variations), a stone 'barrel' vault, which continued the nave walls upward until they met in a continuous arch that unified the interior space of the church, was introduced and the function of supporting it was expressed at ground-floor level. In many cases, open galleries were also introduced above the main arcade (Fig. 2.12). At this point the long stretch of many naves, already articulated by the main arcade, was divided into a series of distinct bays at every level. The use of ridged 'groins' and applied 'ribs' to support the vaults of individual bays (both in naves and in side-aisles) was

FIGURE 2.10: San Michele, Oleggio, late 10th–11th century. Photo: Enrico Engelmann.

one of a number of innovations that led to the introduction of pointed arches. Already suggested visually by the intersection of rounded arches in Romanesque churches, the pointed arch was one of the definitive signs of the Gothic style. By traversing the different spans of a single space – the width, depth and diagonals of a bay – without having to alter their heights (by varying the degree of sharpness), pointed arches enabled builders to expand and compress interior spaces with unprecedented freedom; this feature was especially necessary in the growing number of irregular bays in ambulatories that circled around the east ends of churches giving access to the new side chapels. Pointed arches also enabled builders to introduce complex, affective vistas into their buildings, that were, arguably, consonant with the inclination towards emotional fervour in contemporary imagery (Fig. 2.13).

Especially in the Ile de France, around Paris, where the upper walls of churches were increasingly configured as a gallery, clerestory and triforium surmounted by a rib-vault, each of the supportive functions of the main arcade was identified by an independent column, sometimes resulting in dense clusters of fine colonettes at ground-floor level. One of the offshoots of articulating the functional elements of the structure so clearly was that the supportive aspect of the wall became ever more concentrated around the columns and piers, and that other areas of wall, in which no significant function was performed, could be dramatically reduced, leaving the area free for apertures and windows. This reduction of wall surface was facilitated by the use of stone vaults. While vaults were much heavier than the wooden roofs they replaced, and required more support, the lateral thrust that they exerted on the walls below them meant that a considerable amount of the supportive structure of the buildings could be displaced to the outside walls of the building, reducing the supportive role of the main arcade wall in the middle of the church. As cathedrals grew in height, the invention of flying buttresses enabled the weight of the vaults to be displaced even

FIGURE 2.11: St Michael's, Hildesheim, 1001–33 (with a 13th-century ceiling), restored in 1950.

FIGURE 2.12: St Sernin, Toulouse, around 1080–1120.

FIGURE 2.13: Laon Cathedral, around 1160–90.

further towards the sides of the building beyond the outside walls of the church which, once relieved of their function as support, could also be opened up for glazing (Fig. 2.14). Eventually, the structural function of the external walls was so minimised that the spaces between columns could be entirely filled by stained glass windows, as they were at *La Sainte Chapelle* in Paris (Fig. 2.9). As a result, the interiors of such buildings – for instance, the cathedrals of Chartres, Bourges, Reims and Amiens – were pervaded by light, in keeping with Grosseteste's theory of light as an agent of spiritual illumination. It was as if the material fabric of their walls was precipitated – by a kind of photosynthesis – towards an ever more articulate expression of its own nature as infinitely divisible, while also remaining subject to a 'functional prerogative' that demanded that its structural functions be expressed visibly. The complex but integrated logic of such structures corresponds to the comprehensive logic of the *Decretals* and of the theology of the sacraments, and they embodied the authority of the Church with equal clarity, coherence and conviction, raising it to the peak of its power.

But, just as the theology of the sacraments was internally coherent but ultimately at odds with the needs of the people it served, resulting in the spontaneous generation of alternative 'popular' forms of communion, so the mythical use of 'structural clarity' in architecture as a metaphor for 'logical truth' in theology also became over-stretched. As a dramatic reflection of this crisis, the choir of Beauvais Cathedral, the tallest of all the High Gothic cathedrals (157 feet or 48 metres), collapsed in 1284, and the cathedral was never completed. Its towering choir was rebuilt and stands as a testimony both to the extraordinary vision of the medieval Church and to its doomed idealism. The clerestory level of the choir (the top range of windows) is transcendent; it resembles *La Sainte Chapelle*, raised above an almighty main arcade. But the main arcade is scarred by in-fills of masonry and extra columns, added as an

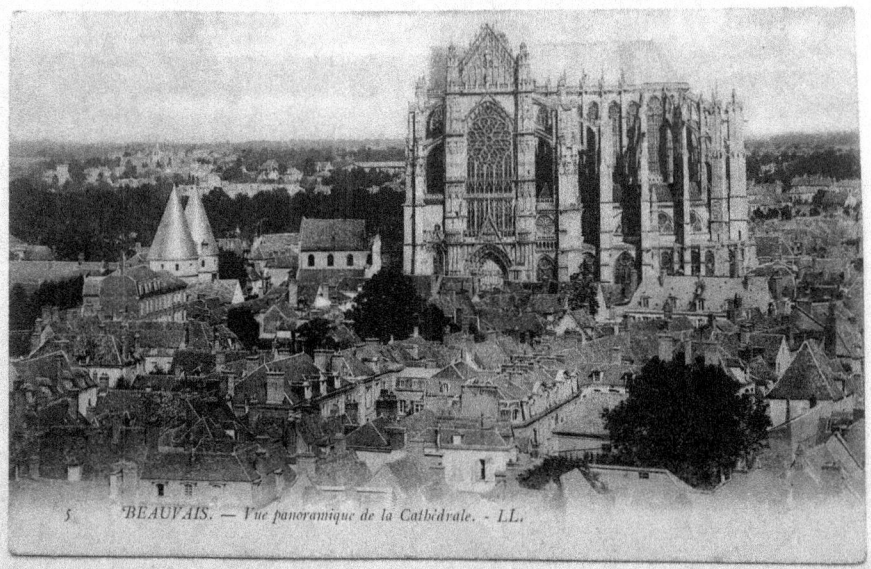

FIGURE 2.14: Beauvais Cathedral. The nave (left, with round-arched windows) is 10th century; the choir is 13th century; the transepts (with the rose window) are 16th century.

emergency measure to shore up the upper walls (Fig. 2.15); and the choir is still abutted by a minuscule nave of the tenth century, which was supposed to have been replaced by a vast Gothic nave, twice the size of the choir – a perfecting of the vision and power of the Church that was never to be (Fig. 2.14). Of course, spectacular churches continued to be built in the Gothic style for two more centuries but they were never as logical as their twelfth- and thirteenth-century forebears; they became more arbitrary and decorative in their design, uninformed by the 'functional prerogative' that had aligned the High Gothic cathedrals to the Church's quest for internal consistency and comprehensive power; columns, for instance, merged with the arch-heads above them, rather than supporting them (Ill. 2.16, lower arcade), and ribs (supporting the vaults) were sometimes unaccountably truncated in mid-air. In extreme examples, such as the Bohemian church of St Barbara at Kutna Hora (1388–c.1530), not only do the ribs that support the main vaults seem to emerge randomly from the columns but, bizarrely, they spring from *behind* the columns in such a way that all traces of a main arcade at that high level (between the columns) are completely swept away (Fig. 2.16). Indeed, it is arguable that, following the consummation of ecclesiastical power in the thirteenth century, the internal coherence of the Church became unsustainable and, like Beauvais Cathedral, began to fracture. Almost as soon as it was achieved, the Church's monopoly over the possibility of salvation began to weaken and the sense of identity that was formerly projected into it began to shift towards other sources of authority.

Significantly, it was at the very moment at which the sacraments were withdrawn from the laity and reserved for the clergy that alternative forms of communion had

FIGURE 2.15: The restored arcade in the choir of Beauvais Cathedral, France, after 1248. Photo: L'oeil de l'écureuil.

begun to develop, empowering the individual and relativising the power of the institution. As we have seen, some of these innovations were accommodated by the Church; others, however, were not. These latter developments were among the earliest expressions of individuality, though as they could only be formulated in the language of the time – that of ecclesiastical supremacy (there was simply no alternative) – they often tended to be expressed negatively, as rejections of the *status quo*. As a result, it was inevitable that they would be considered, by the authorities at least, as 'heresy' – the bane of the late medieval Church and the seed-bed of Renaissance individualism.

FIGURE 2.16: St Barbara, Kutna Hora, Czech Republic, 1388–1530.

Heresies had existed since the origins of Christianity and they maintained a continuous presence in Europe from the eleventh century onwards, but it was not until the thirteenth century, especially in the south of France and northern Italy, that they began to pose a serious threat to the Church. Although there was a wide range of unconnected heretical groups at this period, they tended to fall into two key categories. Some were responding to social and political issues, reacting against the abuses of the Church and the corruption of priests; others were addressing intellectual and philosophical questions about the nature of God (though, in so doing, they were also challenging the theological principles on which the authority of the Church was based). In both cases, it was primarily the threat to ecclesiastical power and authority that led to their being branded as heretics – just as it had been the early Christians' refusal to venerate the emperor that had led the Romans, otherwise tolerant of religious diversity, to persecute them.

The beliefs of heretics took many forms. Initially, reacting against the corruption of the clergy, many people rejected the priestly administration of the sacraments. Some went further and rejected the sacraments altogether, claiming that they were not instituted by Christ but that they were inventions of the papacy and the priesthood for their own gain. Many heretics bypassed the teachings of the Church and advocated a life of poverty, in direct imitation of Christ. Wandering preachers, claiming to have unmediated knowledge of God and attracting huge numbers of followers, became increasingly common, though their right to preach was denied by the Church. Some denied the efficacy of the cross as a redemptive sign and burned crosses in public. Others questioned the necessity of using churches for worship, maintaining that prayers could be said anywhere, including pigsties, and that 'Christ can be adored as well in the mind as in a church'. Ironically, their views – denying the need for material churches – paralleled the collapse of Beauvais Cathedral. It was as if the Church could indeed evolve beyond the state of material manifestation into the unlocatable omnipresence of light.

The persecution of heretics was extreme. While it was genuinely believed, by priests and lay folk alike, that heretics were possessed by Satan and that heresy was a contagious disease that could, in some cases, be transmitted through eye contact, it was also realised that heresy posed a profound threat to the very rationale and identity of the Church. For both reasons, the Church felt compelled to forcibly convert heretics back to the true faith; those that resisted were, in many cases, burned at the stake. Documents relate how some heretics leapt joyfully on to the flames, embracing their destinies, much to the confusion of their accusers. Their courage reflects the vitality of a key aspect of individual identity that was newly emerging at this time: *conscience*. The concept of conscience was not unknown in the ancient world but it was only continuously discussed as an abiding convention of mind from the twelfth century. The debate was initiated by the theologian Peter Lombard (d.1160), whose four books of *Sentences* – exhaustive commentaries on a comprehensive range of scriptures and patristic teachings – became the standard textbook on theology in medieval universities. Peter Lombard's references to conscience were made in relation to a commentary by St Jerome on the prophetic Book of Ezekiel, in which Jerome appeared to differentiate between two forms of innate moral impulse in human beings. On the one hand, he identified a faculty that is naturally and unerringly good, called *synderesis*. This word derives from the Greek words *syn*, meaning 'together', and *heresis*, meaning 'taking' or 'choosing' (which is also, significantly, the source of the word 'heretic' – an individual who *chooses* his or her belief, rather than conform to a prescribed doctrine). On the other hand, he observed the well-intentioned but fallible response to the objective impulse of *synderesis*, called *conscience*, which is conditional and subject to error, thereby making it possible, due to an erring conscience, to commit a sin 'in good faith'. Paralleling the word *synderesis*, the word *conscience* derives from the Latin words *con* (with) and *scientia* (knowledge). Both words suggest 'knowledge with oneself' (or an 'awareness of what one knows to be true'), though they do not guarantee morally positive action on the basis of that knowledge.

Following Peter Lombard's commentary, the debates about conscience that ensued over the next two centuries attempted to define the inborn inclinations of man – the scope of his intellect and free will in matters of moral judgement – with ever greater refinement. For instance, if human beings are free, are they naturally good but 'free' to act wickedly, or are they naturally wicked (due to 'original sin') but 'free' to act virtuously? Is it that the acting will is good and the discriminating intellect is evil, or vice versa? Is it possible to sin deliberately or are all sins simply a form of ignorance and misunderstanding? Innumerable variations on the possible relationships between free will, intellect, nature and grace were explored and every possible combination of impulses, often contradicting each other, was proposed. Most significant here, however, is the fact that, whether one liked it or not, a vocabulary and discourse, in which a new sense of independent and authoritative 'self' was accommodated and exercised, was evolving.

In his *Summa de Bono (Treatise on Goodness)* of around 1230 – the first treatise to be specifically dedicated to the question of conscience – the theologian Philip the Chancellor speculated on the disposition of heretics, saying that

> the effect of *synderesis* is paralysed in them because of the lack of faith, which is the basis of everything good. But, the exercise of *conscientia* thrives in them, the evidence of which is that the man is ready to undergo martyrdom, because he supposes what he believes to be the faith. It is not, however, *synderesis* which does this, but what belongs to free choice or reason.[5]

That is to say, a heretic's primary impulse towards goodness is intact, but it is incapacitated because his intellectual judgement is incorrect and his belief and actions are, therefore, sinful.

The philosopher Peter Abelard (d.1142), on the other hand, respected the moral integrity of conscientious, if misguided, actions, epitomising the shift of identity away from objective authority towards subjective individuality. His treatise *Sic et Non (Yes and No)* famously juxtaposed contradictions from the writings of the Church Fathers, proposing a responsible rationalist method of reconciling them. In drawing attention to these discrepancies, he was not only providing insight into the material at hand; he was also, more importantly, creating cultural conventions and 'psychological space' in which personal discrimination became possible. In the same way, his *Historia Calamitatum (History of My Calamities)*, one of the first ever writings to qualify as 'autobiographical', reflects Abelard's powerful sense of individuality both in the narrative, which reveals much about his passionate nature (not least in relation to his legendary romance with Heloise), and in the fact that he wrote it at all. By regarding himself in this way, Abelard was setting a precedent for appreciating the sense of one's 'self' as a real phenomenon worthy of consideration; he was realising a possibility of experience that others could now also recognise 'in themselves'. Needless to say, he was heavily criticised by the Church and was accused of heresy on many occasions.

Abelard's attitude to conscience anticipates the demise of the medieval worldview and the rise of Renaissance humanism. In contrast to the contemporary theologian, Rupert of Deutz (d.1129), who wrote that he would 'rather sin with

Christ than be virtuous on his own' – epitomising the medieval projection of value away from the individual on to an objective truth – Abelard maintained (in his *Ethics*) that the people who crucified Christ would have committed a greater sin if they had acted against their consciences.[6] With these astonishing words, Abelard clearly proposed that value and identity are to be associated with personal integrity, at the expense of accepted truths if necessary, and, as a result, he represents a step towards a new era of human experience.

While expressions of individuality were initially seen to be threatening, in the thirteenth and fourteenth centuries the potential of personal selfhood was adapted by the Church to its own ends and became a common theme in Christian writing. Indeed, the proliferation of new mystical texts and teachings at this time reflects an increase in the frequency of personal experiences of religious ecstasy and is itself a sign of individualisation. Several such teachings were disseminated among lay people by wandering lay preachers and mystics, many of whom were unauthorised by the Church. They were frequently circulated in vernacular languages rather than Latin (which was the official language of the Church, though little understood by most lay people),[7] thereby further challenging the Church's monopoly on access to salvation and inviting its scorn. To combat breakaway tendencies, the foundation of a number of new preaching orders was approved by the papacy. While the flourishing of these orders (especially the mendicant Dominicans and Franciscans) was itself a sign of the more personal and less institutionalised approach to religious life that was becoming characteristic of the period as a whole, they were promoted partly to keep the preaching fraternity within the Church, and partly to deal with heretics on their own terms. The Dominicans in particular – named after their founder, St Dominic (from *domini canis*, the 'hound of God') – were known for their zeal in hunting down heretics.

Many heretical teachings advocated not only direct communion with God, bypassing the sacraments and other conventions of the Church, but even identification of the soul or self with God. Amaury of Bene, a theologian at the University of Paris, is often credited with popularising the pantheistic doctrine that 'all things are one because everything is God' and that the individual soul is, therefore, already divine. Following his condemnation at the Fourth Lateran Council, Amaury's ideas flourished among heretics of the 'Free Spirit', who claimed to be fully inhabited by, and identified with, the Holy Spirit – the third person of the Trinity – which they believed to have incarnated in, and as, themselves; consequently, they believed themselves to be incapable of committing a sin because everything they did was 'done by God'. This understanding was taken to its most absolute level by the Dominican mystic, Meister Eckhart (d.1328), whose central teaching was that the soul, in its essence, is totally identified with God. Meister Eckhart was accused of being a 'Free Spirit' but he differentiated himself from this heresy on the grounds that it claimed for the ordinary individual what could only be realised in a soul by grace. He maintained that just as there can be no true identity or self without God – as 'only God can say the word "I"' – so there can be no God without self: 'That I am a man is something that other men share with me; that I see and hear, eat and drink, that is the same as with cattle; but that I *am*, that belongs to no man, not even to an angel, nor even to God, except in so far as I am one with Him.'[8]

On account of their commitment to experiencing the presence of spirit in, and as, their own selves, Meister Eckhart and his followers represent further signs of the growing authority of subjectivity, even though they expressed their self-awareness in the language of Christian devotion rather than by developing an independent model of identity. While they presented the identification of 'self with spirit' and 'spirit with self' as an eternal truth, there were also many writers for whom this revelation was not abstract and timeless. It was seen by them to be embedded in the process of history and revealed in historical time. The figure who most clearly recognised the spiritual significance of the perception of historical time was the visionary abbot of the monastery of Fiore in southern Italy, Joachim of Fiore (d.1202). Joachim's fame lies in his radical interpretation of history as the Trinity's progressive revelation of itself to the world and to mankind, culminating in the Second Coming of Christ and the Last Judgement. He unfolded his vision of sacred history in a trilogy of works, written in the 1180s: *A Concordance of the Old and New Testaments*, *An Exposition of the Apocalypse* and *The Ten-Stringed Psaltery*. According to Joachim, the whole of history was divided into three overlapping epochs, associated with God the Father, God the Son (Christ) and God the Holy Spirit respectively (Fig. 2.17). The first epoch, over which God the Father presided, covered the period of the Old Testament,

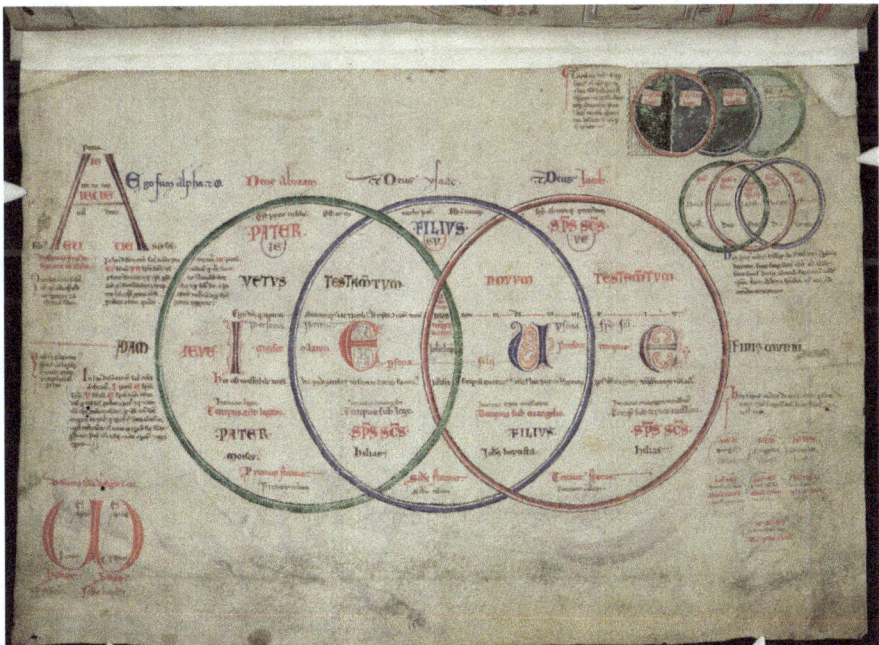

FIGURE 2.17: The Trinitarian Order of History, from the *Liber Figerarum* (*Book of Figures*) by Joachim of Fiore, Southern Italy, early 13th century. Corpus Christi College, Oxford, MS.255A, f7v. By permission of the President and Fellows of Corpus Christi College, Oxford.

from the creation of the world until the time of Christ; the second epoch began with the period of the New Testament and covered the period from the birth of Christ until the 'present time', and the third epoch, the age of the Spirit, was due to begin imminently and would run until the end of the world.

Joachim established a principle of equivalence between the epochs on the basis of correspondences discovered between the Old and New Testaments. In his *Concordance*, he elaborated in exhaustive detail how the structures of the two testaments were unified by their common numerological compositions. Numbers were already important because of the values they acquired from their biblical associations. The number four, for instance, was a grounded number because the earth was created on the fourth day of creation and there were four evangelists, forming a stable square. Seven, adding the trinitarian spirituality of three to the earthy humanity of four, was associated with time and the role of divine influence in human history: the creation of the world took seven days, there are seven days in a week, there were seven seals on the Book of Life in the Book of Revelation, to be opened at the end of time. Apart from their innate symbolic value, numbers also provided the key to recognising the correspondences between the two testaments – reflecting the medieval predilection for patterns and for using them as formulae from which to abstract knowledge. For instance, the twelve patriarchs and tribes of Israel in the Old Testament not only embodied the symbolic value of the number twelve (a multiple of three and four) but also anticipated the twelve apostles and the twelve gates in the New Jerusalem in the New Testament, thereby revealing the principle of equivalence between the two testaments and imbuing their relationship with a sense of logic and necessity.

While Joachim had many ways of deriving meaning from the correspondences that he identified between the two testaments, he also took the process a step further – by abstracting a 'theology of history' from his knowledge of scripture and by applying it to his own time and to the future. For instance, he used the fact that, according to biblical sources, the epoch of God the Father lasted for sixty-three generations (divided into three groups of twenty-one) to help him calculate the length of the epoch of Christ. Allowing thirty years for a generation (unrealistically for the time, but based on 'authoritative' sources) and observing that the first group of twenty-one generations in the epoch of Christ overlapped with the last group of twenty-one generations from the previous epoch (like runners in a relay race), he estimated that the epoch of Christ would come to an end and be superseded by the third epoch approximately forty-two generations (of thirty years each) after Christ – in 1260; that is, imminently.

Joachim's belief in the coming age of the Spirit reflected the legitimisation of individual identity, just as it had for the heretics of the Free Spirit. But, by finding this shift to be both inevitable and imminent, he was also bringing a new dimension of self-awareness to it. By allowing his 'insights' into the hidden laws of scripture and history to activate a prophetic or visionary mode of seeing in him (projecting the patterns of the past on to the future), he experienced a sense of the historical necessity of the present time, and thereby implicitly projected a degree of necessity on to his own capacity, also arising in the present time, to have that experience; no wonder his calculations seemed visionary to him. Moreover, by finding a degree of necessity in his own capacity for such experience, he was implicitly realising the necessity of his own existence as a subject. It is, therefore, arguable that, in Joachim's work, the evolution of selfhood was not only *hypothesised* as a *possibility* (in the forthcoming age of the Spirit); it was also *witnessed* and *seen* to be happening as a *necessity* in the present moment. In fact, the very act of seeing it was a sign of its necessary evolution and existence; it was evolving by *experiencing* itself evolving. In a thoroughly circular and self-referential manner, it was becoming *real* by becoming *aware* of itself – by *realising* itself, in the full double sense of that word. In the context of its time, Joachim's philosophy provided a cultural form in which it was possible to realise such self-awareness.

Joachim was prudent enough, and respectful enough of the 'mystery of God's ways', not to attach the beginning of the age of the Spirit too firmly to a specific year; he was content to be approximate. In the same way, he was careful not to be over-specific in his identification of the signs of the new age. Nevertheless, he did make some actual prophecies. Anticipating the foundation of new monastic orders such as the Dominicans and Franciscans, he predicted that the new 'age of the Spirit' would be led by 'new orders of spiritual men' – contemplative and active monks who corresponded to, but superseded, the laity in the Old Testament and the clergy in the New; there might initially be twelve of them, in keeping with the number of patriarchs and apostles, though he was loath to identify them. At the same time, the Holy Spirit would begin to work inwardly and formlessly in people. For instance, there would be no need for images. Although Joachim (or his close followers) produced a remarkable series of symbolic diagrams (or 'figures') illustrating the various correspondences that his philosophy identified (Fig. 2.17), there would come a time when the spirit of truth would fall directly on men, and images would cease to be necessary – just as the Jewish Passover was superseded by the sacraments in the early days of the Christian Church. Similarly there would be no 'third testament' to complement the Old and New Testaments. Instead, there would simply be a new and more insightful way of understanding the old revelations. Indeed, knowledge through words would be altogether superseded by knowledge through grace.

Although Joachim's views of the immediate presence of the Holy Spirit at work within the individual created a model of personal independence that provides a close parallel to the contemporary model of conscience, he was entirely orthodox and uncontroversial in his faith – voluntarily sending his writings to the pope for approval, defending and supporting the Church, and dissociating from heretics (though he did have one tract posthumously destroyed at the Fourth Lateran Council). The same cannot be said of many of his self-appointed followers, who used his vision as the basis for a range of highly politicised opinions that were vehemently condemned as heretical. Especially as the year 1260 approached, identifications of the new 'spiritual men' – not to mention the antichrist, 'angelic pope' and 'last world emperor' – began to abound. We have already seen how heretics of the Free Spirit considered themselves to be direct incarnations of the third person of the Trinity. With the same visionary fervour, the Holy Roman Emperor Frederick II was hotly tipped to be the antichrist by some and the last world emperor by others, but he died unexpectedly in 1250. Four years later, a

Franciscan monk, Gerard of Borgo San Donnino, became convinced that, despite Joachim's own denial of a third testament, the 'mighty angel' mentioned in the Book of Revelation (10, 2) 'coming down from heaven, clothed with a cloud, with a rainbow upon his head' and 'with a little book in his hand' was Joachim himself, carrying the 'eternal evangel' – a compendium of his own works, with which to enlighten the world at the end of time. Gerard spent the last seventeen years of his life in prison but his eager anticipation of the antichrist never waned. Others in his position soon came to believe that it was the institutional Church that was the heretical 'whore of Babylon', grossly distorting the teachings of Christ for its own benefit, and that the pope himself was the antichrist, usurping Christ's throne. In the meantime, the year 1260 came and went without significant signs and, despite some hopeful recalculations of the date, interest in Joachim's particular interpretation of the shape of things to come began to fade.

This is not to suggest, however, that Joachim's vision of the future was a routine fantasy – a conventional manifestation of the kind of paranoid and apocalyptic psychology that anticipates all auspicious years, or an unconscious projection of tacit knowledge of his own death on to the destiny of the world. On the contrary, surely something of immense significance was indeed taking place during his time, of which he was both evidence and witness. Although the lack of supernatural signs suggested that the age of the Spirit was not about to start after all (and indeed that Joachim's whole scheme was a delusion), his vision of the imminent future was strangely consistent with events as they unfolded. Above all, selfless belief in an external Christ was beginning to be eclipsed by an appreciation of the value of personal experience and, as a result, spiritual agency slowly ceased to be monopolised by the Church and the clergy. Such agency was increasingly beginning to be experienced directly by individuals, thereby extending spiritual legitimacy to their sense of personal identity. In keeping with Joachim's theory of correspondences, the perfect autonomy of the medieval Church and the internal coherence of its self-image and authority were slowly transferred to the individual – generating the self-sense, as a new convention of mind, in the process. Just as the medieval Church had struggled to maintain and propagate itself through a plethora of cultural conventions, so the individual self-sense would now begin to do the same. Before it had time to savour itself and develop its own forms in keeping with its needs, it simply adapted the pre-existing conventions of the Church to its own ends. As it became more sure of itself, it dissociated from the official Church, often heretically, and began to challenge it consciously – even though its own conventions had not yet evolved. But, as soon as it became able to identify itself as a phenomenon in its own right, the language that developed around it began to embody it more independently and authoritatively, shrugging off the trappings of the past and ushering in a new age.

CHAPTER THREE

The Resurrection of the Self: Imaginative Empathy with the Suffering and Death of Christ

The emergent sense of personal self that is reflected in the Christian beliefs and practices of the late Middle Ages is also reflected in its imagery, which was equally dominated by religion. Even images that were commissioned by secular patrons were pervaded by Christian values. Having said that, even within the Church, the earliest Christian images had been controversial: firstly, images were associated with pagan idolatry, which had been practised throughout the ancient world; and, secondly, the veneration of 'graven images' was explicitly condemned in the Old Testament (Exodus 20, 4) and was, therefore, considered to be blasphemous. As a result, many believers rejected the use of imagery and some became 'iconoclasts' (image-breakers). Others however supported images on the grounds that they helped the 'unlearned' understand the sacred mysteries and that the veneration directed towards them is not idolatrously directed at the material objects themselves but is transferred to the sacred personages represented in them (their 'prototypes'). In the year 599, for instance, Bishop Serenus of Marseilles, who felt sympathetic towards the iconoclasts, forbade the displaying of images in churches – believing them to be superstitious – and destroyed them whenever he could. His actions prompted Pope Gregory I to write to him, outlining the official position of the Church on the subject. While Gregory praised Serenus' zeal in combating idolatry, he criticised his extremism, making the case that, while images are not to be adored themselves, it is legitimate for illiterate people to use them to learn what literate people could learn by reading the scriptures. In subsequent centuries, Gregory's words were seen to give papal sanction to the use of images for narrative and didactic purposes.[1]

Despite Gregory's authority, anxiety continued to surround the use of images in the seventh century, exacerbated by the rapid expansion of the new iconoclastic religion of Islam which was thought by some to indicate that God preferred not to be venerated through images and that he was punishing idolatrous Christians by showing favour to their competitors. In the Eastern (Byzantine or Orthodox) Church, which began to separate from the Latin West in the fourth century, the issue flared up into the 'Iconoclastic Controversy' which raged, with one period of respite, between 726 and 843 when it was finally resolved in favour of images. The Orthodox argument for images, subsequently institutionalised in a formal 'theology of icons', maintained that, by choosing to incarnate himself as Jesus Christ, God the Father had himself set a legitimising precedent for the representation of the divine in material form. Consequently, Orthodox images, or icons, were legitimised on the grounds that they were extensions of the Incarnate Christ. As such, they were sacramental objects, physically embodying his divine sanctity. In keeping with this belief, the entire tradition of icon veneration revolves around the physical sanctity of icons. That their aesthetic appeal, symbolic meaning or narrative potential are secondary is reflected both in their relative lack of stylistic development over many centuries, and in the extremely limited range of their subject-matter.

In the West, a very different attitude towards imagery developed in response to these events. In the middle of the Iconoclastic Controversy, an interim formulation of the Orthodox image-supporting position on images had been established (at the Second Council of Nicaea in 787). An account of the proceedings was sent to Pope Adrian I in Rome, where it was translated and sent to the Holy Roman Emperor, Charlemagne. The document suggested that, despite Gregory I's declaration two centuries earlier, Pope Adrian had sanctioned the more devotional 'cultish' Orthodox view, causing much alarm at Charlemagne's court. One of Charlemagne's leading theologians, Theodulf of Orleans, was commissioned to compose a rebuttal. The result was the so-called *Libri Carolini* or *Books of Charlemagne* (written in 791–3), which condemned the Orthodox view as idolatrous and superstitious, offering an alternative view of the appropriate Christian use of images. It later transpired that the version of the text that was sent to Charlemagne had been translated inaccurately, giving the impression that the Orthodox Church did not merely 'venerate' images but that it 'adored' them – whereas the Byzantine authorities had been careful to specify that they condoned the veneration of images (as the honour offered to the image was transferred to its prototype) but not adoration, which was reserved for God alone. Consequently, the *Libri Carolini* were never circulated, and they appear therefore to have had little direct impact on the subsequent development of image theory. Nevertheless, the conflict had happened and attitudes were consolidated around it. The text captures a sense of the suspicion and antipathy that Latin theologians felt towards icon veneration and, after centuries of prevarication, represents a formal statement of contemporary attitudes towards the use of images in the West. Its position was reiterated at the Council of Frankfurt in 794 and the Synod of Paris in 825 and it soon became standard. It is amply borne out by the images themselves.

Besides criticising the Orthodox attitude to icons, the key points in the *Libri Carolini* were that images should teach their viewers about the 'deeds of salvation' and that they should decorate churches, to the greater glory of God – and teaching and decoration are indeed among the most characteristic functions of early medieval imagery in the West. In this context, images were not to be sacramental, as icons were; that role was largely played by relics which, by virtue of their physical contact with the saints, were believed to embody sanctity in their physical form. Nor were they intended to have a psychological or emotional effect on their viewers, as they would in the late Middle Ages. On the contrary, their role was primarily to communicate pre-established doctrine. Image-makers made no effort to render forms or space in a 'realistic' or 'naturalistic' way, based on observation, because they were not attempting to represent the world we live in; they were representing the truths of a 'higher order', as revealed in biblical narrative and Christian history, and as mediated through Church teachings. The authority of images was traditional and, rather like the liturgy, it was to be transmitted through the ages from *within* the tradition. It was not to be enhanced by the subjective choices of artisans and painters; on the contrary, artisans and painters were mere instruments of tradition. As a result, most images were highly stylised, and were copied from earlier images or copy-books. They derived their content – both its subject-matter and its appearance – from approved models or authorised written sources, and not from the imaginations of their makers.

One of the most characteristic ways of articulating pre-existent truths in the Middle Ages was by identifying symmetry and patterns in scripture, history and nature. This was partly because patterns are decorative and regular, reflecting the splendour and intelligence of God's creation. But it was also because the abstract organisation of patterns conferred a sense of coherence and logic on the ideas they were trying to embody, almost as if they were diagrams, making them easier to understand and remember, like rhyme and meter in verse (Fig. 2.3). Even when their ideas were not visualised, medieval thinkers showed a predilection for patterns, developing complex hierarchies of levels at which to interpret the various correspondences they found and elaborating mnemonic structures with which to remember them. Accordingly, one of the most popular ways to extrapolate meaning from the scriptures was by finding hidden correspondences between the Old and New Testaments and by exploring their implications – not only as a key to the future (after Joachim) but for its own sake. For instance, the fact that, according to the Book of Jonah, Jonah was swallowed by a whale and regurgitated three days later was understood to be one of many signs in the Old Testament that 'prefigured' the entombment of Christ and his Resurrection after three days, as described in the gospels (Fig. 3.1, top left roundel). Underlying this 'typological' approach was the fundamental belief that the New Testament is entirely prefigured by the Old Testament and is therefore part of God's original vision of world history. In this way the coherent and self-evident logic of patterns was used to 'prove' the pre-existence of Christian truth. It was designed to demonstrate how everything in nature and history – the entire realm of manifestation, in fact – was a sign of God's wisdom, anticipating the eventual redemption of mankind. In such a context, the responsibility of the theologian or philosopher was to ask not '*what* does a thing signify?' but '*how* does it signify Christ?'

While the presence of meaningful correspondences in scripture, history and nature was taken to be a foregone conclusion, the ability to identify them was by no means a purely rational skill, based on deduction and perfected by study; it also required a *symbolic* mode of vision, rooted in a capacity for insight into the pre-existent unity of the world that was bestowed on the faithful by grace. Something of this capacity to *recognise* the unity of phenomena – rather than learn about it 'for the first time' – is reflected in the origin of the word 'symbol', which derives from the ancient Greek *syn-* (together) and *bol-* (to throw or put), meaning 'bring together'. As early as the fifth century before Christ, the word *symbolon* referred to a token, sometimes a coin, that was broken into two pieces and kept by two people, to be used – by *putting them together* at a later date – as a means of identification. In a world without identity cards,

FIGURE 3.1: Alton Towers triptych, around 1150, wooden core with enamel and gilt copper, 36.2 × 44.7 × 11.8 cm. Cologne. Victoria and Albert Museum, London. The top left roundel, showing the regurgitation of Jonah by the whale, corresponds to the adjacent roundel in the central panel which shows the three Maries at the tomb of the risen Christ).

individuals involved in an agreement could ensure that a go-between, to whom one of the partners had entrusted his half of the coin, could be recognised by the other. The earliest *Christian* use of the word, in the third century, refers to the creed as the distinctive token of a Christian, given to him or her at the time of their baptism and to be used subsequently as proof of their initiation into the inner circle of the cult. Thus the first 'symbols' were not motifs to which static meanings could be ascribed, independent of use, as they later became. As coded signs, they were invested with significance by the capacity for insight that only *initiates* could bring to them. The religious potential of the concept is further reflected by the fact that its opposite – to scatter, fragment, isolate, disperse – is 'diabolic', derived from *bol-* and the Greek prefix *dis-* (apart, away, in all directions). This word was used in early Greek translations of the Old Testament for the Hebrew word 'Satan' and gives rise to the English word 'devil'. Some early Christian Gnostics believed that, when the fallen angel Lucifer stole the light of God, he thrust it into mankind and created lust in order to ensure that it would be *scattered* irretrievably throughout the matter of the world.

The didactic and narrative functions of images remained a priority until the thirteenth and fourteenth centuries, when the first efforts to translate the scriptures into vernacular languages were made. While the scriptures were exclusively available in Latin, images were often used by the clergy, who alone spoke Latin, to teach Christian truths to the undifferentiated community of the faithful. Such images, often designed in a decorative and schematic manner, implicitly identified the viewer as an impersonal believer engaging in a visual ritual of submission and conformity; even the pattern-based logic of the compositions organised the process of looking. No aspect of this experience of imagery overlapped with the experience of 'everyday' life; on the contrary, it exposed the viewer to an otherworldly realm in an otherworldly way. In the middle of the thirteenth century, this began to change. Very slowly (over approximately two centuries), naturalism began to supersede the ritual stylisation of early medieval imagery, and images began to look more 'realistic', inducing their viewers to respond to them in more 'realistic' ways. Key figures were placed in 'realistic' spaces rather than against monochrome backgrounds and the spaces in which they were now placed were frequently filled with 'realistic' details (Figs 3.10, 4.2). Although late medieval imagery continued to revolve around Christian subject-matter and therefore evoke a disposition of belief in its viewers, both its style and setting gradually became more worldly, acknowledging and empowering worldly modes of experience. Such imagery invited viewers to engage in a completely new form of experience – to experience abstract objects of belief as if they were palpably real; but, in order to do this, they had to develop a completely new faculty: *imagination*. It is no accident that the 'imagination' – a mental faculty that is applicable to *all* the senses – should have derived its name from the realm of *visual* experience – images – for it was in conjunction with new uses of visual images that it developed.

The significance of this shift was that whereas the early medieval image-type functioned as 'pictorial text', disseminating pre-existent doctrine – to be believed and interpreted as authorised by the Church and regardless of the subjective disposition of the viewer – the new more realistic type of image encouraged viewers to imagine the life of Christ as a historical reality and to respond to it *personally*; that is, not just to learn from the life of Christ, but to empathise with it. By inducing viewers to respond in this way, this new type of image activated an imaginative and emotional dimension in selfhood – a new *potentiality* – for which there had been no scope in front of the earlier didactic type of image. Moreover, in the most intense states of imagination (stimulated by the most realistic images), episodes from the life of Christ were to be re-lived in the mind with such imaginative power that, to all intents and purposes, they were being experienced, not merely as they had happened in the past (as if remembered), but *as if they were currently happening*. With the power of their imaginations, individuals became able to induce experiences of the historical Christ in themselves – not as fantasies or illusions, which suggest seeing things that are unreal and which were considered in the Middle Ages to be diabolical, but as experiential realisations of immaterial truths in visual form. In this way they became newly able to realise themselves *as imaginative and emotional selves*.

It should be added, however, that the sense of personal identity that is implicit in acts of the imagination is only real to the extent that its imaginative experience is convincing; that is to say, it is only real to the extent that its visualisation is *experienced as real* and not merely believed to be so. For, if the self is not convinced by the reality of the experience that (it imagines) it is having, it will not be induced to have an authentic reaction to it. And if it is not induced to have an authentic reaction to it, its knowledge of itself as a reality will be unsupported by that experience. Its sense of itself, therefore, is invested both in the initial act of *visualisation* which must be *convincing* (exercised in the *creation* of images) and in the secondary act of *responding* to the visualisation which must be *authentic* (exercised in the *use* of images). The state of 'imaginative selfhood' is a somewhat paradoxical and transitory condition because, in order to be functional and effective, the self must react to what it knows to be imaginary *as if* it was real – just as we today can be genuinely moved by films, despite knowing that they are no more than light flickering on a screen and that their stories are contrived.

Because it was necessary for the images visualised in imaginative meditation to be convincing (whether they were actually made, and seen by the eyes, or simply imagined in the mind), it became newly important – even crucial – to know what Christ looked like. There was no mention of his physical appearance in the gospels and the earliest representations of him, produced in the third and fourth centuries, depict him as being short-haired and beardless, in the manner of a classical hero or youth. It was not until the sixth century – *five hundred years after his lifetime* – that the 'conventional' depiction of Christ with shoulder-length hair and a beard became established. The historical 'accuracy' of this facial type was underpinned by a number of contemporary legends, sometimes concerning miraculous 'images not made with human hands' (*acheiropoieta*) in which the actual appearance of Christ was clearly captured. One Byzantine tradition upheld that the ailing King Abgar of Edessa in Syria heard of Christ's miraculous curative powers and sent him a servant, requesting that Christ come to Edessa to heal him. Instead of doing so, Christ is said to have wiped his face on a cloth (the *mandylion*), miraculously leaving an impression of his appearance on it; the cloth was then taken back to the king, who was duly healed by it. By the eleventh century, this legend had spawned an equivalent in the West, according to which St Veronica handed a napkin to Christ as he struggled towards Golgotha, bearing the cross. Christ wiped his face on the napkin, leaving a miraculous likeness on it, and handed it back to Veronica, whose name is – *post factum* – derived from the words *verus*, 'true', and *icon*, 'image' (Fig.3.6, far left). As for the Virgin and Christ-child, a second sixth-century tradition reported that not only did St Luke paint the pair from life (for which reason he is the patron saint of painters) but that the Virgin also blessed the work, still believed by many to survive (Fig. 5.6). According to this way of thinking, painters who copied such images were capturing the true appearance of their subjects *on principle*.

By the thirteenth century, both the veil of Veronica and St Luke's painting had become important relics at the centre of popular cults, and they were consulted as authoritative sources for the actual appearances of the Virgin and Christ. While these traditions did at least have several centuries of legend behind them, and were therefore well placed to stimulate imaginative contemplation of their historical veracity, others appear to have been created much more recently, and – in a highly circular way – by the very imaginations that authenticated them. One such object was the Turin Shroud, in which Christ was said to have been buried and which was believed to have been salvaged from his tomb after the Resurrection. This piece of fabric is still believed by

THE RESURRECTION OF THE SELF

many to retain an impression of Christ's body on it, but it was first documented (and presumably fabricated) in the fourteenth century. Another example was the 'rediscovery', probably in the thirteenth century, of a 'lost' eye-witness account of Christ in which Christ's physical features were described verbally in great detail. The description eventually evolved into the 'Letter of Lentulus' – said to have been sent by Publius Lentulus, Governor of Judaea at the time of Christ, to the Roman Senate, reporting on events in the region (Fig. 3.2). The letter describes Christ as being

> somewhat tall in stature ... with a comely and reverend countenance, such as beholders both fear and love. His hair is the colour of an unripe hazelnut, and is smooth almost down to his ears, but from thence downward, is somewhat curled, darker and shinier, waving about his shoulders; with a parting in the middle of his head in the manner of the Nazarenes. His forehead is very plain and smooth. His face is without wrinkle or spot, beautiful with a comely red; his nose and mouth so formed that nothing can be reprehended. His beard is full, of the same colour as his hair, not long, and forked in form; simple and mature in aspect; his eyes, blue-grey, clear and quick.

This description was clearly designed to facilitate acts of imagination; it was intended not only to inform readers of Christ's appearance but to help them *witness* him in their own minds. Indeed, although it was necessary for people to *believe* that such images and documents were authentic, their debatable origins indicate that it was ultimately in the *imaginative* act that they afforded – the act of experiencing Christ

FIGURE 3.2: Letter of Lentulus, c.1500, Southern Netherlands, oil on wood 38.5 × 27.3 cm. Museum Catharijneconvent, Utrecht.

and the Virgin with total conviction, and responding to that experience with the utmost sincerity – that their redemptive potential lay.

One of the most significant characteristics of imaginative contemplation was that it was innately and intensely personal. Thus, although the process was generally accepted by the Church, it also provided the faithful with a further means of engaging with sanctity that was not monopolised by the authorities. On the contrary, its development generated a range of cultural and psychological conventions in which personal experience was implicitly acknowledged as a legitimate alternative to ecclesiastical tradition. The popularisation of private meditation, from the thirteenth century onwards, was reflected in the evolution of numerous new objects, books, actions and customs, all designed to stimulate and accommodate this experience. Perhaps the most revealing of these innovations was the Book of Hours – a compilation of prayers, psalms and other devotional texts. These private books, mostly used by the laity and often lavishly illuminated with pious images, were structured to provide appropriate meditations for every hour of the day. A miniature in the Book of Hours of Catherine of Cleves, dated to around 1440, shows the unusual scene of Christ as a toddler, learning to walk in a walking frame.[2] Besides clearly sidestepping the institutionalised authority of scripture (in which this imaginative vignette does not appear!), such an image cuts across the ancient idea of Christ as the aloof, triumphant and majestic Son of God (which subtly presumes the insignificance of the viewer), suggesting instead that he is sweet, ordinary, vulnerable and human, and thereby invoking newly validated feelings of motherly tenderness, attentiveness and delight in the viewer. Apart from their intimate subject-matter, the very use of these small and often highly personalised manuscripts eased their users into a disposition of privacy and reflection that contributed towards the shaping and expression of the personalised self. Indeed the outward form of this meditative disposition is itself depicted in many books of hours – in the representations of the Virgin at the Annunciation that they usually include. In many examples of this scene, the Virgin is shown sitting in solitude reading a small book – very similar in form to a Book of Hours – whereupon she is interrupted by the archangel Gabriel (Fig. 3.3). Thus by looking at this image in a Book of Hours, the viewer, usually female, was not only responding as an observer to the sweetness of the theme; she was also entering into a state of *identification* with the Virgin who, in the very moment of observation, is shown doing exactly what she, the viewer, is doing: reading a small book. By extending the pattern of correspondences, she (the viewer) is also being invited to appropriate other attributes associated with the Virgin – most specifically her innocence, humility and receptivity to grace.

While all aspects of Christ's life were subjected to great scrutiny, the most vivid visualisations of his humanity were developed in relation to the Passion, partly because it was through his suffering and death that Christ was believed to have saved mankind and in which man was therefore most implicated, but also because it provided the most emotive material. Indeed, seeing that the iconography of the Passion did not develop into a focus for intense devotion until the thirteenth century, it is arguable that it did so at this time precisely because of the opportunities for affective experience that it offered. In the Orthodox Church, by contrast, the symbiotic relationship between the emergence of the affective self and the popularisation of Passion iconography – in which the former stimulated the latter,

THE RESURRECTION OF THE SELF

FIGURE 3.3: The Annunciation, with the Temptation of Eve (in a roundel, right) and a mother teaching her child to walk (bottom right), from the Françoise Fortin Book of Hours, Rouen, around 1480, by a follower of the Master of the Echevinage of Rouen, f.24v–25r. © Les Enluminures.

and vice versa – simply did not happen. Because the triumph of Christ took precedence over his suffering in the Orthodox Church, reflecting a disregard for the personal identities of the faithful, Byzantine and Orthodox icons continued to dwell on the triumphant image of Christ in Majesty, and devotion to the Passion (and the affective self) never became a cult, as it did in the West. On the contrary, icons of Passion subjects continued to be rare; even the Crucifixion was relatively scarce, only featuring in the cycle of Church feasts rather than as a point of focus in itself.

In the West, the impulse towards imaginative experience of Christ's suffering evolved over many years. Early medieval imagery of the Passion was interpreted in terms of its meanings, as we have seen. Besides telling the story that Christ died on the cross for mankind and triumphed over death, it was made to teach that, in order to be included in the salvation of the world, the faithful had to participate in the sacramental life of the Church. In this context, the death and resurrection of Christ were ritually re-enacted in the celebration of the Eucharist, rather than imaginatively experienced in realistic detail. In line with this position, early medieval images of the crucified Christ were usually presented as stylised statements of doctrine (Fig. 3.4). They had no emotive agenda and the face and posture of the figure of Christ were therefore expressionless (with a few notable exceptions). The figure is typically symmetrical, hieratic, static, frontal and alive; Christ's eyes are usually open and his head is upright. There is no attempt to suggest that Christ suffered on the cross because the image is not attempting to elicit feeling in the viewer. On the contrary, such images only exist as ritual affirmations of a preconceived truth, to which viewers are simply required to surrender, ignorant of the possibility of personal feeling (though *we*, of course, might find them moving, having been habituated to the psychological potential of stylisation by a century of modern art). From the late twelfth century onwards, however, images of the crucified Christ became more visually and emotionally realistic. Christ began to suffer. Initially his head dropped slightly and his body began to droop (Fig. 3.5). Over several decades, his suffering became pain, and his eyes closed (Fig. 3.6). Eventually, his pain became agony, and his agony became excruciating (Fig. 3.7). Especially in northern Europe, where the high-minded idealism of the classical tradition was not indigenous, every moment of his agony was imagined in the minutest detail and was felt intensely. For instance, one fifteenth-century 'witness' of the Flagellation advised his listeners:

> Behold, then, that good Lord shivering and quaking, all his body naked and bound to a pole; about him standing the wicked men, without any reason, full sore scourging that blessed body, without any pity. See how they cease not from their angry strokes, till they see him stand in his blood up to the ankles. From the top of the head to the sole of his foot, [his] whole skin they saved him none. His flesh they razed to the bone, and for weariness of himself, they him left almost for dead . . . A garland of thorns they thrust on his head, till the blood ran down his eyes, nose and mouth and ears.[3]

FIGURE 3.4: Volto Santo (Holy Face), North Italian, 1200–20, wood with polychromy, 226.4 × 204.5 cm. Metropolitan Museum of Art, New York, Fletcher Fund, 1947.

FIGURE 3.5: The Crucifixion, stained glass, Bourges Cathedral, 1215–25.

FIGURE 3.6: Derick Baegert, *The Crucifixion*, with Veronica and a Self-Portrait (wearing a maroon cap, left), Dortmund, Westphalia Propsteikirche, around 1475. Photo: Rolf-Jürgen Spieker, Dortmund

FIGURE 3.7: *The Vision of St Bernard*, 14th century, Rhineland, ink and watercolour, 25.5 × 18 cm. Schnütgen Museum, Cologne. Photo: © Rheinisches Bildarchiv.

In response to highly visualised descriptions of this kind, in which the reader is actively encouraged to 'behold' and 'see' what is being presented to him as if looking at a picture, more and more people began to experience the suffering Christ imaginatively, not only as a historical fact laden with significances but as a living reality in the present moment. In one fifteenth-century print of the Crucifixion with St Bridget in adoration, the blood of Christ was not part of the original concept of the image, which is elegant and composed; it appears to have been added by the viewer, as if Christ was bleeding copiously before her very eyes.[4]

Meditation on the suffering of Christ was facilitated by several cultural conventions that developed around it. One of the most popular and intense devotions of the period revolved around the instruments of the Passion or '*Arma Christi*' – the physical objects that featured in the Passion story. According to a legend, popularised in the thirteenth century, this devotion originated in the sixth century when Pope Gregory the Great was celebrating Mass. At the very moment at which he consecrated the sacred elements of the Eucharist, Gregory had a vision of the suffering Christ standing on the altar, in the place of the paten and chalice, shedding his blood (Fig. 3.8). Surrounding him were the various instruments used at the Passion. These

FIGURE 3.8: *The Mass of St Gregory* with the *Arma Christi* (against the back wall, behind Christ's tomb) by an anonymous painter, around 1500, oil on panel, 66.8 × 62 cm. Rijksmuseum, Amsterdam.

included the spear used to pierce his side, the sponge used to quench his thirst, the dice thrown by the soldiers to see which one of them would claim his seamless garment, the thirty coins for which Judas betrayed him, the nails with which he was pinned to the cross, the ointment jars brought by the three Maries to his tomb to anoint his body, the flail with which he was flagellated, the cockerel that that crowed three times before Peter realised he had betrayed him, the veil of Veronica and various others. From the thirteenth century, images of the *Mass of St Gregory* provided graphic teaching, in the traditional manner, that the bread and wine of the Eucharist are the body and blood of Christ. They also enabled the viewer to enter an imaginative state of focused meditation on the specific details of Christ's suffering and to wring every last drop of devotional potential from them with the utmost feeling. In some cases, worshippers were instructed to enlarge the image by a certain amount – to arrive at the 'exact size' of the actual object in question – in order to perfect the act of imagination; some images of the wound in Christ's side, entirely abstracted from its context to maximise intensity of focus, were depicted 'life-size' (Fig. 3.9). Most significantly, such images enabled the viewer to be activated and

FIGURE 3.9: The wound in Christ's side, with the *Arma Christi*, from the Prayer Book of Bonne of Luxembourg, Duchess of Normandy, attributed to Jean Le Noir and his workshop, France, before 1349, 12.6 × 9 cm. Metropolitan Museum of Art, New York, The Cloisters Collection.

substantiated as an 'affective self'. As St Bonaventure (1221–74) advised in his *On the Perfection of Life, Addressed to Sisters*:

> Since fervour of devotion is nourished and preserved in us by a frequent return of our thoughts to the passion of Christ, anyone who wishes to keep the flame of ardour alive within himself should frequently – or rather incessantly – contemplate in his heart Christ dying upon the cross.[5]

While imaginative contemplation of the suffering of Christ was originally intended to induce pity and repentance in its viewers, it was also practised at other levels. In some contexts, viewers did not merely respond to their experiences of Christ, as if they were separate observers; they began to empathise with him so passionately that they entered into a state of identification with him. Indeed, in the thirteenth century, the 'imitation of Christ' became a devotional ideal. The new mendicant orders, for instance, were largely based on the impulse to follow Christ's example of chastity, poverty, pity and mercy *literally*; they renounced all possessions and served the poor directly (founding the first hospitals and poor-houses, which further instituted the self-sense that generated them). To serve this end, they developed the *Via Dolorosa* – the route in Jerusalem that Christ took on the way to Golgotha – into a contemplative path along which devout Christians could proceed, physically or imaginatively, meditating on each of the fourteen points or 'stations' at which Christ rested the cross. Each station, including the one at which Veronica offered Christ her veil, became an object of meditation and an opportunity to re-live the suffering of Christ.

In the same spirit, 'Passion Plays' became popular throughout Europe. The origin of these plays lay in sung elaborations of Easter celebrations of the Eucharist (itself a ritual re-enactment of the Passion of Christ) that evolved in the tenth and eleventh centuries. By the fifteenth century, these re-enactments had developed into fully fledged dramatisations of the Passion, enhanced by the inclusion of much naturalistic but non-biblical detail in the scripts (for the sake of realism) that often lasted for several days. They were spoken in vernacular languages and were performed by the laity and guilds as popular ritual and entertainment in town centres. While their subject-matter clearly reflected an impulse to visualise the suffering of Christ, the fact that they were performed by lay people also reflects the extent to which imaginative identification had become a means of popular devotion at this time, enabling ordinary people to become personally and dramatically involved in the Passion. Moreover, the fact that each guild was responsible for a scene or play that related thematically to its profession indicates how the experience of identification with the sacred narrative was not simply restricted to the duration of the plays; it was also implicit in their work, pervading their lives and livelihoods. In York, for instance, the Last Supper play was produced by the guild of bakers and the Crucifixion plays by the guilds of pin-makers and butchers. The association of their professions with specific details in the Passion story 'qualified' them to assume these particular roles but it also obliged them to engage their daily work as a continuous contemplative dramatisation of the Passion story.[6]

The condition through which the faithful could most actively and intensely imitate Christ, to the point of identifying with him and becoming one with him, was his suffering. It was only through imaginative identification with his suffering that the alienated suffering of sin (the inheritance of all mankind) could be transformed and redeemed. The way in which identification with the suffering of Christ was seen to be synonymous with the reception of God's grace was iconised in the stigmatisation of St Francis, who was privileged to experience the wounds of Christ in his own body in 1224, as depicted in innumerable images thereafter (Fig. 3.10). To attract a similar state of grace, the most fervent aspirants wore hair shirts and indulged in a host of other methods of inflicting pain on themselves. Particularly to induce identification with Christ at his Flagellation, and to sublimate themselves in his agony, members of the new 'flagellant orders' whipped themselves until they bled (Fig. 3.11). Some mendicants and members of the laity believed that by inducing suffering in themselves, they were not only expressing repentance for their sins, thereby making themselves worthy of God's redemptive grace; they were also imitating Christ – almost to the point of death – in the belief that other aspects of his grace would naturally be realised in them, by the typically medieval logic of correspondence. In the early thirteenth century, the Cistercian monk Caesarius of Heisterbach encouraged his novices to be crucified 'with Christ' by the practice of virtue: 'the three nails by which the body of the monk ought to be affixed to the cross are the three virtues through which ... martyrs are made: obedience, patience and humility'.[7] In convoluted cases like this, the Passion of Christ and the redemption of man became so closely identified and causally inter-dependent that it seemed necessary and even desirable that Christ should die. It could even seem to be virtuous to cause his death – and even to kill him – because it was only through his death that the virtuous process of redemption could occur. In keeping with the complicated 'reverse' logic of this concept, some exceptional images of the Crucifixion show Christ being crucified *by* the virtues (personifications of Obedience, Humility and Love), who are thereby 'creating the possibility of salvation' (Fig. 3.12); they were presumably derived from the analogous notion of the monk 'crucified by the virtues'. Significantly, when the Crucifixion was presented as a pretext for teaching doctrine, as it was almost exclusively until the thirteenth century, it was studied by both sexes; but when it was upheld as a model for imitation, inviting the viewer to empathise with it to the point of identifying with it, it was primarily addressed to men. Women seeking the same affective experience were encouraged to identify with the Virgin suffering at the foot of the cross. There were, of course, exceptions: combining the medieval penchant for finding meanings in patterns, correspondences and inversions with a thoroughly feminised longing to identify with Christ's suffering, the fourteenth-century anchoress, Julian of Norwich (1342–1416), imagined the agonies of the dying Christ as the birth pangs with which he bears the faithful, as their mother, into eternal life.[8] An image in a thirteenth-century bible in Vienna shows Christ giving birth to the Church from the wound in his side – with a second figure of Christ performing the role of midwife – an occurrence that was seen to correspond with the creation of Eve from the rib of Adam (Fig. 3.13).

Because the imaginative and emotional self of the late Middle Ages 'needed' Christ to suffer and die (in order that it might evolve and be born), it was contingent that, in the imaginations of late medieval painters and writers, the triumphant Christ of the early Middle Ages should be made to suffer, and that every moment of his

FIGURE 3.10: Taddeo Gaddi, *The Stigmatisation of St Francis*, Italy, around 1325-30, tempera and gold on panel, 212.1 × 149.5 cm. Harvard Art Museums/Fogg Museum, Friends of the Fogg Art Museum Fund, 1929.234.

FIGURE 3.11: Pietro di Domenico of Montepulciano, *The Virgin of Mercy* (with Flagellants), around 1420, tempera on poplar. Musée du Petit Palais, Avignon.

FIGURE 3.12: The Virtues crucifying Christ, with personifications of Ecclesia and Synagogue (bottom left and right) from the *Bonmont Psalter*, around 1260, MS54 Besançon, f.15v. Image: IRHT CNRS, Bibliothèque municipale de Besançon.

FIGURE 3.13: The Creation of Eve (above) and Christ giving birth to Ecclesia (below), from the *Bible Moralisée*, around 1220, Vienna Codex 2554, f.1v. Osterreichische Nationalbibliothek, Vienna.

suffering should be contemplated in words or images. Over a period of three hundred years, the narrative of Christ's Passion was lived out in pictures. The purpose and effect of these pictures was both to express and to stimulate an emotional dimension of selfhood in their makers and viewers. Indeed, contemporary commentators noticed that many people were incapable of visualising, and therefore responding to, Christ unless they were prompted by paintings.[9] As responses to these images developed over the years, a veritable discourse of affective feeling evolved – involving words, gestures, actions, practices and institutions. Many of these

FIGURE 3.14: *Pietà* (possibly with real human hair), Freiberg Cathedral, around 1430.

conventions, and the values they embody, still provide the ethical and emotional core of western culture.

It is significant that, while images of the suffering Christ were abundant in the late Middle Ages, images of the dead Christ were relatively scarce. Those that do exist (for instance, the *Deposition from the Cross*, the *Lamentation*, the *Pieta*) show him, having very recently died, in the company, and often the arms, of mourners who suffuse the images with feelings of grief (Fig. 3.14). On account of these exemplary witnesses, the expectation of an emotional response on the part of the viewer is implicit in such images; this is especially clear in the three-dimensional life-size tableaus of the *Dead Christ with Plaintive Mourners* that became popular in Italy and France – for instance, the terracotta 'campianto' by Nicolo dell'Arca in Santa Maria della Vita in Bologna, made in 1462–4. For an image of the dead Christ that lies

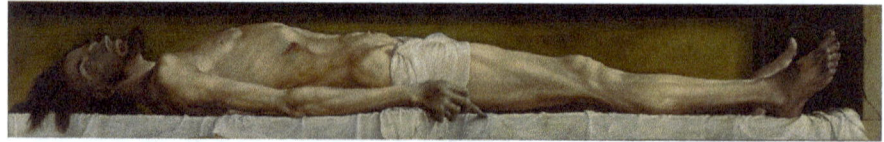

FIGURE 3.15: Hans Holbein, *The Dead Christ in the Tomb*, 1521–2, oil on linden wood, 30.5 × 200 cm. Kunstmuseum, Basel, Inv. 318.

outside of this narrative context, one has to wait until the very end of the Middle Ages. In Mantegna's *Dead Christ* (c.1480), the inert body has finally been laid to rest on the 'stone of unction', observed, but not touched, by the mourning St John, the Virgin Mary and Mary Magdalen. In Carpaccio's version of the scene (1505), these figures have begun to withdraw, albeit faintingly, leaving a single reflective observer with whom to identify. In Holbein's epic *Dead Christ* of 1521, the viewer is no longer invited to feel sorrow (Fig. 3.15). There are no mourning figures around Christ's body to suggest to the viewer how he should respond, and there is no longer any possibility of affective relationship with him; pity is now useless. On the contrary, the picture leaves the viewer stunned and numb. It is too late to repent, too late to identify with Christ's redemptive suffering, for he no longer feels pain. Acknowledging the extraordinary power of the imagination as the key to understanding late medieval imagery of the Passion, the Russian novelist Dostoyevsky responded to the picture by insinuating – ironically – that Christ *must* be dead, because it would be impossible to merely imagine such total and unquestionable deadness, that is, without the painter having *really* witnessed it.[10]

Just as images of the dead Christ were outnumbered by images of the suffering Christ at this period, so images of the Resurrection were also extremely rare. It remains a remarkable fact that the Resurrection, arguably the most significant moment in the life of Christ, was almost never represented in medieval images. The reason for this omission dates back as far as the Iconoclastic Controversy, when iconophile theologians legitimised the use of images on the grounds that representations of God had a precedent in the Incarnation itself. The fact that the Resurrection had not been witnessed by human eyes (the guards attending the tomb were asleep) meant that there was no objective precedent for visualising it; to have represented it therefore would have been tantamount to imagining it, which at that time would have been inappropriate and even heretical. In place of the Resurrection, two scenes that were closely related to the Resurrection, but which *had* been witnessed by human beings, were used: the *Three Maries at the Tomb* and the apocryphal *Descent of Christ into Hell*, witnessed by Adam and Eve on Easter Saturday. One example of this custom can be seen in the Alton Towers Triptych (Fig. 3.1); another is Duccio's *Maesta* (1307–11), which devoted as many as twenty-six panels to the Passion story (Fig. 3.16, the second scene from the right in the top two tiers). However, beyond the doctrinal reason, it is also arguable that the reason that the Resurrection was hardly ever represented in medieval imagery was that the imaginative faculty (and the personal self-sense that underpins it) had not yet *fully* evolved and, therefore, that Christ had not yet died – *in the imagination*. On the contrary, throughout the Middle Ages, his suffering was elaborated and *prolonged*. Indeed the 'medieval mind' needed Christ to suffer, rather than die, because it visualised

THE RESURRECTION OF THE SELF 55

FIGURE 3.16: Duccio, *Maestà*, 1308–11, tempera and gold on wood, 213 × 396 cm. Museo dell'Opera Metropolitana, Siena. Photo: Scala, Florence.

FIGURE 3.17: Piero della Francesca, *The Resurrection*, around 1460, fresco, 225 × 200 cm. Museo Civico, Sansepolcro. Photo: Comune di Sansepolcro.

the possibility of its own salvation *penitentially* in relation to his suffering; it needed him to suffer in order to be able to beg him with tears – or *implore* him (from *pleurer*, French for 'to rain') – for forgiveness. Moreover, as devotional imagery became more imaginative, realistic and subjective, it became less doctrinal, de-necessitating the justification of iconographic types on theological grounds. As a result, images of the Resurrection began to appear in western Europe (in contrast to Orthodox practice which continued to avoid the image, until subjected to Catholic influence in the eighteenth century). Although the image made its first discreet appearance in the twelfth century, it was not until the very end of the Middle Ages that it became not only widespread but central to the iconography of western Europe (Fig. 3.17). It was as if Christ had to die, both in images and in the imagination, before he could be seen to be reborn. Moreover, it was as if the makers and viewers of these images also had to suffer and die, in imaginative identification with the dying Christ, before they too could be reborn – or resurrected – as the men and women of the Renaissance. Indeed it is arguable that the very phenomenon of the Renaissance ('rebirth') constitutes, on the one hand, the occurrence of the Resurrection, or re-arising, of Christ – as realised objectively in the evolution of representations of the scene – and, on the other hand, the 'birth' of the individual self as the subjective capacity to visualise the resurrected Christ.

Throughout the Middle Ages, individuals were initiated into a sense of personal selfhood by the image of Christ's suffering. They learned the language of personal affectivity – 'how to feel' – by engaging with it. First of all, they observed it and responded to it. Because they *believed* themselves to have caused it by sinning – as an obligatory article of faith – they felt implicated by it and were therefore motivated by it to repent. But, as they began to empathise with Christ *imaginatively*, so they began to appropriate and imitate his own capacity for feeling – increasingly dramatising their similarity to him rather than their difference from him – until they finally became identified with him. And paradoxically, as they became increasingly identified with Christ, so their imaginary suffering was indeed consummated – in the realisation of his death as their own; and they were redeemed accordingly, in the sense that the painful separation of the self from the suffering Christ was superseded by its joyful identification with the risen Christ, to the extent that Christ's state of self-awareness was established in (and, ultimately, as) themselves. As Meister Eckhart had said: 'even God can only say "I" in so far as I am one with him.' The image of the resurrected Christ did not evoke a viewer that implicitly needed to imagine and *suffer* the 'truth' in order to be redeemed; that character had suffered and died with the medieval Christ, in keeping with its aspiration and capacity. On the contrary, it addressed a viewer, newly conscious of his own identity, in whom the rational dignity and intelligence of humanity had been awakened – more from ignorance and sleep (as demonstrated by the soldiers that slept as they guarded Christ's tomb) than from medieval sin and guilt. The image of the Resurrection was the reflection of such a man and, as such, it belonged to another age.

CHAPTER FOUR

The Localisation of the Self: the Origins of Perspective and the Accommodation of the Self in Pictorial Space

While the emergent sense of self was coterminous with the development of emotive iconography, this iconography would not have been effective if the manner in which it was conveyed had not also been convincing. Therefore one of the very first signs of the shift away from impersonal experience, mediated through stylised symbols, towards personal experience, mediated through realistic illusions, was the naturalisation of the representation of space in paintings, which began in Italy towards the end of the thirteenth century. Prior to this time, image-makers had shown very little interest in the illusion of pictorial space per se. While naturalism had been inherited from the classical world, by the twelfth century the representation of clothing had become so stylised that drapery folds were to all intents and purposes graphic conventions indicating form, rather than attempts to give a realistic impression of three-dimensional forms in space (Fig. 2.3). Moreover, the backgrounds in images of this period were typically blocked out with expanses of gold leaf, flat colour or pattern; these were either symbolic of a higher spiritual realm or decorative, in keeping with the didactic and decorative priorities of early medieval imagery (Figs 3.10, 3.11).

At the end of the thirteenth century, however, painters began attempting to render space more realistically. There were various ways to do this. The simplest method was to introduce elements of architecture into the image because the straight lines of buildings could be made to seem to recede into space more easily than complex, irregular forms such as clothed bodies. Although this device could be used for outdoor scenes by placing a building in the landscape, it was especially effective in indoor scenes which could be set within the rectilinear space of a room; raftered ceilings and tiled floors were especially helpful here (Figs 3.8, 4.4, 4.5). Secondly, objects that were supposed to seem distant began to be painted smaller – which, in the case of people, conflicted with medieval convention; in most early medieval imagery, figure size was symbolic, reflecting the spiritual importance of a figure rather than his or her physical proximity to the viewer (Figs 2.2, 2.3, 3.11). A third important device was shading. To help the straight lines of buildings seem to recede into the 'background' convincingly, the various walls of monochromatic buildings were often painted in different shades of the same colour, suggesting the presence of light and shadow, and thereby strengthening the impression of a real, unified space. Tentative attempts were also made to introduce modelling into the representation of irregular solids. The depiction of drapery was eventually raised to a virtuosic level of naturalism and, in some cases, takes up as much as half of the picture surface (Fig. 8.2). In the representation of faces, observed gradations of light came to replace the naïve formulaic masks of the twelfth century. The new use of linseed oil as a paint medium was of paramount importance here. Although oil had been used in various circumstances and in combination with other substances for several centuries, it was not until the fifteenth century that it became the primary medium for panel painting, superseding egg tempera. Because oil is viscous and slow-drying, it enabled painters not only to work more slowly, engaging in the new and time-consuming process of observation and changing their minds where necessary, but also to blend their paints with greater subtlety, achieving a wider range of colours and a more nuanced grading of glazes; this in turn encouraged them to use colour descriptively, rather than decoratively or symbolically, enabling them to represent forms in more detail and with more accuracy than any other medium – a characteristic that would eventually help substantiate the claim of painting to be the most expressive and therefore noble of the pictorial arts.

One of the earliest attempts to master pictorial space was the cycle of frescos, depicting scenes from the lives of Christ and the Virgin, painted by Giotto for the Arena Chapel in Padua in around 1305. The scene that depicts Joachim and Anna, future parents of the Virgin, sharing their joy at the news that Anna is to give birth to a child reveals much about the painter's thought process (Fig. 4.1). Giotto capitalised on the fact that the meeting took place at the Golden Gate outside Jerusalem by using the architecture to introduce a modest impression of perspective into the design. He has clearly observed that when a building is seen from an angle (rather than head-on), the top will seem to slope down as it recedes and the ground-line will seem to rise up – even though they are, in actuality, parallel – and so this is how he has depicted the Golden Gate: the top and the base of the tower are made to converge to the left in order to give the impression that the building recedes into real space. This observation, which is reflected in several of the frescos in the cycle, was clearly of great interest to him. As far as the iconography of the scene is concerned, this detail makes no real difference and it would therefore have been of no interest to a twelfth-century painter. Its presence here, by contrast, indicates that Giotto is not relying on the subject-matter alone to convey the content of the picture; he is also prescribing the *manner in which the picture is seen* and investing the 'manner of seeing' with communicative potential. By creating an illusion of depth, he is giving a slight impression that the space in the picture – the 'pictorial space' – is an extension of the space of the viewer – the space we occupy – and therefore that the events that take place in the picture are co-extensive with the events that take place in the viewer's own space. As such, he is acknowledging the existence of the viewer's space and ascribing a degree of cultural value (or at least potential cultural value) to the experiences that are possible there. More importantly, he is acknowledging the existence of the identity of the viewer – the implied subject (or 'self') of the experience he is creating – albeit in its most embryonic form. This position stands in stark contrast to early medieval practice in which sacred events belong to a higher, symbolic realm, on a plane that is not continuous with, or comparable to, the viewer's world; nor is that elevated realm seen to be naturally visible from, or affected by, the viewer's world. The implication of the new mode of seeing, however, is that, if the viewer experiences the event as occurring in his own space (i.e. if he is 'taken in' by the illusion of naturalistic space in the painting, as intended by the painter), he will react to it in a different way – as if it was a real event. This shift, which corresponds exactly to the shift of sacred iconography towards convincingly affective realism, is of immense significance. Firstly, the painter is downplaying the symbolic and didactic *modus operandi* of the image, in favour of its immediate effect on the imagination, and is thereby implicitly relativising the power of the agent that controls the symbolic meanings of images – that is, the Church (though surely without intending to, in this case). And secondly, by presenting the narrative as a real event, worthy of a realistic reaction, he is investing the personal experience of the viewer with potential value, implicitly empowering him as an individual. Even more important than the particular nature of the viewer's reaction to the image is the fact that his existence is registered by it at all. For the first time, the viewer is not only invited to react to a preconceived truth; on the contrary, his world has become an *integral part of the logic of the picture*; the logic of the picture acknowledges the logic of the individual self, and even offers to accommodate it. Indeed, it is as if the sense of self is 'called into being' by the picture – to correspond to the (illusion of) space that is created for it. This is precisely the process that is accomplished by the evolution of linear perspective during the Renaissance. Typically, early medieval images represent self-contained and self-authenticating truths; the viewer is expected to react to the teachings that they convey, but he is thoroughly external and incidental to them; there is nothing in them that implies his presence and there is nothing in his experience that could alter the nature of their truth. In Giotto's work, on the other hand, we see the first examples of paintings in which there is evidence (on the part of the painter) and expectation (on the part of the viewer) that the realistic experience of the viewer is meaningful and legitimate, and therefore that personal identity is meaningful and legitimate.

While Giotto's forays into perspective were groundbreaking, they were nevertheless transitional. For although the solid blue background in *The Meeting of Joachim and Anna* (and throughout the cycle) clearly indicates the sky and is therefore meant to suggest depth, it also belongs to the medieval tradition of simply blocking out the spaces around figures with flat fields of solid colour – frequently in blue but also in other colours. Similar ambiguities are evident in the lighting of the work. Giotto has taken great care to observe that if an object is exposed to a particular light source, the side of the object exposed to the light will be brighter than the side that is not. Reflecting this observation, his draperies are modelled in a newly graded, if still formulaic, manner; this may seem like a basic step but it was not made by his predecessors (Fig. 2.3). Moreover, his understanding of this principle was clearly limited. He was able to observe the play of light and shade within an object, but not

FIGURE 4.1: Giotto, *Meeting of Joachim and Anna at the Golden Gate*, from the Arena Chapel, Padua, 1305.

around it. He appears to have worked out how to depict each object individually, and then to have transposed them, one by one, into the image. As a result, although each object (e.g. the leg of the man in brown to the left of the image) is individually modelled, none of them throw shadows. Giotto's tendency to look at objects in isolation is again reflected in the fact that the two towers are lit from different light sources: the tower on the left is lit from the right (its right side is lighter than the front) while the tower on the right is lit from the left (its right side is darker than the front). Clearly the painter has observed or imagined the towers independently, but he has then placed them in the picture without taking their context, or their relationship to each other, into consideration. He has observed that the sun can be to the left and that it can be to the right, but he has not seen that it cannot be in both places at the same time. He did not synthesise his observations; he did not subject them to a higher abstracted concept or principle in order to unify them and make them consistent. This is not exactly to say that he was 'incapable' of unifying his observations – it would be anachronistic to think this; it is simply that the idea of unifying them in this way had not yet developed. Moreover, it is possible that, by placing the darker areas towards the sides of the picture and the lighter areas towards its centre, he was simply applying the medieval principle of decorative symmetry to the design. More to the point is the fact that the frame of reference within which the convention of perspective acquired meaning – the frame of mind in which personal experience is rooted – had not yet evolved. It was evolving in his hands.

There are several examples in the Arena Chapel cycle in which a *realistic effect* takes priority over the communication of *meaning*. For instance, in the *Pentecost*, one of the apostles' faces is partially obscured by a column and another is shown with his back to the viewer, rendering him unrecognisable. Before the thirteenth century, this practice was extremely rare, for the simple reason that it made the figures impossible to identify – and if one cannot identify the figures and know what their significance is, what is the point in having them? To an early medieval mind, this would have seemed bizarre, even blasphemous. But, to Giotto, the realism of this detail was more important than its meaning, and the identity of the apostle was therefore sacrificed, to make the overall effect of the image more realistic and more likely to induce a 'realistic' reaction in the viewer.

Giotto's works reflect the extraordinary psychological effort that the painter made to allow the truth of observation to challenge the power of tradition and authority. They embody a tension between the impulse to experience the visible world as it is seen with the eyes – in three-dimensional space and lit by locatable light sources – and the force of the pictorial tradition (and the beliefs invested in it) that seems to resist that impulse. It is as if a struggle is taking place between Giotto as an individual self, striving to realise the truth of his own experience for the first time, and Giotto as the impersonal instrument of traditional doctrine. It is for this reason that he is considered to be one of the very first 'artists', and that Giorgio Vasari, the 'first art historian', commenced his *Lives of the Most Excellent Painters, Sculptors and Architects* (1550) with biographies of Giotto and his contemporaries, presenting them as the earliest manifestation of a *rinascita* (or rebirth) in the arts. But beyond the inherent value of his work, Giotto was also a 'prophet' of personal identity because his work transmitted the possibility of personal experience to his viewers. On the one hand, the viewer is expected to respond to the narrative and symbolic dimension of the frescos, acknowledging the truths they present. But on the other hand he is invited to be convinced, on account of the innovative treatment of light and depth, that the pictorial space in which the sacred events appear to be happening is continuous with the space in which he is standing and, therefore, that the sacred events represented there are an extension of his own experience, which is thereby implicitly validated.

Giotto's understanding of perspective was rudimentary and experimental, rooted in observation, and it corresponds to an incipient and partial realisation of personal identity. Throughout the fourteenth century, pictorial space continued to be represented by means of the piecemeal 'trial and error' perspective that he pioneered and, as a result, it continued to seem fragmented and inconsistent. It was not until the beginning of the fifteenth century that a more systematic approach was taken to the art of perspective, resulting in more consistent representations of pictorial space. This more unified sense of space led to a more realistic experience of the events taking place in that space, which in turn corresponded to a more coherent realisation of the sense of self, on the part of both the painter and the viewer. The crucial step was taken by Filippo Brunelleschi (1377–1446), one of the most influential architects of the Renaissance, who formulated a theoretical principle of perspective that enabled subsequent artists to subject their individual observations of space to a single overriding system. The principle, conceived in around 1415 and first published in Leon Battista Alberti's *De Pictura* (*On Painting*) in 1435, simply stated that all the straight lines in a picture that are intended to look parallel to each other as they recede into pictorial space (called 'orthogonals') should be painted in such a way that they converge at a common 'vanishing' point, usually near the centre of the image, despite the fact that, in 'real' space, parallel lines never meet. The important advance in this system was that it enabled painters to create a *unified* impression of pictorial space. This was precisely what Giotto's work in the Arena Chapel lacked. In Giotto's rendering of the *Birth of the Virgin*, for instance, the orthogonals either converge too quickly or they diverge, suggesting that the painter conceived them independently, as was his manner, without subjecting them to a synthetic vision of the picture space as a whole.

Brunelleschi's theory was revelatory and it was immediately adopted by painters all over Italy. The first to apply it systematically was Brunelleschi's friend, Masaccio, who was working in Florence from around 1420. Masaccio's frescos in the Brancacci Chapel in Santa Maria del Carmine, painted in 1424 and depicting scenes from the life of St Peter, are among the earliest works in which the perspective is based on calculation rather than the juxtaposition of independent observations (Fig. 4.2). The cycle occupies the two side walls of the chapel – each decorated with two long frescos, one above the other – and the altar wall that links them. The frescos are clearly indebted to Giotto, whose work Masaccio could have seen elsewhere in Florence, but they also incorporate a number of new features. Above all, Masaccio has rationalised his observations by subjecting them to an overriding principle. For instance, he used architecture in a rigorous and consistent way to create a unified sense of space; all the orthogonals, however small and apparently negligible (i.e. including tiny ledges and steps), converge on a single vanishing point. Moreover, the even and consistent distribution of light and shade on faces, clothing and buildings reflects a single light source, convincingly suggesting that the space they pass through is homogenous. This impression is consolidated by the presence of shadows which help to integrate the lit objects into the space around them. As a result of these devices, the impression that the depicted scenes occupy a space that is continuous with the viewers' space and that they are seen from a specific position in that space, as determined by the perspective, is that much more convincing than it was in Giotto's work; and the implication therefore that a viewer does, or at least could, exist there is that much stronger. The impression of the viewer as a particular 'optical' self, located in a body in space, was gradually cohering – in conjunction with the illusion of pictorial space that co-evolved to accommodate it.

Although Masaccio's approach to naturalism is extremely rational and experiential, he did not use these new pictorial devices simply to increase the illusionism of his work and to 'naturalise' the experience of seeing it, as Giotto had tried to do. He also invested them, rather ingeniously, with a symbolic dimension, highlighting the Christian significance of the commission. His use of linear

FIGURE 4.2: Masaccio, *The Tribute Money*, 1425, Brancacci Chapel, Florence.

perspective serves two purposes. In the fresco of *The Tribute Money* (Fig. 4.2), the convergence of the orthogonals on to a single vanishing point enhances the sense of the unity of the pictorial space, but the fact that the vanishing point coincides with the face of Christ, who stands at the centre of the painting, also ensures that the viewers' eyes are immediately drawn to him as the dramatic centre of the work; there is no question therefore that, although the image acknowledges the value of optical experience, it is ultimately oriented around its Christian message. *The Tribute Money* represents the moment in the gospels at which Christ admonished Peter to render 'what is due to Caesar to Caesar, and what is due to God to God'. It appears that by subjecting his own interests in the independent possibilities of painting to the purposes of Christian iconography, this is exactly what Masaccio himself was trying to do: to honour both his emerging capacity as an individual to value his own experience, and the traditional teachings of Christianity. And this is precisely what was being extended to his viewers: an invitation to become rational and observant individuals, and to use their new potential to deepen their faith.

The role of the light sources in the frescos is also novel. Like the orthogonals, they serve both a visual and symbolic function. Firstly, they are consistent within each of the frescos, reinforcing the sense of unified space. But, more remarkably, they are also consistent within the whole series: the light in all of the scenes seems to come from the end of the chapel where the altar is placed below a window. The significance of this is that, in addition to their individual coherence, the experience of the frescos is harmonised both with the experience of the architectural space, as their light seems to be coming from the window in the altar wall that illumines the chapel, *and* with the spiritual experience of receiving light, albeit symbolically, from the altar. To highlight the spiritual significance of light and shadow – and of Masaccio's mastery of it – one of the frescos, to the immediate left of the altar, shows St Peter healing the sick *with* his shadow (Fig. 4.3). Giotto would have had trouble representing this scene.

The desire of painters to use linear perspective to help create the perfect illusion of three-dimensional space on a two-dimensional surface came to a head with Piero

FIGURE 4.3: Masaccio, *Peter cures a sick man with his shadow*, 1425, Brancacci Chapel, Florence.

della Francesca, who lived and worked in Tuscany from the 1430s until around 1480. Like Masaccio, Piero used linear perspective to enhance the Christian subject-matter of his work. He was, however, a mathematician and geometrician as well as a painter and his use of perspective was both more complex and more subtle than that of his predecessor. His *Flagellation of Christ*, painted in around 1460, is a case in point (Fig. 4.4). Besides employing an elaborate perspectival scheme to create a consistent and convincing impression of depth, the painting is composed around a rigorous system of mathematical proportions or ratios. The fact that Christ is placed in the background of the work and to one side, apparently overshadowed by three worldly grandees in the foreground, is striking, as it dramatically contradicts the medieval requirement that the importance of a figure should be reflected in his size; nor does the vanishing point seem to coincide with the figure of Christ. However, a closer analysis reveals that the location of Christ's face has in fact been specifically calculated in relation to the overall proportions of the painting. Firstly the shape of the painting incorporates the proportions of the 'golden mean': the proportion of the 'height of the picture to its width' is the same as the proportion of the 'width of the picture to its height and width added together' – that is to say, A:B is the same as B:A+B (approximately 1:1.618 = 1.618:2.618). This proportion, which had intrigued philosophers since the time of Pythagoras, was called the 'divine proportion' by one of Piero's pupils, the mathematician Luca Pacioli, who published a treatise on the subject in 1509. Secondly, the location of the face of Christ was determined in the following manner: imagine that the left-hand edge of the painting is the side of a square (the right-hand edge of the square will fall near the central column); join the top left-hand corner of the square to its bottom right-hand corner with a diagonal line; place the point of a compass on the top left-hand corner and draw an arc between the bottom left-hand corner and the top right-hand corner of the square; place the largest possible square within the arc (sharing the top left-hand corner of the first square); draw a second arc, between the bottom left and top right-hand corners of the new square. The point at which the new arc crosses the initial diagonal line (between the top left-hand corner and the bottom right-hand corner) determines the position of Christ's face. Thus, despite the initial impression of randomness, the composition of Piero's *Flagellation* was directly submitted to the Christian function of the picture as a whole. His use of perspective and proportion was thoroughly integrated into the overall dynamics of the painting, introducing elements of complexity and delay into the telling of the story and thereby deepening and prolonging its dramatic impact.

FIGURE 4.4: Piero della Francesca, *The Flagellation*, 1455–60, tempera on panel, 58.4 × 81.5 cm. National Gallery of the Marches, Urbino. Photo: Scala, Florence, courtesy of the Ministero Beni e Att. Culturali e del Turismo.

Considering the fact that Piero cleverly concealed his devices, downplaying their role as mere symbols, what was their significance? Surely it lies in the way they formed part of a pictorial language that reconciled religious belief with a rational experience of nature. The sensory world was no longer seen to be illusory and alienated from the spiritual world; it was seen to grant access to that world by virtue of their shared proportions. For Piero, rational experience did not involve attempting to understand the significance of Christ's life (the subject-matter of most of his paintings) through analysis of scripture and tradition, as it had in the Middle Ages. It involved understanding how the Christian mysteries were fundamentally in harmony with mathematical proportions which he considered to be spontaneous manifestations of the divine intelligence in nature and the universe. Indeed because he regarded proportions as manifestations of divine intelligence, he spoke of them as 'ratios' (from the Latin word *ratio*, meaning 'calculation' or 'reasoning'), implying that man had access to divine intelligence not just by conforming to the precepts of the Church but through his rationality – that is to say, to the extent that he was in harmony, through the natural clarity of his mind, with the proportional relationships in nature and (in his own case) art.

In another painting associated with Piero – *The Ideal City* – which was probably painted by one of his followers in around 1480, the correspondence of proportion and perspective to rational clarity is taken to its limits (Fig. 4.5). Indeed, by adopting the rigorous geometry of the *Flagellation* – but without a narrative or figures – the painting seems precocious; it must have been because it was conceived in conjunction with a piece of furniture, and was therefore seen to be partly decorative, that it was possible. Unlike Giotto and Masaccio, the painter of *The Ideal City* was not maximising the realism of the image in order to make the narrative more realistic, and the meaning more convincing – for there is no narrative or meaning here. He is doing it for its own sake. And the existence of the viewer that is implied by the painting is therefore also validated for his own sake – not as someone to be educated or affected by convincing illusions of Christian truths, but as a subject of rational experience, unencumbered by irrational beliefs, who merely stands in harmony with the natural and rational order of the world. The perspectival scheme is so abstracted and absolute – so far removed from the imperfect appearances of daily life – that it scarcely functions at all as a narrative space 'in which something could happen'; on

FIGURE 4.5: Circle of Piero della Francesca, *The Ideal City*, tempera on panel, 67.7 × 239.4 cm. National Gallery of the Marches, Urbino. Photo: Scala, Florence, courtesy of the Ministero Beni e Att. Culturali e del Turismo.

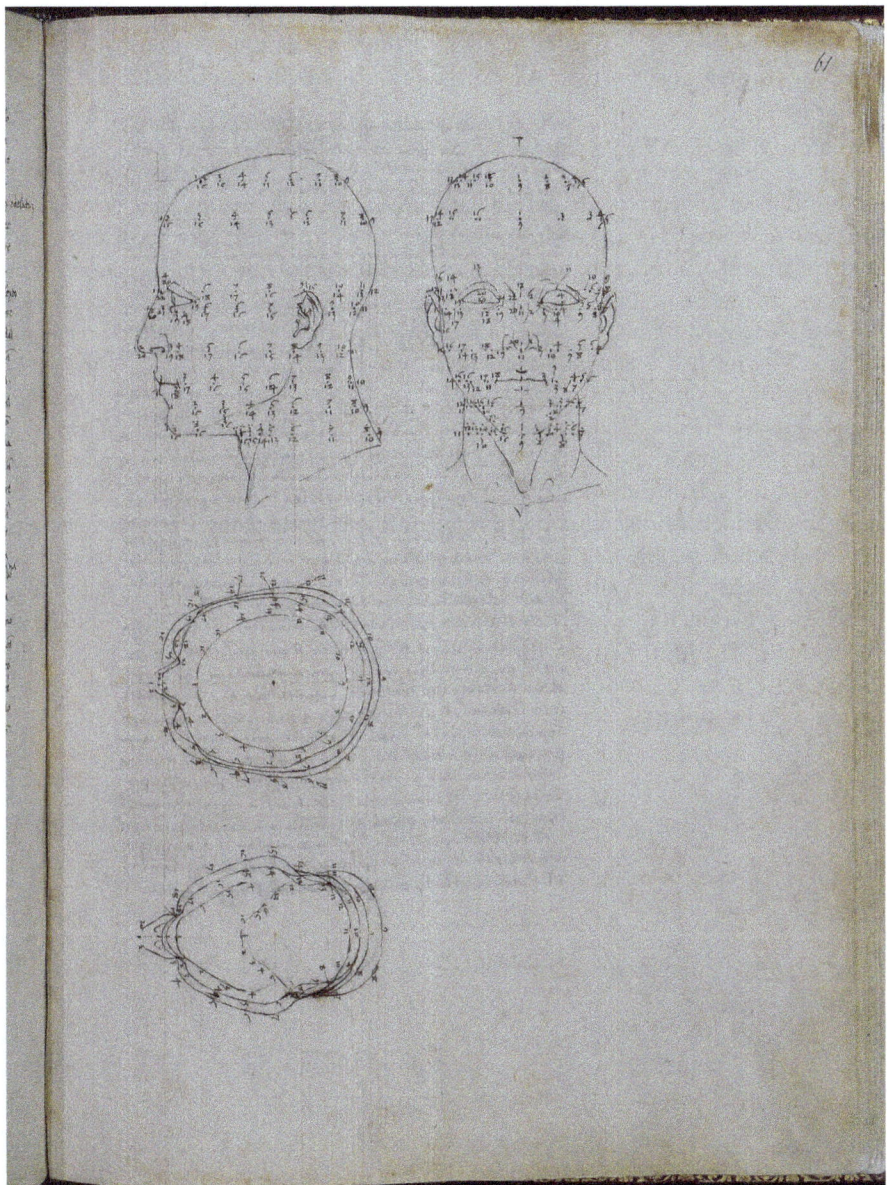

FIGURE 4.6: Piero della Francesca, *Drawing of a Human Head in Perspective*, from *De Prospectiva Pingendi* (*On Perspective in Painting*), book 3, proposition 8, Biblioteca Palatina, Parma, MS 576, folio 64 recto.

the contrary, it functions as a rational 'frame of mind'. It is calculated on the basis of internal considerations, rather than observation of the outside world, and, as such, it represents an 'ideal environment', reflecting and invoking an ideal state of selfhood in its viewers.

Many painters relied on the presence of orthogonals in their works to create a persuasive illusion of space, as in *The Ideal City*. Piero, however, was as adept with non-rectilinear objects, such as human bodies, as with rectilinear ones. Linear perspective was of course of no help to him in this context. To overcome the problem of drawing irregular forms, he devised a laborious system of calculating the coordinates of numerous individual points on the three-dimensional forms in question, as seen from a variety of points of view, before transferring them to a two-dimensional surface. This method is laid out in a treatise, *On Perspective for Painting*, that he wrote in the 1470s. In some of the designs produced to illustrate this treatise, Piero reduced the forms to numerical data, translating them into structures of numbers that anticipate the isometric designs of the digital age. In one image – of a human head, seen from the side, front, top and bottom – Piero abstracts and idealises the face to such an extent that it becomes transpersonal; it is entirely realistic but it appears to have no psychology (Fig. 4.6). This is not to say that it does not represent an individual. On the contrary, it seems to purify and perfect individuality – and the selfhood it implies – by raising it to a level of total objectivity. Indeed, this individual could be an inhabitant of the *Ideal City*. In this respect, the similarity of his face to that of the risen Christ in Piero's fresco of the *Resurrection* – the only frontal figure in Piero's *oeuvre* who looks directly at the viewer – is especially suggestive (Fig. 3.17).

CHAPTER FIVE

The Necessitation of the Self: the Ennoblement of the Artist and the Invention of an Archetype

According to legend, the second sleeping soldier from the left in Piero della Francesca's *Resurrection* is a self-portrait (Fig. 3.17). If this is so, then the painting is a paradox because it represents both a vision of the Resurrection of Christ and Piero's own unconsciousness of that Resurrection. As an ordinary man, Piero depicted himself – in keeping with medieval belief, and like the soldiers guarding Christ's tomb – as being unable and unworthy to see the Resurrection; because this scene was not actually witnessed, and was therefore unprecedented in experience, it was hardly ever represented by medieval painters, who felt disinclined to 'invent' images. But although Piero considered himself to be asleep as a man, *as a painter* he allowed himself to see what his ancestors had not been able to see. While Piero's 'waking up' to the fact of the Resurrection is in itself momentous, reflecting the unprecedented awakening of a new capacity in himself, it is also of immense significance that this awakening was accomplished, not in his identity as a mere man but in his identity as a painter, and through his art. Moreover, by allowing viewers to share his vision – through his art – he (and other painters of the scene) enabled them too to wake up and *see the Resurrection*, thereby realising the birth of a new self-sense in themselves.

By 'revealing itself' through painting, the image of the Resurrection implicitly conferred a unique status on that art and its practitioners, for it legitimised the presence of individuals at an occasion which, according to the gospels, was not experienced by human eyes. In due course, the legitimacy that was extended to individual identity by this image would become part of the currency of European culture. But, in order for this to occur, the language and conventions of individuality – the forms in which a sense of individuality could be accommodated and sustained – needed to evolve and become institutionalised in cultural life. We have already seen how both the content and the form of late medieval and early Renaissance imagery evolved in conjunction with this development. At first, these new conventions continued to serve a traditional model of identity, ultimately submitted to the Church, albeit in a newly realistic way. The fragments of personal experience that they invoked in their users were insufficiently substantial to effect a wholesale shift in their centre of gravity away from the communal identity of the Church towards a self-conscious sense of personal identity; besides, at this early stage, these innovations were still used to enhance the purposes of the Church. But, as the role that these conventions played in the articulation of a new model of identity became increasingly established, so their significance also began to change, to the extent that they eventually became independent cultural functions, institutionalising an independent model of selfhood. With regard to the production of imagery, these independent functions would eventually crystallise into the discourse of 'art', whereupon the notion of the 'artist' and of the 'consumer of art' would become primary manifestations and agents of personal identity in Europe and beyond.

In the event, the legitimacy of personal identity was first exercised not by painters but by the socially superior *patrons* of painters. As with the other self-reflecting innovations of the period, this initiative evolved within the context of the Church. Since the fourteenth century, it had been common for patrons to have themselves represented in the sacred images that they commissioned, often paying homage to Christ or the Virgin (Fig. 3.8, 6.4). Despite occurring occasionally in the early Middle Ages (mostly among royalty), the trend did not reach its full potential until the fifteenth century, when the development of naturalism enabled depicted patrons to be recognised. Despite the presence of patrons, such images were primarily conceived as objects of devotion for the benefit of viewers, though they were of course also expressions of the patrons' piety; indeed, the fact that the patrons were 'immortalised' in images reflects their wish that their devotion to the Virgin and Christ should continue to be expressed perpetually – through their representations – both during and after their lifetimes. However, besides being genuine expressions of piety, donor-pictures also reflected the patrons' wish to *demonstrate* their Christian devotion to the viewer of the painting and to sanctify their authority: by having themselves shown in positions of reverence towards the holy figures, and by showing themselves to have generously patronised the painting in question, they communicated to the viewer how humble, devoted and munificent they were (or considered themselves to be). As a result, besides serving as devotional objects both for viewers and for themselves, such pictures also functioned in some sense as *portraits* of the donors, reflecting their sense of personal identity. They accomplished this in two ways – firstly, in the conventional way, by representing a visual 'likeness' of the donor – itself a novelty – and secondly by promulgating aspects of his or her reputation (devotion, virtue, dignity, generosity). Indeed, to the extent that the subject-matter of such commissions was determined by the donor, such pictures were *self*-portraits – for they were ultimately more expressive of the patron's individuality and inclinations than of the painters'. In fact, the same can be said of regular portraits – another hugely significant innovation of the period (after a millennium of neglect). These images are more likely to bear an inscription or coat of arms identifying the sitter than a signature identifying the painter; it is arguable therefore that they are as much 'works of patronage' as they are 'works of art'. In such a context the painter was a tool or technician, realising the creative idea of the patron, who was representing himself by having himself painted.

A subject that lent itself particularly well to the display of pious affluence was the *Adoration of the Three Kings* or *Magi* (bringing gifts to the infant Christ). In some examples of this scene, the kings or magi are accompanied by, or modelled on, rich patrons and their families, who are thereby shown to be similarly noble, reverent, generous and wise. Indeed, by having himself represented as one of the three kings, a patron could seem to be sacralising his affluence and power by placing it at the service of God. Some patrons took advantage of the scope that the iconography offered to represent a royal entourage by including many members of their own court or family in the image. This was the case in fifteenth-century Florence, where munificent individuals came together in a confraternity dedicated to the Magi (the *Compagnia de' Magi*). First among these was the ruling Medici family, who took a leading role in annual celebrations of the Journey of the Magi, symbolically re-enacted each year on the feast day of Epiphany as a festive procession from 'Jerusalem' (the countryside outside Florence) to 'Bethlehem' (the city centre). In Benozzo Gozzoli's fresco of the *Procession of the Magi* in the Palazzo Medici in Florence (1459–60), set in the landscape around the city, the three kings are followed by a large crowd, led by recognisable members of the Medici family towards an altarpiece of the *Adoration of Christ in the Forest* by Fra Filippo Lippi which, appropriately, does not include its own kings.[1] Occasionally, painters included themselves in such crowd scenes. In these cases, it is not always clear whether they were simply using themselves anonymously as models, or whether their image functioned as a kind of visual signature; certainly in some cases painters 'signed' their work by placing a self-contained picture of themselves, complete with illusionistic frame and inscription, in a discreet position within it. In Benozzo's case, the painter very clearly wanted to be recognised as himself, as he signed his cap *Opus Benotii*, wittily inviting the viewer to 'note well' (*ben noti*) that he was both the talented author of the fresco and included in the courtly entourage. In Botticelli's painting of the *Adoration*, executed for an affiliate of the Medici family fifteen years later, the princes no longer accompany the kings; they have *become* the kings, boldly appropriating the royal honours for themselves (Fig. 5.1). Again, the painter 'signs' the picture with an image of himself at its right-hand edge (if we are to accept the long-standing tradition that the figure cloaked in yellow is indeed him). In both paintings, the narrative is overwhelmingly dominated by the glorification of the patrons and, consequently, it is the identities of the patrons that are being celebrated.

In both cases, however, it is the image of the painter that specifically engages the viewers' attention. This is because, out of the forty or more characters depicted in each picture, the figure of the painter is one of the very few (three or four) – and certainly the most prominent – who make eye contact with the viewer. Eye contact between at least one figure in a picture and the viewer was one of the characteristics of the new 'realistic' painting that Alberti recommended in his treatise *On Painting*. It is of special significance that, in most of the earliest examples in which this feature occurs (until around 1500), the figure that makes eye contact with the viewer is the painter himself, in a discreet act of self-reference; the figure behind St Veronica in Derick Baegert's *Crucifixion* is another example (Fig. 3.6, far left). This may simply be because, when painters looked at themselves in order to depict themselves, they used mirrors, and therefore always saw themselves making eye contact with themselves; but it is also consistent with the fact that it was often considered disrespectful for people of inferior social status (including painters) to make eye

FIGURE 5.1: Sandro Botticelli, *The Adoration of the Magi*, around 1476, tempera on panel, 111 × 134 cm. Uffizi Gallery, Florence.

contact with their superiors (even in paintings). Moreover, prior to this period, the level of intensity and intimacy achieved by eye contact had been reserved for cult images of Christ – as, for instance, in images of the *Salvator Mundi* or *Veil of Veronica*. Thus, a majority of early portraits of sitters other than the painter himself show the sitter looking away from the painter; several of them show impersonal profiles, in imitation of classical coins. Three-quarter-view portraits, in which the first signs of individuality were captured, originated in Flanders and became standard in Italy in the second half of the fifteenth century (Fig. 5.2). This impersonal quality was largely due to the fact that many early portraits were unsentimental statements of status and identity, usually focusing on the head and face, without including any expressive gesture, posture or personal attribute to tell the viewer something secondary about the sitter; rather like passport photos, they documented an individual's identity, in a quasi-existential manner, by simply recording their appearance. According to the German painter and print-maker, Albrecht Dürer, some such pictures were produced to preserve the likeness of a person after their death; others were painted to be sent for approval to prospective spouses. Although they often reflect remarkable powers of observation and were executed with exquisite skill, they do not represent attempts to capture a personality or establish a relationship with the viewer. This is especially

FIGURE 5.2: Jan van Eyck, *Man in a Blue Cap*, around 1430, oil on panel, 22.5 × 16.6 cm. Brukenthal National Museum, Sibiu.

clear in posthumous portraits of medieval saints or kings whose appearances and characters were unknown: as the contract between personal identity and personal appearance was consolidated, plausible likenesses had to be invented for such individuals in order to 'identify' them. As we have seen in the important case of Christ himself, documented knowledge of his features was required not so much to shape his personality as to prove his identity and existence (Fig. 3.2).

By producing portraits of 'other' people, painters were instrumental in creating a convention that accommodated the notion of personal identity. But, by depicting *themselves*, they raised the possibility of self-awareness to a new level. Certainly, as we have seen, the portrait of a patron could be a self-portrait of a kind (if the sitter commissioned it); but in such cases it was only the patron who saw himself reflected in it. By contrast, a self-portrait *of the painter*, which involved a prolonged process of self-observation in a mirror, extended the possibility of self-awareness to *all* viewers. Not only did the self-portrait institutionalise the experience of self-awareness by providing it with a concrete form but, by virtue of the eye contact that it usually made with the viewer, it transferred the experience of 'self-seeing' directly to him or her. For this reason, among others, the art of painting began to acquire a new significance.

Whereas Benozzo's self-representation in the *Procession of the Magi* is an image of sustained, detached scrutiny, acknowledging the viewer but with no sense of psychological drama or challenge, in Botticelli's *Adoration*, the painter clearly involves the viewer in the dramatic implications of his presence; by virtue of the painter's wry expression, the viewer becomes complicit in the painter's self-awareness. Either way, the fact is that, by making eye contact with the viewer, the painted figure explicitly includes the viewer in the iconography of the painting. As we have seen, the illusion of pictorial space per se (whether partial, as in Giotto, or complete, as in *The Ideal City*) presupposes a possible viewer – a located 'optical' self – because it appears to be an extension of the 'real' space in which the viewer is standing; it implicitly includes the viewer's space in the overall space in which the depicted action occurs. However, although *The Ideal City* suggests that its picture space *could* be entered by a viewer standing in front of it (or that a figure in the pictorial space *could* leave the painting and enter the viewer's space), it does not, in itself, imply that a viewer actually *is* standing in front of it. The presence of a viewer is not *explicitly* stated in the painting, as there is nothing in the painting that *explicitly* refers to him, and, as a result, the personal identity of the viewer is also not explicitly realised; it is only realised as a *possibility*. By contrast, a painting in which there is a figure making eye contact with the viewer is specifically and explicitly presupposing the presence of the viewer in front of the picture. As such, the viewer becomes a part of the logic of the picture, an integral part of its iconography. The logic of the figure looking out of the picture depends on the fact that he is seeing the viewer; one can tell, by looking at him, that he is not looking at something else in the viewer's space – he is looking *at the viewer*. Moreover it also depends on the fact – at least in the moment of viewing – that the viewer is seeing him – because it is only in that moment that the viewer can *see* that he (the figure) is seeing him (the viewer). The figure making eye contact with the viewer therefore *necessitates* the existence of the viewer, calling him into being.

The individual through whom these developments came to a head was Albrecht Dürer (1471–1528), who lived and worked for most of his life in Nuremberg. Whereas the association of eye contact with self-portraiture may have evolved in a piecemeal fashion, partly as a practical outcome of the use of mirrors, in Dürer its value was explicit and consciously laden with significance. Dürer's writings indicate that he was highly aware of his status and, somewhat exceptionally for his time, he produced images of himself throughout his life – at least twelve, including three autonomous self-portraits. In all but one of these images, the painter is shown looking at the viewer. The exception is the earliest one, produced in 1484 when Dürer was only thirteen years old, before he could have become aware of the significance of the genre. Much later – when he *was* aware of the significance of the genre – he wrote on the image (a drawing) that he had drawn it 'with a mirror . . . when I was still a child'; in fact, because it shows him looking to the side, he must have used *two* mirrors. In his *Feast of the Rose Garlands* (1506), in which several dignitaries are assembled around the Virgin and Christ, rather as in an *Adoration*,

THE NECESSITATION OF THE SELF 75

FIGURE 5.3: Albrecht Dürer, *The Feast of the Rose Garlands*, 1506, oil on wood, 162 × 192 cm. National Gallery, Prague.

Dürer discreetly but stylishly placed himself in the crowd – though, in his case (unlike the Benozzo and Botticelli *Adorations*), he is the *only* figure looking out at the viewer (at the back of the picture, on the right, Fig. 5.3). In several of his self-portraits, including the *Feast*, Dürer shows himself wearing extravagantly flamboyant clothing – presenting himself not as a craftsman or painter, but as a courtier or poet. Especially following his first visit to Venice in 1495, he expressed an 'Italianate' concern for the elevated status and dignity of painters. No amount of self-styling, however, prepares the viewer for the depth of identity that the painter finds in himself in the celebrated *Self-Portrait* of 1500, in which, although it is not manifestly stated, he clearly represents himself as a likeness of Christ – in the typical frontal format of the medieval *Salvator Mundi* (Saviour of the World) but with the sanctified demeanour and presence of the Risen Christ (Fig. 5.4).

This picture is remarkable for a number of reasons. Firstly, along with Dürer's other representations of himself, it is one of the first ever autonomous self-portraits in the western tradition. In this respect alone, it documents an important moment in the changing status of the art of painting, and in the formation of selfhood. Though the circumstances in which it was made are unknown, the work appears not to have been painted for a particular situation that might explain it (for instance, as a visual

FIGURE 5.4: Albrecht Dürer, *Self-portrait*, 1500, oil on panel, 67.1 × 48.9 cm. Alte Pinakothek, Munich. Photo: bpk Bayerische Staatsgemäldesammlungen.

signature or marriage proposal). In fact, it appears to have been an independent exercise in self-exploration, produced when the painter was at the height of his powers. Dürer's gaze is not merely that of a painter analysing himself in the mirror. On the contrary, by wearing the fur-trimmed coat of a patrician or humanist, he was clearly conscious of the impression he was making on his viewers, not only as a painter but also as a powerful individual with his own dignity and status. This characteristic concern with his status is, however, soon overshadowed by the calm but penetrating quality of his attention and regard. Unlike the complex narratives of Benozzo and Botticelli, the eye contact that he maintains with the viewer does not simply draw the viewer into the picture, as a kind of sub-plot to the main drama; it *is* the main drama, engaging the viewer so directly and intensely that his necessary presence in front of the picture, and his visual contact with the painter, become the core subject-matter of the painting. Having said that, the possibility of a socially or psychologically nuanced dimension to the relationship is eliminated by the severe frontality of the painter's face and body, which differentiates the portrait from all other examples of the period, including Dürer's other self-portraits, in which the painter's face is slightly turned away from the viewer, despite maintaining eye contact with him. As a result, the relationship that the viewer forges with the painter is a purely existential, transpersonal one. He is 'merely necessitated' by the picture; that is to say, he is identified by it as a necessary subjective presence, but as nothing more than that. He is evoked as a pure embodiment of identity, remaining untouched and unqualified by the transience of personal psychology or by other legitimising contexts.

The directness with which Dürer delivers his statement of personal identity in this work is already remarkable; the fact that the painter has clearly based it on an image of Christ raises it to another level. Significantly, if surviving records are anything to go by, neither Dürer nor any of his contemporaries actually commented on this connection; indeed, this observation was not first documented until over one hundred years after the picture was painted.[2] Nevertheless, the symmetrical and frontal format of the pose, the general physiognomy of the painter and the resemblance of his hand to the hand of Christ raised in blessing are all unquestionably derived from medieval devotional images of Christ. By appropriating these elements, Dürer was not simply admiring himself and attempting to attract the glorification aimed at Christ towards himself; as we saw in relation to heretics of the Free Spirit, who believed the Holy Spirit to have incarnated in them, to have done so would have been heretical. On the contrary, in keeping with the biblical teaching that 'God made man in his own image' (Genesis 1, 27), both in his being and in his creativity, Dürer was appropriating the divinity of Christ to the status of his art and to his own identity as an artist. On the one hand, he was framing his art as a potential medium of illumination, capable of bestowing 'blessings' on the viewer by engaging him in transformative acts of the imagination. On the other hand, he was presenting the 'artist' as an archetype of creative potential and personal inspiration in which the viewer might be graced to see himself reflected. This motive was entirely in keeping with attempts by contemporary painters in Italy who were striving to raise painting from the level of a craft to the level of an inspired 'divine' liberal art. But, to *identify* with the risen Christ, rather than confess one's own negligence and unworthiness of him – as implied by Piero's representation of himself sleeping through the *Resurrection* – was unprecedented in painting.[3]

The fact that Dürer merged his monogram AD with the date of the *Self-Portrait* – 1500 AD (*anno domini*) – echoes the way in which he merged his own facial identity with that of Christ. Bearing in the mind the demi-millennial status of the year, it suggests that he was aware of the timing and epoch-making significance of the picture. Having said this, the tradition of identifying with Christ did have historical roots and Dürer was surely aware of them. As we have seen, the 'imitation of Christ' existed as a widespread form of piety throughout the late Middle Ages, not as a means of aggrandising oneself by associating with the majesty of Christ, but as a means sublimating oneself in his suffering. Dürer may have also have made use of this tradition: one of the most popular frontal images of Christ's face – the 'Veil of Veronica' – was generated by this tradition of imaginative, empathetic devotion and, in 1513, Dürer produced a woodcut of the image in which the face of the suffering Christ may be his own. Be that as it may, the fusion of the individual soul with Christ or God became a popular ideal in the late Middle Ages, reflected both in pictorial aids to contemplation and in contemplative texts, and it precipitated changes to the concept and experience of selfhood. Like most of the images designed to facilitate direct unmediated communion of the soul with God, most of the texts written in this context were passionately devotional: these range from the mystical teachings of Meister Eckhart and his disciples John Tauler and Heinrich Suso to the celebrated *Imitation of Christ*, written by Thomas à Kempis in the Netherlands in around 1420. The written source, however, that most closely resonates with Dürer's *Self-Portrait*, and may have inspired it, is a treatise by the mystical philosopher, Nicholas of Cusa, called *On the Vision of God* (*De Visione Dei*), written in 1453 for a community of monks in Tegernsee in southern Germany. Nicholas' text revolves around the observation that, when a viewer looks at a picture of a face in which the eyes are looking at the viewer, the eyes will *always* seem to be looking at the viewer. Even if ten people look at the picture at the same time, each person will have the impression that the face is looking at them alone. Interestingly, one of the images that Nicholas cites as an example of this phenomenon was a self-portrait by Rogier van der Weyden which the painter included in his crowded *Justice of Trajan*, produced for the town hall in Brussels in 1438. According to a late fifteenth-century tapestry copy of the painting (which was destroyed in 1695), the only figure to be making eye contact with the viewer was the painter.[4] Nicholas used this phenomenon as a metaphor for the inter-dependent nature of the relationship between God and man. In order to make his point more clearly, he supplied the monks at Tegernsee with what he called an 'icon of God' – possibly a 'Veil of Veronica', a print of which was included in many early manuscripts of the treatise. The first point to arise is that God's vision (and love) of man is causally linked to man's vision (and love) of God: just as a man cannot look at a frontal image of Christ without Christ seeming to be looking at him, so man cannot see God unless God sees him; and conversely, Christ cannot see the viewer (or rather, cannot be *known* to be seeing the viewer) unless the viewer is seeing Christ. The very phrase *Visione Dei* aptly conflates the meanings of 'seeing God' with 'God seeing' as if there was no difference between them, affirming that 'that which sees God' is 'God seeing' – God seeing himself: 'O Lord, when You look upon me with an eye of graciousness, what is Your seeing, other than Your being seen by me? To see you is not other than that You see the one that sees You.'[5]

Nicholas of Cusa stands on the threshold between the Middle Ages and the Renaissance. Indeed, he has been credited with one of the first ever uses of the term 'the middle ages' (*media tempestas*) – to signify the period of human history that falls between classical antiquity and the revival of classical values in his own time. Nicholas' use of this term indicates that he was himself aware that a 'new time' was currently evolving, to enclose the 'middle time' in the past. And, to some degree, he epitomised the developments in the 'new time' that he was noticing (rather as Joachim of Fiore had, 250 years earlier). Chief among these was his recognition of the integral and active role of man in the spiritual economy of the world. Man was no longer entirely passive to the process of redemption, as dramatised in the late Middle Ages by people's need to induce passive states of suffering in themselves. On the contrary, man was already fundamentally and inherently identified with God through his deepest essence, and especially through his creativity, which Nicholas considered to be divine action in him. However, although Nicholas believed in the infinite unity and indetermination of God and all things, he also explained that man tended involuntarily to differentiate himself from God by unconsciously imposing his limited capacity for self-knowledge on to him (God). That is to say, man's vision of God is determined by his capacity both to see God and to know himself, in such a way that God will appear to him as an image of himself (the viewer) – that is, as a kind of self-portrait:

> Whoever looks unto You with a loving face will find only Your face looking lovingly upon him. And the greater his endeavour to look more lovingly unto You, the more loving he will likewise find Your Face to be. Whoever looks angrily unto You will find Your Face likewise to display anger. Whoever looks unto You joyfully will find Your Face likewise to be joyous, just as is the face of him who is looking unto You. For just as the bodily eye, in looking through a red glass, judges as red whatever it sees, and as green whatever it sees if looking through a green glass, so each mental eye, cloaked with contraction and passion, judges You who are the object of the mind, according to the nature of the contraction and the passion. A man can judge only in a human way. For example, when a man ascribes a face to You, he does not seek it outside the human species; for his judgement is contracted within human nature and does not, in judging, go beyond the passion that belongs to this contractedness. Similarly if a lion were to ascribe to You a face, he would judge it to be only lion-like; an ox, ox-like; and an eagle, eagle-like.[6]

It is in exactly this manner that Dürer saw and painted himself in his *Self-Portrait* of 1500 (Fig. 5.4). He saw himself as a 'vision of God', as determined by his own capacity for self-knowledge. God was revealed to him as his own nature and identity – not as the absolute suffering that was traditionally believed to be a prerequisite of salvation but, at the very core of his being, as a man. Moreover he also saw God 'as God sees Himself'; that is, in the form of himself-as-Christ for, as Meister Eckhardt had said: 'even God can only say "I" in so far as I am one with him.' This is ultimately what is most significant about this picture: it provided a cultural form in which the sense of the individual self was sacralised as a self-authenticating truth. The proliferation of self-portraits (first manifest in portraits of donors commissioned by themselves) established the convention of self-reference as a cultural *possibility*; the introduction of eye contact in portraits (especially in the self-portraits of painters) consolidated it as a cultural *necessity*, and Dürer's Christ-like *Self-Portrait* raised the self-necessitating autonomy of self-awareness to the level of *sanctity*, to the point at which the possibility of knowing God, and therefore of attaining salvation, was determined by it.

It was through a plethora of cultural forms and conventions, including works of art, that the possibility of self-awareness was first mediated to 'ordinary' people. As the dynamics of personal identity began to reverberate throughout society, so it began to leave traces in the cultural, social and psychological contexts that it touched. By slow degrees, the cultural fabric of the time became moulded into shapes that resonated with it. As the sense of self became more established, so a discourse of thoughts, feelings, words, actions, gestures and objects began to cohere around it; and as this discourse began to stabilise, gradually institutionalising the possibilities of self-awareness in its forms, so it became independent, spontaneously precipitating these possibilities in subsequent generations, as norms. Eventually an entire apparatus of self-reflexivity was developed around it, deeply pervading all the forms and conventions of the culture.

One of the most effective of these conventions was – and, to a considerable extent, still is – the notion of the 'artist' as an archetype of creative potential, embodying the ideal of self-authenticating personal selfhood. Another was the concept of 'art' or artistic culture as the archetypal medium in which that sense of selfhood thrives; as we have seen, it was partly through the painter's 'art' that the possibility of self-reference was first realised – explicitly in self-portraiture and implicitly in painters' visions of the resurrected Christ. But, just as the characteristics of works of art had evolved (their style and subject-matter etc.), so the very notion of 'art' was also a convention that needed to develop over time. In the Middle Ages, the concept of 'art', as we know it, did not exist. All practices that required manual skill, including carving, modelling and the painting of panels, were mechanical 'arts', and they were executed by technicians and artisans. From cooper to cordwainer, lorimer to fletcher, artisans required no intellectual abilities, in which the uniquely valuable commodity of *meaning* was invested, and they were therefore unworthy of respect. But, as painters – and sculptors – began to *imagine* and *look* – both at the world and at themselves – and to *express* what they saw, so they began to generate new intellectual contexts around themselves that held them in place as significant selves – not only in their own minds, but also in the expectations of others. The new value they conferred on themselves – and, by extension, on the self-sense per se – became enshrined in a range of new conventions and institutions.

As painters became less required to perpetuate the pictorial traditions of the Middle Ages, and less subject to the detailed dictates of patrons, they became more personally responsible for the appearance and effect of their works; the devices of naturalism and perspective evolved in conjunction with these changes, as we have seen. Even if patrons continued to choose the overall iconography of their commissions, the way in which the iconography was 'interpreted' (by means of composition, setting etc.) was increasingly left to the painter. As a result, painters came to see themselves as creative, rather than simply executive, and therefore more akin to poets than mere craftsmen; and as creators, they aspired to receive credit for their inventions; sculptors felt the same. They demanded both that their skill be elevated to the level of the liberal arts, which had been revered since antiquity, and that they be recognised as 'artists'. In antiquity, the 'liberal arts' – grammar, rhetoric and logic (the *trivium*) and geometry, arithmetic, music and astronomy (the *quadrivium*) – were considered to be the intellectual skills expected of a *free* man (*liber* in Latin) in contrast to a slave. Significantly, no visual medium was included among them; indeed Plato had considered all forms of representation to be a source of illusion rather than of truth. However, painters and sculptors now aspired to appropriate the right to think, feel and act freely and independently, in keeping with this standard, inaugurating an 'era of visuality' – in which unprecedented epistemological value is invested in *visual* representation – that continues to this day. In so doing, they were evolving an archetype of individual creativity and freedom that was to become the keystone of European culture.

Besides reconceiving the status of their respective practices, painters and sculptors also defined their virtues in fierce competition with each other. Painters' belief in the equivalence of painting and poetry had a classical pedigree, associated with the famous saying from the *Ars Poetica* of the Roman poet Horace: *ut pictura poesis* – 'as is painting, so is poetry'. According to this formula, painting and poetry were of equal intellectual dignity, offering the same scope for the expression of noble ideas. One of the earliest Renaissance revivals of this concept occurred in Alberti's treatise *On Painting*, in which the author recommended that painters substantiate their claim to being liberal artists by versing themselves in poetry and classical learning, both for its own sake and for use in their work. Botticelli's *Calumny of Apelles* was self-consciously based on the description by the ancient Greek satirist Lucian of a lost painting (of calumny) by the celebrated painter Apelles. Alberti also claimed that the use of perspective entitled painters to higher status, since this skill (explained in print for the first time elsewhere in the treatise) not only conferred an intellectual dignity on their work, but was also based on geometry and arithmetic which were themselves liberal arts. This trend was reflected in the way several sculptors of the period – including Ghiberti and Donatello – attempted to introduce the benefits of perspective into their work by producing reliefs (in contrast to free-standing figures). Relief sculpture also enabled sculptors to work with another of the qualities of painting that commentators upheld as one of its unique 'ennobling' advantages – evocative backgrounds. In his notes for an (unrealised) *Trattato della pittura* (*Treatise on Painting*), Leonardo da Vinci further extolled the superior virtues of painting – at the expense of both poetry and sculpture – by drawing attention to the unique ability of painters to represent light and colour, depict transparent objects and create convincing simulations of texture.

Some artists, most notably Michelangelo, aspired to appropriate the intellectual status of poetry by actually writing poems – though he did this, ironically, partly because he regarded hours of discomfort on scaffolding in the Sistine Chapel as tiresome and menial. Michelangelo famously maintained that sculpture was more honourable than painting because of its proximity to the classical ideal, its longevity, its realistic (rather than simulated) play with light and shadow, and its ability to capture every aspect of its subject 'in the round'. In order to address the latter criticism, some painters included two views of the same subject in a single painting – one of them reflected in a mirror, or in reflective armour; images of women at their toilette, which often included mirrors, lent themselves particularly well to this kind of virtuosity (Fig. 8.12). Even sculpture did not enable the viewer to see the front and back of its subjects at the same time, as these images did; indeed, unlike poetry and music, painting enabled a viewer to take its content in all at once. Leonardo further rebutted Michelangelo's view, by claiming that sculpting was a sweaty, manual task, unbefitting a dignified man, and that a painter could work while wearing the fine robes of a courtier and poet, and while listening to music or recitals of verse. Indeed, Leonardo clearly aspired to courtly status and, for much of his career, he was respected more as a courtier than as an artist. Significantly, discussion about the relative merits of painting, sculpture and poetry was itself considered worthy of a courtier, and Baldassare Castiglione gave much time to the subject in his contemporary manual of courtly conduct, *The Book of the Courtier*. The fact that architects and artists such as Alberti, Ghiberti (who wrote a book of *Commentaries* on art in around 1450) and Leonardo also wrote treatises on the arts is a further reflection of their aspiration towards literary status, especially when their treatises are peppered with classical references.

Besides highlighting the artistic potential of painting and sculpture, the debate about the relative status of the two skills – called the *paragone* (or comparison) – is significant for two key reasons. Firstly it demonstrates how new cultural values and the corresponding habits of mind were actually created, generating the forms that accommodated them: as experimental conversations and new activities occurred, and were repeated and modified, so patterns began to emerge and crystallise into conventions. And secondly, it shows the extent to which perceptions of personal honour and dignity were of paramount importance at this period – in some instances, more than life itself. It was for this reason that artists strove so ostentatiously to establish and defend their personal dignity and honour. The *paragone* reached a climax in 1547 when the artist Benedetto Varchi sent a series of questions to eight contemporary painters and sculptors, including Michelangelo, Vasari, Cellini, Pontormo and Bronzino, asking for their views on the subject. Regardless of its inconclusive outcome, which Varchi published in Florence in 1550, the debate was a key circumstance in which the concept of the artist was forged into an archetype. When its aim – to defend Catholic representation against Protestant iconoclasm, and to raise the status of art – was sufficiently achieved, it lost momentum, conceding that both painting and sculpture were honourably indebted to *disegno* (which implied 'conceiving' objects as much as 'designing' them).

This diplomatic compromise was accepted by Giorgio Vasari, who firmly and finally enshrined the significant status of the artist in his *Lives of the Most Eminent Painters, Sculptors and Architects*, the first book on the history of art, which, like the *paragone*, was published in Florence in 1550. In this monumental survey of the lives of artists, commencing with Cimabue (c.1240–c.1302) and Giotto, and coming to completion in his own day, Vasari, who was himself an eminent painter, mapped out the history of what he called – for the first time – a *rinascita*, or rebirth, of the arts. Although he clearly had a political agenda, favouring Florence at the expense of Venice and including hardly any non-Italian artists, Vasari's work describes and reflects a shift in the status of art that quickly prevailed across the whole of Europe. His nomination of several artists – especially his master, Michelangelo – as 'divine' reflects their new status as creators and not just executors, of art, though it also recalls the devotional tenor of medieval *Lives of the Saints* which the text resembles both in its basic concept and form, and sometimes in its liberal approach to fact and fiction. More important, however, is the fact that, by identifying the *rinascita* of the arts as a historical phenomenon, Vasari elevated the status of painting and sculpture to a level at which they could be considered worthy of intellectual study. Moreover, because Vasari's *Lives* both *described* the *rinascita* (charting the evolution of art towards a state of pre-eminence) and was itself a *sign* of the *rinascita* (in the novelty and timing of its ratification of art), it was self-reflective; that is to say, because it was historicising art *up to and including the present time*, it was in effect historicising *itself* – explicitly manifesting and instituting the self-awareness that the impulse to historicise the contemporary 'Renaissance' presupposed.

In conjunction with these developments, the associations of the workplaces of artists also began to change. By the middle of the fifteenth century, the notion that painters were 'poets without words' was reflected in the embellishment of some craftsmen's 'workshops' with the associations of a 'studio', which implied a degree of intellectual *study*. In Florence and Rome, some institutions, dedicated to the study of a variety of literary and scientific subjects, refashioned themselves as 'academies', based on Plato's philosophical Academy in Athens. Following the example of Marsilio Ficino's Platonic Academy, which was founded in Florence in 1462 to foster discussion and translation of Platonic philosophy, the word 'academy' also began to be used in the context of the training of artists, as it still is. In keeping with the classical associations of this word, characteristically 'academic' practices, such as studying anatomy and learning to draw by copying antique sculpture, became current at this time; the sculptor Baccio Bandinelli referred to his studio as an 'academy' in 1531 (Fig. 5.5). The first of many formally established art academies – the *Accademia delle Arti del*

FIGURE 5.5: Enea Vico, *The Academy of Baccio Bandinelli in Rome*, around 1544, engraving, 30.6 × 43.8 cm. Metropolitan Museum, New York, Purchase, Joseph Pulitzer Bequest, 1917.

Disegno (Academy of the Art of Drawing) – was founded in Florence in 1562. Conceived by Vasari and others under the patronage of the Medici prince Cosimo I, it superseded the Guild of St Luke, founded in 1339. In Rome the painters' guild became an academy in 1577.[7]

Although the Florentine and Roman drawing academies were modelled on Plato's Academy, and were therefore typical examples of the Renaissance revival of classical precedents, they are also typical examples of the way in which ancient sources were used throughout the fifteenth and sixteenth centuries to facilitate and contextualise the evolution of new cultural values. Various features of the arts of this period – naturalism, portraiture etc. – can be explained as 'revivals' of classical conventions, and plenty of humanists did in some sense attempt to reinvent the past – for instance by forging classical literature or recreating antique works of art that had only survived in verbal descriptions. Even the new notion of the 'artist' was legitimised by reference to classical precedents such as Praxiteles, Zeuxis, Apelles and Phidias (who was even said, by Plutarch, to have depicted himself). By reconstructing the lost painting of *Calumny* by Apelles, Botticelli was not only demonstrating his knowledge of classical literature in which the painting was recorded; he was also assuming the position of the master who painted it. The humanist scholar Erasmus claimed that Dürer surpassed Apelles because he could do with black lines what the classical painter could only do with colour; a stone relief of 1522 shows Dürer in allegorical combat with Apelles, vying for supremacy.[8] But classical sources were not revived for their own sake; they were revived because they provided contemporary culture with the vocabulary, techniques, ideas, associations, values etc. with which to effect and legitimise change: in the present context, they served to substantiate the discourse of art and, above all, the emerging sense of personal identity that art facilitated. The significance of the Academy as an incubator for the 'artist as an archetype of self-awareness' is reflected in a picture of St Luke as the personification of painting that Vasari was commissioned to produce for the Chapel of St Luke – which belonged to the new *Accademia* – in the Santissima Annunziata in Florence (1567–73, Fig. 5.6). The chapel was dedicated to St Luke because he was the patron saint of painting, anciently believed to have painted the Virgin and Christ from life, and thus to have initiated and authorised the entire tradition of religious imagery. The painting is nominally an expression of piety (via St Luke) and the dignity of antiquity (via the Academy); but the fact that it was also a self-portrait underlines Vasari's complicity and pride in appropriating the sacred and newly academic status of 'art' as a function of his own identity.

The academies of art were conceived to accommodate the intellectual ambitions and potential of artists, and to differentiate them from traditional craftsmen whose training and work was regulated by guilds. Until well into the fifteenth century, painters had trained in workshops as apprentices, as did all craftsmen, learning and practising the technical skill or 'art' of painting – as recorded, for instance, in Cennino Cennini's *Craftsman's Handbook*. Written in around 1400, at a time at which the intellectual content of images was determined by patrons, Cennino's *Handbook* was primarily a technical manual for guild members, though he did also offer some early comments on the painter's need to imitate nature and use his sense of fantasy or 'invention' in the manner of a poet – in contrast to the typically medieval copyist. This shift towards the association of the intellectual potential of

FIGURE 5.6: Giorgio Vasari, *St Luke Painting the Virgin and Christ*, 1565, fresco. Santissima Annunziata, Florence.

image-making with painters had a profound effect on the other traditional crafts, polarising them, by contrast, as purely utilitarian and technical activities. Indeed, to some extent, the elevation of painting to the level of a liberal art was coterminous with the divestment of the applied arts of intellectual potential because it depended on the formulation of the imaginative faculties of the mind as distinctive from, and superior to, those skills that were subject to the practical needs of the body and society, and were not, therefore, entirely 'free'. Just as 'art' required the realm of the imagination to be independent of any practical application that might seem to limit its value as an intellectual activity, so it implicitly needed the utilitarian crafts to be alienated from that realm.

During the Middle Ages, the designs for images in all media (ceramics, silver, textiles etc.) had been conceived by the *makers* of objects; their compositions were often based on precedents but they were also determined by the nature of the materials and techniques in which they were made. The design process was therefore part and parcel of a process of production in which decoration and form came together as an integrated whole. This was the case, for instance, in relation to stained-glass windows, one of the glories of the Middle Ages, especially in England and France. In the twelfth and thirteenth centuries – the heyday of the medium – stained-glass windows had been made out of solid sheets of coloured glass; these sheets were made from what was called – confusingly – 'pot metal', molten glass of a single colour. They were then cut into the required shapes before being assembled and held in place by lead strips called 'cames', with a cross-section resembling an H, in order to hold two pieces of glass (Fig. 3.5). The significance of this detail is that the design of the image was to a large extent determined by the technique in which it was executed – and therefore the image was, to a significant degree, designed by its maker. With the exception of some details applied to the surface of the glass shapes in a black charcoal-based medium, the element of drawing in the design was provided by the lead strips which inevitably imposed their own character on it – bold, stiff and stylised, but visible from a distance and therefore entirely fit for purpose. In the fourteenth century, however, this inter-relationship began to change. Improvements to the design of furnaces and kilns enabled glaziers to control the temperatures of the glass to such an extent that they could both apply thin glazes of translucent colour to the surface of separate sheets of clear glass without cracking them and also produce a wider range of colours. The first glaze that they were able to control in this way was yellow, derived from silver sulphide – accounting for the many black, white and yellow painted glass windows of the period (Fig. 5.7); but several other colours were also soon discovered. This innovation meant that glaziers could begin to paint *on* sheets of glass, in a naturalistic style and with a full range of colours, without having to submit to the physical requirements of the 'pot metal' and 'cames' technique. As a result, the design was no longer determined by the technique. For the first time, it became possible for glaziers to transfer designs conceived for other media (often engravings or drawings, provided by 'artists') directly to their own medium (Fig. 5.8). In this way, they, and other craftsmen like them, began to institutionalise the difference between artists (who were responsible for the 'respectable' intellectual or poetic content of objects) and technicians (who were 'merely' responsible for making them) *in* their practice and products. They were also subtly contributing to the elevation of the role of the artist (albeit in an inverted manner, and at their own expense) and to the setting of the parameters of selfhood that the role incorporated.

The new technique of copper-plate engraving – the dominant medium through which designs were disseminated from the sixteenth century onwards – prospered both as a cause of, and a response to, the growing independence of subject-matter from the physical medium of manufacture. As drawing became more sophisticated and craftsmen became less disposed to produce their own imagery, source books of printed designs became common. At the same time, the reputations of artists were spread through the dissemination of prints of their work, many of which were used as designs for the decoration of objects in a wide range of media, whether the prints had been designed to be adapted to other materials or not, and regardless of the technical properties of those materials. Dürer's prints, for instance, were frequently used in this capacity. The most extreme case of the association of the prestige of a

FIGURE 5.7: *Workshop of Veit Hirsvogel the Elder*, St Augustine (after Hans von Kulmbach), around 1507, stained glass, 45.7 × 40.6 cm. Germanisches Nationalmuseum, Nuremberg.

FIGURE 5.8: Hans von Kulmbach, St Augustine, design for a stained-glass window, around 1507, ink with wash and chalk on paper, 33.5 × 31.2 cm. Erlangen, Graphische Sammlung der Universität, inv B235.

product with its artistic and poetic content, at the expense of its actual manufacture, was the life-size painted designs, or 'cartoons', that Raphael produced in 1515–16 for a series of tapestries to hang in the Sistine Chapel in Rome. Although the cartoons were originally made as templates to be copied, the fact that they were produced by an 'artist' ensured that they eventually became more highly prized than the artefacts for which they were made, produced by a mere craftsman. For several centuries, tapestry makers had produced objects that were many times more expensive and prestigious than paintings, due both to the cost of the materials and the quality of their workmanship; but as the status and autonomy of 'artists' began to gather momentum – due to their learning rather than their wealth, according to Alberti – so the status of merely technical craftsmen began to decline, making way for the notion of 'art', and for the sense of an aspirational self that it accommodated. It is no accident that the ultimate depletion of the functional arts in the eighteenth century – during the Industrial Revolution, when manufacturing processes were mechanised – coincided with the perfection of the Romantic ideal of the artist – at the other end of the scale – as an inspired 'genius'. Through the development of this archetype, the self-sense that the notion of art implicitly accommodated was finally liberated from the functional constraints of utilitarian culture, ultimately enabling it to dissociate from the mortality of the body altogether and to 'transcendentalise' itself.

CHAPTER SIX

The Abstraction of the Self: the Secularisation of Subject-Matter and the Commodification of Art

The development of the art of perspective raised the perception of space to a level at which it acquired cultural value and became cultural currency, mediating new meaning among the people that engaged with it. By offering a convincing illusion of space, perspectivally calculated paintings blurred the boundary between the pictorial world and the 'real' spatial world of the viewer, implicitly accommodating the viewer within themselves. Integrally related to this shift in the *manner* of perception was a shift in the *content* of perception. For, just as a new or different pair of spectacles makes the world seem different (as Nicholas of Cusa pointed out in 1453), so changes in 'how people looked' resulted in changes to 'what people saw'. Indeed, it is no accident that the first eyeglasses were produced in Italy at the end of the thirteenth century when it first became possible to make lenses, for it was precisely at this time that people began to value what they saw with their *physical eyes*, rather than the *eyes of the imagination*; they began to *observe* the physical world, rather than *visualise* the path to their redemption. As a result, painters began to include naturalistic details of the physical world in the illusions of space they created. Moreover, as the external world and its contents were increasingly registered as independent objects of attention, without always needing to be seen as symbols of Christian meaning, so the principle of subjectivity that observed them – and indeed evolved in conjunction with that observation – became increasingly autonomous and naturalised in the realm of experience.

Early medieval imagery had made little use of naturalistic detail. Despite attaining high levels of complexity and virtuosity, most images from this period consisted of decorative signs and symbols, and graphic conventions – affirming truths, divulging meanings and telling stories. There was no need or desire to reproduce the world for its own sake. In fact, the world was generally considered to be sinful and corrupt; the role of images was to represent a higher and otherwise invisible realm of being. Even when medieval thinkers did attempt to account for the natural world, they tended to transform it into an object of the imagination and invest it with Christian symbolism. According to Thomas Aquinas, 'sacred doctrine does not treat of God

THE ABSTRACTION OF THE SELF

and creatures equally, but of God primarily, and of creatures only so far as they are referable to God as their beginning or end.'[1] Thus in *bestiaries* – medieval 'dictionaries' of animals, sometimes included in psalters – creatures were seen as symbols. Pelicans, for instance, were seen to be symbolic of Christ sacrificing himself, because they were thought to peck at themselves till they bleed and then feed their young with their own flesh (presumably because they do indeed preen their chests with their beaks and feed their young by regurgitating food from their pouches), rather than as specimens of natural history. Likewise, in medieval and early Renaissance *herbals*, it was the symbolic, medicinal and magical potential of plants that attracted attention, rather than their botanical properties. Purely experiential, rather than credulous, dimensions of selfhood were yet to develop.

From the thirteenth century onwards, an eye for realistic detail began to evolve. Although this shift required observation of the physical dimension of things on its own terms, its first fruits – realised by Giotto and his contemporaries – were applied within the context of belief. The purpose of such details was to make 'objects of belief' seem more real – to *normalise* them, making them seem familiar and therefore accessible to the viewer. For pictorial space to be convincing, it was not enough for it to simply *look* real; it also had to *behave* in a realistic way. It could not therefore only contain things that had religious meaning or were pious; like real space, it also had to contain things that were ordinary and even meaningless.

By the end of the fourteenth century, painters were being increasingly admired for the visual realism of their work, as well as their orthodoxy. Giotto, for instance, was praised, somewhat idealistically, for producing images that were so realistic that it was at first impossible to tell if they were real or not. In his *Craftsman's Handbook*, written a hundred years or so after Giotto, the Tuscan painter Cennino Cennini stressed the value of working 'from nature'. In contrast to the time-honoured practice of copying models, which perpetuated the belief that value was enshrined in tradition, the new inclusion of everyday details in pictures required painters to make their own decisions based on their own experience. Moreover, for the first time since antiquity, painters had to observe and record the visual appearance of the world – the way light actually falls on objects. Increasingly painters used a new and experimental practice – that of making preparatory sketches and drawings (often on the newly available and highly versatile medium of paper) to document their observations and work out their ideas; Stefano da Verona and Pisanello were two of the first painters to use this technique. However, the types of decision to be made were not merely technical; they also required discrimination with regard to the propriety of the details to be included in their works. Even when the subject-matter was traditional, the selection and placement of detail required imagination or *invenzione*. More extravagant *invenzioni*, in which the artist's work became so distinctive and subjective that it seemed to interpret and modify the iconography, rather than merely naturalise it – expressing the artist's feelings and ideas rather than a pre-existent truth – would follow.

A transitional state of balance between unnaturalistic 'objects of vision' (for instance, spiritual phenomena like angels or haloes) and an increasingly naturalistic 'mode of vision' was reached towards the end of the fifteenth century. This brief moment of poise was captured perfectly in the work of Pietro Perugino and in the

FIGURE 6.1: Raphael Sanzio, *Madonna del Cardellino*, 1505–6, oil on wood, 107 × 77 cm. Uffizi Gallery, Florence.

early work of his pupil, Raphael. Raphael's *Madonna of the Goldfinch*, painted in around 1505–6, is a typical example (Fig. 6.1). While the painting represents the haloed Madonna and Christ, with John the Baptist, as objects of devotion, in a traditionally hieratic centralised position, the innocent informality of their expressions and postures, and the playful interactions of the children, magnify the impression of their ordinary humanity. The artist sets the trio against an idyllic Umbrian landscape in which distant buildings and a bridge can just be made out, exactly as one might see in a real landscape. With the exception of the goldfinch (which symbolises the passion on account of the red spot on its face), these details have no meaning or significance; they merely add touches of naturalness to the scene. The painting perfectly documents the transition to a new paradigm in that it looks at a typically 'medieval' sight (a belief-dependent Christian subject which could not be seen in everyday life) in a quintessentially 'Renaissance' way (modelled and contextualised in keeping with the experience of optical seeing). As such, it marks a moment in the emergence of the self-sense at which the possibilities of human experience – both observation and reason – are perfectly balanced with the demands of Christian belief. Moreover, while the naturalistic way of seeing made the divine subject-matter appear realistic and convincing, so, conversely, the divine subject-matter conferred a sense of grace on the medium of 'naturalistic seeing'. Through sacred images of this kind, natural sensory experience was acknowledged to be a legitimate means of witnessing the revelation of Christian truths, in contrast to the penitential and self-deprecating contortions expected of viewers by medieval images of Christ in agony. As a result, viewers gradually became habituated to the independent existence of the physical world and to their experience of it; and the subject and centre of that experience – a sense of personal self, intimately at peace with the divine order of things – was acknowledged and raised to a level of legitimacy and sanctity accordingly.

While the *rationale* for realism was developed in service to religion, the necessary *techniques* for achieving it were developed in relation to the arts of modelling and perspective, especially as practised by painters, as we have seen. And it was in the hands of painters that the association of optical realism (as a *mode* of seeing) with the purely visible world (as the *object* of seeing) was eventually taken to its logical conclusion – in realistic paintings of physical objects that did not presuppose an invisible legitimising frame of reference. It was, however, through the technique of decorative wood inlay, or *intarsia*, which was especially well suited to the development of linear perspective, that the convention of optical realism *for its own sake* was first established. Significantly, but perhaps not surprisingly, *intarsia* was the only medium other than painting in which rigorously perspectival images of idealised architectural spaces (like *The Ideal City*, Fig. 4.5) occur – albeit mostly as decorative panels on pieces of furniture. Just as the style of images made in stained glass was to some degree determined by the techniques of the craft, so the compatibility of *intarsia* work with linear perspective was partly due to its technical properties: firstly, it is much easier, when working to a very high level of precision, to cut a piece of wood in a straight line than in a curve; and secondly, it is much easier to juxtapose several differently coloured pieces of wood – each piece of a single shade – than it is to create gradations of shade within a single piece of wood. Understandably, therefore, wood-inlayers, or *intarsiatori*, were especially attracted to content that revolved around distinct geometrical shapes and orthogonals, rather than modelling (though very fine examples of *intarsia* work using curved and shaded pieces of wood were also made).

One of the earliest surviving examples of images of 'meaningless' objects was made in *intarsia* in around 1435 for an ecclesiastical context – the panelling and cupboard doors that line the north sacristy of Florence Cathedral (Fig. 6.2). A number of these doors are wittily decorated with *trompe l'oeil* representations of the contents of the cupboard spaces they conceal, most of which are rectilinear (books, altar crosses and candlesticks – what one would expect to find in actual sacristy cupboards), as well as representations of the cupboard doors themselves (simulated latticework panels, each one at a different angle of openness). Although they are mostly rectilinear and therefore relatively simple to calculate, if arduous to cut, the designs of the panels are highly complex, and even virtuoso. But, because they were semi-decorative playful conceits, they were not considered to be 'works of art' as such; they carried no status, and were invested with minimal imaginative potential. Indeed, when the fifteenth-century painter Paolo Uccello produced designs for

FIGURE 6.2: Intarsia panels in the vestry of Florence Cathedral, Italy, around 1435, various woods.

intarsia work, Vasari, who said that Uccello was 'obsessed' with perspective, castigated him for wasting his time on designs for objects that he (Vasari) considered to be fit only for worms and fire.

It was in fact precisely because they were *not* 'works of art' that it was possible to decorate *intarsia* panels with such inconsequential images. It would not be for at least another century that the experience of seeing the natural world for its own sake would acquire its own cultural value, and be deemed worthy of registration in art – as the genre of 'still life' painting. In the meantime, the unself-conscious representation of ordinary objects in a decorative context reflected an embryonic acknowledgement of their independent existence, even if the inclination to confer value on that experience remained unformed. When the capacity to value this mode of experience eventually developed in the sixteenth century, so its principle or centre slowly acquired its own identity as an autonomous and independent subject of awareness, paving the way for the fully self-conscious and culturally validated apprehension of the physical world that would in due course become the subject-matter of art.

As painters' powers of representation developed, so their dependence on linear perspective for a sense of optical realism became less formulaic, and objects were increasingly made to look real by virtue of the intensely detailed way in which they were observed and modelled. As a result, the reliance on architecture and orthogonals, which could become crude if over-used, became less necessary as a means with which to create pictorial space. Significantly both Albrecht Dürer and Leonardo da Vinci, who perfected the arts of observation and modelling, were also adept in the use of linear perspective. Dürer studied perspective on his visits to Italy in 1494 and 1506 and wrote a treatise introducing it to German artists and craftsmen in 1525, while Leonardo's notebooks are full of new observations on the subject. In 1497, Leonardo produced a series of illustrations of geometrical bodies for *De Divina Proportione* by his mathematician friend Luca Pacioli, who learned about perspective from Piero della Francesca and may have taught it to Dürer. But while both artists embodied the rational and optical self-sense that mastery of perspective presupposed, neither of them indulged it by using it in a facile or formulaic way. Both of them preferred to use it as a means with which to intensify the experience of personal observation. However, even in their cases, in which the details of a blade of grass or of a rabbit's paw are recorded with meticulous attention to detail, the drawings were often informal studies that were not intended to be seen as works of art in their own right; they were to be included, as 'naturalistic enhancement', in formal pictures that had higher legitimising religious or moral meanings – for instance, Leonardo's unfinished *Adoration of the Magi* (1481) and Dürer's *Feast of the Rose Garlands* (1506. Fig. 5.3), both of which include numerous naturalistic details. Dürer's narrative engravings are typically populated by a wide range of plants and animals, and Leonardo's fascination with light effects, air pressure, rock formations and the musculature of animals – to name but a few of his interests – contributed very directly to his paintings. Many of Leonardo's sketches of natural phenomena were also produced in anticipation of a comprehensive *Treatise on Painting* that he intended to write, but never did. Even so, despite the legitimising contexts of Leonardo and Dürer's studies of natural phenomena, their sensitivity to the subject was a reflection of their very highly developed sense of their own experience as a criterion of knowledge and understanding and, arguably, of their strong sense of personal identity.

In the fifteenth and early sixteenth centuries the evidence of reason and observation were mostly used to compliment the message of the Church; but as these modes of knowing became more established, they challenged the devotional precepts and authority of Church doctrine, and were increasingly seen to assert an alternative source of authority – the authority of individual experience. That the proliferation of secular subject-matter marked a radical shift in the location of identity and authority from the Church to the individual is reflected in the resistance of the Church to these changes. The authority of the Church came under particular attack in 1517 when Martin Luther famously nailed his ninety-five 'theses' – rational criticisms of the Church – to the doors of the Church of the University of Wittenberg in Saxony. Luther's criticisms revolved around a variety of clerical abuses, principally relating to the sale of indulgences (which guaranteed concessions with regard to the amount of time spent in purgatory) and simony (the politically motivated buying and selling of ecclesiastical posts). The discontents that Luther voiced resonated with simmering resentments that were widely felt throughout society and, although he only meant to instigate a process of reform, the controversy that followed led to a radical and irreversible split within the Church. The unresolvable differences of opinion between the various parties resulted in the 'Reformation' of the Protestant Churches, mostly in Switzerland and northern Europe, in which many of the traditional positions of the Catholic Church – the offering of indulgences, the concept of purgatory, veneration of the Virgin and saints, the absolute authority of the pope and various others – were jettisoned. Changes of attitude towards the doctrine of transubstantiation and the cult value of images were especially far-reaching. The Protestant churches rejected the credulous notion that the bread and wine of the sacraments were mystically transubstantiated into the actual body and blood of Christ at the moment of consecration, replacing it with the more rational practice of consuming the sacraments in simple but profound remembrance of Christ's sacrifice; in 1553, the Protestant Simon de Kramer was burned at the stake for refusing to bow to the Eucharist during a procession (Fig. 6.3). The Protestant extension of the Eucharistic elements to the whole congregation, as practised before they were reserved for the celebrating priest in the twelfth century (as described in chapter 2), resulted in the replacing of small chalices and patens with large communion cups and alms dishes, supplemented with large flagons to replenish the cups as necessary – all based on secular non-cultish forms. In this way, the material infrastructure of ecclesiastical power was challenged at its heart. The use of relics also came under scrutiny. The belief that relics were empowered to effect miraculous change, on account of their physical sanctity, was seen to be contrary to the teachings of Christ. It was seen to stimulate magical and

FIGURE 6.3: *The Defiance of Simon de Kramer*, engraved by Jan Luiken from *Martyrs Mirror*, Bergen op Zoom, 1553, p. 49. Rijksmuseum, Amsterdam.

superstitious thoughts in people and was rejected. Similarly, the theology of images came in for radical re-inspection. Indeed, the recently rediscovered *Libri Carolini* was used to prove the traditionally anti-cultish attitude of the early medieval Church towards imagery. While all Protestant factions shared a virulent hatred of Catholic cultism, superstition and 'popery', there existed many different degrees of rigour in their attitudes towards imagery, ranging from tolerance of images as detached aids to reflection (Luther) to zealous acts of destruction and iconoclasm, regardless of circumstances (Calvin). Some iconoclasts nervously scratched out the eyes of the 'offending idols', as if to blind them, reflecting a desire for change but also a degree of ambivalence (Fig. 6.4). Even so, the Protestants generally prided themselves on being individual, rational and morally upright – in contrast to the supposedly hysterical, credulous and corrupt Catholics.

The Catholic Church responded to these challenges by instigating its own programme of self-reformation. Gathering at the Council of Trent in northern Italy between 1545 and 1563, it aimed to clarify the key doctrines of the Catholic faith and consolidate its institutional power. It clamped down on many of the liberties that had evolved during the humanist period of the Renaissance and, with regard to the arts, reversed current trends by introducing much stricter controls. The most fully documented case of its attempt to control the content of images involved the Venetian painter Paolo Veronese who, in 1573, was interrogated by the Tribunal of the Inquisition about a painting of *The Last Supper* that he had produced for the refectory of Santi Giovanni e Paolo in Venice (now in the Gallerie dell'Accademia, Venice). The painting was conceived as if the occasion had been a grand banquet. The inquisitors objected to the fact that it included so many secular figures unaccounted for in the gospels, such as buffoons and dwarfs, a servant with a nose-bleed, another dressed as a jester with a parrot on his wrist, some drunken German soldiers holding halberds, and a dog. There were also 'disrespectful' details such as the apostle Peter shown carving lamb and another apostle picking his teeth with a knife. Such details, the Tribunal argued, were used by heretics (rife in Germany) to discredit the Church. Veronese defended his inclusion of abundant servants in the work on the grounds of naturalism, explaining that 'it seemed to me suitable and possible that the master of the house, who I have been told was rich and magnificent, would have such servants.' In response to the question as to whether he was ordered to include these figures in the work, he demonstrated the growing autonomy and authority of the artist by answering: 'No, but I was commissioned to adorn it as I thought proper . . .' and 'when I have some space left over in a picture I adorn it with figures of my own invention.' Regarding the relevance of these details to the subject-matter, he added: 'I paint my pictures with all the considerations which are natural to my intelligence, and according as my intelligence understands them.' At the end of the procedure, Veronese was let off fairly lightly, by the standards of the time. He was merely required to make certain unspecified 'corrections' to the painting, which he appears to have avoided doing by changing its title to *The Feast in the House of Levi*, in reference to another biblical feast but one that was more worldly and less charged with doctrinal and liturgical implications.[2]

While the Catholic Church reasserted itself by enforcing conformity to traditional iconographic conventions, in which its own authority was vested, the Protestant

FIGURE 6.4: *The Annunciate Virgin*, 1470–90, defaced after 1534, Bury St Edmunds, oil on oak, 110.5 × 45.6 cm. Victoria and Albert Museum, London.

Church moved in the opposite direction. Many Protestants rejected the use of religious imagery altogether, regarding it as idolatrous. Consistent with this view was a far greater dependence on the text of the Bible, which came to be seen as the unique source of original Christian teaching, pre-dating what were believed to be the politically motivated efforts of the Catholic clergy to distort it over the centuries.

THE ABSTRACTION OF THE SELF 97

By cleaving to the biblical text, many Protestants attempted to bypass the institutional Church's desire to monopolise access to salvation. The value of the Bible was magnified, firstly by the translation of the scriptures from Latin into indigenous languages (increasingly widespread since the fourteenth century) and, secondly, by the equally revolutionary circulation of the scriptures in print – both of which made them directly accessible to the laity for the first time (Fig. 6.5). In the Protestant regions that tolerated religious pictures, imagery was directed away from the emotive cult potential of the suffering Christ towards more rational reflections on the Christian story. In the seventeenth century, this shift resulted in a proliferation of representations of Old Testament scenes, which were biblical without being cultish, as well as scenes from the parables and teaching of Christ (sometimes painted like domesticated genre scenes) which were considered exemplary and educational

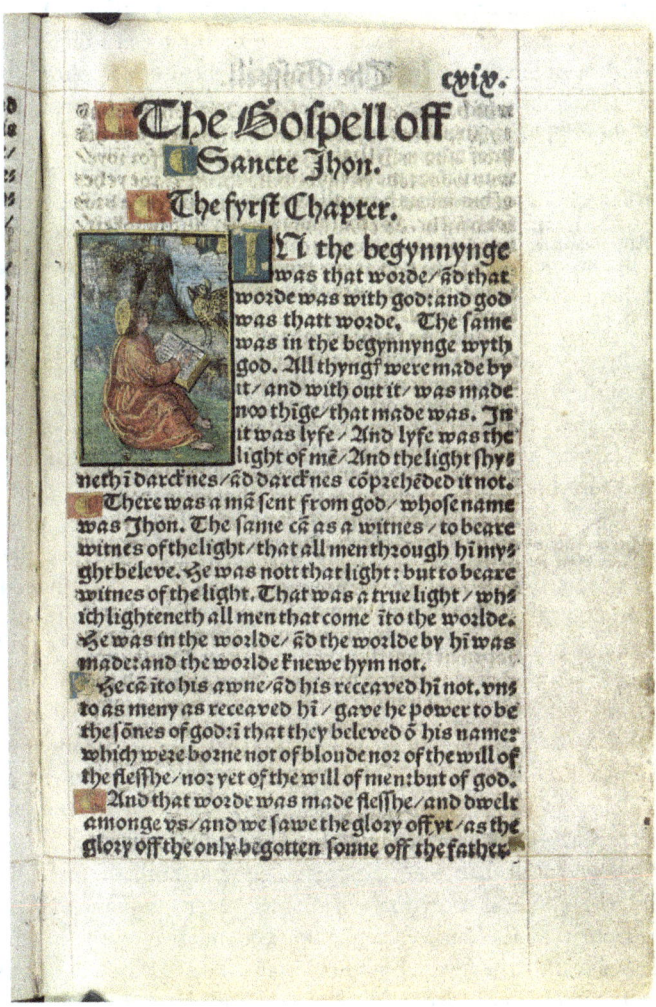

FIGURE 6.5: The Tyndale Bible, 1525. The British Library.

rather than melodramatic and manipulative. Rembrandt painted many such works. Despite these adaptations, the number of commissions coming from ecclesiastical sources, and for paintings of religious subjects, was on the decline in northern Europe and, consequently, many Protestant artists turned their hand to representations of the natural world – portraits, genre scenes, still lives and landscapes – accelerating a trend that had begun before the Reformation.

Some of the earliest depictions of natural phenomena, made for their own sake without a symbolic or religious agenda, appeared in botanical treatises. Many of these treatises were written by Protestants (including converts from Catholicism), and those that were written by Catholics often brought their authors into conflict with the Church.[3] Significantly, in some of the earliest examples, the representations of plants were more accurate than their accompanying texts, reflecting how visual conventions frequently preceded verbal ones in the accommodation of new values. In Otto Brunfels' *Herbarum vivae eicones* (*Living Images of Plants*), published in Strasbourg in 1532 and widely considered to be the first quasi-objective botanical treatise, the author of the text was preoccupied with the useful applications of plants and with self-consciously ensuring that his descriptions were consistent with his authoritative (but often incorrect) classical sources, whereas the illustrator, Hans Weiditz, was clearly working from nature, providing much more accurate information about the actual specimens (Fig. 6.6). The author was at a loss to account for some of the plants that Weiditz illustrated because his ancient sources (based around the Mediterranean and therefore ignorant of northern European flora) were 'as silent as fishes' about them. This problem was exacerbated when plants from the New World, unknown to classical authors, were introduced to Europe. Significantly, Weiditz was a pupil of Dürer, whose powers of observation also took him far beyond the requirements of the narrative context of his work. The near-contemporary physician and botanist Leonhart Fuchs (1501–66) took exception to what he considered to be the excessively artistic style of Weiditz. Fuchs claimed that Weiditz's naturalistic use of shading and foreshortening (clearly learned from Dürer) glorified the painter at the expense of showing the plant clearly. In his own *De Historia Stirpium* (*On the History of Plants*) of 1542 – which includes over five hundred specially prepared woodcuts – he stated his intention to avoid all such 'artifices'; indeed the very processes of observing and drawing the plants, and of transferring the drawings to woodblocks to be printed, is documented in the publication (Fig. 6.7). Fuchs' emphasis on conveying technical information rather than an artistic impression is also reflected in his insistence that no plant should appear damaged and that each example should be composed in such a way that no part of it obscures the part behind it. He also allowed for the inclusion of both fruit and flowers in the same illustration, further prioritising the communication of detailed information over the creation of a correct general effect (Fig. 6.8).

Brunfels and Fuchs both trained as physicians and both of them were partly motivated by the medical potential of plants, even though the illustrations accompanying their work showed an unprecedented interest in their actual appearance; significantly they were both Protestant. The first system of classification in which plants were categorised exclusively according to their intrinsic physical properties rather than their 'accidental' medical effects (let alone their symbolic

FIGURE 6.6: Hans Weiditz, woodcut design from *Herbarum vivae eicones* (*Living Images of Plants*), by Otto Brunfels, Strasbourg, 1530–6. Wellcome Collection, London.

meanings) was devised by the Tuscan physician and philosopher Andrea Cesalpino (1519–1603) and published in his *De Plantis Libri XVI* in 1583. Cesalpino's attempt to identify plants on their own terms, especially in relation to the forms of their seeds and fruit, reflects the extent to which he was no longer subscribing to a worldview according to which the characteristics and identity of a phenomenon are determined by reference to a preconceived set of values (and are therefore implicitly subject to the power that authorises that set of values). Such a view subtly enforced the belief that man's deficiencies and neediness are coded into the structure of nature, and that he is constitutionally dependent and incomplete. On the contrary, by developing a system of classifying objects on the basis of their *innate characteristics* rather than their possible meanings and uses, Cesalpino was establishing conditions under which the observer was no longer implicated, and formed, by a prejudiced

FIGURE 6.7: Portraits of the three artisans employed in drawing plants, transferring the drawings to woodblocks and carving the woodblocks for *De Historia Stirpium* (*On the History of Plants*), Leonard Fuchs, Basel, 1542. Wellcome Collection, London.

interpretation of the outside world; he was free to see the world 'as it is' and to be identified, accordingly, on his own terms; as such, Cesalpino was tacitly inaugurating a form of discourse in which a sense of 'autonomous' self became cultural currency. Being Catholic, it is not surprising that he was suspected of heresy.

This shift was further facilitated by the evolution of 'still life' painting towards the end of the sixteenth century, in both Catholic and Protestant countries. Under this label – not identified as a coherent genre until the middle of the following century – everyday objects were represented in works of art without a narrative context for the first time; they were identified not merely as objects of natural philosophy, for the sake of understanding, but as objects of artistic contemplation. The difficulty with which artists and patrons took this crucial step is reflected in

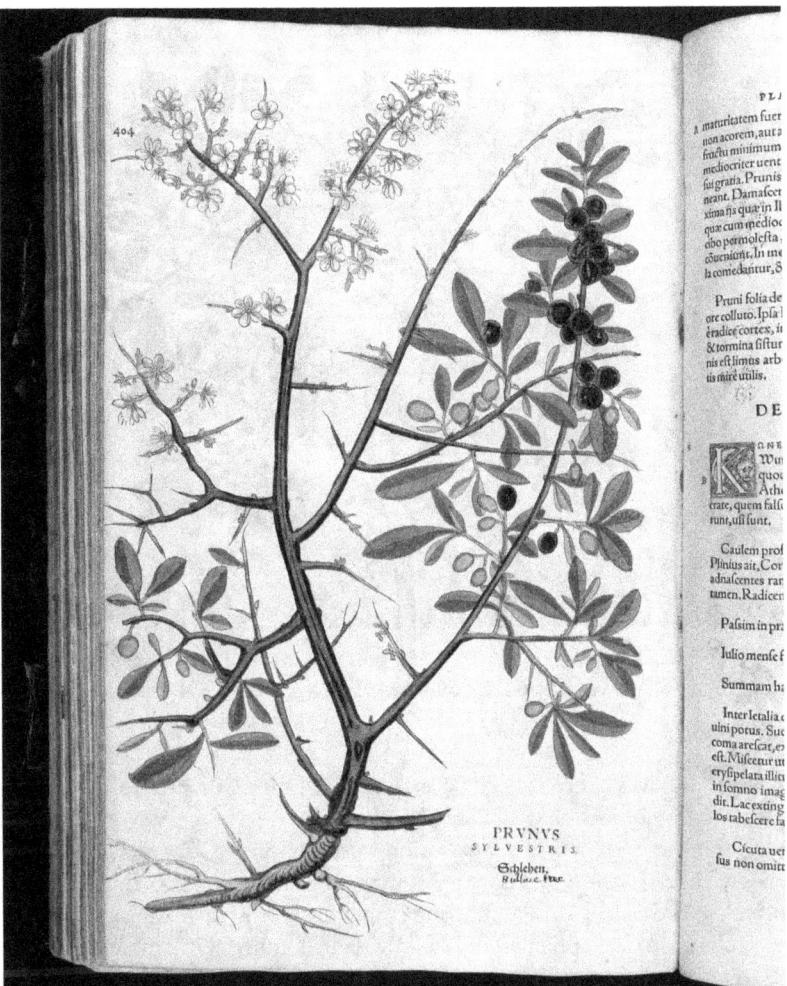

FIGURE 6.8: A plant at different stages of fruition and flowering from *De Historia Stirpium* (*On the History of Plants*), Leonard Fuchs, Basel, 1542. Wellcome Collection, London.

monumental paintings of market scenes – for instance, Pieter Aertsen's *Christ and the Adulteress* (1559) or Joachim Beuckelaer's *Well-Stocked Kitchen* (1566). These early works consist of immense piles of natural produce – like giant 'still lives' – and seem to revel in the sensuous abundance of nature for its own sake; but closer inspection reveals that, in the background, episodes from the life of Christ also appear in miniature (Fig. 6.9). Without such legitimising references – tokenistic though they are – it would have seemed anarchic to find value in such mundane and meaningless phenomena.

Even when such religious details were absent, representations of the physical world continued to be justified by moralising associations. A significant number of

FIGURE 6.9: Joachim Beuckelaer, *The Well-Stocked Kitchen, with Jesus in the House of Mary and Martha*, Antwerp, 1566, oil on panel, 171 × 250 cm. Rijksmuseum, Amsterdam.

the earliest 'still lives' were conceived as *vanitas* paintings, incorporating objects that are highly commodified but which also demonstrate the brevity of life and the spiritual emptiness of worldly possessions. In addition to fragile insects, wilting flowers and dead game, such objects include candles (alight or extinguished), timepieces (representing order and control, but also transience), books (representing education, but also the ephemerality of knowledge), musical instruments (generating sounds that are harmonious and sweet, but which immediately fade) and, most commonly, skulls (Fig. 6.10). The pictures are paradoxical because, despite warning against the impermanence of the material world, they also promote and indulge a taste for that world. While they claim to teach detachment from the passing pleasures of the mind and senses, they are – as objects – blatant contradictions of this teaching, capitalising on the absence of narrative to ravish the senses, thereby intensifying the viewer's interest in the experience of sensation while also claiming to weaken it. Indeed, the virtuosity of many of the paintings is so exquisite and prolonged that any pretensions to moralising are quickly forgotten. As the eye is beguiled by the suave virtuosity of the painting, it builds up confidence in its independence and authority – without necessarily realising it – to the point at which its subjection to external criteria of value falls away. Pure 'still life' painting, in which all explicit references to moral significance have been removed, evolved to accommodate this inclination.

Although the genre of 'still life' painting epitomises the venerable tradition of European Old Master painting – now a benchmark of cultural conservatism – it is surely one of the most exceptional, and even bizarre, manifestations of human

THE ABSTRACTION OF THE SELF 103

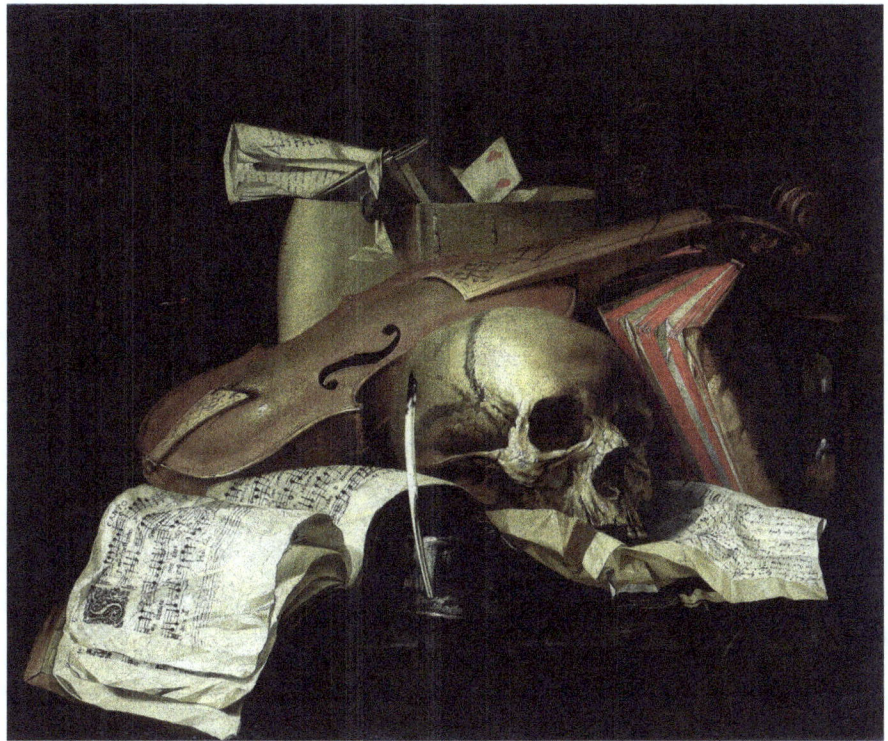

FIGURE 6.10: N. L. Peschier, *Vanitas Still Life*, 1660, oil on canvas, 57 × 70 cm. Rijksmuseum, Amsterdam.

culture, not only in Europe but throughout the world. From the perspective of human civilisation as a whole, the aspiration to reproduce the optical appearance of ordinary, often meaningless, things with as much verisimilitude as possible is unique. Almost all other civilisations at all other times in human history have, to one degree or another, *stylised* their representations of the visible world. The emergence of hyper-realistic 'still life' painting therefore reflects a significant moment in the history of art, raising the question: *what do pictures of ordinary objects have that the objects themselves do not have?* Such representations are not exactly more 'exquisite' or 'curious' than their models (for instance, a real insect or a flower), and they have no practical potential to recommend them. Nor can they be explained on the grounds that they made the invisible visible for, unlike imagined narratives or portraits of absent family members, most of the objects they represent were common; and, as we have seen, their moralising programmes were easily exhausted. What was it then that made them so compelling? Was it not because they provided a convention, or way of seeing the world, through which the random incomprehensibility of mere existence and the banality of ordinariness could be apprehended as a medium of cultural value *without recourse to external frames of reference*? On the one hand, they translated the raw data of experience into the language and currency of contemporary culture, offering a model of autonomy that enabled the self-sense to find itself reflected in the world without having to contextualise itself in relation to religion, morality or status; on the other hand, they conferred cultural legitimacy on that experience and, above all, on the personal autonomy and self-sufficiency that it both presupposed and precipitated in its subjects. In front of such works, the viewer was not invited to venerate Christ, understand significant meanings, reflect on his mortality or fantasise about his status; he was simply invited to apprehend the world as it appeared to him, and to be identified by it, not on the basis of any meanings that it might offer, but on the basis of its existence.

The emergence of 'still life' painting was significant because, despite any formulaic pretensions to symbolism that it may have had, it liberated art appreciation from the superstructures of belief and knowledge in which identity had been conventionally invested, sacrificing the monumental securities of tradition for the fact of existence in the present moment. Although the painters of 'still lives' were mostly Christian, in keeping with the conventions of the time, the value of their work implicitly depended on the suspension of all mental frames of reference in which subtle principles of knowledge and meaning were already tacitly presumed, in favour of pure experience; they were simply painting what they were seeing. As such, the genre provides a close parallel to Descartes' epoch-making articulation of the self-sufficient truth, *cogito ergo sum – I think, therefore I am* – first formulated in 1637. The significance of Descartes' revolutionary statement lay in the fact that he totally withdrew his sense of identity from the conventions of belief and knowledge, and invested it uniquely in experience itself and in the subject of experience – the self, 'I'. He maintained that although the *content* of experience could be an elaborate illusion or dream, and should therefore be subjected to scrutiny and doubt, the *fact* of experience and the *subject* of experience – 'I' – were self-evident truths. In radically establishing present self-awareness as the only legitimate 'proof of existence' and as the ultimate 'principle of identity' – independent of sensation, memory and conceptual interpretation, all of which are subject to change and are therefore fallible – Descartes divested the Church, the state and all other 'repositories of truths' of their power to define and control the individual's sense of him- or herself. The self stood free, as an existential and self-authenticating fact. That he realised and established the autonomy of self-reflective thought – in defiance of the forces of politics, religion and history, not to mention his own conditioning – is an almighty achievement, by any standards (even if – in a moment of anxiety about the radicality of his own realisation – he upheld that God must exist, as an *a priori* matter of principle).

The obverse of Descartes' realisation was the notion that, if consciousness is proof of subjectivity, and *vice versa*, then everything that is perceived not to be subjectivity, everything that is not the conscious self or 'I' – that is, the objective world or 'non-self' – must be *un*conscious. Moreover, if the objective world is activated neither by a known subjective self ('I') nor an imagined objective one (God), it must be automatic – subject to its own laws – and therefore mindlessly mechanical. On the basis of this belief, Descartes formulated a materialistic and mechanistic model of man and nature, crystallising a theory of mind–body dualism. To hold him responsible, however, for the mechanistic materialism of the modern world would be anachronistic – just as it would be anachronistic to judge seventeenth-century behaviour and medical practices by the moral and medical standards of the twenty-first century. Whether one considers his conclusions to be right or wrong, most important is the fact that they were based on 1) direct experience of the identification of subjectivity with *consciousness* and 2) a sincere attempt to challenge the monumental but untested belief that the objective world is guided by an external agent (God), on the grounds that there was simply no evidence (other than amazement) to support it. Just as the subject of experience was realised as an 'existential and self-authenticating fact', so the 'object of experience' – that which was perceived to be 'other' than the self – also came into focus, as its corollary and coordinate, reflecting the independent self to itself. This capacity to appreciate the apparent autonomy of the objective world – independent of meanings and legitimising contexts – surely precipitated the representation of inanimate 'things' in 'still life' paintings, and vice versa.

The growing autonomy of art, and its correspondence to the autonomy of the self, is even more clear – and is indeed consummate – in the popular genre of *trompe l'oeil* painting; for it was only in relation to *trompe l'oeil* painting that the 'experience of art' was *specifically* and *self-consciously* identified, and differentiated from the 'experience of the world'. Although our experience of all images is of course different from our experience of what they represent, it was only in relation to *trompe l'oeil* painting that this understanding was expressed *explicitly,* and that the notion of 'art' was realised as a distinctive and *consciously* self-legitimising convention. Even more important in the present context is the fact that by realising the notion of art in this uniquely self-referential way, the sense of self that was implicit in it was also realising *itself* as a 'distinctive and consciously self-legitimising convention'.

The difference between a *trompe l'oeil* painting and a conventionally realistic 'still life' painting lies not so much in the manner of painting as in the different states of mind that each type of painting presupposes in the viewer. With regard to conventional painting, the differences between the pictorial world and the real world are so fundamentally taken for granted that viewers are able to suspend their sense of realism in order to be convincingly effected by a work of art as if it offers, at least to some degree, a 'real' experience of the subject-matter it depicts; for instance, no one seeing a realistic painting of a bowl of lemons hanging on a wall would be deceived into thinking that the bowl was actually there, no matter how realistic it was, and yet they could nevertheless engage with it as a thoroughly effective presentation of the subject. But, in *trompe l'oeil* works, viewers are not required to make this imaginative leap as a precondition of their understanding the work. On the contrary, although the subject-matter is entirely plausible and the style extremely realistic, the images were deliberately conceived and displayed in such a way as to deceive the viewer into *not noticing that they were paintings* (Fig. 6.11). To achieve this effect, artists had to erase any differences between the subject-matter as it appears in the painting and the subject-matter as it would appear in reality; the represented objects had to be painted life-size and could have no symbolic or iconographic meaning, as to have given them one would have noticeably differentiated them from their real equivalents which have no meaning as such. Indeed, any feature that might have suggested an intention to convey meaning, beauty, expression, amusement or pleasure had to be erased, for if the work had any

FIGURE 6.11: Samuel van Hoogstraten, *Trompe-l'Oeil Still Life*, 1664, oil on canvas, 45.5 × 57.5 cm. Dordrechts Museum.

such explicitly 'artistic' qualities, it would not have resembled reality perfectly enough to deceive the viewer. Not surprisingly, therefore, bulletin boards stuffed with letters and prints were a favourite subject of *trompe l'oeil* painters – for their flatness coincided with the flatness of the picture surface. In extreme cases, artists depicted 'anti-artistic' subject-matter that was so clearly alien to the familiar canon of artistic iconography – and, in Cornelius Gijsbrechts' highly ironic painting of the *Back of a Painting* (1670), the very 'opposite' of it – that it could not possibly be 'mistaken for art'.

The implication of this deception is that it is only in the act of recognising it *as art* that a *trompe l'oeil* painting becomes a work of art. Unlike a conventional 'still life' painting, which presents itself as a work of art from the outset, regardless of the viewer, a *trompe l'oeil* painting is only art *from the moment at which it is identified as art*. Indeed, because a *trompe l'oeil* painting has no meaning or expressive purpose, the characteristic that essentially identifies it as a work of art is the fact that it is *recognised* as such. The significant moment of recognition that transforms an apparent 'experience of reality' into a self-conscious 'experience of art' is cleverly pinpointed in Adriaen van der Spelt's *Still Life of Flowers with Curtain* (1658), which presents a hyper-real image of a silk curtain drawn back to reveal a 'still life' painting of flowers (Fig. 6.12). The clear indication that the flowers are worth protecting, and are therefore a precious painting rather than real flowers (which are

FIGURE 6.12: Adriaen van der Spelt, *Trompe-l'Oeil Still Life with a Flower Garland and a Curtain*, 1658, 46.5 × 63.9 cm. Art Institute of Chicago. © Photo SCALA, Florence.

not typically kept in the dark!), indicates that the artist has no intention of deceiving the viewer into thinking that the flowers are real and that this is a *trompe l'oeil* painting; moreover, in real homes, it was not unusual for precious paintings to be protected behind curtains and to be exposed only when being looked at. But the artist is dissembling here, because his apparent confessional honesty with regard to the flowers is clearly designed to lend plausibility to the impression that the curtain is also 'what it seems to be' – a real curtain – though it is in fact also painted, in a deliberately deceptive *trompe l'oeil* manner. Thus the flowers are initially conceived to be seen as 'art' while the curtain is to be seen as 'real', until – in a shift of experience that consummates the dramatic intention of the painting as a whole – it too is seen to be 'art'.

The important point here is that, two hundred and fifty years before Kandinsky and Malevich popularised the notion of 'absolute art', the status of 'art' as a self-referential and self-authenticating abstraction, independent of its potential as a medium of communication, was formally established as a cultural convention, albeit in a somewhat ludic way. While the overall genre of 'still life' painting conferred cultural value on ordinary objects and thereby contributed towards the legitimisation of enjoyment of the physical world for its own sake, the genre of the *trompe l'oeil* painting conferred autonomy on the practice of art itself, and on the practice of looking at art, celebrating it as a direct function of personal experience or identity, regardless of its content. That is to say, the identity of art, and experience of art, became the subjects of art. This is not to suggest that *trompe l'oeil* paintings were produced as 'art for art's sake' in the modern sense; on the contrary, as soon as their deception was recognised, the conventional parameters of art interpretation (iconography, symbolism etc.) could be applied to them. It is more to convey that the concept of art was no longer being universally subjected to extraneous agendas (communication, decoration etc.). Albeit on an embryonic scale, it had become the self-conscious and self-authenticating source of its own identity.

Having established that the dramatic core of a *trompe l'oeil* painting lies principally in its identity as a work of art rather than in its possible meanings, it is equally important to point out that the characteristic that determines the painting's status as art – the conscious act of recognising it as such – is not a property of the painting; it is a *property of the viewer*. It is the outcome of a shift in the viewer's experience. And yet this shift is precipitated by the painting; for as soon as the viewer recognises that the *trompe l'oeil* objects do not actually occupy a space that is continuous with the 'real space' in which he stands, but exist in an artificial pictorial space, he spontaneously differentiates himself from it, and re-identifies himself in relation to it. Moreover, as the seventeenth-century viewer acknowledged the independent, self-authenticating capacity of the art object, realising its status as art by simply experiencing it as such, he was also creating and entering a frame of reference in which a principle of self-authentication was realised, not on the basis of approved content (meaning, morality, style etc.), but merely on existential grounds. And in so doing, he was also establishing parameters within which the subject of experience – or self – was validated and made current on purely existential grounds – exactly as Descartes had achieved at precisely the same time, by realising 'I think therefore I am.'

CHAPTER SEVEN

The Imaginary Environments of the Self: its Physical and Intellectual Frames of Mind

Today, the physical and psychological environments in which personal identity thrives are so conventionalised that it is difficult for us to see how they might be cultural constructions. It is natural for us, for instance, to spend time alone – at home, in private rooms, going for walks etc. – but in the early Middle Ages, this was not the case, for the conditions in which a personalised self-sense could be propagated – the concepts, language, social conventions, spaces and objects that accommodate and articulate it – simply did not exist. The possibility of retreating to one's bedroom to read a book was inconceivable because, for most people, books, reading and bedrooms were non-existent. Most people were illiterate and, even among the nobility, books were rare. Similarly, most people slept in common multi-functional rooms alongside other family members, co-workers and, in many cases, strangers (as many people still do, in various parts of the world). Many of them slept on the floor, in their clothes; where there were beds, they were often shared. According to the tympanum of the twelfth-century cathedral of Autun in Burgundy, even the three kings journeying to visit the infant Christ shared a bed (Fig. 7.1). Similarly, even for the nobility, certain freedoms such as the freedom to choose a profession or a spouse – fundamental expectations of modern individuality – had not yet evolved. On the contrary, work and marriage were functions of community and family identity, rather than matters for personal choice. Consequently, the dynamics of personal identity were not inscribed in the fabric of language and material culture, and could not therefore be activated in behaviour or sustained in the imagination. Something of this radically different orientation towards identity can be sensed from some traditional non-European cultures in which community or family values are still stronger than individual preferences. In India, for instance, it is not, generally speaking, culturally meaningful to 'wander lonely as a cloud' as it has been in picturesque England since the Romantic period; nor was it, in early medieval Europe. On the contrary, solitude was a dangerous state, leaving people vulnerable to 'demons' – the only explanation, at the time, for fantasies, dreams, or subjective flights of the imagination.

FIGURE 7.1: Gislebertus, *The Dream of the Three Magi*, from a capital at Autun Cathedral, 1120–35, stone.

Throughout the Middle Ages, the one state in which it was considered meaningful to be alone was monasticism. The word itself (from the Greek *monos* for 'one' or 'alone') suggests singularity, originally referring to the solitary hermits who, in the third and fourth centuries after Christ, took refuge from the perceived degeneration of the pagan world in the Syrian and Egyptian deserts. But such monasticism did not remain solitary for long. In the fourth century, many Christian hermits were formed into loose 'cenobitic' communities of monks who came together to pray, work and eat. In the Latin Church, this trend towards community was formalised by St Benedict, whose *Rule*, a collection of core precepts for monks written in around 530, underpins the entire tradition of monasticism in the West. The *Rule* stresses each monk's obligation to practise unconditional obedience to his monastic superior, trumping any aspiration to solitude with self-sacrifice. With the exception of the superiors, monks were to eat together in refectories and sleep together in dormitories; they prayed together in church and, from around the ninth century, read and meditated together in cloisters. Segregation from the community was used as a form of punishment rather than privilege, associated more with deprivation than with privacy; to be solitary was to be desolate. It was also associated with illness, providing sick monks with comfortable conditions in which to recover (though hospital beds were also sometimes shared).

The scope for developing a personal or 'private' sense of identity was, therefore, minimal at this time. Even when solitude did occur, it did not necessarily support it. As late as the sixteenth century, children were instructed to observe etiquette even when they thought they were alone because they were always in the company of angels who watched over them. Moreover, when some privileged individuals described themselves as being 'alone', it often transpired that they were 'alone with their servants', who did not count as significant people. According to Gregory the Great, St Benedict himself, when living 'in solitude' before composing the *Rule*, was accompanied by his old nurse.[1] In the same way, individuals who slept 'alone' in their own beds in their own bedchambers were often accompanied by a servant or servants who slept fully dressed on the floor or maybe on a pallet or truckle bed (kept under the master bed or in an adjacent space in the daytime). When Pope Gregory IX was visited in a dream by St Francis (as represented in Giotto's fresco cycle of the *Legend of St Francis*, painted in San Francesco in Assisi in around 1290), he was accompanied by four attendants (Fig. 7.2).

FIGURE 7.2: Giotto, *The Dream of St Gregory*, Upper Chapel, San Francesco of Assisi, around 1300, fresco.

Some of the earliest signs of a shift away from communality towards a sense of personal identity are reflected in changes associated with reading. The practice of reading has not always involved reading to oneself in silence. On the contrary, it was rooted in ancient oral traditions of memorisation and recitation. It seems likely that many of the earliest written narratives were records of stories that were intended to be *voiced*. As such, reading was originally a communal phenomenon. In the ancient world, public speakers or 'lectors' were trained to read out loud to groups of listeners, many of whom would be illiterate. Even 'solitary reading' might entail spoken communication, in that privileged individuals were frequently read to by their slaves; indeed some auditors considered the actual act of reading to be a menial task.[2] For several centuries, therefore, texts were often designed to be heard rather than read – like the lyrics of songs – and were structured according to their rhetorical potential rather than the information they incorporated.[3] They were written down as continuous strings of syllables – without punctuation, spaces between words or other lexical paraphernalia to help articulate the sense of the text – and they thereby resembled the unbroken texture of speech (Fig. 7.3). The articulation of the text, achieved by vocalising the words, was provided by the lector.

FIGURE 7.3: The *Vergilius Augusteus*, before 400, Staatsbibliothek, Berlin, Lat. fol. 416. Photo: bpk / Staatsbibliothek zu Berlin.

Silent reading, on the other hand, appears to have been relatively uncommon in antiquity, though it was not unknown. Certainly, when St Augustine saw St Ambrose reading in silence at the end of the fourth century, he found it sufficiently unusual to warrant speculation as to why he was doing it. Maybe he was 'resting from the din of other people's affairs and reluctant to be called away to other business'; maybe he was avoiding the curiosity of listeners who might be perplexed by the content of what he was reading, if he read it out loud; or maybe he was simply resting his voice.[4] Whatever the case, while public reading survived in the liturgy and in prescribed readings during communal meals, the contemplative act of reading silently became increasingly associated with Christian meditation, and eventually became one of the definitive practices of Christian monasticism. But it was not originally practised in solitude. While St Ambrose was reading in silence, St Augustine and his companions did not want to disturb him but were content to sit with him, also in silence, 'for a long time'. According to the *Rule* of St Benedict, monks were required to spend a certain amount of time each day reading – as a form of prayer rather than as a form of study – but they were not expected to do this in isolation. The fact that they were instructed to read 'without disturbing others' suggests that they may have been required to read *quietly* – still enabling them to *hear* the words they were reading – rather than in total silence. Between the ninth and twelfth centuries, such gatherings for prayerful reading took place in cloisters, which became integral features of monasteries at this time. Most monasteries had relatively modest collections of books; for the sake of convenience, they were often stored in chests or presses (*armaria*) in the cloister, rather than in a library.

The practice of silent reading – without murmuring or moving one's lips – became widespread among monks from the twelfth century and it is arguable that this change reflected a significant step in the development of personal identity. The classical orientation towards 'performable texts', in which the venerable truth of an authoritative work was delivered to receptive listeners, was superseded by an orientation towards texts that were designed to address the individual silent reader directly. Above all, reading ceased to be an implicitly 'social' act – which it had been in the sense that texts were designed to be exteriorised and heard (if sometimes only by oneself); it became a more interior, contemplative act. While vocalised reading had been slow but articulated and expressive, silent reading was rapid, allowing the reader to skim over the surface of the words, perusing them 'with the silent eyes of the heart', moving back and forth between them. This shift was partly prompted by technical changes to the very fabric of the texts being read. For instance, the replacement of scrolls by codices or books, which coincided exactly with the development of early Christianity and was complete by the time of St Augustine, compacted and structured the way in which the processing of knowledge was undertaken, giving shape to the subjective 'knower'. By newly enabling readers to move from one part of a text to another with ease, books also facilitated more reflective ways of thinking. Moreover, over a period of several centuries, culminating in the twelfth century, the ancient form of text, which had consisted of an unbroken and unpunctuated string of words – to be recited ritually – was replaced by a body of text that was articulated by means of punctuation marks, spaces between words and differentiated upper and lower case letters (Fig. 7.6). For instance, a dot-and-dash convention, thought to have originated in the ninth century as a quasi-musical sign prompting lectors to change intonation, morphed into the question mark at this time, instituting a questioning mode of mentation.[5] Books were increasingly furnished with reference aids, such as lists of contents, section headings, pagination and alphabetical indexes. Without such short cuts, it was difficult to make use of a text without reading it from cover to cover.

While such tools facilitated a more analytical approach to written texts, they also allowed for greater structural complexity in the conception of the works themselves. As with the presentation of images, changes to the *form* of the work reflected changes in its *content*. The new types of text took various forms. On the one hand, there was a proliferation of devotional works, expressing the aspirations of the individual soul to be united with God. Especially in a monastic context, these texts – for instance, St Anselm's *Meditations and Prayers* and St Bernard's *Meditations on the Song of Songs* – made a direct contribution to the development of a new discourse that revolved around the functions of personal experience and psychology: the nature of the soul, mind, love, self-knowledge, feeling etc.. On the other hand, there was also a proliferation of analytical texts. The invitation to the individual reader to navigate his own route through the material he was reading is clearly reflected in the writings of St Anselm and Peter Abelard, and of the scholastic theologians of the thirteenth century, especially the Dominicans Thomas Aquinas and Albert Magnus, whose ideas were both a cause and an effect of the increased capacity of written text to articulate complex meanings. Their use of the medium to establish a comprehensive system of doctrines, based on an intricate network of logical necessities and cross-references, has led to comparison with the architecture of the High Gothic cathedrals, which were being constructed in exactly the same spirit – as complex articulations of Christian truths – and at exactly the same time. Such texts invited contemplation and study rather than recital, activating an imaginative, rather than compliant, mode of being in their readers. By desocialising and internalising the practice of reading, they became *aids to* meditation rather than *objects of* meditation. They encouraged readers to bring their own experience to bear on their reflections, validating that experience – *and the subject of that experience* (the personal self) – in the process.

It was not until the eleventh and twelfth centuries that monastic inclination towards solitude became institutionalised, as a positive experience, in material and architectural form. This is reflected in the revival of interest in 'eremitical' (solitary) monasticism, leading to the founding, in 1084, of the Carthusian order which, unlike other orders of the period, allotted individual cells to its monks. But the trend is also evident in cenobitic monasteries, which increasingly made provision for monks to spend time in physical solitude, away from the cloister (the 'social' centre of the monastery). Significantly, the earliest justification for solitude (other than illness and punishment) was not sleep, which continued to take place in dormitories; nor was it meditation and prayer, which took place communally in the church or cloister. It was primarily to facilitate concentration, while studying.

Among the earliest signs of the allowances for privacy that were made for scholars, scribes and students were rows of 'carrels' – shallow cubicles that were specifically made, from the thirteenth century onwards, for undisturbed reading. Carrels were semi-enclosed, free-standing structures, made of wood, and they comprised a seat, a

FIGURE 7.4: Carrels in the south wing of the cloister of Gloucester Cathedral, late fourteenth to early fifteenth century. Photo: David Walsh.

desk and sometimes a shelf. In English monasteries, they were ranged along one of the open arcaded sides of the cloister to ensure enough light from the central courtyard. The inner boundary of the carrel – facing the cloister gallery – was open, sometimes with a door, to enable readers to be seen and supervised by their superiors. A sixteenth-century description of Durham Cathedral records how the carrels in the cloister were no wider than the distance between the mullions (uprights) in the arcade openings – less than three feet wide. In Gloucester Cathedral, which was a monastic priory until the Reformation, the placing of the carrels was made semi-permanent by masonry settings which were constructed for them between 1370 and 1412 and which still survive (Fig. 7.4).[6]

The most studious of the medieval religious orders were the Dominicans, founded by Dominic de Guzman in 1216 expressly to combat the rising tide of heresy, by means of preaching and persuasion. Unlike the Benedictines, whose lives were spent secluded in prayer and manual work, the Dominicans were dedicated to bringing the word of God to the lay folk of the growing cities and, as a result, they consecrated their time to preparatory study rather than manual work, living from the fruits of charity and begging rather than labour. The most qualified of them studied at the new secular universities and the most eminent – Albert Magnus and Thomas Aquinas – taught there. Although they took vows of poverty, renouncing personal property, and spent much of their lives travelling, Dominican priories were also founded and their characteristic orientation towards study was reflected in them. Their libraries, for instance, which they viewed as a 'teaching resource', became renowned throughout Europe. Like Benedictine monks, Dominican friars slept in dormitories; but, in order to provide them with the conditions necessary for undisturbed study, their beds were separated by partitions, creating cells that were conducive both to study and to sleep. These cells were not conceived as opportunities for privacy, and on one occasion Dominic, returning from travel, castigated the friars for 'abandoning poverty and creating palaces' by raising the divisions between some of the cells by the 'length of an arm'.[7] Moreover, in later cases, like the Dominican priory of San Marco in Florence, consecrated in 1443, where individual cells were incorporated into the permanent architecture of the dormitory, it was required that doors remain open and that the contents of the cells – beds and furnishings provided for study – be visible from the corridor. The fact that most of the cells in San Marco were decorated (by Fra Angelico) with a different image from the life of Christ suggests that the friars circulated between them, meditating on each of the images, and were not allowed to become attached to any particular one (Fig. 7.5). Having

FIGURE 7.5: Fra Angelico, *The Annunciation*, after 1437, fresco. San Marco, Florence.

FIGURE 7.6: 'Prostration' from *Modi Orandi Sancti Dominici* ('St Dominic's ways of praying'), *Codex Rossianus* 3, 1450. The Vatican Apostolic Library, Rome.

said this, Dominican cells were specifically designed to be used in solitude and, as such, they constitute a new cultural form in which the psychological potential of solitude is implicitly acknowledged. Dominic himself was clearly sensitive to this and one of his nine 'ways of praying', as recorded by his disciples who secretly watched him, involved withdrawing 'to some solitary place, to his cell or elsewhere' to read and meditate. Some manuscripts of the text in which Dominic's modes of prayer are recorded (*De Modo Orandi* or 'On the Way to Pray', composed in around 1280) included illustrations of the saint's various postures (Fig. 7.6). These were described for the benefit of readers who were encouraged to imitate them, with a view to inducing the disposition of devotion that generated them, in themselves; the very gestures of the saint were considered to embody a particular psychological dynamic that could be 'retro-activated' in the friar who copied him.

The growing association of study with solitude is further reflected in a series of frescos painted by Tommaso da Modena in the chapter house of the Dominican Church of San Nicolo in Treviso in around 1350 (Fig. 7.7). The frescos depict forty eminent members of the Dominican order (popes, cardinals and saints as well as the philosopher-theologians Thomas Aquinas and Albert Magnus), each sitting in his

FIGURE 7.7: Tommaso da Modena, paintings of Dominican scholars from the Chapter House of the Church of St Nicholas, Treviso, 1352, fresco.

own wooden cubicle – a cross between a carrel and a cell – reading, probably in silence, or writing. The figures are equipped with an array of scholarly accessories – books, quill-pens, penknives, inkwells, an hourglass, a mirror, spectacles (a relatively new invention, especially valued by readers and represented here for the very first time) – all of which facilitate the actions of a solitary individual and thereby contribute towards the evolution of a range of conventions and behaviour in which the personal self-sense is implicitly embodied and propagated.

While the Dominicans established study as one of the core activities of the Church, the individual that raised the image of the scholar to the level of an archetype, and came to epitomise the role in a general capacity throughout the Renaissance, was St Jerome – who was singled out accordingly by Tommaso for a dedicated fresco in the church of San Nicolo, adjacent to the chapter house. The fourth-century ascetic, St Jerome, was credited throughout the Middle Ages with having produced the Vulgate – the definitive translation of the Bible from early Greek and Hebrew versions into Latin, the common or 'vulgar' tongue. This task was not simply a question of translating from one language to another; it also required immense amounts of comparing, collating, editing and correcting texts, and it presupposed phenomenal knowledge of scripture, languages, history and geography. St Jerome's cult was promoted in the late thirteenth century when his relics were moved to Rome from Bethlehem, which had been under Muslim rule since the seventh century. Throughout the fourteenth century, the saint was revered for his extreme penitence and self-mortification, which established him as a model for the growing numbers of ascetics and flagellants among the mendicant orders. Paintings of him from this period tend to show him as a hermit in a rocky desert, beating his breast with a stone; he is usually accompanied by a lion from whose paw he is said to have removed a thorn. Because he was a priest and became one of the 'doctors of the Church', he is also shown as a cardinal, with a cardinal's distinctive red hat, though the role of cardinal did not actually evolve until many centuries after his death. As the humanist interest in ancient literature gathered momentum in the fifteenth century, he was increasingly revered for his work on the text of the Bible, and was therefore shown as a scholar at work in his study. Jerome's erudition was not valued for its own sake; it was valued for the way he applied it to Christianity, enabling the saint to rescue the ancient texts of the Bible and make them available to the Latin world. His training in classical literature – Virgil, Cicero and Plautus were among his favourite authors – was frowned upon by purists, but was valued in a scholarly context because it both enabled him to write in clear and elegant Latin, and set a legitimising precedent for the reconciliation of Christian and classical values that pervaded humanist idealism.

Although St Jerome was not a monk, his study is often reminiscent of the cells and carrels used by solitary monks (though it is usually more elaborate) and it appropriates the associations of legitimate solitude from them. In several examples, the fixed fittings of the room – a seat or bench, a desk, a lectern, some shelving – impose a kind of three-dimensional grid on the space occupied by the saint. These fittings are furnished with all the typical accoutrements of reading and writing. In Antonello da Messina's version of the image, painted in around 1475, the saint is shown seated in strict profile at a fitted desk that is integral to an elaborate structure that constitutes his overall study-space (Fig. 7.8). The sense of space in the study, which is itself free-standing in a vaulted church-like interior, is rigorously unified and geometrical; it is carefully constructed from a network of interacting horizontals, verticals, diagonals, planes and curves. The figure of Jerome, who is immobile at the physical centre of the composition but who is also its iconographic centre, appears to be held in place by the rigid framework around him. It is as if the geometrical structure and the objects within it serve together as the descriptors of a function in space; they are spatial and iconographically suggestive coordinates that plot the saint's position at the centre of a three-dimensional graph and call him into being as an embodiment of the rational principle that unites them.

The image of St Jerome in his study conflated the associations of solitude, study and receptivity to grace. Just as nuns identified with the Virgin reading at the moment of the Annunciation (Fig. 3.3), in order to be receptive – like her – to the Holy Spirit, so humanists and theologians identified with St Jerome in order to be open – like him – to the wisdom of Christ. Some scholars believe Antonello's representation of St Jerome, for instance, to be a disguised portrait of the philosopher-cardinal Nicholas of Cusa, who is known to have admired the saint.[8] Another humanist scholar who explicitly identified with St Jerome was Albrecht of Brandenburg, who became a cardinal in 1518 and commissioned Lucas Cranach to paint him as the saint, both emulating his scholarship and invoking his protection and blessing, to mark the occasion (Fig. 7.9). Several examples survive.[9] Closely based on Dürer's famous engraving of the saint from 1514, they are further examples of how

FIGURE 7.8: Antonello da Messina, *St Jerome in his Study*, around 1475, oil on limewood, 45.7 × 36.2 cm. National Gallery, London.

identification with an eminent or sacred character could be a sign of admiration, and an aspiration to resemble the figure in question, rather than (or as well as) a sign of self-importance.

By the end of the fifteenth century, the relationship between solitary study and the possibility of graceful illumination was fully forged, and the condition of solitude came to be invested with positive potential on its own account. After three hundred years of monastic and scholastic transformation, the practice of studying on one's own was extended to the laity, becoming one of the earliest forms in which solitude was legitimised in a secular context. The fourteenth-century poet Petrarch is often associated with this shift. Inspired by classical precedents, Petrarch made a point of retreating from the bustle of the city to a secluded villa in the countryside to study and meditate. In due course, the material accessories of study became associated with the wisdom and gravitas of studying and, for this reason, they were consciously used to shape the identities of scholars. In around 1475, the humanist duke Federico da Montefeltro of Urbino – a mercenary who used his earnings to build up a substantial library and become a scholar – had himself portrayed in the act of formal reading (Fig. 7.10). His ceremonial attire, his heavy, unwieldy book and his stiff, upright posture in front of an awkwardly high and rigid lectern (boxing him in like

THE IMAGINARY ENVIRONMENTS OF THE SELF 121

FIGURE 7.9: Lucas Cranach, *Albrecht of Brandenburg as St Jerome*, 1525, oil and tempera on limewood, 117 × 78 cm. Hessisches Landesmuseum, Darmstadt.

a carrel) all suggest that, although the painting is secular, its 'rhetoric' – the associations of its conventions – is derived from, and charged with meaning by, religious precedents. Indeed, although there is no evidence to suggest a direct connection between the two paintings, the duke's posture bears a striking resemblance to that of Antonello's St Jerome, painted at exactly the same time. The portrait was clearly intended to complement the duke's status as a steadfast man of the world with signs of his high-minded sense of justice, his learned intelligence and his reverent openness to instruction from respected sources of wisdom. His literacy and privileged access to privacy (his son Guidobaldo is present as his heir but is not otherwise acknowledged) are clearly offered as signs, or coordinates, of his identity.

Federico further projected his self-image as a powerful but reflective, magnanimous and just ruler – both to himself and to his privileged guests – into the two *studioli* (studies) that he had built for himself in his palaces in Urbino and Gubbio in central Italy, in around 1476 and 1480 respectively (Fig. 7.11). Such private spaces soon became common in the courtly palaces of Renaissance Italy (though few survive intact) and, through them, the possibility of privacy and solitude became conventionalised among the princely elite. They were usually built in a remote part

FIGURE 7.10: Pedro Berruguete, *Federico da Montefeltro and his son Guido*, around 1475, tempera on panel, 134 × 77 cm. National Gallery of the Marches, Urbino.

of a residence, away from public spaces. Images and inventories document how they were fitted out with the utensils of literacy and learning, each of which contributed towards the materialisation of the self-image of their owner as a learned individual, investing his sense of himself in the trappings of his lifestyle.

Federico's *studioli* consist of small cabinet rooms, a little more than three metres square each, entirely lined with *intarsia* (wood inlay) panels – exercises in virtuoso observation, imagination and craftsmanship that place them among the greatest masterpieces of Renaissance art.[10] Like the *intarsia* panels in the sacristy of Florence Cathedral, to which they are indebted (Fig. 6.2), Federico's panels are decorated with *trompe l'oeil* representations of cupboards, with complex latticework doors that are either ajar at different angles, showing the latticework at different degrees of foreshortening, or open, revealing the apparent contents of the cupboards. Benches, with objects placed on some of them, appear to be ranged all round both rooms though they are in fact flush with the rest of the panelling. As a sign of the frame of mind that the *studioli* were designed to reflect and inspire, both schemes of panelling were surmounted by a series of painted portraits of intellectual characters (now much dispersed in museums). In Urbino, the paintings consisted of

FIGURE 7.11: The *studiolo* from the Ducal Palace of Gubbio, made by Giulio and Benedetto da Maiano, 1478–82, walnut inlaid with various woods. Metropolitan Museum, New York, Rogers Fund, 1939.

two rows of 'portraits' of famous scholars, philosophers, theologians and poets from Christian and pagan history (including St Jerome and Petrarch), while the Gubbio panels, which were dismantled in 1631 and are now in the Metropolitan Museum in New York, were accompanied by a series of painted personifications of the Liberal Arts.

Apart from their technical virtuosity, the *intarsia* panels in the *studioli* incorporate a number of innovations. On the one hand, they provide early examples of naturalism, rigorously worked out in keeping with the new science of perspective (as explored in chapter 4); on the other hand, because they have no narrative, they confer value on physical objects for their own sake (as explored in chapter 6). But, besides their naturalism and lack of narrative, their most important feature – in the present context at least – is the way they accommodate their patron's heightened sense of personal identity and reflect it both to himself and to their other viewers.

Besides giving an immediate impression of Federico's wealth, power and fashionability on account of their cost and novelty, the role of the *studioli* in the process of his identity-formation occurs at four levels: 1) the actual physical space and function of the rooms; 2) the optical illusion of pictorial space in the panels; 3) the meaning of the individual images; and 4) the overall principle according to which the images are organised into a whole.

Firstly, at a purely physical level, the rooms were conceived as places of retreat, for solitary study and meditation. While inheriting the semantic structures of monastic cells and secularising them, they are also indebted to the conventions associated with images of St Jerome in his study. Secondly, the perspectival schemes of each room are internally consistent – not only within each panel but also between the panels as a whole. They thereby presuppose a particular viewpoint in the rooms from which to be seen, and imply the presence of an individual viewer at that point – not as a detached and disembodied observer of the scheme but as an integral part of its *modus operandi*. Thirdly, the iconographic details of the schemes symbolise personal values that are attributable to their owner. Representing a wide range of objects and figures to signify the entire spectrum of intellectual disciplines and virtues, they define Federico's self-image as a perfect humanist, reflecting him to himself and to his guests like a mirror with a memory. The *intarsia* objects that appear to be in the cupboards include books, scientific and musical instruments, an hourglass, a clock, a candle, a sword, a mace and some armour, and various literary accessories. Each item has a meaning, often underpinned by textual references. One panel depicts a polygonal birdcage, symbolising the need to tame the thoughts that 'fly around' in the mind.[11] Each of the many bars of the cage – including those at the back and sides, seen through those at the front – is convincingly represented at a very slightly different angle, reflecting its minutely different position in relation to the viewer; in the Gubbio version of the image, the overall design of the cage, which is itself comprised of an immensely complex web of lines, is partly seen through the latticework of the fictive cupboard door (Fig. 7.11, right). On other panels, an astrolabe and armillary sphere refer to astronomy; a mathematical writing tablet refers to arithmetic; and a *mazzocchio* (originally a multi-faceted hoop used for forming hats but also of interest to perspectivists on account of its complex structure) refers to geometry. The books, writing implements and inkwell are reminiscent of the contents of the shelves in paintings of St Jerome in his study and are generally suggestive of scholarship. The fact that the Urbino inkwell, which is octagonal, has the first four letters of Federico's name – F, E, D and E – inscribed on its four visible sides (implying that R, I, C and O occupy the other four) links it, and him, with the theological virtue of 'faith' (*fides* in Latin), and therefore with the devotional rosary beads that hang from the shelf above it. That the panel is intended to convey a sense of the harmony between Federico's Christian faith and his respect for secular knowledge is also suggested by its location between panels representing an organ symbolising harmony (on the left) and a human personification of faith (on the right).

As *trompe l'oeil* works, the iconography of these schemes operates in two ways – firstly, as (apparently) real *objects,* with *uses* that refer to the practical activities of their owner; and secondly, as symbolic *pictures,* with *meanings* that refer to his inner disposition. Whether the images are descriptive or symbolic, the overall schemes of the *studioli* are thoroughly humanist. For instance, while the presence of weapons among the books *demonstrates* Federico's role as a powerful ruler and military strategist, it also *symbolises* his adaptation of the monastic ideal of balance between the active and contemplative lives to a secular humanist context. Equally central to the philosophy of humanism is the belief in the compatibility of Christian wisdom with classical philosophy, expressed by Federico in his choice of luminaries painted in the two upper tiers of the *studiolo* at Urbino. This series of figures, which recalls the series of Dominican scholars in Treviso, consists of both great sages from the history of the Church (including Old Testament precursors such as Moses and Solomon) and scholar-philosophers from antiquity. Besides attempting to reconcile belief and reason, they also represent each of the key intellectual disciplines of the time – logic, mathematics, music, astronomy, geometry, rhetoric, law, medicine and poetry.[12] On the one hand, these figures personify Federico's interests; on the other hand, they *historicise* them, placing them in an ennobling context that extends from antiquity to the threshold of the present time (represented by Petrarch and Federico's teacher Vittorino da Feltre) and therefore implicitly to himself. In both senses – through their individual associations and through the overall logic of the group – they conspire to identify Federico as an heir to the classical and Christian traditions.

While the individual objects in the *studioli* can be said to reflect the distinctive qualities of their patron, the way in which they were *organised into a whole* constitutes a fourth way in which the *studioli* function as instruments of identity-formation; for, by subjecting the diverse possibilities of knowledge and virtue to a coherent and rational system of organisation, the *studioli* evoke a rational unity in the mind that apprehends them, and thereby 'construct' that mind as a unified and rational centre of apprehension and identity. By functioning as 'frames of mind' in this way, they realise the configuration of beliefs and associations that constitutes the humanist mindset in the form of a coherent three-dimensional structure. Indeed they could also be regarded as three-dimensional diagrams of the mind, attempting to understand the mind by identifying and organising its functions in space, rather as contemporary drawings of the brain attempted to understand the functions of sensation, imagination (*imaginativa* and *fantasia*), intellect (*cogitatio* and *estimatio*) and memory by representing them diagrammatically (Fig. 7.12).

Although Federico's *studioli* functioned as the parameters of his own identity, the process by which they transferred their meanings and associations to him was of course entirely imaginative, not least because the sources of those values – the visual contents of the rooms – were themselves illusory (despite pretending not to be). Indeed, to the extent that his sense of self was articulated by the associations of objects and environments (whether imaginary of not), it is arguable that his sense of identity was itself a product of the imagination – most perfectly evoked in him by his experience when he was in one of his *studioli*. Considering the fact that Federico is likely to have been alone for much of the time that he spent in his *studioli*, it seems plausible that the affirmation of identity that they represent was as much for his own good as for that of his guests, acting like halls of mirrors, in which each mirror was pre-conditioned to reflect and sustain a different fragment of his sophisticated and multi-faceted sense of himself. It was as if he was semi-consciously constructing himself by creating an environment of suggestive coordinates in which a specific configuration of values, amounting to a coherent model of personal identity, was implicitly plotted. His near-contemporary Erasmus was certainly aware of the capacity of the built environment to act as a surrogate memory; in 1528, Erasmus

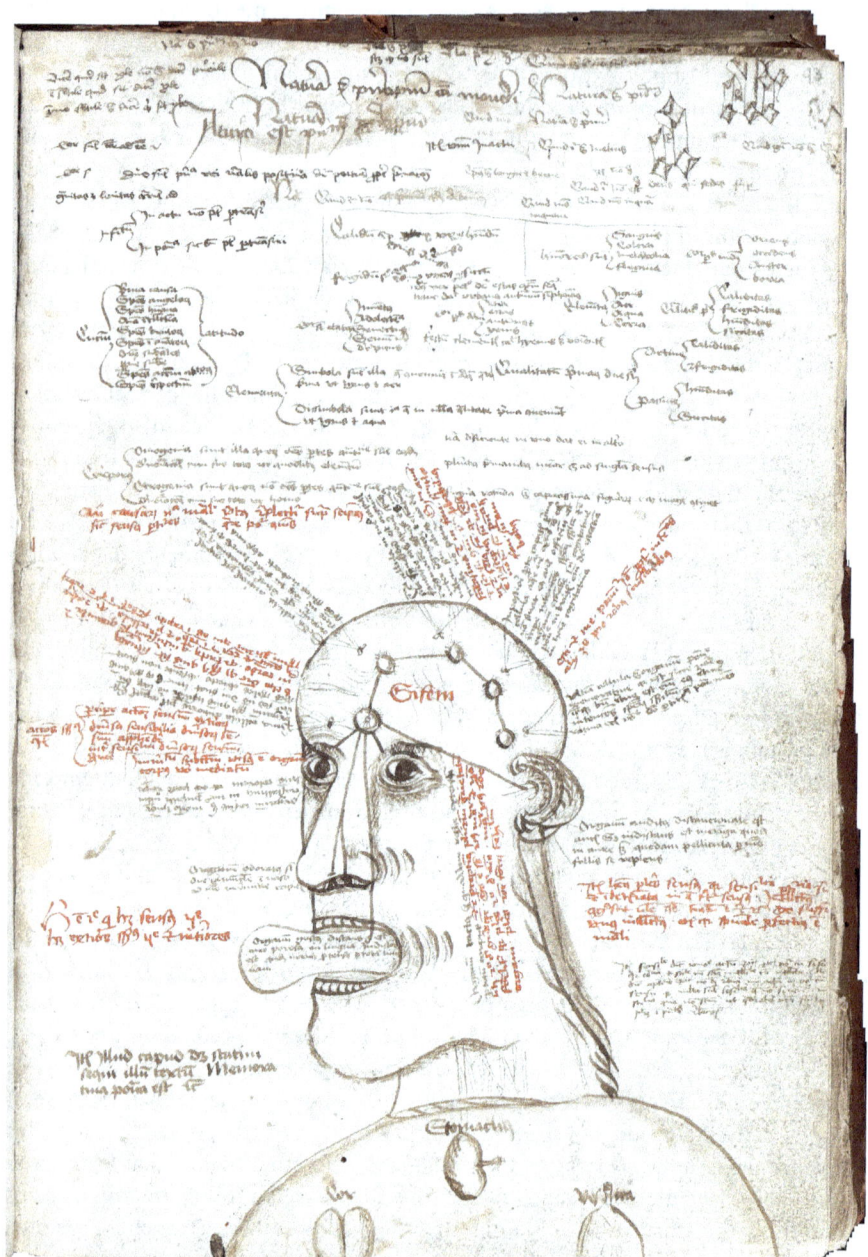

FIGURE 7.12: Aristotle, *De Anima*, Johann Lindner of Mönchburg, Leipzig, 1472–4, MS 55, f.93. Wellcome Collection, London.

imagined (through a character in one of his dialogues) a 'whole house [that was] most eloquent everywhere, so that gates and doors and window-frames and every pane of glass and beams and ceilings and floor-tiles and walls ... should all say something that it should be useful not to forget'.[13] And when, fifty years later, the French writer Michel de Montaigne retreated from public life to his chateau near Bordeaux to reflect and write about his experience of life, he transformed a room on the top floor of one of its towers into a library that he self-consciously regarded as an embodiment of his private identity. The beams on the ceiling of the room were inscribed with maxims, mostly quotations from antiquity, that exteriorised his disposition of solitude and scepticism, forming it as a physical environment. Montaigne was one of the first of a new genre of writers who actively made a point of incorporating their own subjectivity into their reflections. Although his book of *Essays*, written in his library and published in 1581, includes opinions on an immensely wide and diverse range of subjects, he acknowledged that 'I am myself the subject of my book.' Reflecting on the whole project, he mused that what he created *created him*:

> In modelling this figure on myself, I have so often had to prepare and compose my self, in order to draw it out, that a master copy of it has been firmed up and has, in some sense, formed itself. In painting myself for others, I have painted myself in clearer colours than I originally had. *I have no more made my book than my book has made me*; the book is consubstantial with its author – a proper function, or limb, of my life.[14]

The process of creating environments, inbuilt with coded prompts to accommodate and evoke knowledge and ideas (including knowledge and ideas of one's 'self'), was not unprecedented. Of course, at one level, all architecture and built environments embody and communicate values, deliberately or otherwise. It is, however, arguable that environments like the *studioli*, which were programmed to summarise the *totality* of knowledge, do not simply evoke 'knowledge and ideas'; they also evoke a sense of the mind itself. In this context, it is not as if the mind *has* ideas, as if it is a separate entity that pre-exists its contents; on the contrary, it *is* its ideas. A sense of how the sense of mind or self may not only be reflected *in* its environments but may also exist *as* an environment is suggested by the classical *art of memory*, revived and adapted in the fifteenth and sixteenth centuries. According to this art, ideas and memories are not necessarily formless interior abstractions that exist independently of the environments and phenomena that stimulate them; they can also *be* environments of a kind, instituting knowledge as an internal, psychological 'frame of mind' that is highly *suggestive* of a sense of self at its centre.

The art of memory developed in antiquity, to help orators remember their speeches. According to Cicero, and subsequently believed throughout the Middle Ages, it originated in the fifth century BC when a Greek poet, Simonides of Ceos, was said to have remembered the names of the guests at a feast, all of whom had been suddenly killed by the collapse of the roof, by recalling the order in which they sat round the dining table. As he moved round the table in his imagination, Simonides was able to identify which individual was sitting at each of the places. On the basis of this experience, he developed a mnemonic 'art' whereby individuals could be trained to systematically remember huge quantities of ideas by associating them with objects placed in an ordered manner in an imagined environment. The earliest known text in which the traditional techniques of systematic memory training were described was a treatise on rhetoric, the so-called *Rhetorica ad Herennium* (*Rhetoric for Herennius*), written in the first century BC. It was wrongly attributed to Cicero, who therefore lent it prestige, until the fifteenth century.[15] In the Middle Ages, the art was revived to facilitate the memorisation of scriptural texts. By the thirteenth century, it was also being promoted, largely due to the Dominican order (especially Albert Magnus and Thomas Aquinas), to help the growing numbers of preachers and teachers in the new universities remember their sermons and presentations.

The first step of the art was to visualise an environment or place (*locus*). This was usually a structured space like an architectural interior or courtyard, and could be real or imaginary. It was preferable that memory places should be relatively secluded, or even solitary, because the impression of random people moving through them could be distracting. The *Ideal City* would have been highly suitable in this role (Fig. 4.5). Secondly, it was necessary to imagine a range of specific objects or people (*imagines*), selected for their associations with the ideas that the memoriser wished to remember, and to place them, in the order in which they were to be remembered, in the imaginary environment. These *imagines* should be striking – for instance, figures 'wearing crowns or purple cloaks, blood-stained or smeared with paint' – in order to be memorable. By today's standards, some of the examples given in the text seem positively surreal. For instance, in order to remember the *testament* of witnesses, a man holding a ram's *testicles* was suggested. Individuals were, however, encouraged to invent their own images, to ensure that they would have personal resonance for them.[16] Finally, when the remembered ideas were to be recalled, the practitioner was to move around the imaginary environment in his mind, retrieving them from the suggestive objects to which they had been attached in the order in which he encountered them.

Medieval notions of memory differed radically from our own. For most of the population, especially the laity, physical repositories of information (documents, books, libraries, archives and personal mementos) were exceptionally rare or non-existent and memory, therefore, was a unique resource. Thus, in the absence of maps, young children were sometimes taught the boundaries of their parish by being subjected to minor ordeals at significant marking points (such as jumping into a stream, or out of a tree) in order to help them remember those locations and create mental 'maps of memories'. At the other end of the scale, if an educated monk or priest had a single opportunity to read a text, he might memorise it in its entirety. Every monk was expected to know at least the psalter 'by heart' – to re*cor*d it (from the Latin *cor*, 'heart') – and many of them memorised much, much more. But memory was not just a resource; it was also an *instrument* of knowledge. In a literary context, individuals were encouraged to formulate their knowledge and understanding in terms of precedents that were approved by the Church. It was for this reason that medieval writers made so many citations. A notion could be *proven*, not by logic or experience, but by reference to biblical or patristic sources that functioned as pre-fabricated expositions of true doctrine. It was therefore in the interest of every educated man to memorise as much text as possible, furnishing himself with references with which to support his arguments. In using such sources, thinkers were not merely submitting to authority; they were also accessing what they believed to be a fount of truth. To have expressed themselves independently as individuals – without reference to remembered sources – would have been controversial; and to contradict them, as Peter Abelard did in his *Sic et Non* (*Yes and No*) – which compiled apparent contradictions among the writings of the Church Fathers – would have been heretical.

It was partly to facilitate memorisation that medieval books were so lavishly decorated. Illuminated initials, marginal grotesques and complex schemes of alternating colours were not simply wayward eccentricities or doodles; they were also mnemonic devices. Readers were advised to attach their memory of a passage in a text to a visual feature on the page – whether it was naturally there, like the location of the passage on the page (top/bottom, left/right), or contrived, like a monkey firing an arrow at a snail in the margin – and to remember the visual feature. They were also encouraged to memorise a text from a single manuscript – not from more than one version of the same text – to ensure that the mnemonic prompts associated with that manuscript would not change.[17] Some texts – even utilitarian ones such as primers of grammar and collections of laws – were written in verse, as the structured rhythm of metre and rhyme is easier to memorise than prose.[18] Patterns and diagrams, both drawn and imagined, were also important aids to memorisation because they enabled readers to remember clusters of ideas as coherent inter-connected systems. The coherence of these systems made them easy to remember as single entities, like a 'compressed' computer file, which could then be imaginatively 'decompressed', disclosing the texts that had been pre-attached to its various parts. Such mnemonic systems ranged from the simple – for instance, attaching a sequence of ideas to the letters of the alphabet – to the immensely complex and comprehensive. Hugh of St Victor's *De arca Noe pro arca sapientiae* (*On Noah's Ark as an Ark of Wisdom*), written in around 1130, describes Noah's ark as a vast virtual three-dimensional diagram or map of the totality of knowledge; by remembering the principle of the diagram rather than its content, the reader's attention could move though it in any direction, like a librarian walking along corridors of library stacks. It also describes the ark as a metaphor for a mind that is systematically structured by the extensive configuration of texts remembered in it: 'I give you the ark of Noah as a model of spiritual building, which your eyes may see outwardly *so that your soul may be built inwardly in its likeness.*'[19]

It is arguable that the proliferation of printed books in the Renaissance contributed towards the undermining of the medieval art of memory. Especially from the seventeenth century, 'source' books increasingly functioned as *alternatives* to memory, like 'offshore' repositories of information and ideas, rather than as *aids* to memory, as in the Middle Ages. The increasing investment of authority in experience rather than in tradition also resulted in less dependence on authoritative texts and, therefore, on memorisation as a mode of knowing. Having said this, although the prescribed values that were enshrined in traditional sources slowly ceased to apply at this time, the psychological processes and mechanisms by which objects and environments were invested with ideas and required to function as mnemonics continued to operate. Images continued to communicate by 'releasing' the associations projected into them, but they were no longer necessarily attached to a preconceived body of beliefs, as prescribed by the Church. On the contrary, to the extent that they were used to organise and store the content of personal experience, so they began to reflect the parameters of personal identity – reason and observation – tacitly reminding the viewer of his own subjectivity.

Although the highly structured and programmed *studioli* of Federico do not appear to have been conceived in relation to specific texts, it is arguable that they were nevertheless designed to encapsulate a particular set of values in a series of mnemonic prompts, tacitly reflecting the thoughts of the patron *as if* they were memory *loci*. Federico was familiar with the art of memory as an instrument of knowledge. He is known to have developed his memory as a child and to have studied rhetoric at the humanist Academy of Vittorino da Feltre (whose portrait was included among the luminaries at Urbino) in Mantua. As a leader and public speaker, it was necessary for him to be able to remember texts and information, especially for use in the delivery of speeches. While the symbolic content of his *studioli* evokes the ideal with which Federico aspired to be identified, it is even more significant that, by manifesting as a surrogate frame of mind, it also re-minded him of *himself*, reflecting his sense of himself to himself, so that 'his soul might be built inwardly in its likeness'. Moreover, by projecting his values into a psychological environment that existed in a physical form outside of himself, Federico was also transmitting them, as a 'frame of mind' – invested with conventions of identity-formation – to his successors, who would then be induced to 'remember' them as the frames of their own minds. Most important among these successors was his son, Guidobaldo, who was also renowned for his prodigious powers of memory (in which he too was formally trained). Significantly, a treatise on the art of memory, written by Johannes Host von Romberch and published in Venice in 1533, includes a rare page of illustrated mnemonic prompts associated with the contents of a *studiolo*, as well as those of a hall and a chapel (Fig. 7.13). The scholarly objects that were selected to be loaded with memorable associations are precisely those objects that are common in images of St Jerome in his study, most of which also appear in Federico's *studioli*. In this context, the study with its contents was no longer a mere room. It had become a psychological environment in which inclinations and ideas appeared *as* things, unified by the space that seemed to contain them; it had become an imaginary place – a frame of mind or mode of experience that realised itself as a subject by seeing its perceived contents not as inert objects but as psychological functions of itself.

Federico's *studioli* constituted a schematic organisation of his ideal image of himself, as a spatial environment. This impulse to realise the identity of man as a comprehensive structure, centred in itself, was more elaborately and explicitly reflected in a broadsheet, *The Order of the Universe and the First Monuments of Human Knowledge*, conceived sixty years later by the Italian philosopher and physician, Andrea Bacci (Fig. 7.14).[20] The text of this broadsheet, which was composed in the 1540s but not printed until 1581, covers the key components of humanist cosmology, ranging from the planets, elements and seasons to the humours, senses and intellectual faculties of man. Central to Bacci's thought was the notion that the various levels of life in the universe correspond with each other, by virtue of the rational proportions between them, and therefore that the highest principle of divine intelligence is microcosmically present both in the operations of nature and in the mind of man. Despite its humanist aspirations, Bacci's diagram is based on

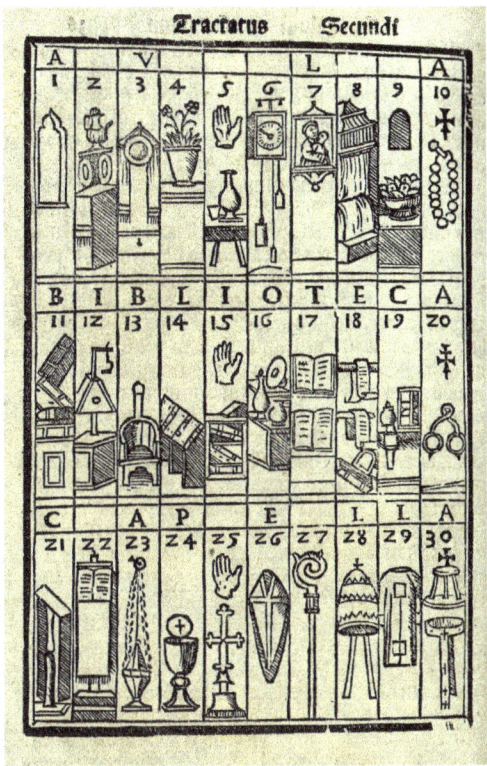

FIGURE 7.13: Johann Romberch, *Congestorium artificiose memorie* (*Compendium of Artificial Memory*), Venice, 1533, folio 36v. Wellcome Collection, London.

medieval representations of the human mind in which the brain is divided into three ventricles – with sensation and imagination (producing images) towards the front of the head near the sense organs; cogitation and 'estimation' at the centre, and memory at the back. This division of the brain into three zones was not based on observation. On the contrary it was based on its perceived correspondence, in a typically medieval manner, to a pre-established convention or 'truth'. Although mental activity was sometimes divided into three modes or phases in antiquity, the tidy tripartite structure of the brain (which even Leonardo da Vinci accepted until he had an opportunity to dissect one) was developed by analogy with working buildings in which material was received through the 'front door' of the senses, before being processed in the centre, and stored at the back. This concept was inherited by medieval physicians from the ancient Greeks who called the brain the 'temple of the spirit' on account of its apparent similarity to the architectural layout of chambers in their temples. Thus not only was the humanist sense of the self evoked by the suggestive intellectual environments that it created for itself, but the very structure and operation of the brain was conceived by analogy with exemplars in the outside world. According to one twelfth-century commentator,

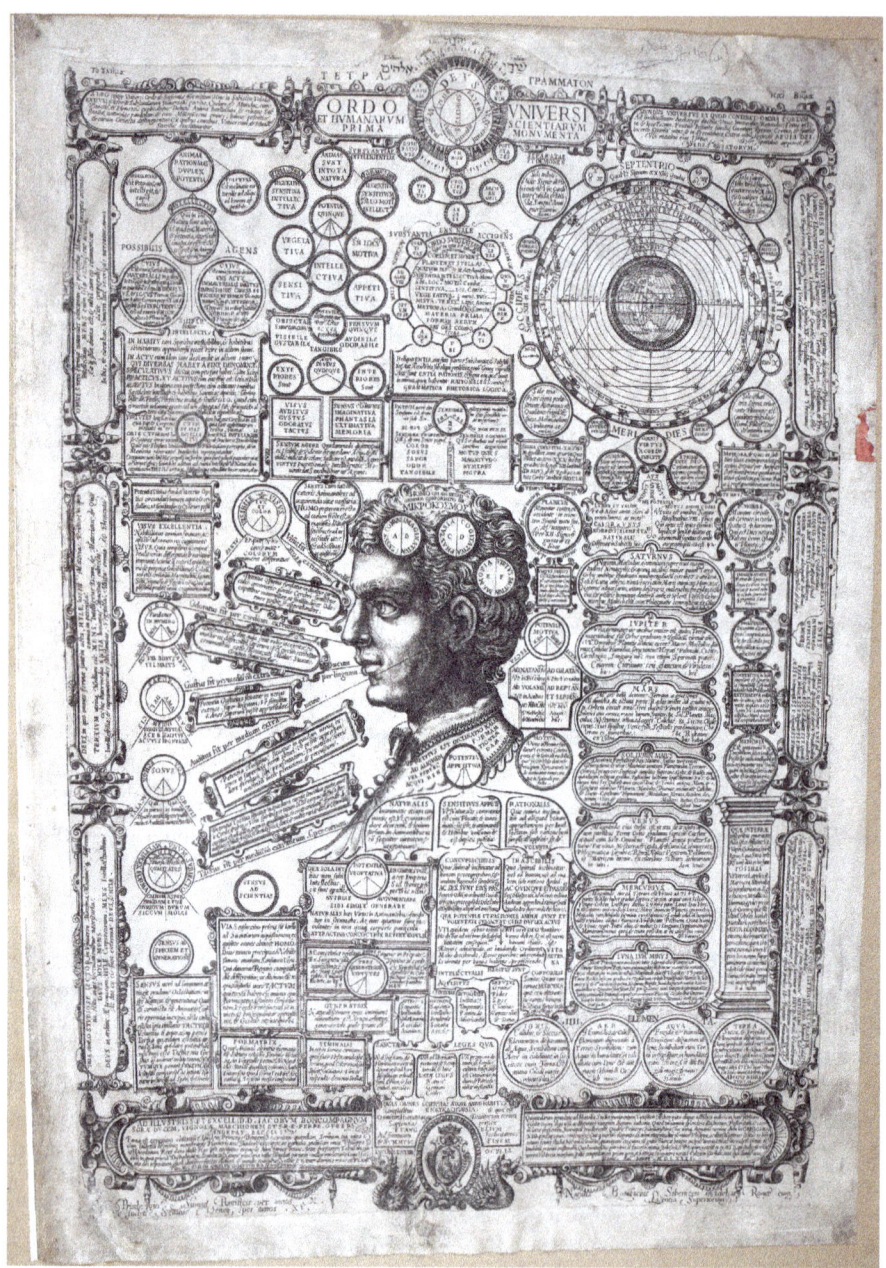

FIGURE 7.14: Andrea Bacci, *De Ordo Universi et Humanarum Scientiarum Prima Monumenta* (*The Order of the Universe and the First Monuments of Human Knowledge*), Vaccarius, 1581. British Library, London.

the ancients had three chambers in their temples, first the *vestibulum*, then the *consistorium*, finally the *apotheca*. In the first, the declarations were made in law cases; in the second, the statements were sifted; in the third, final sentence was laid down. The ancients said that the same processes occur in the temple of the spirit, that is the brain. First, we gather ideas into the *cellula phantastica*; in the second cell we think them over; in the third we lay down our thoughts; that is we commit to memory.[21]

While the content of Bacci's ideas is significant, more pertinent in the present context is the manner in which he created and presented them. To ensure that he communicated not only the content of his philosophy but the fact that it revolved around a central unifying principle – 'man as microcosm' – Bacci represented it in diagrammatic form. Capitalising on the organisational potential of the medium, he sought to demonstrate how the various different levels of life relate to each other, not only in a linear and temporal sequence – as represented by text, to be harvested by reading – but also *simultaneously*, as conveyed by the diagram as a whole. As Leonardo argued in the *Paragone*, one of the advantages that painting had over poetry and music was that it could present its content simultaneously, rather than in extended 'delayed' form. In some sense, therefore, Bacci was doing with words – as representations of ideas – what Federico da Montefeltro had been doing with images of his possessions – capitalising on the capacity of spatial relationships to organise data into coherent structures of knowledge that revolve around a unifying principle and are manifest in their totality at any given time. Just as a comprehensive collection of meaningful possessions (as imagined in the *studioli*) could serve to embody a fully formed and present sense of self in Federico, undistended into the past and future, so a comprehensive body of ideas, rationally organised as a 'collection' (rather than a sequence), could constitute a universal structure in which the mind of man is presently sustained – not partially, in a state of becoming (in time), but completely, in a state of being (in space).

While the design and decoration of *studioli* were clearly programmed to reflect the complex identities of their patrons, so were their *actual* possessions. Having originated as places in which to read in silence and solitude, *studioli* were also places in which to keep, and meditate on, precious objects. Reflecting a shift away from the domination of religious values, antiquities and exotica became especially popular among collectors. Roman coins and bronzes and curiosities from the New World were highly prized. Inexplicable *naturalia*, such as bezoars and lodestones, were transitional in the sense that they were natural, rather than religious, but they were still believed to have magical powers. While the changing character of collected objects reflected changing perceptions of personal identity very directly, so also did the logistics of storage and display. The two phenomena unfolded together.

Before considering the ways in which privileged individuals used the selection and organisation of possessions as a means of identity-formation, it is worth remembering that, at the beginning of the period under consideration here, a vast majority of the population will have owned very few chattels, mostly to meet their immediate needs, and the question of storage will have scarcely arisen for them. Moreover, although the Church was immensely wealthy, Christian doctrine advocated a life of modesty, and even poverty. Indeed, belief in the salvific value of renouncing material goods was one of the factors that led to the spawning of mendicant orders of monks in the twelfth and thirteenth centuries. Another factor, however, was the growth of the merchant class, whose disposable wealth was seen by some to be excessive. While wealthy merchants attempted to legitimise their affluence by engaging in religious commissions (sometimes as acts of self-representation, as we saw in chapter 5), they also began to consume fashionable items, such as fine fabric and costumes; indeed, in the thirteenth century, sumptuary laws, which had previously been used to identify clergymen, criminals and heathens, were applied to the laity for the first time.[22]

Paradoxically, the obverse of these constraints was the fact that it became increasingly possible for lay people other than the gentry to acquire possessions at this time, not just to meet their needs but to reflect their personal inclinations and exercise some immediate control over their world. With commodities came the need – first – to protect them and – second – to organise them. For the few who were able, and entitled, to acquire luxury goods (fabrics, jewellery, silver utensils, books), it was initially common to store them in portable, lockable hold-all strongboxes and coffers (Fig. 7.15). The size, elaborate design and technical ingenuity of the locks on such coffers testify both to the need for the physical enforcement of security, even in the home, and to the high status of the key-holder; such was their authority that, if

FIGURE 7.15: Chest, fifteenth to sixteenth century, iron, Europe, 21.3 × 19.4 × 29.8 cm. Metropolitan Museum of Art, New York, The Cloisters.

decorated with coats of arms, some keys could be used as an early form of passport. For added security at night, chests were often kept near the bed, sometimes doubling up as bedside tables (Fig. 7.2). The coffers' handles, and sometimes wheels, reflect the fact that, in the days when the elite were constantly on the move between their various residences (in order to be known to their tenants or subjects, and to consume the local produce to which they were entitled), it was customary for them to travel with their mobile chattels, including their tapestries and furniture (still called *meubles* – or 'movables' – in France). In the fifteenth century, chests became more refined in style and were often mounted on stands, whereupon they were given front-opening lockable doors, and sometimes a shelf (Fig. 8.4). Particularly in the context of social dining – one of the key arenas of self-presentation – the top surfaces, or 'boards', of mounted chests were 'dressed' for the display of fine utensils such as dishes, flagons, ewers and cups; hence their names – 'cupboard' ('cup-board') and 'dresser' (Fig. 7.16).

FIGURE 7.16: Wedding Feast from *L'histoire d'Olivier de Castille et d'Artus d'Algarbe*, 1445–65. Département des manuscrits, Français 12574, folio 181v, Bibliothèque Nationale de France, Paris.

In the following century, portable chests were increasingly furnished with *drawers* – a new invention that reflected less immediate concern with physical security and more concern with the variety and meaningful organisation of their contents (Fig. 7.17). Indeed, the contents of collections became ever more varied and marvellous at this time, supplementing the traditional attachment to objects of practical or devotional value with man-made and natural wonders – antique figurines, medals, table clocks, cameos, shells, minerals and other curiosities (Fig. 7.18). Some chests of drawers were given falling fronts in place of doors, enabling them to also function as writing desks; this suggests that it was more as instruments of knowledge and understanding than for convenience and security that they were compartmentalised in this way (Fig. 7.19).

Besides reflecting wealth and influence, the acquisition of possessions was instrumental in the process of identity-formation on two fronts. Firstly, the choice of objects enabled the collector to exercise his interest in prestigious items; and secondly, the organisation and display of his possessions enabled him to exercise his understanding of them. While seeming to reflect an interest in the world for its own sake, both parts of the process also reflect the collector's impulse to shape his world in such a way that he sees his own mind reflected in it. As such his collection was a physical embodiment of his mind, just as the Gubbio and Urbino *studioli* were virtual embodiments of Federico da Montefeltro's mind. Significantly, the earliest tract on the ideal way to display a collection of objects – *Inscriptiones vel tituli teatri amplissimi* (*Inscriptions or labels for the most complete theatre*), written by Samuel van Quiccheberg in Munich in 1565 – was partly inspired by a treatise on the art of

FIGURE 7.17: Travelling cabinet, with designs after Lorenz Stoer, Innsbruck, late sixteenth century, pine carcass, 52 × 67 × 35 cm. Image: Blumka Gallery, New York.

THE IMAGINARY ENVIRONMENTS OF THE SELF   137

FIGURE 7.18: Ferrante Imperato, *Dell'historia naturale* (*On Natural History*), Naples, 1599. Wellcome Collection, London.

FIGURE 7.19: Hercules (or 'Plus Oultra') cabinet, around 1530, walnut inlaid with various woods, 81.3 × 134 × 44.4 cm. Victoria and Albert Museum, London.

memory in which a model classical amphitheatre was proposed as a three-dimensional memory *locus* for objects to be used as mnemonics. The miniature amphitheatre, conceived by Giulio Camillo in the 1520s and described in *L'Idea del Teatro* (published in 1550), consisted of seven tiers of seats, divided by seven aisles. Each of the forty-nine sections of the fan-shaped 'auditorium', to be viewed by a person standing on the stage, was associated with a different aspect of the cosmos. Not unlike Bacci's *Order of the Universe*, these aspects ranged from the planets and elements to the inclinations of the human mind and products of human culture – each one logically related to its neighbour. As such, the model was a kind of interactive diagram; it represented a coded embodiment of all possible knowledge, systematically organised into an architectural resource – *storing* ideas (like a memory) on the one hand, while also *generating* them (like an imagination) on the other. One writer, who saw the model, described how Camillo

> calls this theatre of his by many names, saying now that it is a built or constructed mind and soul, and now that it is a windowed one. He pretends that all things that the human mind can conceive and which we cannot see with the corporeal eye, after being collected together by diligent meditation may be expressed by certain corporeal signs in such a way that the beholder may at once perceive with his eyes everything that is otherwise hidden in the depths of the human mind. And it is because of this corporeal looking that he calls it a theatre.[23]

Based on this model, Quiccheberg (who adopted his predecessor's use of the word 'theatre' to mean 'display') recommended that collectors divide their possessions into artificial man-made wonders and miracles of nature. Following in the steps of Camillo, he clearly indicated that such material should be organised into meaningfully conceived categories and sub-categories (identified by the 'inscriptions' and 'labels' in the title of his work) that reflect the unity and coherence of the universe – according to the patron's judgement and therefore as an expression of his self-sense.

As personal collecting became more fashionable, the functions of storage and display became more important, and chests with drawers developed into independent cabinets. The most spectacular cabinets were so grandly conceived and lavishly decorated that the very use of them – opening them, and accessing the drawers, in the company of privileged friends and acquaintances – became a theatrical act of self-promotion. One example, commissioned by Duke Philip II of Pomerania in 1616–17, contains a highly self-referential (and anticipatory) panel that represents the Duke showing his new possession to a large gathering of impressed and obsequious admirers (Fig. 7.20). Some of the interiors of such cabinets were even designed as miniature stages with columns and tiled floors – on which possessions became conspirators in the drama of sophisticated selfhood. Moreover, as collections of objects grew, so cabinets were moved out of the private space of the study into a more social space – either a pre-existing hall or, in some cases, a new room developed especially for them, also called a 'cabinet' (of curiosities) or *kunstkammer* (Fig. 7.18). For instance, many of the objects that Francesco I, Grand Duke of Tuscany, had displayed in his small one-room *studiolo* in the Palazzo Vecchio in the early 1570s were transferred to the galleries of the Uffizi in 1584.[24] The most extreme cabinets of curiosity, such as those of Archduke Ferdinand II at Schloss Ambras in Innsbruck or Emperor Rudolph II in

FIGURE 7.20: A painted panel from a Pomeranian cabinet (represented on the panel), commissioned from Philip Hainhofer by Duke Philip II of Pomerania, c.1616–17. Kunstgewerbemuseum, Berlin.

Prague, extended into long chains of rooms. Fusing the rationality of the *studiolo* and the transformative potential of church treasuries on a vast scale, they were highly elaborate and exclusive theatres of self-construction. Indeed Rudolph's collection has been seen to be so subjective that it borders on the pathological. It was as if he assembled it as an alternative to the real world, which constantly eluded his control and frustrated his efforts to find himself reflected in it; by amassing a comprehensive collection of possessions, he created a microcosm of the world which he *could* control and organise, and therefore seem to understand as an apparently natural function of his own existence. The proposition that collections served as much to create identity as to gratify the curiosity of the collector is supported by the simple fact that, as some object-types, such as certain types of shell, became well known and were de-mystified, they ceased to be collected; such a change of fortune indicates that it was their rarity and mystique, rather than any inherent quality, that gave them cultural value, and therefore that it was their rarity and mystique that owners wished to appropriate from them, to enhance their own individuality.

While some natural objects fell out of favour with seventeenth-century collectors as they became commonplace, *paintings* were increasingly commodified, and collections of paintings became prestigious. The extent to which such collections were conceived, not only because of their particular merits, but also to give substance and structure to the identity of their owners is reflected in the way that the collections themselves became the subject of paintings and were represented as commodities, in cabinets or galleries – a genre that became especially popular in Flanders. This agenda is clearly reflected in the 'gallery paintings' themselves. Firstly, the contents of the galleries are usually displayed decoratively and symmetrically, according to their size and regardless of their specific theme (religion, mythology, portrait, still life etc.). The fact that even masterpieces by Giorgione and Titian were subjected to this treatment (for instance, in David Teniers the Younger's imaginative painting of the Hapsburg Archduke Leopold Wilhelm's collection of 1651) demonstrates how the overall impression of a collection took precedence over the individual characteristics of its contents (Fig. 7.21).[25] And secondly, the collectors themselves are usually shown in the midst of their possessions, admiring and discussing them with friends, thereby 'redeeming' the potential of collections to serve as instruments of identity-formation. Between 1651 and 1653, Archduke Leopold had Teniers paint about ten pictures of him visiting his collection, to be sent, in place of portraits, to members of his circle. As court painter and keeper of the archduke's collections,

FIGURE 7.21: David Teniers the Younger, *Archduke Leopold Wilhelm in his Gallery*, around 1651, oil on canvas, 123 × 163 cm. Kunsthistorischesmuseum, Vienna.

Teniers was frequently present at these occasions and he included himself in the paintings accordingly, investing them with yet another degree of self-reference.

The fact that art collecting was becoming common at this time is a testimony to the extent to which the idea of 'art' had acquired autonomous cultural value, regardless of its content. But the fact that *collections* of paintings were also being documented *in* works of art is a sign of the way in which the concept of 'art' did not only refer to art objects; it had also become a highly self-conscious and self-referential index of personal identity among its consumers and collectors. That is to say, besides legitimising the act of painting in a thoroughly circular manner by painting 'pictures of paintings', paintings of art collections also conferred legitimacy on the practice of *collecting* art, by framing and presenting it as 'a subject worthy of artistic representation'; and, by extension, they conferred status on the sense of self that constructed and defined itself by collecting art. Although it was only the financial and intellectual elites who were able to construct their identities by owning art – and by *showing* themselves to be owning art – it is arguable that, as the potential of art as an 'archetype of self-determination' became established in public awareness, participation in the growing 'discourse of art' – in one capacity or another – became a primary medium through which the notion of personal identity began to thrive in society as a whole. As the notion of art crystallised into a corollary of subjective selfhood, it became the authoritative medium of self-expression and cultural exchange that it continues to be today.

CHAPTER EIGHT

The Privatisation of the Self: Fireplaces, Beds and Mirrors

The development of the monastic cell, study and collectors' cabinet epitomised how specialist environments evolved to accommodate a burgeoning sense of personal identity among the elite. The same changes can also be observed in a more domesticated context. An affluent medieval household consisted of a lord and his family, retinue and servants. Especially in northern Europe, most daily activities – cooking, eating, gaming and, when necessary, administering justice – took place communally in a single all-purpose space – the hall. Indeed, writing in the eighth century, the Venerable Bede compared life itself to the swift flight of a sparrow through a hall – in through one door and immediately out through another, back into the unknown.[1] Of course, domestic spaces varied enormously from one region to another but, generally speaking, the household revolved around a large multifunctional space of this kind. In England, halls were originally built on the first floor, above a cellar or storage area, but, as fortification became less necessary in the thirteenth century, they became one-storey buildings on the ground floor, leading to a range of smaller functional spaces. At first, they had no chimneys but revolved around an open hearth in the middle of the room, used for light, heat and cooking, as at Penshurst Place in Kent (Fig. 8.1). The roof, supported by rafters, was pitched and high, and was fitted with vents to allow the smoke from the fire to escape. For meals, plain trestle-tables covered with fine linen were set up, with a 'high table' on a raised dais at one end for the lord and his entourage, and a series of tables, set at right angles to the high table, for the rest of his household, seated strictly according to rank. In this respect, halls resembled monastic refectories, from which they may have partly evolved. The lord, and maybe his immediate companions, would sit on chairs, which were rare and carried status accordingly. Even in his absence, the lord's chair, sometimes framed by a canopy, would symbolise his authority – just as the spiritual authority of a bishop was present in the bishop's throne (*cathedra* in Latin) in a cathedral. Everyone else would sit on stools or benches (hence 'banquet'); three-legged stools were common because they were more stable on uneven floors than four-legged ones. The hierarchical structure of this set-up, demonstrated through the spatial organisation of people and ritually re-enforced through repeated social actions, was of paramount importance.

FIGURE 8.1: The Great Hall, Penshurst Place, Kent, around 1340. By kind permission of Viscount De L'Isle from his private collection at Penshurst Place, Kent, England.

At night, it was not unusual for the servants and knights of a household to sleep on straw on the floor of the hall, in their clothes. In castles, their armour would be hung on the walls in readiness for defensive action; traces of this tradition can still be seen in the panels of stained glass, decorated with coats of arms, that were used to grace halls in more peaceful times. For such serving people, the idea of 'retreating to sleep in comfort and privacy' – not to mention the notion of personal selfhood that such an idea reflects and fosters – was yet to evolve. Even at the end of the sixteenth century, an English clergyman William Harrison could write, in his book *A Description of England* (published in 1577), that there were 'old men yet dwelling in the village where I remain' who noted that several aspects of life in England had 'marvellously altered . . . within their sound remembrance'. Recording the words of these 'old men', Harrison comments that one of these changes was:

> the great (although not general) amendment of lodging; for, said they, our fathers, yea and we ourselves also, have lain full oft upon straw pallets, on rough mats covered only with a sheet, under coverlets made of dagswain or hopharlots (I use

their own terms), and a good round log under their heads instead of a bolster or pillow . . . Pillows (said they) were thought meet only for women in childbed. As for servants, if they had any sheet above them, it was well, for seldom had they any under their bodies to keep them from the pricking straws that ran oft through the canvas of the pallet and rased their hardened hides.

Halls were supplemented by a number of smaller 'service' rooms. In England a buttery and pantry, supplying the staple diets of wine, ale and bread, were often placed beyond the entrance to the low end of the hall, away from the dais. The names of these rooms, derived from the French words for 'bottle' (*bouteille*) and 'bread' (*pain*), demonstrate how, following the Norman Conquest in 1066, many prestigious customs that developed among the English elite were of French origin. Moreover, as the identities of the elite became more individuated, so their environments began to accommodate their more articulated social and psychological personas in function-specific rooms. 'Oriels' – projecting bay windows – were added to some halls in the fourteenth century to make allowance for private conversation. At the top end of the hall beyond the dais were the lord's parlour, chamber and closet, accessible through a private door. These smaller, privileged rooms were primarily for receiving guests, private entertainment and sleeping. Again, their French origin is reflected in their names – from *parler*, to speak, and *chambre*, a bedchamber – in contrast to the early medieval Saxon 'hall'. They may have derived from the private quarters of abbots in medieval monasteries. Indeed, at the dissolution of the monasteries in England in 1536, several monastic foundations were given to Henry VIII's favourites to be converted into noble houses. In some cases, such as Muchelney Abbey in Somerset, it was only the abbot's quarters that were considered capable of adaptation to a domestic lifestyle and have therefore survived.[2] When halls in English houses moved from the first floor to the ground floor, a private space called a *solar* was often retained on the first floor in an adjacent part of the building, over a cellar which in due course also evolved into the parlour or chamber where the lord of the manor would eat in private. In his allegorical *Vision of Piers Plowman*, written in around 1362, William Langland documented the lord of the manor's growing distaste for eating with his entire household in the hall and his preference for privacy with his lady:

> Wretched is the hall each day in the week,
> There the lord and lady liketh not to sit;
> Now have the rich a rule to eat by themselves
> In a privy parlour for poor men's sake,
> Or in a chamber with a chimney [fireplace], and leave the chief hall
> That was made for meals, for men to eat in.[3]

From the fourteenth century, private rooms, which were too small for open hearths, were increasingly heated by chimney fireplaces. These novel installations were prestigious because they required a sophisticated reconceiving of the wall-structures of buildings and were therefore expensive, but they were also instrumental in the commodification of comfort in the form of a guaranteed source of relatively safe, reliable heat and light. Fireplaces were eventually integrated into the design of halls, obviating the need for open hearths and capacious high-pitched roofs, which could then be replaced by lower ceilings supporting a second floor of rooms. Indeed, another of the 'alterations' to English homes that William Harrison noted in 1577 was

> the multitude of chimneys lately erected, whereas in their young days there were not above two or three, if so many, in most uplandish towns of the realm (the religious houses and manor places of their lords always excepted, and peradventure some great personages), but each one made his fire against a reredos [supporting the hearth] in the hall, where he dined and dressed his meat.

The continued prestige of fireplaces was reflected in the lavish ornamentation of their over-mantels, which often reached up to the ceiling; whether the fire was lit or not, they could be used as honorific frames (Fig. 7.16, behind the central canopy). Proximity to the fire was determined by seniority; even in the seventeenth century, it was felt that

> in the presence of well bred company, it is uncomely to turn one's back to the fire, or to approach nigher than others, for the one and the other savoureth of preheminence. It is not permitted but to the chief in quality, or to him that hath charge of the fire-fork, to kindle it, take it away, or put fuel on it.[4]

The development of private rooms precipitated the development of a personal sense of self. This shift is reflected in numerous representations of such spaces, in which the characteristics of the rooms are used to enhance and contextualise the identities of the individuals within them. For instance, the *Annunciation* from Robert Campin's *Merode Altarpiece* – painted in Tournai in around 1425 – is set, unusually, in a domestic closet with a substantial window and fireplace (Fig. 8.2). Although it uses the conventional image of the Virgin reading in solitude (and maybe silently) as a sign of her receptivity to the Holy Spirit, it does not cast her as a renunciate, appealing to renunciates, as Fra Angelico's *Annunciation* in San Marco does (Fig. 7.5); it casts her as a privileged householder. Besides naturalising the sacred by making it familiar, the image sanctions the privilege of domestic comfort and the personal self-sense that enjoys it. Besides the fireplace, the most coveted commodity in the Virgin's closet is the glazed windows, owned only by the wealthy. The value of clear glass was such that it was not unusual for the elite to take their glazed window panels with them when they travelled. In the early Middle Ages, and in poorer homes, interiors were dark. Window openings were narrow and were covered by wooden shutters, if at all (Fig. 8.2); parchment, greased to become more translucent, was sometimes used. Beeswax for candles was expensive and not readily available. The alternative – tallow candles, using the 'dripping' or fat from beef – was horribly smoky and smelly, and highly inefficient. In poor households, tallow candles were made at home, using the dried stems of long grass as wicks. People would visit their neighbours in the evenings to share light. Consistent with these limitations, most people worked outdoors in the daytime, rising at dawn and going to bed at dusk; their social lives revolved around the community and the Church rather than the home.

By allowing increased light into interiors, glazed windows became a key determinant in the construction of the 'domesticated individual' for they increased the individual's potential for private socialising and self-oriented actions such as

FIGURE 8.2: Workshop of Robert Campin, *The Annunciation* from the Merode Altarpiece, Tournai, around 1427–32, oil on oak, 64.1 × 63.2 cm. Metropolitan Museum of Art, New York.

reading. Indeed, the *solar* – one of the earliest private spaces in English houses – appears to have been named from the French word *sol* (sun) on account of its windows and light. Glass that was sufficiently clear to be used in windows was available from the fourteenth century, but it was initially expensive, difficult to make and relatively ineffective. In the fifteenth century, the possibility of enjoying daylight and warmth at the same time became a reality but clear window glass was still a luxury and was used sparingly – as reflected in Campin's *Annunciation*, in which a variety of window coverings can be seen – shutters and latticework screens, covering unglazed openings and, only at the top, the latest option – glazed panels, decorated here with family coats of arms. Significantly, the Virgin has supplemented the light received from the window with a candle (though the fact that the candle on the table has just been extinguished suggests that physical light, and the texts it illuminates, have just been superseded by grace). It was not until the late sixteenth century that the huge quantities of window glass that had traditionally been used in churches (where the difficulty of producing clear glass was turned into a virtue through staining) began to appear in prestigious houses – for instance, at Hardwick Hall ('more glass than wall') in Derbyshire (Fig. 8.3). Indeed, chimneys and windows epitomised domestic privilege and luxury until the seventeenth and nineteenth

FIGURE 8.3: Hardwick Hall, Derbyshire, 1590–7.

centuries respectively. In medieval Normandy, households were taxed according to the number of hearths (chimneys) they had. In Britain, a 'hearth tax', introduced in 1662, was replaced thirty years later by a 'window tax' which was not superseded until 1851. Windows that were bricked up to avoid the tax can still be seen in houses all over the country.

While Campin's *Annunciation* shows the Virgin in a private closet, most fifteenth-century *Annunciations* from northern Europe – for instance, those of Rogier van der Weyden and Hans Memling – show her in her bedchamber, reading prayerfully at a *prie-dieu*, thereby realising the potential of the bedroom as a place of privacy (Fig. 8.4). It was not unusual for literate individuals to read in their bedchambers. Indeed collections of books were sometimes kept there. In Carlo Crivelli's *Annunciation* of 1486, the Virgin's books are kept on a shelf above the bed. Because books were valuable, they were also kept beside the bed in low chests. In St Ursula's well-lit bedchamber, as depicted by the Venetian painter Vittore Carpaccio (in *The Dream of St Ursula* of around 1500), one of the corners of the room has been designated a study area, with a table, set up with a portable sloping desk for reading and writing, and a cupboard full of books (plus a candle, suggesting night reading) – exactly as in a dedicated study. In affluent houses, studies or cabinets were sometimes situated near the bedchamber, enabling their insomniac owners to contemplate their collections at night.

Besides a *prie-dieu* and the obligatory vase of lilies, symbolising purity and virginity, the Virgin's bedchamber was often furnished with such comforts as a cupboard, dressed with a variety of utensils, and a bench with cushions. But by far

FIGURE 8.4: Hans Memling, *The Annunciation*, 1480–9, oil on panel, transferred to canvas, 76.5 × 54.6 cm. Metropolitan Museum of Art, New York, Robert Lehman Collection.

the most important feature in the room – and often in the late medieval house altogether – was the bed itself. The 'bed' referred not only to the wooden bedstead on which an individual slept, but also to the bedding used to dress the bedstead which, with the help of a canopy, was conceived as a highly distinguishing space (Figs 7.2, 8.4). Inventories and wills indicate that beds were the most valuable chattels in many houses. In the sixteenth century, the most extravagant examples, lavishly draped with silks and velvets, rose from the floor to the ceiling, and were several times more expensive than oil paintings by contemporary artists such as Raphael and Leonardo da Vinci.

In the thirteenth century, canopies or 'testers' first appeared over beds. The earliest examples hung from cords attached to the walls and ceiling, and frequently supported drawable curtains that could be rolled up into bulbous pendants during the daytime. Especially while suspended in this way, testers are comparable with the canopies that were hung over honorific chairs in halls and elsewhere, or held over the heads of royalty, and relics, during processions (Fig. 7.16). They were temporary features, conferring honour on their users while also accommodating the peripatetic nature of a grand household, with which they would travel, as required. It was not until the end of the fifteenth century that the support of the canopy was integrated into the structure of beds, as bed-posts – as in Carpaccio's *St Ursula* (albeit without the hangings in this case) – and that the association of the bed with the possibility of personal identity became innate in the object. Having said that, as with the collapsible trestle-tables used for dining, it was usually the textiles dressing a piece of furniture that were decorative, expensive and prestigious, rather than the woodwork, which might be a fairly rudimentary piece of carpentry. Bearing in mind that windows were not curtained at this time and might not even be glazed, and that servants might have slept in an elite bedchamber, such fabrics also served a practical purpose; they closed the bed off at night. Especially before the invention of corridors, which enabled people to circulate around a house without having to go through each room, this sense of a 'room within a room' was contrived to ensure a degree of privacy, protection and comfort.

Having said this, beds were not always associated with privacy. Indeed, at one end of the social spectrum they were purely utilitarian – for sleeping in. In numerous houses, there was more than one bed to a room and, as we have seen, beds were frequently shared. Erasmus, for instance, commented that he occasionally 'shared a mattress' with Giulio Camillo (author of *L'Idea del Teatro*).[5] In fact, well into the eighteenth century, travellers staying at roadside inns might find themselves sharing their bed not just with their companions but with total strangers. At the other end of the spectrum, beds represented the height of luxury. However, while they consolidated the privileged experience of personal identity by creating a definitive space for it, they were not originally private; they were also designed to ensure that the prestige associated with personal identity was broadcast to the wider world. It was not until the eighteenth century, when dedicated dining rooms and drawing rooms evolved – to stage specific social functions – that bedrooms finally settled into being private spaces. Until such time, grand beds were used to affirm dynastic power and demonstrate the continuity of the family lineage; many of them were emblazoned with the family's coat of arms accordingly. This political function was especially important during pregnancy and childbirth, when the expectant or new mother would receive guests in her bedchamber. In fifteenth-century Tuscany, a new birth was ritually celebrated with the giving of auspicious gifts, some of which were ceremoniously brought to the mother on specially conceived 'birth trays' (Fig. 8.5). Images of the *Birth of the Virgin* and the *Birth of John the Baptist*, both of which were set in bedchambers, sometimes show as many as ten or twelve people in attendance, usually women. In important cases (remembering that infant deaths were common at the time), the birth itself would be witnessed by lawyers to ensure that babies were not swapped. An astrologer might also be present to document the exact moment of the birth and to calculate its significance. In such a context, beds were not merely for sleeping in; they were the very source and spring of a family's honour, the stage on which its identity was performed and perpetuated.

In many representations of births, the infant is depicted being washed, in a portable tub or with a ewer and basin, or being suckled by a wet-nurse. Partly because it was feared that breastfeeding would prevent a woman from becoming pregnant with another child (another potential heir), it was common for the infants of noble families to be put out to wet-nurses for the first years of their lives. Despite being an occupational hazard, multiple births were expected of virtuous wives but they put an enormous strain on women and many sought to avoid them. Catherine de Vivonne-Savelli, the Marquise de Rambouillet, who was born in Rome

FIGURE 8.5: Masaccio, a *Desco da parto* (birth tray) showing a birthing scene, with a man holding a birth tray (far left), 1428, tempera on wood. Gemäldegalerie, Berlin. Photo: bpk/Gemäldegalerie, SMB/Jorg P. Anders.

in 1588 but married a French noble and moved to Paris, was one such woman. After the birth of her first (of seven) daughters in 1607, she prolonged her confinement, on the grounds of illness, and contrived that the gatherings of women around her bed should become independent meetings for the discussion of literary, linguistic and philosophical issues. These occasions were called *ruelles* after the confined spaces ('little alleys') between her bed and the wall. They attracted the social and intellectual elite of Paris and, by offering an alternative and informal forum for the exploration of culture and ideas – independent of the court – they eventually developed into the *salons* of the Enlightenment. In 1618, the marquise redesigned the interior of her house to create a more intimate environment for her guests – alterations that anticipated the relaxation of social mores and the privatisation of cultural life that characterised the following century.

In grand houses in England – for instance at Knole in Kent – immensely expensive 'state beds' were produced throughout the sixteenth and seventeenth centuries in case the ever-itinerant monarch should deign to visit. Such visits, which could require the host to entertain a substantial entourage for several days, were both an honour and an ordeal, as they were partly conceived to control the wealth of the nobility by sapping it. State beds were conceived as much for holding audiences as for sleeping but many of them were never used and, as a result, they became symbols of royal identity and family allegiance. In many cases they functioned like thrones. A painting of Gian Gastone de' Medici, the last Medici to be Grand Duke of Tuscany, receiving guests in bed shortly before his death in 1737 gives some impression of the use of 'beds-as-thrones', albeit in a late, debauched, example of the tradition (Fig. 8.6). They could also stand in for the presence of the absent authority. For

FIGURE 8.6: Pseudo-Marcuola, *Gian Gastone de' Medici in bed receiving the young Cosimo Riccardi*, around 1735, oil on canvas. Museo degli Argenti, Pitti Palace, Florence.

instance, in 1701, Louis XIV had his grand bedchamber at Versailles moved to the centre of the palace, where it overlooked the Marble Courtyard in the front and was aligned with the central axis of the formal gardens at the back – making his bed the focal point of all the approaches to the palace.[6] However, for much of his reign – especially following the death of his wife Maria Theresa in 1683 – the king slept in a small room next to this iconic space, only getting into the state bed in the morning, to perform the famed *grand levée* – his highly ritualised and structured process of getting up and getting dressed in the morning. As a result of this elaborate ritual, at which privileged courtiers seeking favours served like acolytes, his bed became increasingly invested with an aura of sanctity. Like an altar, it was surrounded by a low rail which kept the 'congregation' – of up to one hundred people – at an appropriate distance (Fig. 8.7). Visitors to the room honoured it with genuflections, whether the bed was occupied or not, as if it contained the holy sacrament. The king's *levée* not only paralleled the rising of the sun – after which Louis named himself the 'Sun King', as if to relocate the physical centre of the universe to his own person – but it also mimicked the elevation of the host, thereby implying his identification with its spiritual centre too. By performing his identity in this way, Louis became not only the consummate embodiment of personal selfhood but also a sanctification of it; the archetype of personal selfhood reached its most complete and exaggerated glorification in him. Incarnating an ideal of independence from

FIGURE 8.7: The King's Bedchamber, Chateau de Versailles, 1701. Photo: © Château de Versailles, Dist. RMN-Grand Palais/Christophe Fouin.

external constraints, it was subsequently to become an absolute in the western imagination.

Louis' claim to absolute rule was underpinned by the theory of the 'Divine Right of Kings', which had evolved in England under James I earlier in the seventeenth century and which formed a secular equivalent – with its equivalent liturgy – to the medieval notion of papal infallibility. Louis dramatised the absolute power of his self by ensuring that daily events at court revolved around him like clockwork and were minutely programmed down to the finest details. Nobles were required to attend court, in person; while it was difficult for them to receive favours otherwise, the interminable ceremonies also stifled the possibility of their developing power bases elsewhere. From 1682, Louis relocated the court from Paris to the Chateau of Versailles, just outside the city. In the previous two decades, the building had been transformed from a relatively modest hunting lodge into one of the grandest baroque palaces in Europe.

The decoration of the palace was supervised by the painter–designer Charles Le Brun, who was later to become director of the Royal Academy of Painting and Sculpture in Paris. Le Brun's master-stroke at Versailles was the Hall of Mirrors, the grandest hall in the palace, begun in 1678 (Fig. 8.8). This hall consists of a 240-foot long gallery, decorated along one wall with a monumental arcade of seventeen arches, each one containing twenty-one panes of mirror glass, amounting to a total surface area of approximately 700 square feet of glass. The arcade faces and reflects an equivalent arcade of windows that look out over the famous palace gardens. The ceiling of the gallery, adorned with paintings of Louis' triumphs by Le Brun, revolves

FIGURE 8.8: Galerie des Glaces (Hall of Mirrors), Chateau de Versailles, 1678–9.

around an image of the twenty-three-year-old king accepting sole rule of France in 1661, following the long regency of Cardinal Mazarin. The painting, called *The King Governs by Himself* (i.e. without interference from his court), represents a kind of 'coronation of the archetype of the individual self' (Fig. 12.12). While the room was principally conceived for court, family and ambassadorial functions, it also consummated the evolution of Louis' sense of identity towards a state of absolute self-authenticating autonomy. 'L'etat, c'est moi,' he said, subjecting the state of France to a single king, a single faith and a single law ('un roi, une foi, une loi'). Surrounding itself by an unprecedented expanse of mirrors, the personal 'self' seemed to prove its own existence to itself by seeing itself everywhere.

The Hall of Mirrors was a perfect manifestation of Louis's self-oriented and self-affirming sense of identity – partly because of the optical effect of mirrors, reflective of himself, but also because of their novelty, rarity and expense, which in themselves highlighted his unique status. Indeed, the technology of mirror-making at this period was still extremely experimental. It required a huge investment in the material and technical infrastructure of the craft which only the king could afford, and the success rate of production was low: for every mirror plate that was made successfully, several failed. The struggle to make mirrors was itself a reflection of the impulse at the time to evolve forms through which the self could become conscious of itself. The *Manufacture royale de glaces de miroirs* which produced the mirrors for the Hall of Mirrors was one such initiative. The company was set up by Louis' finance minister, Jean-Baptiste Colbert, in 1665. Beyond its deeper significance as an instrument of self-awareness, it was part of a strategic policy to boost the national economy by keeping the production of luxury products within the country. Until this time, French patrons had been paying a fortune for mirrors from Venice, which had monopolised the trade in clear glass since the thirteenth century. Colbert had to entice glass-makers from Venice, often risking their lives, to help him. For several years, the trade was surrounded by mystique and intrigue, as Venetian glass-workers were forbidden from emigrating and had therefore to be smuggled out of the city amidst huge amounts of secrecy and subterfuge; indeed they had been relocated to the island of Murano in the thirteenth century, partly to reduce the threat of fire to the city but also to prevent them from disseminating the secrets of their trade. By the end of the seventeenth century, a knowledge of the craft had taken root in French soil, and when Bernard Perrot eventually discovered how to make extremely large sheets of glass (larger than those in the Hall of Mirrors) by casting them instead of blowing them, the industry in France was able to overcome the Venetian monopoly. By 1700, production had grown and prices had dropped; the ownership of mirrors became more common and the possibility of self-awareness that they afforded was hugely increased across the entire spectrum of society.

FIGURE 8.9: Mirror, late fifteenth century, wood lined with canvas, parchment and gold leaf, 85 × 65 cm. Musée historique de Vevey, Vevey, Switzerland.

Mirrors, of course, had been known since ancient times. In antiquity and throughout the Middle Ages, they were largely made of polished metal or obsidian. The production of coloured glass had also been mastered in antiquity (mostly for vessels), as it was by the makers of the stained-glass windows in medieval churches. However, the ability to make expanses of flat, transparent glass remained elusive. While the technique for making sheets of clear glass from unrolled sections of blown-glass cylinders was described by the artisan-monk Theophilus in the twelfth century, use of the material for mirrors (and windows) did not stabilise until the fourteenth century. The earliest glazed mirrors were backed with molten lead, but because they were made from sections of blown-glass bubbles, they were convex, distorting the reflected image (Fig. 8.9). A mirror of this kind can be seen in Jan van Eyck's *Arnolfini Portrait* of 1434. It was not only the technical challenges that impeded the evolution of glass mirrors; it was also the significance of their effect, for the understanding of what was actually seen in these beguiling objects was, for many centuries, a source of concern. Although reflective surfaces were used for cosmetic reasons in ancient Greece, their auspicious or threatening potential – leading to self-knowledge or vanity respectively – was also recorded in Greek mythology. On the one hand, Perseus was saved from the petrifying effect of seeing the hideous gorgon Medusa by looking at her reflection in the shiny surface of his shield; on the other hand, Narcissus fell in love with his own reflection in a pond, neglecting the pleas of his lover Echo, who pined away until she became no more than a voice. In the Middle Ages, the technicalities of seeing were not understood at all clearly and optical mirrors were usually considered to be the devil's work (Fig. 8.10, left). The 'true' mirrors – that is, the objects that reflected the truth of Christianity – were the scriptures and compendia of Christian knowledge. To the extent, therefore, that mirrors could be used to reinforce Christianity they were accepted, albeit with some ambivalence. For instance, before inventing movable type in around 1439, Johannes Gutenberg was involved in a plan to produce 'pilgrim-mirrors', sometimes worn as hat badges, that enabled pilgrims to 'capture' and take away the healing radiance of relics that was seen to have entered them. The *miracles* that such objects performed, and the *admiration* they stimulated, gave them their name; it may even have been the sight of text reversed in mirrors that led Gutenberg to his better-known invention. But mirrors that operated outside of Christianity were seen to be dangerous, giving rise to innumerable myths in an attempt to explain and neutralise them. 'Speculation' (from *speculum*, a 'mirror' in Latin) involved the use of mirrors to reveal the otherwise invisible significance of objects. To speculate about how material phenomena are reflections of the divine realm, *as if* seen in a mirror, was subsequently considered to be a legitimate form of contemplating the world. But an object that *only* reflected the corporeal and transient dimension of a person – that is, his or her mere appearance – was considered to be diabolical and deceptive; it showed an illusion. Many such 'diabolical' objects existed. When used as instruments of self-fashioning, and set in frames depicting scenes of courtly romance – for instance, the 'Castle of Love', or lovers playing chess or out hawking together (Fig. 8.11) – mirrors were seen to promote vanity, lust, curiosity and pride. But they were also invested with magical and prophetic properties. Unnervingly, concave mirrors could make things seem to disappear. Moreover, devils could be invoked and snared in them by witches (as in

FIGURE 8.10: Hieronymus Bosch, panels showing Pride, Lust and Dejection from *The Seven Deadly Sins*, 1505–10, oil on poplar panel, 119.5 × 139.5 cm (whole panel). © Photographic Archive Museo Nacional del Prado.

other reflective surfaces, like the shiny blades of daggers or polished fingernails),[7] and they could then be used to corrupt weak and easily fascinated souls. Although the sight of one's own face could be used positively to remind one of one's own ageing and eventual death, prompting a virtuous reconsideration of one's priorities during life, a bewitched mirror could also induce a vision of the actual face of death, leading to madness. Catoptromancy – divination by mirror-reading – was widespread and was condemned by the Church.

During the Renaissance, mirrors gradually ceased to be seen as fearful instruments of damnation – at least among the cultural elite – but continued to function as symbols of insight into 'the true nature of things'. The humanists, for instance, saw man as a 'mirror of God', reflecting his dignity rather than distorting it (as he had been seen to do in the medieval world). But new attitudes towards mirrors also evolved. This was partly because people began to understand their technical properties, without projecting religious beliefs on to them. Convex mirrors, for instance, were sometimes used in *studioli* to magnify the text of books.[8] By 1400, it was possible to make flat mirror glass which reflected an 'accurate' visual image. The mirror that Brunelleschi used to check his pioneering theory of perspective in 1413 was flat; the mirrors that Alberti recommended painters use to assess their compositions must also have been flat. But the ultimate significance of mirrors at this period was not their mysterious evocation of intangible and hidden truths; nor was it their ability to magnify and clarify the visible world. On the contrary, at a time when the individual was beginning to value his own experience as a 'subject', beyond the doctrines of the Church, and when the natural world was beginning to be seen as an 'object' for its own sake, rather than as a symbol of a Christian truth, the potential of the mirror was more profound. On the one hand, it was a discrete physical object in which the experience of literally 'seeing oneself' was fully and

FIGURE 8.11: The back of a mirror-case showing an *Attack on the Castle of Love*, ivory, 1325–50, 12.9 cm. Victoria and Albert Museum, London.

fundamentally instituted; as such, it became integral to the experience of daily life. In this capacity, it was instrumental in consolidating the identification of the sense of individual self with the physical body. On the other hand, it provided a precedent and principle for all forms of experience in which the subject – the self – believed its own objectivity to be a self-evident, and therefore necessary and sacrosanct, fact. While seeing itself in the mirror, the self became both the subject *and* the object of its own experience; as a result, the mirror became an instrument and archetype of self-awareness, objectifying the principle of personal identity. Moreover, because when looking at itself in a mirror, the subject could not *not* see itself, the experience of seeing itself in a mirror initiated a process of 'automatic self-reflection' which increasingly functioned thereafter (or seemed to function) as the hidden principle of *all* constructed or conventionalised experience and discourse; for, to the extent that cultural conventions were predicated on the dynamics of personal identity, they functioned, metaphorically speaking, as its mirrors, reflecting it to itself, in keeping with its capacity for self-awareness.

Of all the cultural forms that evolved in conjunction with the sense of a personal self, it was surely the experience of seeing oneself in a mirror – especially of making eye contact with oneself – that paralleled the experience of self-awareness most closely, for it was through the experience of mirrors that the subject of experience most clearly came to be seen, as an object, by itself; it was surely this experience that most suggestively institutionalised the moment of self-reference that constitutes personal identity, initially nurturing the burgeoning impulse towards self-awareness among the precocious elite, but eventually precipitating it throughout society. To the extent that mirrors facilitated this experience, they captured the very essence of personal identity. Not only did they seem to objectify the subject; they also seemed to *necessitate* the objectivity of the subject, for it is impossible to look at oneself in a mirror without being seen by oneself. In such circumstances, the self-sense became a function of the mirror, to the point at which its existence seemed to be 'proven' by it; the mirror presented the subject to itself as a self-evident necessity, inducing it to say: 'I see myself seeing myself, therefore I must exist.'

While the *actual* experience of self-awareness is only precipitated by a mirror when the viewer is looking at himself in it, the *possibility* of self-awareness that the proliferation of mirrors created in a more general sense was disseminated throughout the culture, via the wide variety of self-reflective conventions that were generated around it. Most immediate among these was the self-portrait. In contrast to early medieval 'author portraits' which were imagined rather than observed, most of the self-portraits of the fifteenth and sixteenth centuries must – at least in part – have been made using mirrors; as we have seen, this circumstance part-explains why, in so many Renaissance self-portraits, the sitter seems to be looking at the viewer.

While mirrors facilitated the *experience* of self-awareness, they were also used to *symbolise* it and they were included in portraits as personal attributes accordingly. In allegorical pictures, mirrors referred to a variety of abstract ideas – prudence (arising from self-understanding), luxury, vanity, the sense of 'sight' and the illusoriness of worldly pleasure. In portraits, however, they were used to help shape the personas of their sitters. Most immediately, they conveyed a sense of their sitters' attention to their personal appearance, enabling people to see themselves – and thereby experience themselves – in completely new ways. A portrait by the Venetian artist Giovanni Bellini, painted in 1515, shows a noblewoman using two mirrors to see the arrangement of her hair at the back of her head – an experience that very few people before her can have ever had (Fig. 8.12). But mirrors did not only reflect physical appearances. Because physical beauty was believed by many to be an outward sign of interior virtue – and needed therefore to be maintained, on quasi-moral grounds – they also communicated a sense of their sitters' integrity. This was especially evident in the distinctive genre of portraits of women bathing, or at the *toilette*, in which mirrors feature prominently (Fig. 8.13). While these images reflect the beginnings of a newly liberal attitude towards sexuality, their nudity refers as much to purity and fertility as it does to eroticism. They show women whose self-consciousness is a sign of their sophistication, rather than their vanity, and who are permitted, but also *obliged*, to fashion themselves in keeping with their personal and family status.

Although many mirrors were produced during the Renaissance, it is important to remember that they continued to be extremely rare objects until the seventeenth century and it is quite conceivable that, until this time, many peasants – the majority of the population – will have never seen one, let alone owned one; some people may

THE PRIVATISATION OF THE SELF

FIGURE 8.12: Giovanni Bellini, *Young Woman at her Toilet*, 1515, oil on poplar, 62.9 × 78.3 cm. Kunsthistorisches Museum, Vienna.

FIGURE 8.13: School of Fontainebleau, *Woman at her Toilette*, 1550–70, oil on panel, 111.7 × 87.6 cm. Worcester Art Museum.

FIGURE 8.14: Emanuel de Witte, *Interior with a Woman at the Virginal*, 1665–70, oil on canvas, 77.5 × 104.5 cm. Museum Boijmans van Beuningen, Rotterdam.

not have even known what their own faces looked like. It is difficult for us today to imagine how their self-awareness can have developed without having this experience, and without the conventions of mind and behaviour that developed around it. Even more important is the fact that, without the 'infrastructure' of self-awareness that was precipitated by the use of mirrors, the development of a discourse around the notion of a personal self must also have been limited. In the absence of this discourse, it is unlikely that even the meagre experience of seeing oneself in a pail of water, or a puddle or a pond, will have been meaningful to them. It therefore seems likely that, for most people living during the Middle Ages and Renaissance, the so-called 'mirror stage' identified by the psychoanalyst Jacques Lacan, at which a child first notices him- or herself as an 'other' in the mirror, and therefore realises a sense of his or her own self as a distinctive entity, cannot have happened as Lacan suggested. For it was not until the middle of the seventeenth century that mirrors began to appear in bourgeois homes. Their new popularity is recorded in numerous paintings of bourgeois interiors, especially in the Netherlands where the genre flourished (Fig. 8.14). Inventories taken of Parisian homes at the beginning of the seventeenth century also indicate a rise in the ownership of small mirrors (usually one per household) from a mere fifteen per cent between 1581 and 1622, to thirty-three per cent between 1638 and 1648, and sixty-six per cent after 1650.[9] By this time, mirrors were no longer objects of intense fascination; they were beginning to be taken for granted – just as the existence of personal identity, which was implicit in them, was beginning to be taken for granted.

CHAPTER NINE

The Automation of the Self: the Material Culture of Time-keeping

Although a sense of personal self had been growing in European culture since the Middle Ages, it was only in the seventeenth century that it became conscious of itself as a self-authenticating abstraction, independent of its contexts. We have seen how self-awareness became explicit in Descartes' *cogito*, in *trompe l'oeil* pictures and in the proliferation of mirrors. Another area in which it was definitively enshrined was time-keeping. It was not until the mid-seventeenth century that the conventions surrounding the measurement of time became abstracted from the natural world. This process enabled the self-sense to disengage from the temporal cycles of nature and religion, in which it had been invested, and, for the first time, to imagine its past and future independently.

In the Middle Ages, time was typically measured in relation to natural and religious phenomena, reflecting society's dependence on natural resources (for food, warmth and light), and on the Church (for its spiritual well-being). The dating of events was largely calculated in relation to the occurrence of 'landmark' events, such as feast days, births or deaths. To the extent that it was necessary to measure them at all, individual periods of time such as the length of a sermon could be measured by burning candles, marked at regular intervals, or, from the fourteenth century, by hourglasses (Fig. 7.9). Daylight, measured by sundials on public buildings (if the sun was shining), was divided into twelve hours, regardless of the length of the day; hours, therefore, became longer in summer and shorter in winter. From the sixteenth century, stained-glass sundials enabled people to read the time from inside a building (Fig. 9.1); in the seventeenth century, some elaborate interiors were used as 'catoptric sundials' to be used in conjunction with a spot of light reflected into the room by a mirror, or bowl of water, placed on the windowsill.[1] The day was also structured according to a sacred rationale. This was principally manifest in 'books of hours', which evolved in the thirteenth century to provide lay people with daily programmes of private devotion (Fig. 3.3). The structure of these programmes was based on the divine 'offices' followed in monasteries, where monks were called to prayer at three-hour intervals – at prime, terce, sext and none ('noon'). Some books of hours aligned the various times of the day to episodes in Christ's life and offered relevant prayers accordingly, such that a day's events could be imaginatively reconceived as a continuous symbolic re-enactment of the life of Christ.

FIGURE 9.1: Stained-glass sundial, from Schloss Ambras, 1555. 38.5 cm. MAK–Österreichisches Museum für angewandte Kunst. © MAK/Georg Mayer

As a result of this dependence on nature and the Church, the structure of most people's lives revolved around the seasons, the weather and religious festivals. The entire population of a village would work in the fields in the summer, and do more domesticated tasks in the winter; they rose at dawn and went to bed at dusk. The various pastimes associated with the different times of year are recorded in images of the 'labours of the months' which frequently accompany the calendar pages of books of hours (Fig. 9.2). From the tenth or eleventh century, significant times were communicated by bells (*cloches* in French, hence 'clocks'), mounted in bell towers that were attached, or adjacent, to churches. The earliest bell towers had no faces from which to read the hour; their bells were rung when required – for instance, at curfew (*couvre-feu* – the time to cover the domestic hearth in the evening) and before church services. Many of these times were sacred rather than utilitarian. The consecration of the Eucharist was traditionally marked by bell-ringing for the sake of those unable to attend the service; at such a moment, the sick and other indisposed people could become part of an extended congregation and be receptive to the grace

THE AUTOMATION OF THE SELF 163

FIGURE 9.2: Page from a Book of Hours showing September with a man sowing seeds, from the workshop of the Rohan Master, around 1415–20, tempera, gold paint and gold leaf on parchment, 20.5 × 14.8 cm. The J. Paul Getty Museum, Los Angeles, Ms. 22, fol. 9v.

bestowed on it. Three times a day, individuals within earshot of a church were exhorted to remember the Annunciation by the ringing of the 'Angelus' bell, named after the archangel Gabriel who announced the advent of Christ to Mary. People would stop working to say an 'Ave Maria' (the archangel's 'salutation' to Mary, often inscribed on Angelus bells). In rural areas, this tradition continued well into the nineteenth century, as recorded in Jean-François Millet's celebrated *Angelus* (1857–9) in which, on hearing the church bells in the distance, two peasants stop working in a field to pray (Fig. 9.3). Indeed some people associated the Latin word for a bell (*campana*) with the fact that they were heard by people working in the fields (*campus*). Some landscape paintings of the period include churches with real watches fitted into their towers, set to strike the hours at times of prayer, thereby bringing the Angelus devotion into the home (Fig. 9.4). In such circumstances, an individual's

FIGURE 9.3: Charles-Albert Waltner, *The Angelus*, after the original painting by Jean-François Millet (1881), 1881, etching on wove paper, 44 × 50.8 cm. Metropolitan Museum of Art, New York. Gift of J. R. Watkins.

self-sense was shaped by conventions that were rooted in a medieval Christian world-view; for most people, the cultural and psychological forms through which to realise an independent sense of self simply did not exist. They had to evolve.

Among those forms were modes of perceiving and measuring time. Attempts to mechanise and regulate time-keeping, reflecting an impulse to evolve towards abstraction and autonomy, first bore fruit in the thirteenth century. This was achieved through the invention of the 'verge escapement', a device that made mechanical clockwork possible by regulating the expenditure of the driving force (created by a hanging weight) that powered the mechanism, thereby preventing it from being spent all at once. This ingenious device consisted of a toothed 'crown wheel' attached to a horizontal axle that was rotated by the driving force (Fig. 9.5). The rotation of the crown wheel was interrupted by a pivoted rod (the 'verge'), from which two projecting pallets, at an angle of approximately ninety degrees to each other, alternately engaged with the teeth of the crown wheel, one at the top and one at the bottom. As the crown

FIGURE 9.4: Landscape with a Church, nineteenth century, France, oil on canvas with a functioning clock. Private collection.

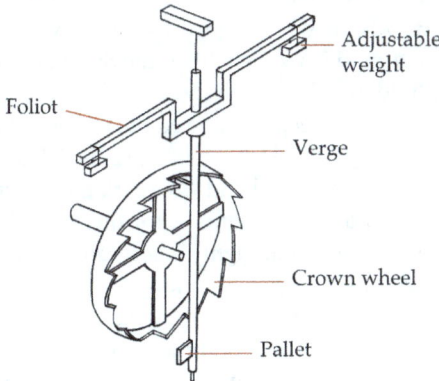

FIGURE 9.5: Diagram of a verge escapement. Image: Ye Bing.

wheel rotated (in response to the driving force), the pallet that was engaged with it at the top was forced aside ('escaping'), causing the verge to turn approximately ninety degrees, which in turn caused the second pallet to engage with the crown wheel at the bottom, thereby inhibiting its rotation momentarily until that pallet was also pushed aside, causing the first pallet to re-engage with the crown wheel at the top, and so on. The rate at which the crown wheel rotated (one tooth at a time), determining the rate of the movement of the rest of the mechanism, was determined by the speed at which the verge oscillated, backwards and forwards; this was regulated by a horizontal 'foliot' attached to the top of the verge. Weights placed at the ends of the foliot could be moved inwards or outwards (held in place by notches), thereby altering their centrifugal force and the speed of their oscillation; the further the weights were from the centre, the slower the foliot would oscillate. This flexibility may have been built into the design to allow for changes to be made to the length of hours at different seasons, indicating how clocks were not used to record *the* time – as if there was an objective correct standard; they were simply used to structure and regulate the otherwise inconceivable passing of time and above all to communicate it for practical purposes.

While such devices reflected the origins of temporal autonomy, the earliest clocks were characteristically seen in a sacred context. For instance, the Dominic mystic Henry Suso had a vision in which Wisdom appeared to him in the form of a beautiful woman with a mechanical clock symbolising the logical, regular nature of the universe and the measured temperance that the Christian should bring to his or her life of contemplation. The division of his meditative text *Horologium Sapientiae* (*The Clock of Wisdom*, of around 1335) into twenty-four chapters reflects his desire to see the twenty-four hours of a day as a programme of meditation. According to a fifteenth-century miniature of Suso's vision, Wisdom's revelation included a large weight-driven clock (with a twenty-four-hour face), an astrolabe (hanging from the clock), a bell-ringing mechanism (on which is inscribed: 'God, who precedes time and the ages, became incarnate in Mary') and, on the table, two horizontal sundials, a sprung table clock, a hanging cylindrical 'shepherd's' sundial and a quadrant (Fig. 9.6).[2] Reflecting the same sacred priority, the earliest actually surviving mechanical clock, dated to around 1386, was made for Salisbury Cathedral (Fig. 9.7). It was designed to chime every hour and has no face. One could not therefore turn to it asking 'what is the time?', on the basis of an abstract desire to know; it only 'told' the time when its bells tolled.

In the fifteenth century, time-keeping entered the home and domestic wall clocks, and table clocks with springs in place of hanging weights, became increasingly common. They had a face and a single hand – to mark the hours – but were probably valued as much for their curiosity and status as for their time-keeping capabilities as they were elaborately ornamented but highly inaccurate. They were often decorated with astrological iconography (the planets and signs of the zodiac) reflecting their primary role as instruments of natural philosophy, but allegorical images of transience and death (e.g. the Four Ages of Man) were also typical, reflecting the moralising context in which such novelties were legitimised. Spring-driven watches, often in the form of a cross or a skull, tended to be worn on chains or ribbons around the neck as ostentatious jewellery. On clocks with alarms, it was often the skeletal figure of death who rang the bells.

The drawback of the verge escapement was that the gradual diminishing of the driving force caused the mechanism to slow down. Efforts were made to compensate for this loss of power by introducing new devices: the snail-shaped 'stackfreed' which evened out the diminishing force of the mainspring in watches by applying diminishing degrees of resistance to it as it unwound; and the quasi-conical *fusée* which increased the leverage of the mechanism as its power decreased. But, despite the development of ever more complex and ingenious devices to overcome this and other problems of

FIGURE 9.6: The *Horologium Sapientum* (*Clock of Wisdom*) by Henry Suso, around 1450. Bibliothèque royale de Belgique, Brussels, ms. IV 111, f. 13v. © Bibliothèque royale de Belgique.

FIGURE 9.7: Clock mechanism, Salisbury Cathedral, around 1386. Photo: David Walsh.

interference from extraneous sources (the effects of friction, changing temperature etc.), total accuracy continued to elude clockmakers, and traditional systems of time-keeping remained in place for several centuries. It was not until the middle of the seventeenth century that clocks became sufficiently accurate and reliable to be used in isolation as functional time-keeping instruments. This was principally due to the invention of two new devices – the pendulum, adapted for use with clocks in 1656 (Fig. 9.8), and the balance-spring, invented in 1657 (Fig. 9.9) – which superseded the foliot. The foliot had been made to oscillate back and forth by the engagement of the projecting pallets with the teeth of the weight-driven crown wheel; it would have simply ground to a halt if it had not been powered in this way. The balance-spring and the pendulum, on the other hand, not only passively regulated the rotation of the crown wheel by limiting it; they were also *actively* inclined to oscillate at a regular rate. The balance-spring was attached to a balance-wheel (which oscillated like a foliot) but exerted an independent counter-force on the spinning of the wheel when wound up or unwound beyond its natural state of rest; similarly, the pendulum (mounted vertically, unlike the foliot) was independently caused to swing back and forth by gravity, acting as an independent determinant of regularity for the mechanism

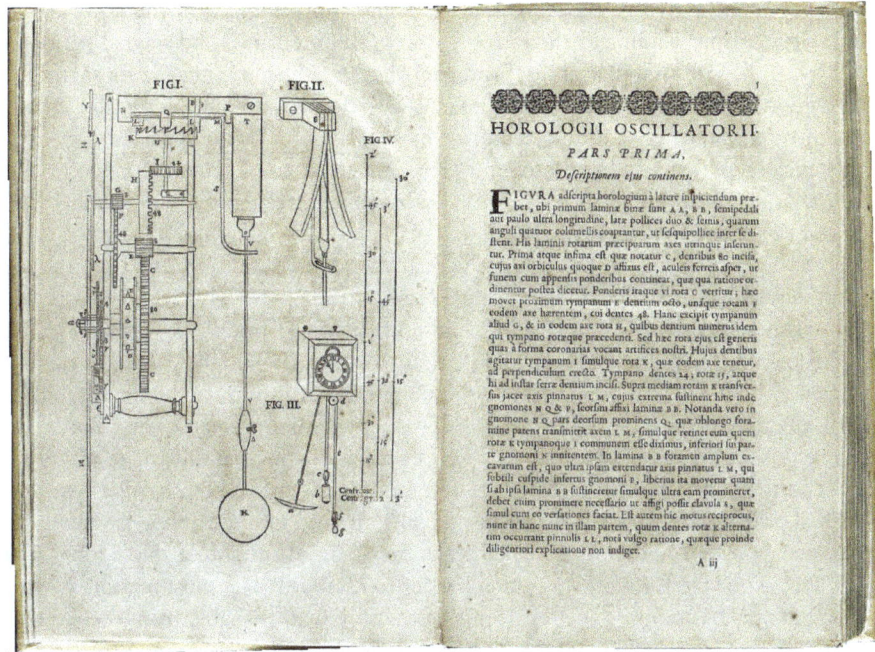

FIGURE 9.8: Diagram for a pendulum, by Christiaan Huygens, from *Horologii Oscillatorii*, Paris, 1673.

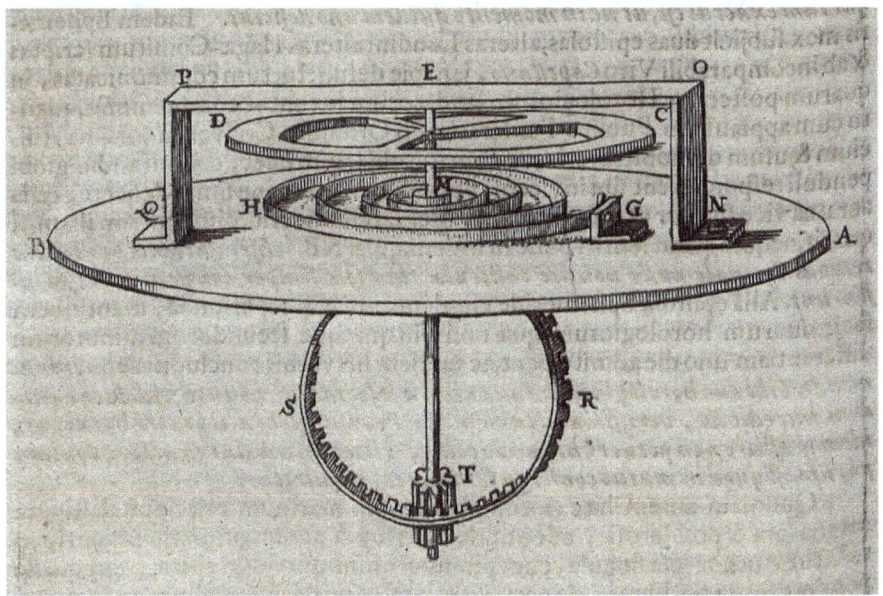

FIGURE 9.9: Design for a balance-spring, by Christiaan Huygens, from *Collegium Experimental sive Curiosum*, published by Johann Christoph Sturm, Nuremberg, 1676, p. 118.

as a whole. These two improvements had an enormous impact on the accuracy of clock mechanisms, leading to the introduction of minute hands and second hands to clocks; significantly, minutes and seconds only became meaningful as units of time at this date (as will be discussed in chapter 12). Pendulum-regulated long-case clocks subsequently became common features in respectable households, and pocket watches came to be worn by fashionable gentlemen, enabling them to personalise the way they related to time; waistcoat pockets, which appeared in the 1660s, may have evolved especially to hold them.

The quest for a means of absolutely accurate time-keeping reached its apogee with the work of the clockmaker John Harrison (1693–1776). Harrison was not only seeking accuracy; he was also seeking *autonomy*. Indeed the challenge he undertook was specifically to invent a time-keeping device that was maximally independent both of the properties of the materials used to make the device and of environmental circumstances (especially temperature and gravity). The impulse to achieve this aim was the need to find a way to measure the longitude of ships at sea. For centuries, the inability to calculate longitude had caused ships to get lost and wrecked, with much loss of life. While local time and latitude (how far north or south a ship was) could be established from the angle of the sun, a ship's longitude (how far east or west it was) was much harder to establish. The most feasible way of doing this was to compare the local time of the ship (establishable from the relative position of sun) to the time of a fixed departure location. But how could the time of this fixed location be known? The answer was a time-keeping device that was independently constant and reliable on the basis of the perfect accuracy and autonomy of its mechanism. It could be set to tell the time at the point of a ship's departure, which could then be related to the ship's local time, known from the sun, at any given moment. To design such an instrument was the challenge (for which British Parliament offered a prize of £20,000) that Harrison set out to meet in around 1730 and which he succeeded in doing, after three decades of experimentation, in 1759. During this period, he designed and made four instruments, each of which is a veritable meditation on the possibility of perfect autonomy.

Each of Harrison's innovations represented a step towards greater independence. In his early 'gridiron' pendulums, combinations of steel and zinc rods were used in such a way that the different expansion rates of the metals in different temperatures counteracted each other, ensuring that, even though the individual rods changed length, the overall length (and swing rate) of the pendulum remained the same. The use of an automatic 'maintaining device' enabled clocks to continue working while being wound up. In his chronometers, a pair of connected 'bar-balances' was used in place of a pendulum, thereby containing the oscillatory action that determined the rate at which the force of the spring was spent, *within* the mechanism, rather than subjecting it to the external force of gravity which constantly changed on a pitching ship. The avoidance of sliding parts and the use of roller bearings eliminated friction and removed the need for lubrication.

Besides saving countless lives (and enabling Britain to 'rule the waves'), Harrison's time-keeping devices represented a decisive point in the abstraction of the concept of time. Above all, the achievement of autonomy in time-keeping occurred in tandem with the evolution of the abstracted sense of self. Both phenomena were evolving towards a state of internal coherence and autonomy that appeared to release them from dependence on external conditions; as the units of temporal measurement – hours and minutes – became more absolute and independent of worldly circumstances, so the very notion of time became abstract, subject only to its own laws. As such, it became the perfect 'environment' for the independent self, enabling the self to fantasise its own extension – in time – without having to subscribe to any associated systems of value that might qualify its individuality or render its freedom conditional. Having said this, while the notions of abstract 'time' and 'self' appear to have evolved simultaneously as two separate phenomena, there is a case for asserting that they actually evolved as co-terminous functions of each other. Just as the abstract self 'needed' the parameters of abstract time in order to sustain itself independently of circumstances, so the notion of abstract time inevitably generated a sense of self whose identity was rooted abstractly in an awareness of itself rather than in the wayward and inconsistent rhythms of the natural world. At the end of the eighteenth century, the notion of abstract time as a logically necessary solipsism was explicitly codified by Immanuel Kant (1724–1804), who maintained that the self-sense does not merely exist *in time* or *in relation to time*, but that it generates the impression, or experience, of time as an *a priori* function of its own existence – to the extent that it exists *as* the experience of time; time and self are one and the same, merely seen in terms of objectivity and subjectivity respectively. From this perspective, linear time is merely the medium in which consciousness reflects on itself as a 'self with possibilities'; conversely, the self-sense is the state of consciousness in which the experience of linear time, and the apparent possibility of times 'other than now', seem to arise.

Most significantly, the concept of time accommodates the self's vision of its *possibilities*. Without the impression of time, nothing is *possible*; everything is only actual. Indeed, to the extent that experience only occurs 'now' and cannot be otherwise without introducing the notion of the future and the past, it appears to be inevitable and fundamentally *necessary*; in the moment, nothing can change it. The self-sense cannot exist under such circumstances, for its vision of itself as a centre of subjective freedom, and as the seat of identity, depends on the perception that it has possibilities; and possibilities only exist in time. Thus, to avoid the antithetical experience of timeless necessity (sometimes artificially conceptualised as 'predestination'), the emergent self spontaneously generated the impression of abstract time as the *illusory medium through which it experiences the possibility of its own freedom*. It enshrined the notion of abstract time in ever more autonomous and infinitely predictable time-keeping devices in order to find its own autonomy and freedom infinitely reflected in them – a goal that was first achieved in the middle of the seventeenth century.

CHAPTER TEN

The Sensibilities of the Self: Courtesy, Conversation, Letter-writing and Novel-reading

While mirrors invited individuals to reflect on themselves as *selves* – from the 'inside' – they also enabled them to see themselves as *others* – from the 'outside' – as other people saw them. Thus, although the self was seen to be self-evident and self-authenticating on account of its self-consciousness, it was also seen to be defined by its *relationships*, and by the conventions that structured those relationships. And because relationships involved other selves – in their own diverse states of formation – these conventions embodied degrees of mutual, social sensibility. This sensibility was originally enshrined in codes of behaviour and manners but it was eventually appropriated by the self to the extent that it was fully interiorised and seen to be one of its innate functions.

The evolution of a language of manners can be traced back to the monastic rules conceived in the early Middle Ages to regulate the lives of monks. By far the most influential of these was the *Rule* of St Benedict, written at the beginning of the sixth century and used in the Latin Church for the next millennium. Besides offering instruction relating to interior discipline and prayer, the earliest monastic rules offered guidelines for the organisation of monastic communities, including simple principles to be followed in connection with purely practical matters such as eating, talking, sleeping and receiving guests, all of which were strictly disciplined. While eating, for instance, monks were admonished not to look around at each other, not to stretch beyond the food that was in front of them towards something more appealing, not to spit indiscreetly, and not to start eating before their superior started. But these precepts were scarcely enough to support a culture of social courtesy. On the contrary, their abiding characteristic is the way they were oriented towards the attainment of salvation. They were designed to minimise distraction from the main purpose of monastic life, which was prayer. Each practice was to be engaged as an embodiment of virtue and, as such, was charged with ethical significance. Nothing was to be practised for the sake of appearances or politeness, which reflected the vices of pride and flattery. Clothing was to be practical and impersonal, affording no opportunity to impress or deceive viewers. Although monks were encouraged to show respect for each other, all scope for purely social interaction was undermined. The only form of relationship that was actively approved was with a superior, requiring unquestioning humility and obedience. Similarly, the *Rule* warned monks not to 'defend each other' out of a sense of social loyalty, ensuring that absolute openness and honesty took precedence over 'protectionism', even for family members. The implication here was that there was to be no 'hidden self', with its own agenda, concealed behind an opaque show of behaviour. On the contrary, the physical form of the monks' lifestyle was designed to be transparent to their selflessness. To all intents and purposes, the *Rule* made no provision for courtesy or manners – codes of behaviour that were independently invested with social value and meaning.

In the twelfth century this highly unsocial approach to communal living was supplemented by a range of new developments that reflected the introduction of a more socially self-conscious dimension to monastic life. These developments suggest that the secular conventions that grew up around courtesy and manners in the later Middle Ages may have – at least in part – originated in monasteries. Indeed, medieval 'customaries' (compilations of customs produced in each monastery or convent to record its own particular practices) include many precepts that became the staple contents of secular courtesy manuals, especially regarding eating: wipe one's hands on a napkin, not on one's clothes or the tablecloth; do not put one's elbows on the table; do not throw food or eat noisily etc.. Some monastic customaries describe celebratory occasions that resemble their equivalents in secular courts. The 'order of precedence' at a festive meal, for instance, was structured hierarchically around the abbot or abbess sitting at the high table (or an image of the Virgin Mary) in exactly the same way that the seating plan for a feast in a domestic hall revolved around the lord of the manor.[1] Indeed, even Christ was seen to conform to the highest standards of behaviour, reflecting the extent to which medieval courtesy was seen to be a direct manifestation of virtue. Responding to the precept that bread should be cut with a knife and not broken, one fourteenth-century writer helpfully explained that when Christ 'broke the bread' during the supper at Emmaus, it was 'as if he cut it with the sharpest blade' (Fig. 10.1).[2]

Moreover, from the twelfth century onwards, a number of influential churchmen wrote texts, elaborating on the instructions given by St Benedict, that prescribed appropriate behaviour for monks in a variety of social situations. Hugh of St Victor, for instance, is credited with a text, *De Institutione Novitiorum* (*On the Formation of Novices*), that explains how good manners are an essential part of the discipline that leads to virtue and beatitude.[3] Robert Grosseteste (d.1253), best known as a philosopher and theologian (referenced in chapter 2), also wrote a poem on courtly behaviour and a list of *Statutes for the Household*.[4] The poem was partly influenced by the Old Testament books of *Proverbs* and *Ecclesiasticus*, which include precepts relating to a range of practical issues such as table manners but which also lent biblical dignity to the subject of decorum.[5] Despite his humble birth, Grosseteste was well known for his refined manners, which he claimed to have learned from the scriptures.[6] Indeed, his reputation was such that nobles lodged their sons in his house, to have them learn courtesy as a part of their education. It was not unusual at this time for the children of nobles to be brought up in the households of bishops and other nobles of high office; that some of them were also farmed out to be educated in monasteries and

FIGURE 10.1: Follower of Stefan Lochner, *Supper at Emmaus*, 1450–60, canvas on oak, Cologne. Bavarian State Painting Collections, Alte Pinakothek, Munich, GM 871, on loan to the Germanisches Nationalmuseum, Nuremberg.

convents also reflects the extent to which monastic institutions were seen as sources of courtesy and good conduct. Monastic life had always been seen as a suitable destiny for a noble child; but, as the Benedictine *Rule* indicates, the infant sons of noblemen who were offered to monasteries in the sixth century were expected to live cloistered lives as monks for the rest of their days, sacrificing social contact with their families.

By the twelfth century, the good conduct promoted in monastic environments was also being appreciated as a secular virtue and could be taken back into the outside world. Indeed, a noble boy who spent his youth in a monastery at this period was likely to live apart from the monks, in the abbot's household – which could be as worldly as that of a bishop – and to leave the monastery, suitably educated in manners, when he reached maturity.[7] Clergymen did not always welcome the responsibilities that came with this role. Thomas Becket, Archbishop of Canterbury, housed a number of noble youths in his household but could only pretend to enjoy their feasts, 'simulating civility'.[8]

Although the notion of courtesy underwent a kind of pre-history in the form of 'instructions for novices' throughout the early Middle Ages, it was not until the twelfth century that it crystallised in the western imagination as an independent concept. First of all, it acquired its name, reflecting the context in which it evolved; 'courtesy' was adapted from the French *corteis* (meaning 'courtly'), which ultimately derived from the Latin *curialis* (from *curia*), meaning a great household with a court. And secondly, it became the subject of secular manuals which instructed readers in refined conduct with increasing independence from Christian morality. Early 'courtesy books' tended to focus on the proper behaviour of lords, knights and servants (who might include the sons of nobles) in the context of the courtly household, revolving around ceremonial functions such as welcoming guests, feasting and washing. The immediate household of a lord would consist of a rigid hierarchy of nobles, each with his own privileged role, seeking preferment on the basis of loyal service. Originally, even such personal tasks as holding the lord's drinking cup or holding the cloth or straw with which to dry his hands (or even wipe his backside after defecating) were considered honourable duties to be performed, amidst much ritual, by favourites.

In return for their service, the lord's vassals would receive provision, protection and education. This bond of mutual obligation constituted the medieval system of feudalism. In times of war, male members of the household were required to fight for their lord. In anticipation of such service, their education included training in the arts of war, often inculcated in them through the 'sport' of the tournament – mock battles. When they came of age, they would be initiated ceremonially into the noble order of chivalry or knighthood and granted the gift of arms – horse, helmet, lance, sword, shield and crest – the possession of which confirmed their noble status; indeed, the concept of 'investiture' derives from the honorific conferment of significant 'vestments' or clothing (Fig. 10.2). Moreover, their knowledge of horsemanship – from which the notion of chivalry arises (from *cheval*, the French word for horse) – became one of the determining characteristics of the role. To ensure the loyalty of their knights, lords also rewarded them with gifts of money or land. The granting of land was especially important as it could be passed down through the family, thereby consolidating the tradition that nobility could be – and indeed, according to some commentators, could *only* be – inherited. The notion that the right to inherit nobility was associated with knighthood was continued, long after the age of chivalry, in heraldic crests and coats of arms. These had originally been used in the twelfth century to decorate the shields of participants in tournaments (who were otherwise fully covered by armour), enabling them to identify each other, and to help spectators identify them (Fig. 10.3). But they soon came to adorn possessions in general and to advertise family lineage, for instance on tapestries and in stained-glass windows (Fig. 8.2). Indeed, they continued to be a primary indicator of identity until the end of the seventeenth century, when more personalised forms of self-representation became established.

The status of a knight depended on his prowess, strength, valour, perseverance, loyalty and, crucially, his ancestry. Having said this, despite the magnanimous ideal of peace-keeping, knights could make huge profits from war and they were not necessarily motivated to prevent it. From the point of view of the Church, therefore, they were a mixed blessing, as much inclined to wreak havoc on the land as to maintain peace. At the end of the eleventh century, the reputation of knighthood was somewhat redeemed and raised to a new level of dignity by the Crusades, which

FIGURE 10.2: Thanor knighting Apollo, from the prose *Roman de Tristan*, MS.648, f.13v., French, 1440–60. Musée Condé, Chantilly. Photo: © RMN-Grand Palais (domaine de Chantilly)/René-Gabriel Ojéda.

combined the appetite for military combat with a Christian impulse – to go on pilgrimage and regain the holy city of Jerusalem, captured by Muslims in the eighth century. In this context, the knight became a metaphor for Christian courage and vigilance, perfected in the legend of the Holy Grail, and, as a result, the perception of knighthood began to change. With the establishment of the military orders (the Templars and Hospitallers), founded in the twelfth and thirteenth centuries to defend and care for pilgrims on their way to Jerusalem, the two impulses – military and moral – were fused into a single role in which the impulse to fight was seen to be positively virtuous. The abundance of effigies of knights on church tombs, through which individuals presented themselves in the form that they considered to be most worthy of remembrance and salvation, reflects the extent to which the image of knighthood was sacralised at this period (Fig. 10.4).

The rehabilitation of military prowess by association with the Crusades elevated it beyond the utilitarian function of conquest and defence to a level at which it could function symbolically and morally. This shift was crucial because it provided the

FIGURE 10.3: *The Tournament of Inglevert* from The Harley Froissart, Bruges, 1470–2, Harley MS.4379, f.43. British Library, London.

background against which the language of knighthood could be translated, via the notion of chivalry, into the discourse of courtly love, giving rise to a complex of relational conventions that would eventually become the basis of modern etiquette. Above all, the possibilities of chivalry added a new and powerful motive for engaging in the physical realities of warfare to the two already established (conquest and salvation): to impress and seduce women. In tournaments, which were watched by women, knights had an opportunity to use their courage (from *coeur*, French for 'heart') to make a direct impression on their spectators (Fig. 10.3). In one twelfth-century account (fictional but nonetheless significant), the ladies of the court pledged themselves in advance to marry those who showed the greatest courage.[9] One fourteenth-century writer of a number of treatises on chivalry, Geoffrey de Charney, maintained that it was good for a knight to be in love while at war because he would be inspired to greater feats of heroism in order to do honour to his lady.[10]

Women were not only to be impressed by conquest; they were also the objects of conquest, to be invaded by men using all the weaponry at their disposal. Images of

FIGURE 10.4: Effigy of Gilbert Marshal, 4th Earl of Pembroke, died 1241. Temple Church, London.

ladies defending the 'Castle of Love' and perhaps their own chastity – the citadel of their virtue – by emptying baskets of roses from the parapets on to the heads of their male assailants were a common form of decoration for medieval mirror backs and other luxury objects, especially those associated with vanity and romance (Fig. 8.11). A fifteenth-century parade shield makes the connection between military victory and romance explicit by combining an object that was probably made as a prize for winning a tournament or joust with an image of an armed knight on his knees before his prized lady (Fig. 10.5). In this context, it was not enough for a knight to be courageous, bold and strong; to win this additional prize, he also had to be courteous, modest and genteel – a 'gentleman'. It is no accident therefore that, in this and other such images, the knight resembles the archangel Gabriel at the Annunciation, for Gabriel was revered as a model of courtesy. Indeed, according to one fifteenth-century source of advice, *The Lytylle Childrenes Lytil Boke*, it was through archangel Gabriel's gracious sensitivity to the Virgin Mary at the moment of the Annunciation that the very possibility of courtesy was given by God to humanity.[11] From the fourteenth century onwards, when the new naturalism in painting began to allow realistic feelings

FIGURE 10.5: A parade shield with a knight in Italian armour kneeling before a lady, around 1470, Flanders or France, 82.7 cm. British Museum, London. © The Trustees of the British Museum.

to be naturalistically represented, Gabriel's courteous understanding of the fact that the Virgin was 'troubled at his saying, and cast in her mind what manner of salutation this should be'[12] was delicately conveyed in numerous images of the scene (Figs 3.3, 7.5, 8.2, 8.4).

Although courteous behaviour was cultivated in the contexts of monasticism, household service and chivalry, it was in 'courtesy books', written from the late twelfth century onwards, that the ideal of courtesy found its fullest and most direct expression. Where monastic life prioritised obedience and humility, a life of service to a lord prioritised loyalty, and a life of chivalry prioritised courage and honour, the 'courtesy books' promoted a new virtue: social self-awareness or sociability. The appreciation of sociability was new. Monastic precepts had shown no interest in sociability as such; they were focused, without distraction, on spiritual practice. In the courtly household, relational obligations had tended to revolve around the lord himself; behaviour *between* courtiers was of secondary importance. And while knights might have shared a sense of camaraderie, they were not noted for their politeness to each other. Courtesy books, by contrast, begin to place importance on the impression that an individual makes on the company around him, partly to avoid conflict and offence, and partly to please. The earliest known courtesy book, the *Urbanus Magnus* or *Liber Urbani* ('Book of the Civilised Man') is thought to have been composed in the late twelfth century by Daniel of Beccles, a courtier (possibly a knight) in the household of Henry II. It was written in Latin verse and is three thousand lines long. The often random jumbling-up of situations that it addresses suggests that it may have been compiled from a variety of sources; this would have been entirely in keeping with the overall predilection that medieval writers felt for the authority of precedents. The earliest known manuscript of the poem was produced for an Augustinian monastery, indicating that it may have been used for the instruction of novices, but there is nothing religious about the text, which is distinctly unmonastic in character, and the fact that it spawned numerous copies and adaptations, none of which claim to serve a religious purpose, suggests that it is a new and distinctive type of work, probably written for the benefit of young boys.

Despite its inconsistent structure, the poem is preoccupied by a number of principal themes. The first of these, reflecting the courtly ambience in which it appears to have been written, concerns respect for social hierarchy. The reader was instructed to demonstrate his awareness of his lord's authority by means of a series of highly visible actions and gestures, especially at meals (Fig. 7.16). These included serving his lord first, not turning his back towards his lord at table, not sitting in front of him with crossed legs, kneeling and bowing in front of him whenever appropriate, and bathing him. A second preoccupation concerned 'things entering or leaving the body'. With the exception of the lord, urinating should not take place in the hall. Defecating should take place outdoors in a remote place; it was shameful to attack an enemy who was in this position. Farting indoors should also be avoided; and if one had to belch one should take care to look up at the ceiling (as if to absent oneself) while doing so. If one had to blow one's nose, one should not examine the contents in public.[13] Spitting was slightly more acceptable but should not be done over the table – it should be done away from the table or into a cloth.

Of the numerous precepts concerning eating, many recommended restraint or personal dignity: do not put your elbows on the table, do not put excessively large morsels of food into your mouth, do not talk with your mouth full, do not play with your knife or spoon. But others were more immediately sociable: carve meat for your neighbour, do not take a tasty morsel from under his nose; and, bearing in mind that, throughout the Middle Ages, diners shared food from a common plate (still reflecting the relative absence of the notion of personal space), some of them concerned hygiene: for instance, 'do not dip bread that you have already touched with your tooth back into the soup' and 'do not share your spoon with a neighbour'. This latter instruction could clearly be problematic as cutlery was not provided for each individual at a meal until the beginning of the seventeenth century. Indeed, it was customary for affluent individuals to bring their own cutlery, often taking the opportunity to show off their wealth and taste in highly personalised designs. Further down the social scale, it was not uncommon for men to wear knives as part of their personal attire, using them to cut food when necessary. Diners were instructed not to pick their teeth with their cutlery, a recommendation that was not heeded – as we have seen – by one of the apostles in Veronese's *Feast in the House of Levi* (behind the second column from the left). Indeed the exquisitely bejewelled pendant toothpicks that survive from at least as early as the sixteenth century suggest that it was, in some circumstances, acceptable to pick one's teeth in public; some were even worn as luxuriously set pendants.[14] Forks for eating were rare; they were principally used to hold meat down while cutting it. It was not unusual for individuals to eat with their fingers, preferably wiping them on napkins or, if they were well-to-do, washing them in ewers and basins, brought to them by servants (as frequently shown in images of Pontius Pilate washing his hands of Christ). In the seventeenth century, forks became more common, reducing the need for napkins, though when they first came to England, from Italy, they met with some resistance. One Englishman associated them with pitchforks, disdainfully commenting: 'We need no little forks to make hay with our mouths!'[15]

Courtesy books proliferated throughout the Middle Ages and examples from all over Europe survive from the thirteenth century onwards – written, significantly, in indigenous languages as well as in Latin. There is a huge amount of variety between these texts – of form, length and emphasis – but, broadly speaking, they reflect the same fundamental orientation, revolving around the lord of the manor and underpinned by a principle of loyalty from which both lords and servants benefited. Well into the fifteenth century, many such texts were produced, recycling precepts that had been used in earlier sources. In sixteenth-century Italy, however, when humanist values began to establish themselves among the educated elite, significant changes began to take place. For instance, the medieval inclination towards self-abasement in front of God (and other external authorities) was challenged by a new belief in the dignity and autonomy of the individual. This change was inevitably accompanied by a new awareness that individuals could have of their own status, not only within the context of court hierarchy, but also beyond that context, in relation to other individuals. This development corresponds to a shift of focus, among writers on manners, away from the tightly structured conventions of feasting and entertaining in the great hall, towards a more diffused theatre of social relationships in a multitude of different situations that could include acquaintances and even strangers.

Significantly, this shift was accompanied by the gradual replacement of the word 'courtesy' by 'civility'. While 'courtesy' referred to the courtly context in which manners were originally cultivated, 'civility' was derived from the Latin word *civis*, meaning a citizen or inhabitant of a city. The association of refined conduct with urban culture developed in early medieval Italy, where thriving trade had favoured the growth of rich city states, ruled by semi-elected councils in place of feudal lords. Bearing in mind that, in the most insular medieval towns and villages, life revolved around a sense of community, and encounters with strangers were relatively rare, it is easy to see how the rapid growth of urban populations could have generated a need for new principles of social cohesion that were not based on personal familiarity. Nor, indeed, could they be unduly based on religious values, as personal experience began to challenge the power of belief, and the association of behaviour with status and personal space began to eclipse its traditional association with morality. In the long term, the codification of manners provided a common language of interaction that made the harmonious cohabitation of large numbers of strangers in a relatively confined space possible. Refined manners had been associated with cities in the classical world, as reflected in the ancient use of the word 'urbanus' (from the Latin *urbs*, a city) to mean sophisticated behaviour and wit. By the ninth and tenth centuries, by which time the word 'urbanus' had lost its association with city culture (just as the English word 'urbane' has), it was still being used to describe the manners of the prince-bishops at the court of Charlemagne and his successors,[16] and it continued to be used as a general descriptor of courtesy throughout the Middle Ages (for instance, in the *Liber Urbani*).

The shift from 'courtesy' to 'civility' was also facilitated by the increased use of gunpowder in the fifteenth century. Because gunpowder, which was first mentioned in Europe in the thirteenth century, rendered man-to-man combat redundant, it also undermined the context in which the image of the courtly knight fighting for the sake of his lady's love derived its cultural value. In his *Orlando Furioso* (1516), a late example of the genre of chivalrous literature, the poet Ludovico Ariosto lamented:

> How did this infamous and ugly invention [firearms] ever find a place in human hearts? Because of it the glory of war is destroyed and the profession of arms is without honour . . . valour and virtue are so debased that evil often seems better than good, and boldness and daring can no longer be put to the test in the field.[17]

In fact, a general demilitarisation of courtly style began to occur at this time. In domestic architecture, the defensiveness of crenellations and arrow-slits was replaced by the graciousness of classical proportions and ornament. Diplomacy became an important and desirable quality in a courtier. Instead of resorting to violence, scores could increasingly be settled by means of written agreements, recorded in official documents that were sometimes folded into two parts or 'double-plied' (hence 'diplo-macy'). In the seventeenth century, duelling was outlawed.

The notion of 'civility' was spread by the publication of a short treatise on manners, *De Civilitate Morum Puerilium* ('On Civility in Boys'), written by Erasmus in 1530 and translated into most European languages within ten years of its publication. In many ways, the treatise, which was written for the son of a noble but was probably always intended for wider circulation, is traditional. It refers to many of the hotspots of possible transgression that had filled the medieval texts, especially behaviour at table, treating them in a typically direct and down-to-earth manner: avoid putting one's elbows on the table, picking at half-eaten bones, dipping bread that one has bitten into the soup, licking one's plate, gobbling and gulping. It also openly addresses belching, farting, spitting, crossing one's legs and talking too much. But it differs from its sources in significant ways. Some of these are formal. For instance, unlike many of its precedents, the book is structured systematically; its contents are divided into individual body parts (eyes, nose, face, mouth, hair, private parts), clothing, behaviour in church, table manners, playing games, meeting people and the bedroom. Also, its style is elegant and clear, reflecting Erasmus's humanist background. These points are important because they contribute towards the re-contextualisation of civility within the sphere of humanism and a liberal education, at the expense of chivalrous militarism. Indeed, although Erasmus does not elaborate on this theme in the main body of the text, in the introduction he states that the duty of shaping the young includes ensuring that they develop a thorough knowledge of the liberal arts. Although knowledge per se is not a form of behaviour, he does contrast it with the traditional chivalrous signs of nobility which focus on the display of family lineage: 'Let other people emblazon their shields with lions, eagles, bulls and leopards; the emblems of the intellect, acquired by an education in the liberal arts, bear a truer nobility.'

For all its elegance, *De Civilitate Morum Puerilium* was written in a didactic style for boys and, as such, is a technical manual, rooted in the tradition of 'instructions for novices'. In this respect, it differs from a new body of writing about manners, written for adults in a more discursive manner, that was also becoming popular at this time. These new works emanated from Italy – increasingly seen as the pinnacle of cultural sophistication – and they were also translated into most European languages, whereupon they became the universal benchmark for refined behaviour for the next two centuries; indeed, one English treatise on manners, Simon Robson's *The Courte of Civill Courtesie* of 1578, was falsely presented as the translation of an Italian work to ensure that it received the respect the author thought it deserved.

The most influential Italian text on courtesy was Baldassare Castiglione's *Il libro del cortegiano* or *The Book of the Courtier*, begun in 1508 but not published until 1528. The book sets out to define the image and behaviour of the perfect courtier. Despite its originality, it too was indebted to the past. For instance, its concept of the courtier includes skill at arms and physical prowess in sports, though it does not focus on them. Similarly, it favours noble birth, while also acknowledging that there have, in the past, been many distinguished men born into ordinary families and many ordinary men born into distinguished ones. Several of the preconceptions about the subservience of women that it raises and challenges were clearly derived from traditional attitudes towards courtesy, and it makes several references to examples of men whose valour in battle was inspired by their wish to impress their lovers.[18] However, *The Courtier* also marked an important turning point. Above all, whereas a majority of medieval texts on manners had presented a relatively disjointed sequence of behavioural precepts, it presented an integrated vision of an ideal type of man with a comprehensive exposition of the way in which his various qualities should manifest in social life. As Castiglione himself stated: 'In these books we shall not follow any strict order or list a series of precepts, as is the normal practice in teaching.'[19] The didactic and insistent tone of many medieval courtesy books – 'if such and such happens, you should do this', 'make sure you do that . . .' – implicitly casts the reader in the role of a passive recipient, entrenched in vulgar habits and clearly in need of instruction; they make no allowance for discrimination on the reader's part. The fact that such texts were sometimes written in rhyming verse to facilitate memorisation reinforces the impression that they were meant to be learned and adopted by their audience without questioning. *The Courtier*, by contrast, is presented in a completely different style and it makes completely different presumptions about its reader. For instance, Castiglione adopted the conceit of presenting his ideas in the form of four dramatised conversations, held between an eminent group of courtiers and ladies on four consecutive evenings at the court of Urbino, where Castiglione had himself been a courtier from 1504 to 1516. Besides linking itself with Plato's *Republic* and Cicero's *On the Orator*, which also take this form, the conceit of a staged conversation enabled Castiglione both to include ideas that he did not condone himself and to be as inconclusive as he wanted to be about any given idea – for instance, by staging an interruption. The outcome of this discursive open-ended format was that enquiry was extended to the reader, who was thus required to make his own assessment of the ideas presented and to form his own conclusions, as if he was himself engaging in the conversations; indeed, embedded in the text is the implication that the reader is himself an accomplished or aspiring courtier. Significantly, such conversations were themselves a form of courtly practice – preferably peppered with classical references, as in this case. After a festive dinner in a grand household, it was not uncommon for the host or hostess to propose a subject for a witty and educated discussion in which the guests would be invited – or challenged – to demonstrate their erudition, literary skills, humour and repartee as if they were dancing or fencing. The writer and poet Pietro Bembo, who travelled with his collection of curiosities, had his dining companions pick antique coins from a bag and discourse upon them spontaneously. In some cases, spice was added to these games by requiring participants to speak in rhyming couplets or some other poetic form.

This subtle shift in the presumed identity of the reader of *The Courtier* was also reflected in the novelty of its content. Of course, the most definitive characteristic of the ideal courtier was his role at court and the relationship he developed with his prince, around whom the court revolved. In direct descent from the medieval notion that a knight should be entirely at the beck and call of his lord, Castiglione strongly represents the view that a courtier should 'devote all his thoughts and strength to loving and almost adoring the prince he serves above all else, devoting all his ambitions, actions and behaviour to pleasing him'.[20] Indeed, the pleasure of the prince, and the honour to be gained from ensuring that it is always achieved, is the courtier's key aim, at the expense of his own preferences. He should obey his prince

> even if it is against his nature, in such a way that whenever his prince sees him he believes that his courtier will have something agreeable to say. And this will be the case if he has the discretion to discern what pleases his prince, and the wit and judgement to know how to act accordingly, and the considered resolve to make himself like what he may instinctively dislike.[21]

Of course, advocating such devotion presupposes that the prince in question is himself a model of beneficence. *The Courtier* also gives several examples of situations in which individuals have conflicting agendas, and discusses the numerous ways in which personal boundaries should be negotiated in such cases. On one occasion it addresses a situation in which the courtier becomes 'convinced that by departing more or less from the detailed instructions [of his prince] he can achieve a better or more profitable result for the master who gave him the orders'.[22] Should the courtier give precedence to his own judgement, even with the prince's interests in mind, or should he surrender to his prince's will as a matter of principle? And what should he do in the case of an evil prince who orders him to commit a 'treacherous deed'? In this instance, Castiglione concedes that the courtier is not obliged to perform the deed and even that he is obliged *not* to do it; however, he advances this view not on account of the inherent immorality of the act but 'for the courtier's own sake' and 'to avoid ministering to his prince's shame'.[23] In the extreme, but all too common, case of a 'prince whose nature is so degraded that he is completely sapped by evil, like consumptives by their disease', the courtier should 'withdraw his allegiance in order to escape blame for the misdeeds of his master and not experience the anguish of all good men who serve the wicked'.[24] But, in more natural cases, in which the prince is benign, his aim should be to exemplify the virtues of honour, propriety and magnanimity that will orientate his prince toward his own virtuous actions, like 'a whetstone that is used to sharpen iron, though it cuts nothing itself'.[25]

Despite prioritising the prince at every opportunity, the book is also pervaded by a sense of the courtier's concern for his own personal honour and for the impression he makes on the people around him. This is a crucial moment, for it identifies the point at which the difference between an inner, invisible self and an outer, visible self is institutionalised in cultural conventions. Thus, although the ideal courtier is required to embody virtue for its own sake, it is also clear that his honour is determined by the judgements of others. Thus besides knowing 'how to avail himself of all the virtues', he should 'sometimes set one [virtue] in contrast or opposition to another in order to draw more attention to it'.[26] He should be 'able to change his style and method from day to day, according to the nature of those with whom he wants to converse'.[27] Indeed he is advised to construct his persona with regard to its effect on other people, as if he was a work of art:

> This is what a good painter does when by the use of shadow he distinguishes clearly the lights on his reliefs, and similarly by the use of lights deepens the shadows of plane surfaces and brings different colours together in such a way that each one is brought out more sharply through the contrast; and the placing of figures in opposition to each other assists the painter in his purpose. In the same way, gentleness is most impressive in a man who is a capable and courageous warrior; and just as his boldness is magnified by his modesty, so his modesty is enhanced and more apparent on account of his boldness.[28]

With the same concern for his image, a courtier who finds himself 'in a skirmish or pitched battle, or something of that nature' should 'arrange ... to accomplish the bold and notable exploits he has to perform ... in view of all the noblest and most eminent men of the army, and, above all, in the presence, or if possible under the very eyes, of the prince he is serving'.[29] At jousts or similar spectacles, he should make sure 'that he is as elegant and attractive in the exercise of arms as he is competent, and that he feeds the eyes of those that are looking on with everything that can give him added grace ... attracting the eyes of the onlookers in his direction as surely as the loadstone attracts iron'.[30] Popular occasions at which he might lose such a sporting contest to a peasant – a shocking and undignified outcome – should be avoided, 'at least when there are many onlookers'. His attitude to dress epitomises the strategic way in which he constructs himself in the eyes of others, for the sake of propriety and honour: in this context, he should decide 'what sort of man he wants to seem, and then dress accordingly, so that his clothes help him to be taken as such'.[31]

The quality that best captures the courtier's aspiration to perfect his performance of behavioural conventions, sometimes at the expense of his actual feelings, was *sprezzatura*, which 'conceals all artistry and makes whatever one says or does seem uncontrived and effortless ... So we can truthfully say that true art is what does not seem to be art; the most important thing is to conceal it, because if it is revealed this discredits a man completely and ruins his reputation'.[32] The aim of *sprezzatura* was to give the impression that virtuosity and grace came naturally to the courtier, unaided by the artifice of practice. The implication here was that credit for these qualities should truly go to him – in acknowledgement of his courtly identity – and should not be diluted by explanations that might suggest alternative origins for them (such as good parenting or a good teacher).[33] Even though would-be courtiers were warned against 'affectation', the mastery of *sprezzatura* inevitably involved a certain amount of dissembling, false modesty and hypocrisy. This paradox highlights the extent to which the search for perfect civility among elite citizens was becoming detached from its roots in obedience and conformity, in favour of a language of behaviour that reflected more directly on the moral and social sensibility of the individual. Significantly Castiglione's courtiers do not even discuss the subject of religion, let alone suggest whether their ideal courtier should be a Christian, as if belief in a higher principle would somehow undermine the basis of his self-sufficiency and self-esteem.

In the arts, effortless *sprezzatura* was complimented by the seemingly contradictory cult of *difficultà*, which inspired artists and craftsmen to introduce technical challenges into their work in order to highlight their 'heroic' virtuosity in overcoming them. This preoccupation with the means of producing art, and the impulse to elaborate or exaggerate it for the sake of its effect, sometimes at the expense of a work's function or meaning, was first observed by Giorgio Vasari, whose use of the word '*maniera*' – to identify a style of art that was sophisticated, or mannered, for its own sake – gave rise to the art historical notion of 'mannerism'.[34] In keeping with this new self-consciousness in the arts, *The Courtier* gave substantial attention to the ways in which a knowledge of literature and an appreciation of (and even competence in) the arts of music and painting could be used to enhance the image of the courtier as a humanist and man of culture. This development was in line with current efforts to raise the status of painting to that of a liberal art – a subject that Castiglione also discusses.

Some luxury artefacts of the period epitomise the way in which virtuoso 'mannerist' objects implicitly demand to be handled in a virtuoso 'mannerist' way that presupposes the accomplished elegance and grace of their users. For instance, the *tazza*, a wide but shallow drinking-bowl mounted on a slender stem over a disproportionately narrow foot, is especially top-heavy when full and difficult to handle with *sprezzatura* – though, according to a celebrated painting by Caravaggio from around 1595 (Ufizzi Gallery, Florence), the god Bacchus managed with ease. Many patrons had themselves depicted as the kind of individual who would excel in such circumstances. The Florentine painter Agnolo Bronzino was a master of such portraiture, ensuring more than any other artist that his sitters appeared to be magnificently at ease with (their sense of) their own importance (Fig. 10.6). In many cases, Bronzino achieved this by giving his sitters powerful but relaxed eye contact with their viewers, immediately establishing them on equal or superior terms. The right to look at someone so intently was itself a privilege, entitling an individual to inhabit and expand a sense of personal, psychological space. As the English Jesuit Thomas Wright wrote in *The Passions of the Minde* (1601): 'neither doe wee holde it for good manners, that the inferior should fixe his eies upon his superiors countenance; and the reason is, because it were presumption for him to attempt the entrance or privie passage into his superiors minde, as contrariwise it is lawfull for the superior to attempt the knowledge of his inferior.'[35]

The postures of Bronzino's sitters were proud and erect, and their garments were solemn, rich and restrained, discreetly but confidently projecting *gravitas*. This

FIGURE 10.6: Agnolo Bronzino (Agnolo di Cosimo di Mariano), *Portrait of a Young Man*, 1530s, oil on wood, 95.6 × 74.9 cm. Metropolitan Museum of Art, New York, H. O. Havemeyer Collection, Bequest of Mrs. H. O. Havemeyer.

impression of imposing self-assurance was enhanced by the artist's own *sprezzatura* – the ostentatious panache with which he used his extremely controlled and understated style to demonstrate his virtuosity as a painter. Having said this, he intensified the sense of self-containment in his sitters by introducing elements that subtly seem to challenge or subvert it, qualifying 'with his left hand' what he asserted 'with his right'. Firstly, he uses *contrapposto*, a sophisticated new convention used by figure painters in which the head of a sitter is turned in one direction while the body is turned in the other. This device gives the impression that the sitter's attention is subtly divided between a number of concerns, thereby creating a sense of dynamism and sophistication. And secondly, he includes details that go beyond mere sophistication towards psychological depth. While his sitters are convincingly presented as models of composure, the attributes around them often leak undercurrents of internal tension – as if following Castiglione's advice to 'set one virtue in contrast or opposition to another in order to draw more attention to it'; this internal tension constitutes a kind of 'psychological *contrapposto*'. Thus the way in which his male patrons repeatedly insert their fingers between the pages of a book has a sensuous and even erotic quality that undermines the impression of serenity and self-control that the portraits otherwise exude. Similarly, the presence of sculpted figurines, nominally intended to suggest a refined interest in classical antiquity, evokes a sense of hidden passion (especially when partly curtained). Indeed such features concentrate the feeling of passion in themselves as if to free the visible persona of the sitter from the dangers that passion gives rise to, thereby enabling him to wear the mask of 'honourable dissimulation' that is so important to Castiglione's ideal courtier. This vestigial appetite for internal conflict is rooted in a newly self-conscious and *complicated* sense of individuality that is completely absent from the homogenous and harmonious world that Perugino, Giovanni Bellini and the young Raphael were inhabiting at the turn of the sixteenth century (Fig. 6.1). Newly ennobled by association with the mythological labours of the demigod Hercules, who was archetypally obliged to make a difficult choice between virtue and pleasure, this impression of interior complexity generated an ideal of 'heroic struggle' that epitomised the independent spirit of the Renaissance self-sense in its state of emergency, and quickened its art. Although only monarchs (such as Cosimo I, Francis I, Charles V and Henry IV of France) could presume to model themselves openly on the demigod, a definitive tension between the inner and outer dimensions of the self was becoming endemic among the elite as a whole.

The Courtier gave rise to a number of new trends. For instance, by virtue of its dramatised form, it contributed towards the cultivation of *conversation* as a formal medium of social exchange. The importance of propriety in speech, which had not featured prominently in medieval courtesy books, was stressed by two further treatises, both written in Italy in the second half of the sixteenth century and disseminated throughout Europe.[36] Giovanni della Casa's *Il Galateo* (1558) offers a typical sequence of didactic instructions about bodily functions (albeit enriched with congenial explanations and classical references, unlike its medieval equivalents) but also gives unprecedented attention to appropriate ways of speaking. Stefano Guazzo's *La Civile Converzatione* (1574) not only adopts the form of a series of conversations but also begins the work with a celebration of the virtues of conversation itself, in preference to silence and solitude, which the author considered to be a melancholy malaise at the opposite end of the scale (though this disposition was also a sign of the new selfhood, as we shall see in chapter 12). The treatise then moves on to a discussion of the various conventions that should be observed in conversations between individuals of different rank (masters and servants, men and women, laymen and clergy, acquaintances and strangers). In so doing, it demonstrates how speech can function as an adaptive medium to facilitate communication between a multitude of different types of people, enabling the identities of those people to accrue cultural value and propagate themselves in a culturally legitimised form, while also respecting the appropriate prerogatives of personal space. The discursive nature of conversation, which conflicts with the one-way dynamics of 'command and obedience', inevitably involved a transition from a strictly 'vertical' structure of status-relations (between lord and vassal, prince and courtier) to a more 'horizontal' one, in which appropriate forms of address had to be negotiated. This adaptation did not take place at court; on the contrary, it was partly fuelled by a desire to establish a cultural environment away from the court and the autocratic principles that the court represented. Indeed, the fact that 'absolute courtiership' presupposed a degree of dissimulation, affectation and even hypocrisy led to a reaction against it, giving rise to a number of new courtesy books (including *La Civile Conversazione*) that rejected the manipulative and sycophantic self-interest of courtly strategy and promoted a more honest and genuinely sociable form of civility.

Guazzo had commented that the reason that Italians had fared so disastrously in recent wars was the excessive gentility of their menfolk; the French, by contrast, had flourished because they were more chivalrous and warlike than civil and cultured in their codes of honour. This was about to change. The regency of the Florentine Marie de Medici (widow of the French king Henry IV), who ruled France in place of her underage son Louis XIII between 1610 and 1614, ensured a degree of Italian influence at the French court. Italianate forms of civility were also introduced to France by the Marquise de Rambouillet, whose elevation of her bedside gatherings into high social occasions was mentioned in chapter 8. The marquise's father was the French ambassador to Rome, where she was born in 1588. Her mother was a member of the noble Roman families of Strozzi and Savelli and a relative of Marie de Medici who had accommodated the family in the Palazzo Madama in Rome. According to one contemporary source, the marquise 'trained her mind by reading good Italian and Spanish books',[37] disliked the vulgarity and intrigue of the French court and, in around 1613, opened up a salon – known as the 'Blue Room' – in her own home in Paris as an alternative centre of cultural and intellectual life.

Originating as the kind of setting in which Castiglione's conversations were imagined, the Blue Room was a place where individuals could meet to converse about literary and theatrical issues, read poetry, play literary games and gossip. They were judged as much by their wit, composure, charm, manners and loyalty – fused into the untranslatable virtue of *honnêteté* – as by their social status. Even subject-matter was secondary; intense, academic subjects such as war, politics and religion were not welcome because they raised ponderous ethical issues that disturbed the smooth flow of the conversation. Above all, it was the quality of participation that mattered – the ability to be sensitive to the ever-changing dynamic of the assembled company and to engage in it in a spontaneous but judicious manner. This skill was based on a subtle awareness of the nuanced signals of others, and a discreet insight into their psychology and affections. It required an ability to sense their expectations and appetites, and the wherewithal to feed them. Although books of model correspondences were produced to help aspirants acquire the necessary skills, it involved a certain *je ne sais quoi* ('I don't know what') and could only be learned by imitation. Above all, it was important to please one's companions – to be *complaisant* or obliging. Indeed, the impulse to please and be pleased (but not to please *oneself*) became the currency into which all other impulses could be exchanged (as still reflected in the French expression *s'il vous plait* – 'if it pleases you' or 'please'). The value of this ideal was sustained by the group as a whole. Depending, as it did, on a culture, or elegant conspiracy, of mutual gratification, it could not be sustained by the group members individually. On the contrary, individuals aspired to conform themselves to the ideal and were judged, and credited with legitimate identity, accordingly.

Among the many subjects discussed at the hôtel de Rambouillet was the potential of language to express the subtle nuances of feeling and meaning that members of the salon were savouring – an initiative that eventually led to the foundation of the *Académie Francaise* by Cardinal Richelieu in 1635 to protect and promote the French language. The significance of these conversations lay not only in the conclusions the participants reached but in the way that they used conversation as a medium through which to evolve and refine the linguistic forms (and thought-forms) in which they considered their own notions of themselves to be most satisfactorily accommodated. They spent much time playing with the ideas of sociability – creating, and becoming conscious of, new possibilities of selfhood – and crafting new words to embody them. Given the importance of good breeding, it is no accident that it was from the vocabulary of family allegiance that much of the vocabulary of virtuous behaviour evolved. Both in French and English, the words 'gentle' and 'generous' derive from the Latin *genus*, meaning family stock or race – which also gives rise to 'gentry', 'gentleman' (originally a man of high birth) and 'generations' of 'genitals'! 'Benign' derives from *bene-genus*, 'well-born'; and 'noble' behaviour originated in people who were *known* on account of their social distinction. Similarly, the word 'kindness' derives from *kin* or *kindred* (hence *Kind*, 'child' in German), reflecting the 'kind' of person one is (i.e. of what lineage) and the 'kind' of loyal, 'generous' behaviour one would be expected to show to members of one's own family.

Not surprisingly the role of women in the development of this new sensibility was of immense significance; but whether it was the evolution of a more sensitive, domesticated and graceful form of cultural life that led to women's more active and visible engagement in the cultural process or vice versa is debatable. Clearly, the two processes served each other. Certainly, the more sensitive and sociable nature of women was conducive to the development of salon culture, which was largely hosted by women for the entirety of its two-hundred-year history – in contrast to the culture of the academies which evolved over the same period but which tended to be run by men. Indeed it was argued at the time that women's lack of formal education had ensured, albeit accidentally, that they had remained free of the pedantry that had characterised, and almost crippled, courtly and academic culture – to which they were now offering an alternative.[38]

If natural disposition was not seen to be excuse enough to absent women from court, pregnancy *was*. As we have seen, the Marquise de Rambouillet had several children but she may also have exploited the fact to avoid participation in what she perceived to be the crude tedium of court life. Whatever her reason, one of the most influential signs of the newly civil self, upheld in conversation, was the very building in which the first salons took place – the hôtel de Rambouillet – in rue Saint Thomas du Louvre (no longer extant), which the marquise had had reconstructed in 1618. The exterior of the house was built in a well-proportioned Italianate classical style. It was the marquise's express wish, however, that the interior of the house should be designed to accommodate the intimate meetings of her salon, placing comfort before magnificence in a way that 'even the ancients did not know'.[39] According to one contemporary witness, Gédéon Tallemant des Réaux, the design that she was seeking came to her in a moment of inspiration: 'Dissatisfied with all the drawings made for her, one evening after having reflected at length, she began to shout: "Quick! Some paper! I have found the way to do what I wanted". Within the hour, she had done the drawing, for she naturally knows how to draw ... Madame de Rambouillet's drawing was followed to the detail ...'[40] As a result of the marquise's inspiration, the grand staircase, a feature that was laden with status in sixteenth-century houses, was relocated away from the centre of the building and was made to serve a more utilitarian than status-seeking purpose. The grand and vacuous hall of the earlier house on the site was replaced by a series of smaller *enfilade* rooms – antechambers, chambers and cabinets – enabling guests to circulate between a number of smaller spaces that were more conducive to intimate conversation. The Blue Room itself marked a break with tradition in that it was decorated with airy blue velvet panels, interwoven with threads of gold and silver, instead of the rich, regal red that was customary in such houses. Contemporary sources record that the Marquise de Rambouillet also invented a new type of window which extended from the ceiling to the floor, opening on to the gardens and bringing new quantities of light to the rooms (the 'French window'). As we have seen, the bedchamber was used, not as a place for sleeping (which took place in a nearby closet), but as an audience chamber, accommodating guests in the *ruelles* between the bed and the walls. The creation of an environment that explicitly accommodated the new institution of congenial sociability and conversation at the expense of intimidating grandeur was unprecedented, and it initiated a trend that reverberated throughout Paris and Europe (Fig. 10.7). Indeed, Tallemant reported that 'when the Queen Mother [Marie de Medici] had the Palais de Luxembourg built, she sent the architects to see the

FIGURE 10.7: Abraham Bosse, *A Visit to the New Mother*, 1633, published by Melchior Tavernier, etching with engraving, 26.7 × 35 cm. Metropolitan Museum of Art, New York, Harris Brisbane Dick Fund.

hôtel de Rambouillet, and such attention did not prove to be useless'.[41] By slow degrees, the possibility and expectation of personal sociability would become coded into the material fabric of the domestic interior.

Although the *raison d'être* of the Blue Room was spoken conversation, absentees could participate by sending letters, to be read out loud to the assembled company – whereupon reports would be sent back to them, extending the conversations to include written forms. The scope of letter-writing corresponded perfectly with the spirit of the salons. The lightness, mobility and small scale of letters were conducive to delicate expressions of personal feeling, executed in a gracious and intimate manner, and they were therefore instrumental in the evocation of a newly sensitised dimension of selfhood; reflecting the primacy of sociability at salons, even love letters were copied and circulated, admired and discussed. When actually penned by their authors (rather than dictated to scribes), letters induced correspondents to communicate in the language of silent thought rather than vocalised speech, thereby easing them into a state of silent inwardness. Prior to the popularisation of letter-writing, the only circumstance to have offered such an experience – accommodating such a personal, and private, form of selfhood – had been prayer or study. Significantly, a rare altarpiece dating back to as early as the fourteenth century includes a depiction of the Annunciation in which the archangel Gabriel – the sacred source of courtesy, as we have seen – delivers his message to the Virgin by means of a sealed letter rather than by spoken words (Fig. 10.8, top left). In letters, it was as if thoughts and feelings could be transmitted directly from one interior to another without having to materialise in sound and pass through the exterior world of publicity and sensation; for this reason, one contemporary writer commented that letters were better suited than speech to the expression of passion.[42] A deep contentment with the sense of the silence, privacy, intimacy and freedom from interference that letters provided is beautifully captured in the numerous paintings of individuals reading and writing letters that were produced in the Netherlands throughout this period. For instance, in Vermeer's *Woman Reading* – which bears a resemblance to an Annunciation – the interior of the room is deeply supportive of the state of the woman's mind, holding her thoughts and feelings in itself as its own atmosphere and thereby transmitting them to the viewer wordlessly (Fig. 10.9). The extent to which a new class of individuals, especially women, identified with this state is reflected in the way some aristocratic women in Paris chose to correspond with their close neighbours on a daily basis by letter rather than by visiting them. Tallemant recorded how an esteemed noblewoman, the wife of the maréchal de La Meilleraye, 'had the fantasy that there is nothing so beautiful as to write well; and that, without this, one is only a beast; she persuaded three other sensible women of this; and all four of them practise good writing, often in the four corners of a room, each with a table, writing sweet nothings to each other'.[43]

Although the classical art of familiar letter-writing had been revived by the humanists in the fifteenth century – supplementing the official, administrative letters of the Middle Ages – most humanist letter-writers used the genre as a way of disseminating ideas, often with a view to posterity, rather than as a medium of intimate sociability. As the genre of letter-writing became established as a medium of *sociable* communication in the seventeenth century, collections of letters were assembled and

FIGURE 10.8: Meister Konrad, *Altarpiece with scenes from the Life of the Virgin*, from Schloss Tirol, Innsbruck, 1370–3, oil on panel. Tiroler Landesmuseum Ferdinandeum, Photo: Innsbruck, Tiroler Landesmuseen.

published. One regular at the hôtel de Rambouillet, Jean-Louis Guez de Balzac, used the letter format to give his philosophical reflections a semblance of personality and informality, though his letters, first published in 1624, were later criticised for their moralising and heavy-handed tone and their indulgent acknowledgement of social rank. By the middle of the century, the genre had been raised to an unprecedented level of delicacy and refinement: the letters of Vincent Voiture (who also attended the Rambouillet salons) were not written to be published but, because they were seen to embody the highest level of propriety and wit, they were published after their author's death in 1648. Significantly, because they could now be read out of context by strangers from a wide range of social ranks, they no longer functioned as instruments of real social exchange; they became technical aids, inviting readers not only to admire them as literature, but also to copy them as models. In some cases, collected letters were specifically edited to serve this purpose.[44] Anthologies of historical letters, which lacked the coherence of single-author collections, were even more overtly published to serve as examples. They consisted of collections of exemplary letters written by a range of eminent French authors in a variety of situations, to be adapted to contemporary circumstances (sending congratulations or condolences, offering

FIGURE 10.9: Johannes Vermeer, *Girl Reading a Letter at an Open Window*, 1657–9, oil on canvas, 83 × 64.5 cm. Gemäldegalerie, Dresden.

service, acceptances to invitations, declarations of romantic interest etc.); different styles of script were sometimes recommended for different types of letter. Such anthologies were produced to make the possibility of civil socialisation and self-awareness, to which the delicate craft of letter-writing was so well suited, available to ever-broader sections of society. The genre became so popular that, in 1661, Colbert established a state postal service, institutionalising the new sociablility and self-sense that the genre facilitated, on a national scale.

Among the most influential advocates of the new sociability was the prolific Madeleine de Scudéry (1607–1701), who frequented the hôtel de Rambouillet from 1637 before setting up her own salon in the Marais in Paris in around 1653. Scudéry not only engaged in letter-writing and conversation; she wrote letters and had conversations *about* letter-writing and conversation. Several of her *Amorous Letters by Various Contemporary Authors* (1641) dwell on the formal characteristics of letters – their length, quality, frequency, tone – questioning the way each of these features communicates a different shade of intimacy and affection. Similarly, her *Conversations on Diverse Subjects* (1680) consists of a series of themed conversations (descendants of Castiglione's *Courtier*) on various subjects, including conversation itself. In the latter case, eight women discuss the unseemliness of talking too much or too little, too rashly or ponderously, too much about oneself, too much about trivial subjects etc., as well as the propriety of speaking with pleasing wit, judgement, clarity and (apparent) naturalness. The second, of ten, volumes of *Conversations* (1684) includes a *Conversation on the Manner of Writing Letters* in which four women friends attempt to persuade a fifth friend to engage in letter-writing. After extolling the sociable virtues of letter-writing, the women debate the relative abilities of both sexes to write exemplary letters; they then discuss how different situations require different styles of letter: business, consolation, congratulation, compliment, news, gallantry and love. The important point here is not so much the content that Scudéry discusses (revealing though it is), but the thoroughly self-referential way in which the content describes and thereby validates the manner in which it is discussed. By using the *content* of her communication to legitimise the *mode* of her communication, she was inventing a convention in which her sense of herself, as a sociable and sensitive being, seemed to be self-authenticating. Moreover, by exchanging these ideas with her friends, she was manufacturing a frame of reference in which their refined and obliging activity, and *the sense of selfhood it embodied*, acquired cultural value and became cultural currency.[45]

The sensibility that Scudéry aimed to promote was most exquisitely experienced in friendship. The purest friendships were platonic because sexual love was seen to arouse passions that were rooted in self-interest. They could, therefore, occur between members of the same sex (especially women), as well as between men and women. At their most refined, they could reach such a level of mutual consideration and empathy that the integrity of one's personal identity came to depend on the well-being of one's friends. As Scudéry's sensitivity to the many nuances of personal relationships deepened, so her use of language became more articulated and precise. This involved considerable analysis of the meaning of words and, in some cases, the invention of new words. Several degrees of intimacy were newly identified and named – 'agreeable acquaintances', 'new friends', 'habitual friends', 'solid friends', 'tender friends' – each characterised by a subtly different feeling. By formulating new types of relationship – and new ways of *feeling* in relationships – Scudéry was not simply describing abstract conditions; she was creating a new discourse of sensitivity which, in turn, created new possibilities of experience and selfhood. This is reflected in her *Carte de Tendre*, an allegorical map that she co-created to chart the mysterious territory of friendship, affection and love, and to give form to the experiential, developmental process to be undertaken by anyone journeying towards it (Fig. 10.10). The map was originally conceived in 1653 in response to an admirer, the author Paul Pellisson, who sought to enter the sphere of her intimacy. She used the device as a playful means with which to articulate the various different states of feeling that Pellisson would have to experience in order to approach her. In so doing, she furnished the self-sense with a programme of feelings through which to process an urge that had previously been processed in keeping with a completely different set of values (associated with status and rank rather than feeling) and which therefore accommodated a completely different notion of the self. The map charts the territory between 'New Friendship' and 'Tender Friendship', identifying a direct central route along 'Inclination River' towards 'Tender Inclinations', and two overland routes, progressing from the villages

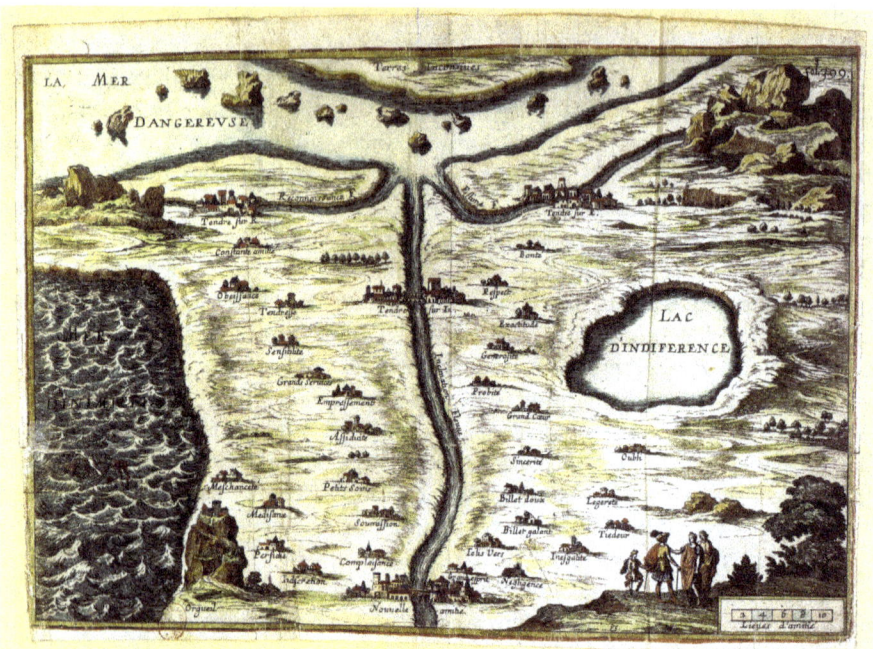

FIGURE 10.10: The *Carte de Tendre*, from *Clélie, histoire romaine*, by Madeleine de Scudéry, 1654, Paris.

of 'Gratification' and 'Submission' towards 'Tender Reconnaissance' and 'Tender Esteem'. The territory also presents many opportunities to get lost. The route via 'Negligence' leads to the 'Lake of Indifference' and the route via 'Indiscretion' leads to the 'Sea of Enmity'. The three rivers of 'Inclination', 'Reconnaissance' and 'Esteem' flow into 'The Dangerous Sea', beyond which lies the *Terra Incognita* – the land of passionate love which Scudéry was careful to differentiate from the most tender friendship. By framing the experience of feeling in a positive light rather than as an aberrant departure from the safe territory of reason and conformity, the *Carte de Tendre* charted the psychological territory of the newly sensitive self, conceiving it diagrammatically as a frame of mind, or *locus* – rather as the *studioli* in Gubbio and Urbino had provided Federico da Montefeltro with a humanist frame of mind, or diagrammatic embodiment of his own self-image.

Besides discussing the virtues of sensitive identity and experience directly, Scudéry also addressed them in her fictional writing. In fact, the *Amorous Letters* mentioned above were fictive, and the *Conversations* were originally printed, in a slightly different form, in her novels *Artamène, ou Le grand Cyrus* (1653) and *Clélie* (1655) – the epic (ten-volume) allegorical romances set in antiquity for which she is best known; the *Carte de Tendre* was also first published in *Clélie*. That these works presented her ideas as 'entertaining fiction' rather than as 'instructive teaching' reflected a change not so much in the purpose of writing, which, broadly speaking, remained didactic (disguised as allegory), as in the manner of reading and in the nature of the expected readership, which became less studious and more discursive and sociable. That is to say, the very act of reading – its social and psychological circumstances – became more accommodating to the type of experience and sensibility that Scudéry was exploring in the works themselves. The fact that she later decided to publish excerpts from the conversations as independent texts reflects the primary importance they held for her, over and above their original narrative settings, a priority that is also suggested by the neglect of characterisation in the novels and the relative indifference of their plots.

One of the many subjects of conversation in *Clélie* is the notion of the possible 'truthfulness of fiction' and the relative merits of fiction and historical writing. The discussion documents the shift of opinion away from an appreciation of the objective, but pedantic, 'truth' of history, conveyed in history books, towards an appreciation of the subjective, and pleasing, 'truth' of sociable sensitivity and feeling, conveyed in fiction. Just as she had done with letter-writing and conversation, so once again – this time by writing fiction about writing fiction – Scudéry was establishing a self-legitimising literary convention in which to experience and animate her own sense of selfhood – as sensitive, obliging and cultured – and to substantiate that sense of selfhood as a possible experience for her readers. One of the participants in the discussion, Herminius, compares the respective qualities necessary for writing 'histories' and 'fables', proposing that

> when a man is provided with faithful memorials, has liv'd himself in the world, and has part of the qualities necessary to an Historian, 'tis easie to make a History not wholly bad ... But, to compose an accurate Fable, adorned with all that can render it agreeable or profitable, I conceive it necessary, not only to have a hundred knowledges more comprehensive and particular. Such a writer must be (as I may so speak) the Creator of his Works; he must understand the art of setting forth Virtue, and exhibiting it as a thing not difficult to be practis'd. He must know the World, not only as the Author of a History ought, but he must understand the handsome mode of the World perfectly, politeness of conversation, the art of ingenious raillery, and that of making innocent Satyrs [satires]; nor must he be ignorant of that composing of Verses, writing Letters, and making Orations.[46]

While fiction could be presented as if it was real history – as in Scudéry's 'historical' novels – so reality could also be lived as fiction. The members of Scudéry's salon gave themselves mythical pseudo-historical names that resonated with their aspirations – for instance, Scudéry called herself 'Sappho', after the ancient Greek poetess. Moreover, when using this persona in her real-life non-fictional correspondence, she sometimes referred to herself in the third person singular – as 'she', as if she was another person, other than herself – reflecting the extent to which she and her circle felt constrained to adopt legitimising personas through which to dramatise a life of feeling, and to experience it 'as if vicariously'. By displacing themselves in this way, they were fictionalising themselves, entitling themselves to appropriate the possibilities of fictional characters and to act as if they were in a novel. It was as if the form of fiction, itself justified by its pretensions to being historical, in turn justified the feeling and expression of intimate affection that was not otherwise accommodated in the cultural language of the time.

Because it accommodated the possibility of emotional sensitivity, the creation of the novel was of immense importance for the development of the notion of an independent 'self'. Indeed, it is arguable that the evolution of the genre was a function of the evolution of the emotional dimension of selfhood, providing it with a medium in which it could develop and thrive. Although the precise nature of the novel (in the modern sense of realistic prose fiction) remained amorphous until the end of the following century, the tracing of its emergence as a 'genre' to the second half of the seventeenth century gains credibility from the fact that the first history of prose fiction – Pierre Daniel Huet's *Trait[t]é de l'origine des Romans* – was itself written at this time, in conscious recognition of a shift in its significance. Huet's treatise, which was first published in 1670, both *describes* a change in the nature of prose fiction, identifying Scudéry's novels as the pinnacle of the genre, and *reflects* it – by virtue of its very existence (rather as Vasari's *Lives of the Artists* had both described and reflected the re-birth of art in his own time). The importance of the treatise as a sign of the new self-consciousness of the genre is compounded by the fact that it was first published as the preface for the historical romance *Zayde* by Madame de la Fayette, who is often considered to be the writer of the first 'true' novel.

Despite the fact that the genre was still embroiled in the traditions of the past, the features that Huet identifies as being characteristic of modern fiction (which he calls 'romance') are revealing. First of all, he established that

> we esteem nothing to be properly Romance but Fictions of Love Adventures, disposed into an Elegant Style in Prose, for the Delight and Instruction of the Reader. I call them Fictions, to discriminate them from True Histories; and I add, of Love Adventures, because Love ought to be the Principal Subject of Romance. It is required to be in Prose by the Humour of the Times. It must be compos'd with Art and Elegance, lest it should appear to be a rude undigested Mass, without Order or Beauty.[47]

Having distinguished fiction from history (which he admits was often so mythologised in the past that it rates as a precursor of actual fiction), Huet then makes an important distinction between the realism of romance (fiction) and the fantasy of fable (or legend), stating that 'Romance is a Fiction of Things which may, but never have happen'd; whereas the Matter of Fables is what never has, nor ever will be perform'd.' The fact that fiction involves the visualisation of realistic events that *could* happen is a new observation that presupposes the existence of an imaginative dimension in the self – the self as a seat of *possibilities*, as considered in the previous chapter – that is not confined (like memory, history and prophecy) to the rehearsal of fixed narratives. Huet then goes on to claim that the original purpose of stories was to protect ancient wisdom; even Christ taught in parables. But, in his own time, people were no longer so inclined to apply themselves to 'intricate speculations and occult sciences':

> the Soul is not carried to Hard and Spinous Learning, unless in Prospect of some Advantage, or Hope of some remote Amusement, or else by Necessity. But, the Knowledge which attracts and delights it most, is that which is acquired without Pain and where the Imagination alone acts on Subjects which fall under our Sense,

> ravish our Passions, and are great Movers in all the Affairs of Life. Such are Romances, which require no great Intention or Dispense of Mind, to understand them. No long Reasonings are exacted; the Memory is not overburthened: Nothing is demanded, but Fancy and Imagination. They move our Passions; but 'tis on purpose to sooth and calm them again: They excite neither Fear nor Compassion; [u]nless it be to display to us the Pleasure of seeing those we are afraid, or concern'd for, out of Reach of Danger or Distress. In short, all our Emotions there find themselves agreeably provoked and appeased. 'Tis hence, that those who act more by [Passion than Reason], and labour more with their Imagination than Understanding, are affected by them.[48]

Having identified the duty of romances to delight the soul and move the passions, Huet then goes on to trace 'the Excellent Degree of Art and Elegance, to which the French Nation is now arrived in Romances . . . to the Refinement and Politeness of our Gallantry; which proceeds, in my Opinion, from the great Liberty which the Men of France allow to the Ladies'. The new genre was originally popular among women, at the expense of history and the classics. In contrast to Spain and Italy, where

> Men have neglected the Art of Engaging the Tender Sex . . . in France, the Ladies go at large upon their Parole; and being under no Custody but that of their own Heart, erect it into a Fort, more strong and secure than all the Keys, Grates, and Vigilance of the *Douegnas* [governesses]. The Men are obliged to make a Regular and Formal Assault against this Fort, to employ so much Industry and Address to reduce it, that they have formed it into an Art scarce known to other Nations. 'Tis this Art which distinguishes the French from other Romances, and renders the Reading of them so Delicious, that they cause more Profitable Studies to be neglected. The Ladies were first taken with this Lure: They made Romances their Study; and have despised the Ancient Fable and History so far, that they now no longer understand those Works.[49]

While the modern romance appealed to the sensitivity of women at the expense of classical authority, it was out of obliging 'complaisance' to women that some men, initiated into the civility of salon culture by women, were also constrained to reject austere knowledge of antiquity in favour of politeness and moderation. While it was regrettable to them that what was once considered to be an 'Essential Part of Politeness' (in the age of humanism) was now being regarded as 'Pedantry', the romance did have much to recommend it. Indeed, in the famous 'Quarrel between the Ancients and the Moderns' that was currently dividing opinion over the relative importance of classical or modern standards in French culture, the rise of the romance was presented as key evidence in support of the Moderns' cause. With regard to manners, for instance, the Moderns were seen to present an improvement on the Ancients. Pointing out that even history is full of 'pernicious examples' and that, in classical mythology, 'crimes are authorised by the Practice of the Gods', Huet states that, in the ancient world,

> Little Regard was had to Sobriety of manners, in most Part of the Greek and Old French Romances, by Reason of the Vice of the Times in which they were composed . . . But, the Modern Romances (I speak of the Good ones) are so far

from this Fault, that you'll scarce find an Expression, or Word, which may shock Chaste Ears, or one single Action which may give Offence to Modesty.[50]

Not only were romances (the good ones) exemplary in their manners but they were also useful and even necessary as guides to tender hearts in the ways of the 'dangerous passion' of love, enabling them to 'stop their Ears to that which is Criminal, and be better fortified against its Artifices; and know their Conduct, in that which has an Honest and Sacred End ... Experience lays before us, that such as are least acquainted with Love, are the most unguarded to its Assaults, that the most Ignorant are soonest decoyed'.[51] Indeed, by providing examples of virtuous characters with which to identify, romances could serve as 'Dumb Tutors, which succeed those of the College, and teach us how to Live and Speak by a more Persuasive and Instructive method than theirs'.

The scope for readers to identify with exemplary characters in novels and to learn from their experience was one of the key grounds for justifying such books morally. As a result, many authors of novels adapted the content of civility manuals to the new genre. The importance of this shift lies not only in itself, but in the corresponding shift that it implies in the disposition of the reader. Where the reader of the manual had used the text as a source to be studied and practised – presupposing an impulse towards 'complaisance' – the reader of novels was more inclined, as Huet suggested, to abandon the posture of study, and to empathise with the characters. Moreover, while civility manuals were read out of a sense of obligation, novels were read for 'delight' – thereby legitimising the experience of pleasure in their readers and ascribing cultural value to it. While the readers of manuals and novels might both wish to be civil and polite individuals, the reading of novels presupposed a very different fundamental impulse on the reader's part – a shift towards imaginative and even fantasised experience which, in turn, reflected new imaginative and fantasised capacities in the self-sense. Indeed, because the reading of novels offered an experience that was entirely imagined, and often occurred in silence and solitude, the sense of identity that it implied was activated and dramatised *inwardly* and often *invisibly*. That is to say, the institutionalisation of realistic fiction in novels created psychological space which enabled the sense of self to become fully identified with a sense of interiority, to withdraw from the world of sensation, to hide 'within the body'. In such a space, the possibilities of identity were no longer determined by objective phenomena – traditional obligations and codes of behaviour – they were determined by purely subjective criteria; above all, by the capacity for interior feeling, experienced directly and personally by the individual subject. Unlike the 'imaginative self' of the medieval flagellants who sought to visualise something they believed to have already *happened* (the historical narrative of Christ's suffering) or *would* happen (the Last Judgement), the self-sense evoked by the novel was encouraged to imagine 'what *could* happen' or 'what *could* have happened', unsubjected to exterior constraints. As such, the determinants of personal identity were interiorised as the *capacity of the imagination* – to the extent indeed that the self-sense became a *function* of that capacity. The earliest examples of realistic fiction revolved around individual characters who were newly motivated by their feelings, and who thereby ascribed cultural value to an inwardly perceived principle of self-identification. By engaging with such individuals, readers were invited to subscribe to the same principle of self-identification, and to expand themselves, imaginatively, into the realm of unlimited possible narratives that it validated.

Scudéry's novels were epic performances, showing little interest in the dramatic potential of their plots, or in the personal psychology of their participants. None of her characters experience introversion or interiority. Although they spend much time discriminating between subtle shades of feeling, implicitly including the reader in their discussions, they do not actually experience the complexity of emotion themselves; nor do they strive to stimulate emotional responses in their readers. On the contrary, it is arguable that the novels were read more as compendia of stimulating conversations and letters than as engrossing literary dramas. The opposite is true of Madame de la Fayette's *La Princesse de Clèves* (1678), which explores the reactions of its protagonists to the vicissitudes of its plot, and is therefore widely regarded as the first truly psychological novel. While this groundbreaking work is set historically (if somewhat tokenistically) in the sixteenth-century court of Henry II of France, its key preoccupation is with its characters' psychological confusion and emotional ambivalence and their efforts to understand these experiences. Indeed, in the case of the princess of the title, Fayette documents the experience of feeling certain emotions for the very first time, charting the way in which she discovers and processes them, not only on her own behalf but also on behalf of her readers; it is as if her readers are being inducted into a new realm of feeling just as her characters are. In the story, a young girl, Mademoiselle de Chartres, gets married to the Prince of Clèves, but falls in love with the Duc de Nemours. In a parallel development, the Duc de Nemours pretends to be the recipient of a compromising letter that was written to a friend of his by his friend's spurned mistress, in order to conceal his friend's history from his new lover; but the letter falls into the hands of the princess, who is inevitably upset by it, though the intrigue it reveals does not actually relate to the Duc. After much soul-searching, she confesses her feelings for the Duc to her husband, who eventually dies of distress, mortifying the princess and inhibiting her in the further development of her relationship with the Duc.

The fact that *La Princesse de Clèves* engages with the feelings and psychology of its protagonists indicates that it is inhabiting a completely different realm of experience to that of its predecessors and that it expects its readers to engage with it at this new level – as emotionally aware and active individuals. This expectation of a more subjective manner of engagement with the novel, reflecting a more subjective point of view or principle of identity in its readers, is not only present in the content of the work; it is also coded into the material characteristics of its production and use. Above all, the novel is *much* shorter than Scudéry's *Le grand Cyrus* and *Clélie* and could be read in a relatively short time, reflecting a movement away from the ponderous academic associations of the epic 'tome', towards a medium that was altogether more delicate and agile in its manner of communication. As a result, the book is small and light, and can be held comfortably in the hands. Moreover, the act of reading novels was a largely solitary process; indeed, much to the chagrin of the conservative 'Ancients', it was increasingly eclipsing the collective act of watching tragic drama at the theatre. Thus, the very format of the novel was conducive to private experiences of interiority and fantasy. It instituted a change in the 'anthropology' of reading, creating material objects (the books themselves), a social practice (the act of solitary reading) and a psychological state (of imagining narratives) that implicitly provided the new sense of emotional selfhood with a material, cultural and psychological form.

It is no accident that many early novels were 'epistolary' – taking the form of sequences of letters. Directly reflecting the 'sensitisation' and 'interiorisation' of the self, the epistolary novel thrived from the second half of the seventeenth century until the end of the eighteenth century. The use of the letter format was especially apt in this context. Not only was it closely associated with sensitivity to intimate feeling, but the very nature of letters made them conducive to emotional identification. Firstly, letters are *direct expressions* of feeling by the protagonist, rather than *recollections* of feeling by the protagonist or another narrator, as in reported stories; this makes them seem more immediate, and therefore more affecting. Secondly, they are inherently created *to be read* – often in silence and solitude. By reading epistolary novels, therefore, the reader is drawn into a position of identification with the letters' original readers; indeed, the very act of reading eases her body into the posture of the original correspondents as if she was one of them. From this position of identification, she is primed to become involved in their emotional predicaments; regardless of their content, she is induced, by the 'capacity for feelings' that has been coded into the material culture of writing and reading letters over many years, to function as a 'sensitive self'. It was as if particular feelings do not necessarily exist as pre-existent absolutes but are precipitated and shaped in their subjects by the conventions that contain and define them. As François de la Rochefoucauld proposed in one of his maxims, published in 1665: 'There are people who would never have fallen in love if they had never heard of the idea of love.'[52]

The most widely read collection of fictional letters was a short collection of five passionate love letters, said to have been written by an anonymous Portuguese nun to a French officer who had seduced her while serving near her convent, and then abandoned her. Published in Paris in 1669, *Les Lettres Portugaises* consists of the impulsive outpourings of their writer's turbulent emotions, veering from passionate love, to scorn, self-pity, remorse, anger, despair and forgiveness in rapid succession. As such, they offer the reader a series of direct glimpses into an individual's deeply interiorised experience of uninhibited feeling. However, although the letters are fictional and dramatic, they do not amount to a true epistolary novel because they were originally presented, and read, as a collection of *real* letters. By seeming to subscribe to the convention of publishing historical letters, their author (the *real* author – probably the Frenchman Gabriel-Joseph de La Vergne, comte de Guilleragues) relieved himself of the obligation to invest his work with an overall narrative or moral intention, hoping instead that the responses it elicited in his readers (mostly women) would be experienced as authentic responses to real life, rather than to some meaningfully contrived scenario or allegory. In this respect – to the extent that the reader was not able to tell the difference between 'a letter' and 'a representation of a letter' – the publication is comparable to *trompe l'oeil* paintings which, as we have seen, were also divested of signification in order to seem real.

The work that most effectively combined the expressive potential of letter-writing with the interiority of the imagination – artificially and self-consciously induced in

THE SENSIBILITIES OF THE SELF

the mind of the reader by literature – was what was perhaps the most widely read of all eighteenth-century epistolary novels (an English work, but also known throughout Europe): *Pamela, or Virtue Rewarded*, written by Samuel Richardson and first published, in two volumes, in 1740. In *Pamela*, a novel is, for the first time, oriented not only towards the expression of feelings but towards the development of character based on the expression of feelings. Broadly speaking, *Pamela* tells the story, via a series of letters from the heroine to her parents, of a humble and pious servant girl, Pamela Andrews, whose master, the squire Mr B, attempts to seduce her – at first unsuccessfully, causing her much consternation, but eventually successfully, causing agitation among the local gentry who look down on her (Fig. 10.11). The novel revolves around relationships between people of different social classes with different personal agendas. The suggested moral of the tale – its legitimising principle – is that virtue will eventually triumph over vice because it is inherently good and therefore favoured by fortune. The importance of *Pamela* in the present context lies in the fact that it originated as a conduct book – as a book of letters, commissioned by two of Richardson's friends, to instruct young girls how to relate in polite society. Richardson described how the new novelistic type of writing evolved out of an impulse to keep his message simple and accessible – neither too didactic and moralising in its manner

FIGURE 10.11: Louis Truchy, *Mr B finds Pamela writing in her Dressing Room*, after the original painting by Joseph Highmore (of 1743–4), 1762, engraving, 29.8 × 37.6 cm. Yale Center for British Art, London, Paul Mellon Collection.

of address, nor too ponderous and archaic in its style and subject-matter:

> And hence sprung *Pamela* . . . Little did I think, at first, of making one, much less two volumes of it . . . I thought the story, if written in an easy and natural manner, suitable to the simplicity of it, might possibly introduce a new species of writing, that might possibly turn young people into a course of reading different from the pomp and parade of romance-writing and, dismissing the improbable and marvellous with which novels generally abound, might tend to promote the cause of religion and virtue.[53]

The letter format was clearly conducive to the kind of prolonged dramatisations of interiority that Richardson wanted to convey. Moreover, significantly, the insights that enabled Richardson to write with such conviction about the romantic inclinations of the female heart were also bound up with the technicalities of letter-writing. Having shown an aptitude for reading and writing as a child, he was, by the age of thirteen, in demand as a scribe for illiterate young girls who wanted to reply to love letters from their sweethearts. During these years, he acquired first-hand experience of the complex and layered nature of women's feelings, while also learning how to craft letters that were sufficiently nuanced to do justice to them. Sensitive to the subtleties and paradoxes that the situation required, he explained how, on some occasions, he was 'directed to chide, and even repulse, when an offence was either taken or given, at the very time that the heart of the chider or repulser was open before me, overflowing with esteem and affect'.[54]

The immense popularity of *Pamela* reflects the extent to which the novel met a new appetite and capacity in the reading public. As such, it was a milestone in the history of cultural experience, generating and institutionalising imaginative, interior dimensions in the notion of selfhood. It did this not only by addressing the world of imaginary interiority as its subject-matter, but also by evoking the space of imaginary interiority in its readers. Even as material objects, novels became the focal point of a psychological environment or state of mind – accessed only through the physical act of reading them – in which the notion of personal identity could be substantiated and expanded along avenues of realistic but imaginary narratives. In this capacity, novels were magically transparent to the imaginary possibility of a new depth of personal freedom and self-determination. Having been evoked by precedents like *Pamela*, this new dimension of selfhood was quickly interiorised in its readers, whereupon it became autonomous in them.

The way in which people responded to *Pamela* not merely as a story to be observed but also as a frame of reference in which to operate as a 'fantasised and psychological self' is reflected in the way that many individuals felt moved to continue and extend the story of *Pamela*, as if it was their own story, appropriating it as a vehicle through which to dramatise and unfold the narratives of their own 'virtue, rewarded'. Even the author could not control his heroine's destiny. Accordingly, some editions of the book include printed illustrations of scenes that did not even happen in the original. The book was also emulated and caricatured. Jean-Jacques Rousseau's epistolary novel *Julie, ou La Nouvelle Héloïse* (1761) combined a romantic narrative with a didactic message, but gave unprecedented value to personal sincerity and authenticity of feeling over politeness and compliance. *Julie* stimulated intensely felt responses from its readers, many of whom reacted to the story as if it was real. A decade later, some readers of Goethe's *The Sorrows of Young Werther* (1774) became so identified with the letter-writing hero, driven by unrequited love to commit suicide, that they followed him to his death, cleaving to the consummate fantasy of personal identity that he seemed to offer, in preference to life itself. On the other hand, reacting against the perceived idealism and superficiality of *Pamela*, Henry Fielding's *Shamela* (1741) purported to tell the story of the 'real' Pamela, who he revealed to be a scheming and lascivious wench, manipulating Squire Booby to marry her for her own benefit. *Shamela* dispensed with both the moral intention and the intimate associations of the letter form that are fundamental to *Pamela*, replacing them with a more straightforward narrative that was primarily meant to be enjoyed. This development is important because it demonstrates how the novel eventually became established as an independent literary form without having to be justified on moral grounds. The motive of pure pleasure was becoming increasingly acceptable, to the extent that even amoral and immoral characters could be developed as heroes. Initially, the stories of such heroes were presented as cautionary tales or prefaced by disclaimers to the effect that they were 'true' and therefore instructive; many of them were supported by the evidence of 'documentary letters'. But, as the century progressed, such claims became increasingly tokenistic. Towards the end of the eighteenth century, when the epistolary novel was on the brink of redundancy, Pierre Choderlos de Laclos' *Les Liaisons Dangereuses* (1782), consisting of letters between a wide range of characters, capitalised on the potential for privacy in letters but replaced the exemplary virtues of sensitivity, confidence and trust with the more entertaining intrigues of secrecy, seduction and sabotage. The deliberate transgression of moral norms in the pursuit of undiluted pleasure was taken to extremes in the libertine novels of the Marquis de Sade (1740–1814, Fig. 13.20).

As the principle of civility became increasingly interiorised as a natural function of the self, so the external scaffolding of formal convention was progressively dismantled. During the Renaissance, religious conformity to Christian models of virtue was challenged, and sometimes contradicted, by a powerful attachment to personal dignity; indeed, one seventeenth-century writer recommended that 'if any man of your owne Ranke doe you an affront, shew that you are sensible of your Honour', ruefully adding that 'this is not so consonant to the doctrine of Christ, as I would it were.'[55] In due course, social status and military prowess were overshadowed by more educated and cultivated refinements. In the eighteenth century, courtly ritual was challenged by salon geniality; moral obligation – an external principle of behaviour, honoured for the sake of social cohesion – was replaced by the pleasurable application of sensitive and discriminating taste – an internal principle of behaviour, appropriated and naturalised by the self and identified as one of its innate functions. This shift was accomplished in conjunction with the relaxation of dependence on preconceived narratives that were pre-legitimised by their classical or historical associations, and the rise of the novel. Although formal codes of manners continued to be written and read throughout the eighteenth century, novels provided an important blueprint for the development of personal fantasies, and they thereby made a fundamental contribution towards the establishment and consolidation of a highly interiorised sense of self that thrived in the imagination. On the one hand, they furnished individuals with the means with which to read and interpret their experience of the world in imaginative ways that presupposed their existence as subjective selves on the threshold of an infinity of possible personal narratives. On the other hand, they provided a conventional form for the process of imaginative self-construction; by conferring a collective cultural value on this process, they normalised it to the point at which it became unnoticeable.

CHAPTER ELEVEN

The Behaviour of the Self: the Codification of Sensibility in Domestic Life

The apparent 'civilisation of the self' reached its apogee in the eighteenth century when the principle of sociable conduct was interiorised as personal *sensibility* – that is to say, when sociable conduct seemed to arise not simply through conformity to an exterior code of practice but as an apparently natural and spontaneous function of the self. But while civil sensibility seemed to become a natural function of the self, it was nevertheless evoked by, and held in place by, the practices of sociable conduct, and even its environments. While the new self-sense manifested itself in new modes of thinking and feeling which gave rise to new behaviours, objects and types of room so, at a more subtle level, these behaviours, objects and rooms precipitated new modes of thinking and feeling which, in turn, determined the possibilities of identity-formation. As the poet Edmund Spenser observed of clothing, as early as 1596:

> Mens apparell is comonly made according to theire condicons, and theire condicons are oftentymes goverened by theire garmentes: for the person that is gowned is, by his gowne, put in minde of gravitie, and also restraynd from lightnes by the very aptnes of his weede . . . there is not a little in the garment to the fashioninge of the mynde and condicons.[1]

What was true of dress was also true of interior spaces and furniture; possibilities of self-perception were coded into them and the two evolved together. Numerous images of seventeenth-century interiors demonstrate that, even in affluent houses, permanent room fittings were relatively simple at this time, making little allowance for the shaping of a highly personalised sense of self. (Fig. 10.7). Even in important rooms where salons were held, such fittings were limited to the prestigious but somewhat austere commodities that had become popular in the previous century: tapestries, glazed windows, substantial decorated fireplaces and overmantels, and sometimes beds. These features were sources of light, heat and comfort but they were also signs of status and identity. In the grandest halls, large cabinets, veneered with precious materials, would be used for the ostentatious display of curiosities; many of these cabinets were adorned with plaques showing allegorical scenes that

FIGURE 11.1: Armchair, around 1680, England, walnut, 120.7 × 44.5 × 64.1 cm. Metropolitan Museum of Art, New York, Fletcher Fund.

served the same legitimising purpose as the high-minded iconography of contemporary academic painting.

The overall effect of such rooms is that of a large rectilinear space, fitted with secondary rectilinear shapes and forms (Fig. 8.14). The presence of windows, panelling, paintings, tiled floors, cabinets, tables and even creases, ironed into table linen, adds to the impression that the rooms are translucent three-dimensional grids. Chairs, traditionally associated with elite status, became more common at this time (unlike benches which, promoting an absence of personal space, became more rare); however, they continued to be seen as formal objects and were usually ranged in a strictly ordered manner around the exterior walls of a room – unless they were being used. The majority of chairs were still conceived as 'backed stools' and, like the rooms they occupied, they were designed as spatial grids, constructed out of vertical, horizontal and perpendicular elements; cushions would sometimes be used. To ensure rigid strength, their legs were linked just above the ground by 'stretchers' (Figs 8.14, 10.7, 11.1). The grandest examples of the type were solid and fully upholstered. Tassels and fringes were sometimes attached to their seat-rails to add to their splendour and give them a sumptuous, ceremonial air (Fig. 11.2). These details were highly refined, suggesting civility; but, by covering the parts of the chairs where one would normally place one's hands to lift them, they also made it difficult to move the objects, subtly reinforcing the statuesque immobility of the values they were intended to project. Such chairs were not designed to be comfortable; they were designed to uphold a proper hierarchy of social and political relationships. Their very design imposed a static, upright and frontal posture on the people who used them, inclining them to adopt a formal and unrelaxed frame of mind. Even the ornament used to decorate them – for instance, 'strapwork' on their top-rails or stretchers – tended to be punctuated with complicated angles and articulations, like points of etiquette; the eye is required to stop and start as it moves around them, as if in formal procession. Individuals were invited to take their place on this stage and they were judged by their ability to do so. Their privilege was evinced, not by their comfort, but by the dignity and graciousness of their bearing and the stiff luxuriousness of their clothing. Even in conversational situations, they seem to have occupied their regulated interiors

FIGURE 11.2: Armchair, Paris, around 1675–85, carved and gilded walnut and beech (with modern upholstery), 104 × 69.5 × 70.5 cm. Victoria and Albert Museum, London W.32-1918.

like chess pieces. As in the formal court dances of the period, their movements were made to resemble sequences of articulated postures, shifting from one unit of space to the next in a series of steps rather than in a continuous flow.

These conventions prevailed in affluent residences, from houses to palaces, until the end of the seventeenth century. The growing presence of mirrors and long-case pendulum clocks, signifying interiority, reflected the imminence of change. In 1699, Louis XIV himself requested that the Ménagerie at Versailles be designed in a spirit that was more 'youthful' than that used elsewhere at the chateau. On his death in 1715, his successor, the Duc d'Orleans (regent for Louis XV until 1723), went a step further by disbanding the court at Versailles and relocating his centre of power to the Palais Royal in Paris, thereby releasing the tension that Louis XIV had maintained for half a century between courtly culture at the chateau and salon culture in the city. The demise of Louis XIV's ritualised model of courtly culture at Versailles coincided with the gradual relaxation of the highly structured codes of behaviour that kept a respectable sense of selfhood in place throughout his reign.

An impression of this newly relaxed and congenial atmosphere is conveyed by Jean-François de Troy's *Reading from Molière* (1728), in which a group of privileged *salonnières* gather round informally to read and discuss literature together (but not to *study* it!) and to socialise (Fig. 11.3). The image is transitional. Aspects of it are redolent of the imposing grandeur of the Versailles years: the bold, stiff backs to the chairs, fully upholstered; the fact that the top-rail and upright of the chair on the right meet at a point, rather than flow into each other as a curve; the formal decoration of the silk wall-coverings (articulated with corners, visible near the clock); the voluptuous forms and fabrics of the clothing. But other features in the picture reflect an entirely new sensibility: the informal distribution of the chairs, temporarily moved from their usual locations against the walls of the room (hence the lack of decoration on their backs); their scrolling 'cabriole' legs, projecting out diagonally rather than frontally (reflecting how the chairs have been conceived sculpturally; that is, to be viewed in the round and in motion, rather than as an assembly of static, flat planes); the dispersed attention of the individuals, reflecting the leisurely nature of the gathering; and, above all, their casual positions – especially that of the fashionably detached gentleman on the left, the lady in the ivory-coloured dress who is almost slouching (most unbecoming in a woman!), and the lady on the right who is not only provocatively revealing her ankle but is also immodestly engaging the attention of the viewer without repositioning herself; that is, on equal terms (forcibly demonstrating the changing status of women). The fact that none of these figures are making a show of their respect for each other also indicates an important shift of values. In contrast to the salon gatherings of the Marquise de Rambouillet and Mademoiselle de Scudéry, in which the obligation to please *others* were paramount (Fig. 10.7), in this group the participants seem more inclined to please, or pleasure, *themselves*. Their naturalness and sincerity are more important than their politeness and compliance, and their sociability resides in their integrity and honesty as individuals, only minimally supported by formal codes of behaviour.

Troy's *Reading from Molière* provides an early indication of how domestic interiors were used to embody and evoke the new notion of the individual as an increasingly independent being, cognisant of the conventions of civil behaviour but also motivated

FIGURE 11.3: Jean-François de Troy, *Reading from Molière*, 1728, oil on canvas, 72.4 × 90.8 cm. Private Collection.

by his or her own inclinations. As the eighteenth century unfolded, so the pleasurable interaction of individuals with the domestic environment became increasingly natural and sensuous. This was immediately reflected in changes to the interiors of the *hôtels* in which the elite met to discuss philosophy and art. Firstly, the distribution of rooms became more *convenient*; this was manifest both in the appearance of corridors and service stairwells that enabled servants to circulate around the house without entering the social rooms, and in the increasingly clear differentiation between 'rooms for public display' and 'rooms for private comfort' – as, for instance, in the Chateau de Champs at Champs-sur-Marne, near Paris, built from 1699 to 1706.[2] And secondly the interiors of the rooms became more *elegant*. As if in response to the natural and animated fluency of the civil self, room decoration became more curvaceous and less rectilinear in its treatment of form, and more fluid and less articulated in its movement. The classical description of interior spaces, in which straight lines, often in the form of columns, were used to introduce structure and clarity to a room, and to differentiate between the secondary spaces demarcated within the overall space, was superseded by the 'rococo' style in which sinuous lines were used to link forms and to promote the impression of a single unified space. This sense of unity was sustained by the continuous inter-penetration of forms at the expense of the forms themselves. Even paintings, traditionally elevated by their noble iconography, were fitted into this integrated scheme, as decorative panelling. In extreme cases, rooms were 'shaped' – with no corners, and with rounded coves between the walls and ceilings to ensure that surfaces elided with each other seamlessly; the oval 'Salon de la Princesse' in the Hôtel de Soubise in Paris, designed by Germain Boffrand for the Prince and Princesse de Soubise in 1735, epitomises the type (Fig. 11.4). Conservative critics of the style, such as Etienne La Font Saint-Yenne (one of the first self-styled art critics), complained that such rooms made it difficult to place furniture against the walls; they subtly imposed a degree of informal sociability on their users. In rectangular rooms, bow-fronted corner-cupboards (*encoignures*) were used to conceal the breaks between walls. Occasionally, the curvaceous design and decoration of a piece of furniture – a sofa or a console table – was matched to the panelling behind it, such that its ornamental lines could be picked up and continued beyond it, like a melody passing from one musical instrument to another (Fig. 11.5); in such cases, the eye is naturally inclined to migrate over the surface of the interior without impediment or repose.

Because the rococo style is innately antipathetic towards rationalisation, contemporary theorisations of the style are – almost by definition – rare. Some light can, however, be thrown on its significance by reference to the concept of the 'line of beauty', a serpentine linear element, not unlike a graceful 'S', which the contemporary

FIGURE 11.4: Salon ovale de la Princesse, Hôtel de Soubise, Paris, designed by Germain Boffrand, 1737–9. © RMN-Grand Palais. Agence Bulloz.

FIGURE 11.5: Design for a couch for M. le Comte de Bielenski, from *L'Oeuvre de Juste Aurèle Meissonnier*, 1742–8, etching and engraving, 31.7 × 36.4 cm. Metropolitan Museum of Art, New York, Rogers Fund.

British artist, William Hogarth, considered to be the fundamental principle of good design. Hogarth promoted this principle, in his *Analysis of Beauty* (1753), because he believed it to be rooted in nature and the physiological process of seeing, rather than academic sources. Significantly he advocated its use in the design of ordinary household objects, such as candlesticks or chair legs, to ensure that they corresponded to the dynamic and variegated process of visual perception in human beings, during which the eye naturally moves over the surface of objects, in rapid sequences of minute movements, rather than focusing on them with a fixed stare (Fig. 11.6, frame 14). For candlesticks, he recommended that the diameters of all the horizontal mouldings on the stem, as well as the distances between them, be different – to avoid regularity and repetition, and to maximise variety (Fig. 11.6, frame 32). Chairs were to be fitted with animated S-shaped 'cabriole' legs, with neither too much, nor too little, curvature (Fig. 11.6, frame 50).

From around 1730, pieces of furniture of all kinds were increasingly composed of sinuous elements, absorbing all angles and articulations into themselves. In French commodes, signs of functionality such as the divisions between drawers were understated to the point of invisibility; similarly, drawer-handles were lost in the

FIGURE 11.6: William Hogarth, *The Analysis of Beauty*, Plate I, London, 1753.

animated play of ornament. Chairs were gradually adapted to the sensuous form and movement of the human body. The junctions that had previously punctuated the relationships between static rectilinear elements (Fig. 11.1) were erased. Their legs now descended from the seat to the floor with the lively flourish of a brushstroke (Fig. 11.7). They are no longer interrupted on the way down by utilitarian stretchers; on the contrary, replacing the tense and imperious 'ball-and-claw' feet of the early eighteenth century (Fig. 11.2), their feet meet the ground with delicate poise, tapering to a point like a musical phrase that naturally comes to rest (Fig. 11.8). Similarly, the straight sides of armrests and chair backs were softened into curves. Eventually even the carved floral ornament, intended to lighten up designs in the 1740s but seen to burden them by the 1760s, was erased and absorbed into the flow of the whole (Fig. 11.9). There is none of the 'rhetoric of *gravitas*' that characterised the earlier baroque chairs; nor any attempt to express the structural functions of the various parts of the chair with architectural motifs. On the contrary, the user is engaged as a dynamic subject, rather than a static one; as a result, his or her identity is increasingly located in the ever-changing experience of bodily sensation, rather than the stable realm of mental abstractions. As chairs became softer and fuller, sitters were invited to become comfortable and relaxed, at the expense of self-conscious formality and moral security. Indeed, at the height of the rococo period, one of the daughters of Louis XV ruefully reflected on her refusal to enter into a convent by saying: 'I love the conveniences of life too well; this couch is my destruction!'[3]

FIGURE 11.7: Armchair, 1725–35, France, carved walnut and beech with needlework and damask, 110 × 69 cm. Victoria and Albert Museum, London, W.55-1914.

FIGURE 11.8: Armchair, 1740-60, France, carved and gilded beechwood with Beauvais tapestry, 92.1 × 68.6 × 55.2 cm. Metropolitan Museum of Art, New York, Gift of J. Pierpont Morgan.

FIGURE 11.9: Armchair, Louis Delanois, around 1765, Paris, carved and gilded walnut with silk brocade upholstery, 106 × 71.8 × 59.7 cm. Metropolitan Museum of Art, New York, Gift of J. Pierpont Morgan.

Reflecting a growing affinity for a wider and more consciously articulated range of sensibilities, specific types of chair were increasingly designed to meet specific occasions – watching games, kneeling in prayer or writing at desks. In his *L'Art du Menuisier* ('Art of the Joiner') of 1769–74, the cabinet-maker and writer Andre-Jacob Roubo described a 'desk chair' (*fauteuil de cabinet*) that was specifically designed to be used at a writing desk (Fig. 11.10). Because of the projection of the seat-rail at the front, supported by its own leg, the chair was

> very comfortable for those who are obliged to remain sitting and leaning forward for long periods, as all those who write must do. In such circumstances the thighs are parted and must carry the weight equally, and are not bruised by the front crosspiece of the chair; this, being curved, allows the entire weight of the body to rest on the front part of the seat and thus on the inner part of the thigh, which being the fleshiest is most resistant to fatigue.[4]

In this case, the identity of a 'writer', and the various significations of that social role, are coded into the very design of the chair, and into the posture of the body that the chair is designed to support.

Just as writing chairs were evolved to accommodate the role of the 'writer', so the design of writing desks also became more particular at this time, partly in response to the growing culture of letter-writing. In the sixteenth and early seventeenth centuries, personal desks had been self-contained objects – portable boxes with sloping lids, not unlike the writing surfaces of fitted carrels (Figs 7.8, 7.9, 11.11). The fact that they were often lockable indicates that they were havens of privacy, containing the

FIGURE 11.10: Desk chair, Etienne Meunier, 1760–70, Paris, beechwood, rosewood, purpleheart, kingwood, with gilt bronze mounts, 88.3 × 62.8 × 63.0 cm. Rijksmuseum, Amsterdam.

accessories of a personalised identity, though the fact that they were portable, to be placed on any table, suggests that they were not associated with a particular room in which privacy could be guaranteed. Moreover, their sloping tops, used as a surface for reading and writing, imposed a frontality on their users, suggesting a disposition of impersonal formality, rather than of comfortable relaxation. That they were hinged at the top shows that they were closed when being used and therefore that their interiors served more as storage space than for the interactive theatre of use. On the basis of these characteristics, their appeal as indices of personal identity was best suited to literary intellectual types, and it is not surprising therefore that it was mostly as signs of scholarship that they were included in contemporary portraits (Fig. 11.12).

In cabinet-desks, which evolved in the sixteenth century to combine the functions of collecting and writing, the large front panel that concealed the interior was hinged at its base rather than the top and could be lowered, both to expose sets of drawers on the inside and to serve as a writing surface (Fig. 7.19). Some such cabinets were fitted with iron handles at the sides and were evidently portable. Others were mounted on open-frame stands – usually rigid rectilinear frames like the bases of contemporary chairs – and were clearly designed not to be moved. In the seventeenth century, these designs were developed in tandem with private closets in grand houses, reflecting the

THE BEHAVIOUR OF THE SELF 217

FIGURE 11.11: Table desk, around 1600, England (probably Southwark), oak inlaid with boxwood and bog oak, 31.5 × 69.2 × 50.5 cm. Victoria and Albert Museum, London, W.4-1911.

FIGURE 11.12: Franciabigio, *Portrait of a Young Man Writing*, 1522, oil on panel, 78 × 61 cm. Gemäldegalerie, Berlin. Photo: bpk/Gemäldegalerie, SMB/Jörg P. Anders.

way in which the privacy associated with writing and study (first evinced in the *studioli* of fifteenth-century Italy) was institutionalised, both for men and for women, throughout Europe. Private closets in such houses often served as the culmination of an *enfilade* of rooms – consisting of antechambers, bedchambers and dressing-rooms – increasing progressively in intimacy as they decreased in ease of access to guests. This shift towards sophisticated privacy was undertaken at Burghley House in Lincolnshire, where the suite of ever more privileged and intimate rooms that replaced the Elizabethan 'long galleries' at the end of the seventeenth century can still be seen. Other rare examples, at least one of which was originally furnished with a 'walnut tree scriptore', survive at Ham House near Richmond (Fig. 11.13). Such spaces were clearly perceived to facilitate new possibilities of selfhood, for, as Randall Cotgrave observed in 1611, 'the man is that certainly, that he is secretly. There are many that sweat upon the stage, that are key-cold in their Closets.'[5] That is to say, the true nature and identity of a man is not evident from his performance in society but is – both metaphorically and literally – closeted and secreted, where only he can know it.

In much of eighteenth-century Europe, the cabinet-desk developed into the lean-to bureau, consisting of a desk with a sloping front over a chest of drawers, often surmounted by a cupboard or bookcase; in France, it developed into the *secrétaire*

FIGURE 11.13: The Duchess's Private Closet, around 1675, with writing-cabinet, tea-table and japanned chairs at Ham House, Richmond-upon-Thames. © National Trust Images/John Hammond.

in which private objects or documents could be kept secret (Fig. 11.14). Significantly, the *secrétaire* derived its name from a medieval court official – a notary, clerk or *secretary* who was charged to witness and record private negotiations, keeping them apart (*se-cretus* in Latin) from other business.[6] Its transformation into an *object* reflects a shift away from the kind of social privacy that included the dictating of letters to a servant, towards the more psychological privacy of solitude which involved *writing* them.

The fact that the folding lids or fronts of cabinet-desks and *secrétaires* were hinged at the base indicates that they were used while open. In keeping with the complex choreography of letter-writing, they became increasingly ingenious and self-conscious in their construction, setting the stage for paper, quills, ink, seals and other such literary utensils to play their part in the theatre of intimate communication. Moreover, as desks became less exclusively associated with study and more associated with women, so the paraphernalia of writing became more integrated into the

FIGURE 11.14: Drop-front secrétaire ('*à abattant*' or '*en armoire*'), by various makers supervised by Jean Hauré, Paris, 1786–7, oak carcass, veneered with exotic woods, 161.3 × 81.3 × 38.1 cm. Metropolitan Museum of Art, New York, Gift of Mr and Mrs Charles Wrightsman.

material culture of the civil self, and writing desks were placed in sociable spaces throughout the home. Having said this, many such desks also concealed hidden drawers as if to reflect and objectify their owners' capacity for secrecy – one of the most definitive 'proofs' of private identity (Fig. 11.15). Such drawers, often released by secret buttons, were only known to their owners, and were uniquely accessible to them; as such, they corresponded to, and exteriorised, their owners' deeply interiorised sense of themselves. It is symptomatic of their role in the process of identity-formation that such exquisite embodiments of privacy should have been so ostentatiously decorated and displayed. On the one hand – by virtue of their concealed contents – they promoted a perception of selfhood that was so private that it could not be exposed to the outside world, while on the other hand – by virtue of their appearance and location – they were thoroughly impressive chattels attracting inordinate attention to themselves. This irony highlights the point at which the private and public dimensions of personal identity met, delicately reflecting the extent to which privilege and privacy were commodified as luxuries at this time, partly validated through admiration and envy.

The scenario in which the self-constructive potential of the domestic environment was most explicitly realised was the *toilette*, in which the physical act of self-grooming was transformed into a ritual of identity-formation in a more abstract sense. The increased availability of mirrors in the thirteenth century clearly enabled individuals (especially women) to fashion themselves, and forge a sense of themselves, in their own eyes. But the fact that the act of self-fashioning was considered worthy of representation in pictures (from the fifteenth century) and was performed in public, enabling individuals to be seen in this privileged situation by *others*, indicates that it also presented women with an opportunity to construct their public personas. A number of images of elite women grooming themselves exist from the fifteenth

FIGURE 11.15: Rolltop desk (with detail), David Roentgen, c.1776–9, Germany (Neuwied am Rhein), veneered oak with gilt bronze mounts, 135.9 × 110.5 × 67.3 cm. Metropolitan Museum of Art, New York, Rogers Fund

century – van Eyck is known to have painted one – but they are rare. Moreover, most such images involve moralising narratives (Bathsheba, Susanna and the goddess Diana, Fig. 13.9) in which women are shown bathing in nature and, apart from their maidservants, do not know that they are being watched. It was not until the mid-sixteenth century that the activity was transformed into self-conscious 'theatre' in which the self-sense was staged and performed (Figs 8.12, 8.13). Under the intensified gaze of onlookers, the process of making oneself up became a thoroughly artificial one, revolving around the fixing of clothing, jewellery, hair, perfume and make-up; rather like the formal garden designs of the period, there was nothing 'natural' about it in the modern sense of the word. Initially associated with the elite, the trend became more widespread in the seventeenth century and representations of the *toilette* began to proliferate (Fig. 11.16). The occasion usually required no more than a mirror propped up on a table but, in the most extravagant cases, it involved elaborate and expensive 'toilet services', often made of silver, which were clearly meant to be displayed, and even used, in company (Fig. 11.17). Toilet services, which originated among the accoutrements to Louis XIV's *levée* and became fashionable from around 1680, could consist of as many as seventy items, including caskets, flasks, ewers, basins, tazzas, whisks, brushes, candlesticks, a bell and a table-mounted mirror. Usually placed in, or adjacent to, a bedchamber, possibly in a closet, the toilet service was named after the cloth (*toile* in French) that was used to cover a gentleman's, or (more usually) a lady's, shoulders while his or her hair was being dressed; but it

FIGURE 11.16: Utrecht School, *A Lady at Her Toilet*, around 1650–60, oil on canvas, 135.3 × 176.5 cm. Minneapolis Institute of Arts, The Putnam Dana McMillan Fund.

FIGURE 11.17: The Calverley Toilet service, William Fowle, 1683–4, London, cast, embossed and chased silver. Victoria and Albert Museum, London.

also referred to the cloth that covered the dressing table, or the mirror on it, and eventually to the entire act of being made up and getting dressed. Besides requiring a number of maidservants – to apply patches, set jewels and tie ribbons etc. – the morning *toilette* was cultivated as an opportunity to hold audiences with visitors. Indeed, in the eighteenth century, it became a thoroughly sociable occasion, and some toilet services included pairs of cups and saucers for tea or hot chocolate accordingly. Witnesses to this ritual act of self-affirmation, which could last several hours, ranged from family, friends and lovers at one end of the social spectrum to lawyers, business advisers and the sellers of luxuries at the other (Fig. 11.18).

For two hundred years, the *toilette* ritual constituted a performance of personal identity. The hostess was the heroine, her visitors were her audience. The various objects in her toilet service were her props, providing her with myriad possible micro-narratives through which to refine, exercise and convey her sense of herself; on such a stage, every gesture became a dramatisation of her taste, wealth, status, power, delicacy, beauty and intelligence. But towards the end of the eighteenth century, as the principle of personal identity was increasingly interiorised, it ceased to be necessary to dramatise it in conformity with prescribed routines, and the performance of the *toilette* in public ceased to be expedient; a more 'natural' look became fashionable and, in keeping with the growing appetite for interiority, the creation of that look became more private, eventually giving rise to the 'bathroom'.

FIGURE 11.18: François Boucher, *The Milliner*, 1746, oil on canvas, 64 × 53 cm. Nationalmuseum, Stockholm.

Like the *secrétaire* and *table de toilette*, a plethora of new purpose-specific tables were also conceived to be *performed*. Convertible tea and games tables institutionalised pleasurable sociability and sociable pleasure-seeking in the home, by virtue of their functions; but they also incorporated these inclinations in their very form, for they were *designed* to be moved around, thereby innately accommodating the possibility of spontaneous sociability. Games tables, for instance, were specifically furnished with hinged tops and gate-legs to enable them to be moved from the wall, where they were kept closed, to the centre of the room where they were used open. 'Occasional' tables also became common. Liberally dotted around the intimate spaces of the domestic interior, these petite objects were often dedicated to a single task – perhaps to support a letter, novel or piece of needlework. Beyond their purely aesthetic appeal, their deeper effect was to provide a focus around which an individual's level of behavioural sensitivity could be practised and demonstrated. Not only did their functions reflect the refined activities of their users but the very use of them required a degree of physical dexterity that presupposed a cultivated sense of self-awareness. For instance, their small size and extreme lightness reflect how they could be easily moved by the privileged women who used them (in place of servants), enabling such women to exercise a degree of independence without threatening to compromise their elegance with the indignity of physical effort or strain; it also enabled, and even encouraged them to act whimsically, manifesting a degree of informality – both to themselves and to others – that presupposed an unprecedented level of 'naturalness' and intimacy (Fig. 11.19).

While the precious details of luxury objects (and the environments they belonged to) reflected a high level of refined sensibility in the privileged individuals that enjoyed them, they also laid down the parameters of behaviour and determined the construction of the self-sense. Indeed some objects are so particular that it is as if they *impose* the values they represent on their users, delicately forcing them to behave as genteel selves. For instance, work-tables (*tables en chiffonnière*) sometimes contain a diminutive drawer, or sliding shelf for a candle, with a knob that is so small that it can only be held by two fingers; to pull on the knob too forcefully would cause the entire table to tip over (Fig. 11.20). In the same way, early-eighteenth-century tea bowls – made, in the Chinese manner, of paper-thin porcelain without handles –

FIGURE 11.19: François Nicolas Barthélemy Dequevauviller, *L'Assemblée au Salon*, after Nicolas Lafrensen (or Laureince), etching and engraving, 41 × 50.2 cm. Metropolitan Museum of Art, New York, Harris Brisbane Dick Fund.

FIGURE 11.20: Work and writing table, Léonard Boudin, around 1761–70, France, oak veneers with exotic woods, gilt bronze mounts. Metropolitan Museum of Art, New York, Robert Lehman Collection.

were so delicate that, although some of them had a projecting base and everted rim to hold, it required some skill to use them gracefully, without burning oneself.[7]

The contract of co-dependence that existed between fragile luxury objects and refined, privileged subjects was of course entirely invisible, for the dynamics of civility now seemed to be as naturally and spontaneously scripted into the elite domestic environment as the sensibility itself seemed to be naturally and spontaneously present in its inhabitants. But beneath the relaxed surface, the contents of such environments played a more significant role in the construction of their users' identities than they seemed to, for they tacitly allowed and even prompted them to experience the easy freedom of pleasure, apparently for its own sake, rather than submit to the restrictive demands of a formal code of practice. Indeed it was precisely the feeling and appearance of *naturalness* that these environments were, somewhat unnaturally, required to confer on their users – to the point at which the self-sense that engaged with them seemed, both to itself and to others, to be innate, autonomous and free.

CHAPTER TWELVE

The Portrayal of the Self: Facial Expression and the Language of Personal Emotion

While the nature of personal identity was to some extent determined by its 'external' environments, it was also conditioned by its 'internal' ones – the mental and linguistic conventions associated with the experience of emotion – or the 'passions' and 'affections', as emotions were called until the seventeenth century. The first one hundred and fifty years of portraiture reveal that, until this period, an individual's significance and disposition were largely represented symbolically – by means of attributes and allegory rather than facial expression (Figs 7.10, 10.6, 11.12). In the same way, the *experience* of emotion was usually realised vicariously – as projected into pre-existing narratives (Christian, mythological or historical) through which it could be known indirectly and impersonally (as discussed in chapter 13). In both cases, the passions were processed through a language of signs and symbols that linked them to a preconceived system of meanings, offering limited scope for the unqualified experience and expression of subjectivity. In the latter case, they were experienced as functions of the stories under consideration rather than as functions of the self that viewed them, and were only legitimate, therefore, to the extent that they were interpreted in that context. Because that context was initially controlled by the Church – and, indeed, developed in relation to Christian devotion – the independent expression of emotion was not an arena in which the dynamics of personal selfhood were freely activated at this time. It took many years for the legitimising scaffolding of these moralising conventions to be dismantled, and for new conventions, accommodating the experience of pure subjectivity, to evolve.

During the Middle Ages, the passions were generally thought to be dangerous and threatening. Although they could, in principle, serve a positive end, they were mostly uncontrollable and seen to be subject to demonic influences from outside the soul. As numerous images of the temptation of St Anthony reflect, they could either arise in the imagination as phantasms, or they could appear magically to the senses by assuming a physical form – for instance, that of a satyr, centaur or alluring woman (Fig. 12.1). As such, they were independent forces with their own wills, pursuing their own aims, usually in conflict with the rationality of Christian virtue. Above all,

FIGURE 12.1: Michelangelo Buonarroti, *The Torment of Saint Anthony* (after an engraving by Martin Schongauer), 1487–8, tempera and oil on panel, 47 × 34.9 cm. Kimbell Museum of Art, Fort Worth, Texas.

they were *other*; the rational soul was *passive* to them – suffering them, or allowing them, as Christ 'suffered' his 'Passion'. The individual's defence against the passions was virtue. The medieval repertoire of virtues was largely inherited from Plato and St Paul (the 'cardinal' and 'theological' virtues respectively) and the fifth-century Roman Christian poet Prudentius, whose allegorical poem *Psychomachia* (*The Battle of Souls*) described the virtues in combat with their corresponding vices (Fig. 12.2). When not shown in combat, the virtues were usually depicted in personified form as human figures (as in the thirteenth-century *Roman de la Rose*), or symbolically as birds or animals (as in bestiaries). Such images were not intended to inspire emotional responses in their viewers; nor, indeed, were they designed to impart new knowledge. On the contrary, as with so much medieval imagery, they reinforced traditional networks of ideas that had been instilled in their viewers since childhood.

During the Renaissance, attitudes towards emotional experience became more secular. The passions slowly ceased to be associated with demonic influence and were increasingly identified as physiological phenomena, reflecting a more humanist

FIGURE 12.2: 'The Virtues kill Discord', from Prudentius' *Psychomachia* (The Struggle of the Soul), 1120, St Albans, England. British Library, Cotton Titus D. XVI, f.28v.

assessment of the place of the individual in the world. This did not mean, however, that they became any less magical or dependent on sources beyond the control of the individual will, and so they were not yet seen to be functions of a 'self'. On the contrary, the soul was generally seen to be made of an impersonal substance, housed in a particular body; and the passions were interpreted in terms of the impersonal system of 'humours' and temperaments, originally developed by the ancient Greek physicians Hippocrates and Galen, but now being revived. The system maintained that the experience of the passions – and, indeed, all the fundamental inclinations of an individual's character – were determined by the proportion of four substances or humours that were naturally present in the human body. Each humour was associated with a particular element and temperament: blood was airy and sanguine (light-hearted and sociable but indulgent); yellow bile was fiery and choleric (dynamic and motivated but irascible); black bile was earthy and melancholic (profound and creative but depressive); and phlegm was watery and phlegmatic (rational and detached but cold). The balance between these substances was partly established at birth but it was also subject to age and season, and to the movements of the planets (Fig. 12.3). For instance, people born under the influence of Jove (the planet Jupiter)

THE PORTRAYAL OF THE SELF   229

FIGURE 12.3: The Limbourg Brothers, *Zodiac Man* (with the four humours and their characteristics described in the corners in Latin, in red and blue lettering). From the *Très Riches Heures* of Jean Duc de Berry, around 1410. Musée Condé, Chantilly. Photo © RMN-Grand Palais (domaine de Chantilly)/René-Gabriel Ojéda.

were inclined to be sanguine, or *jovial*; those born under Saturn were inclined to be melancholy, or *saturnine*. Despite their apparent objectivity, each humour was also associated with the specific bodily organ in which it originated – the liver, gall bladder, spleen and brain or lungs (each of which was also linked to a planet). A correct balance between the humours could therefore be maintained through a variety of virtuous life-practices, relating to diet, sleep, air and climate, reflecting how people could newly aspire, as embodied individuals, towards an increased degree of personal responsibility for their emotional disposition. The potential for conflict between this approach, which was at least intended to be based on objective evidence, and unquestioning surrender to the inscrutable will of God was realised in the work of the mathematician and astrologer, Girolamo Cardano, who in 1554 attempted to calculate the horoscope of Christ from the time and place of his birth (which was reflected in the stars, as described in the gospels), thereby prompting the Church to accuse him of heresy (Fig. 12.4).[1]

FIGURE 12.4: Girolamo Cardano, The horoscope of Christ from his Commentary on Ptolemy's *Tetrabiblios*, Basel, Henricus Petri, 1554.

Of all the humours, the one that resonated most closely with the emerging sense of self was melancholy. In the Middle Ages, grief was legitimised, and even encouraged, to the extent that it constituted an appropriate response to Christ's suffering; but melancholy was feared because it appeared to be disengaged from the world and was therefore especially vulnerable to demonic manipulation. With such symptoms as depression, despondency, apathy and withdrawal, it was closely related to 'acedia', an affliction that was, significantly, first associated with early Christian monks who became dejected and estranged from their communities; it reflected a primordial impulse towards solitude, perhaps, before mainstream culture was able to accommodate it (Fig. 8.10, right). In the fifteenth century, the persona of the melancholy type began to acquire more positive associations – parallel to, and arguably as a function of, the emergence of the individual self. With the help of the scholarly St Jerome, who was frequently depicted with his head in his hands, contemplating a skull, its reputation shifted from possessed outcast, resistant to grace, to solitary student, plumbing the depths of philosophy. The early stages of this shift were further inspired by the writings of Marsilio Ficino, founder of the Platonic Academy in Florence. Ficino was a leading neo-Platonic philosopher but he was also a trained physician, identifying the introverted but sometimes frenzied withdrawal of melancholics with the solitude of philosophical study. Citing both Plato and Aristotle, Ficino revived the classical notion that creative intelligence and insight are compensation for a melancholic disposition and, conversely, that melancholy is the price of inspiration – a notion that was personified by Dürer in his famous engraving of 1514 (Fig. 12.5). Accordingly, the association of inspiration with melancholy was woven into the very fabric of selfhood, shadowing the idealistic vision of Renaissance man as the perfect microcosm of the Universe. These two attributes – man as microcosm, and man as melancholic – became key elements in the construction of personal identity. On the one hand, the new sense of the independence of the self

FIGURE 12.5: Albrecht Dürer, *Melencolia I*, 1514, engraving, 24 × 18.8 cm. Metropolitan Museum of Art, New York, Harris Brisbane Dick Fund.

gave rise to the humanist concept of the 'dignity of man', at harmony with the world, as celebrated in Pico della Mirandola's *Oration on the Dignity of Man* (1486); on the other, the experience of melancholy accommodated perceptions of man's self-conscious isolation from the whole, and of his fatal inability, from such a position, to attain the perfection he craved.

Although melancholy was widespread in Italy, it was especially well suited to the detached rationality of Protestantism and it therefore thrived in northern Europe, reaching its apogee in Robert Burton's monumental *Anatomy of Melancholy*, first published in 1621 (Fig. 12.6). While the Catholic Church continued to express its faith in the absolute power of the Eucharist, the Protestant churches attempted to stimulate religiosity by more rational means. On the one hand, they replaced the cult veneration of Christ with a more detached consideration of his exemplary virtues, seeking to be inspired and instructed by them; on the other hand, they replaced what they considered to be hysterical dramatisation of the suffering of Christ with intense but sobering remembrance of the inevitability of their own deaths. Reflecting this shift, morbid objects designed to remind the viewer of the transient vanity of life, and to turn their attention to morality and virtue, became common. Emotive images of the Crucifixion were replaced by *memento mori* – visual 'reminders of death'; these images took many forms but, typically, their iconography included snuffed candles, fragile insects, hourglasses, coffins and, above all, skeletons and skulls. But emblems of death were also used to decorate highly fashionable items, using the look of melancholy to enhance the self-sense: a pendant jewel in the form of an enamelled skeleton in a coffin; a watch mounted in a silver skull; a toothpick formed as a sickle held by the ruby-adorned hand of Death. It was through objects of this kind that the rehabilitated status of melancholy was expressed, for many of them are virtuoso luxuries that testify as much to their owners' wit, privilege and vanity as to their religiosity. While the sombre practice of meditating on death and decay represented melancholy as an undesirable but nevertheless virtuous feeling, it was also contrived to *stimulate* the feeling; for, despite its associations with sorrow and piety, the disposition was now seen to reflect emotional sophistication and individuality, subtly enhancing the status of its 'victims' as modish philosophers and poets.

While the intellectual potential of melancholy was epitomised by St Jerome, its poetic potential was epitomised by Michelangelo, who was widely idealised in this role, even by his contemporaries. Raphael, for instance, honoured his rival by using his features for the figure of the classical philosopher Heraclitus in his fresco *The School of Athens* (1509) in the Vatican. The fact that Heraclitus was said to be unable to finish his works due to his melancholy temperament gave Raphael a pretext for representing Michelangelo, who also struggled to finish his works, as a brooding and despondent loner, slouched disconsolately over a block of stone at the base of the composition with his head in his hands (Fig. 12.7). This melancholy posture was traditionally used for the evangelist John in images of the *Crucifixion* where it functioned as a sign, rather than an expression, of his grief (Fig. 3.5, right); but it was otherwise rare until the sixteenth century. It would eventually become a template for the self-image of numerous individuals, mostly men, as reflected in their portraits. Moretto da Brescia's *Portrait of a Young Scholar*, painted in around 1540, provides an early example of the type (Fig. 12.8). The painting depicts a nobleman taking a

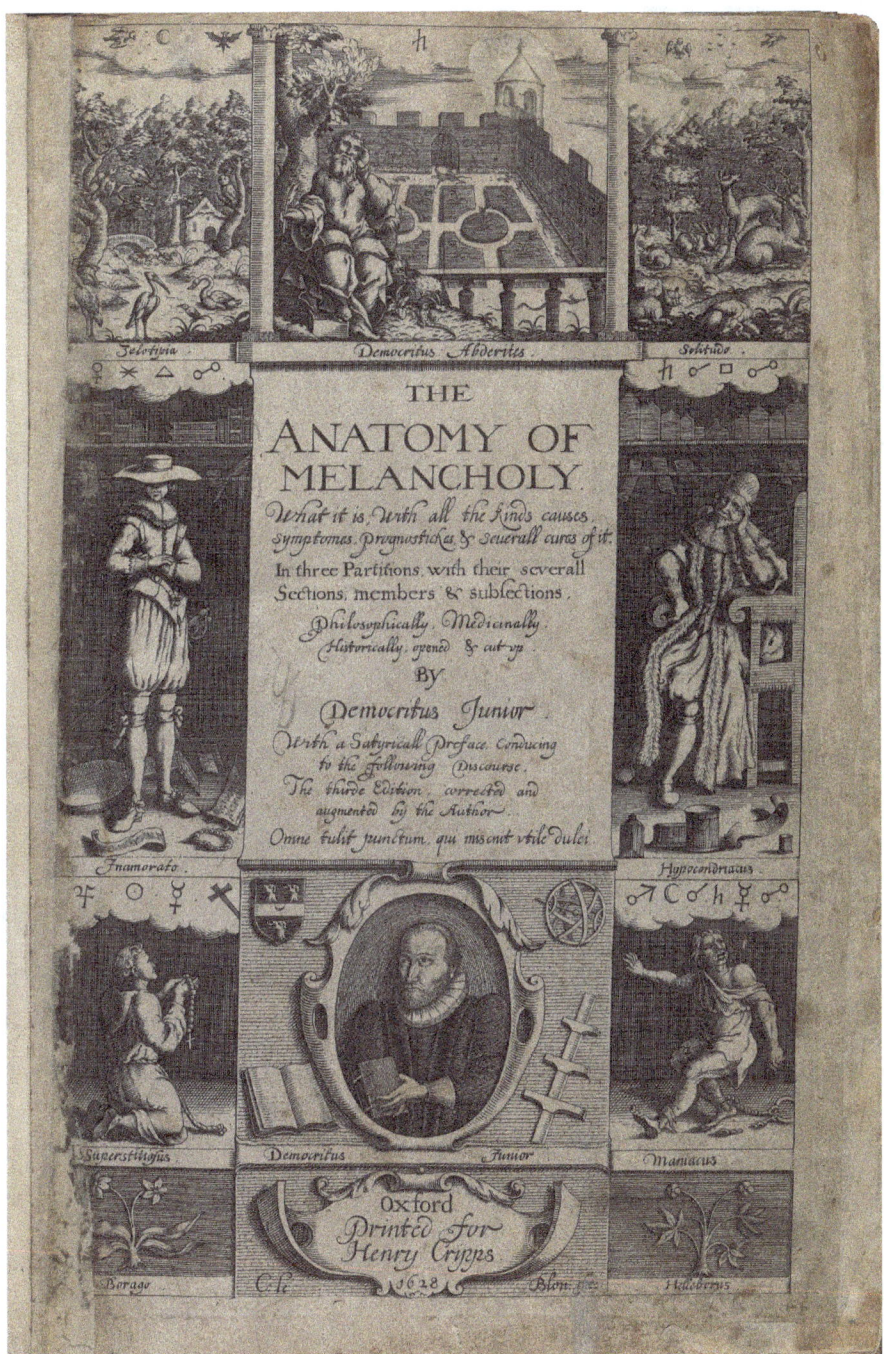

FIGURE 12.6: Robert Burton, *The Anatomy of Melancholy*, 1628 edition. Wellcome Collection.

FIGURE 12.7: Raphael, Michelangelo as Heraclitus, from *The School of Athens*, 1509–11, fresco, the Vatican, Rome.

break from studying his collection of classical antiquities, the attributes of a humanist scholar. While the collection contributes to the sitter's status as a wealthy intellectual, his weary air of resignation suggests that such efforts to classify and rationalise the world are also challenging. Presumably he considered it flattering to be seen in such a state of sophisticated sorrow.

Despite the fashion for melancholy, attempts to express the feeling-dimension of a sitter's character were, nevertheless, rare in the sixteenth century. Sitters for portraits tended to 'sit still', presenting themselves to their viewers as individuals of repute, to be observed. Depicted as timeless statements of static identity – representing a social role or enduring lineage – in which feelings played little part, they were often identified by inscriptions, coats of arms or attributes. Such portraits therefore are both individuated *and* impersonal. Christoph Amberger's portrait of *Matthaus Schwarz*, an accountant working for the Fugger banking family in Augsburg, is a case in point (Fig. 12.9). Staged and unchanging, the sitter's identity is communicated by means of visual 'data' rather than feeling, highlighting the extent to which a socialised persona took precedence over a more psychological sense of self. Significantly, the *raison d'être* of the picture, which was painted in 1542, was Schwarz's ennoblement the previous year. While the glass of wine on the windowsill refers to his family background in the wine trade, his attire – from his expensive but sober clothing to

FIGURE 12.8: Moretto da Brescia, *Portrait of a Young Man (Count Fortunato Martinengo)* – inscribed, in Greek, 'Alas, I desire too much' – 1540, oil on canvas, 114 × 94.4 cm. National Gallery, London.

his dagger and jewellery (which includes a cased toothpick) – documents his rise in fortune. In keeping with his contemporaries, Schwarz projected inordinate significance into his clothing; indeed for forty years he kept a detailed visual record of his life as reflected in the costumes he wore (amounting to 137 annotated illustrations, often dated to a specific year, month and day). Although his interest in dress reflects a high degree of self-consciousness, the fact that dress was regulated by sumptuary laws indicates that it was also interpreted in terms of wealth, status and class; indeed the zealous Philip Stubbes, who considered the appropriate uses of dress in his *Anatomie of Abuses* of 1583, maintained that it was not 'lawfull' for 'priuate subjects' to 'weare silkes, Veluets, Satens, Damaskes, golde, siluer, and what they list . . . except they[,] being in some kind of office in the common wealth, doe use it for the dignifying and innobling of the same'.[2] Similarly, while the inscription in Amberger's painting states that Schwarz was born on 19 February 1497 at 6.30 in the afternoon and that the portrait was painted on March 22 1542 at 4.15 in the afternoon – pinpointing Schwarz's individuality with a precision that was highly

FIGURE 12.9: Christoph Amberger, *Portrait of Mattheus Schwarz*, 1542, oil on panel, 73.5 × 61 cm. Museo Nacional Thyssen-Bornemisza, Madrid. © Fundación Colección Thyssen-Bornemisza, Madrid.

unusual for its time – inclusion of his personal horoscope in the picture indicates that his character is not entirely his own; it is also subject to planetary influences.

While most sixteenth century-sitters of portraits were identified by means of inscriptions, coats of arms and attributes, many of the most elite patrons defined themselves by identifying allegorically with the classical gods whose virtues they claimed to embody. For instance, Diana of Poitiers sought to express her prowess and allure by having herself represented as the goddess Diana. To convey a sense of his universal but multi-faceted nature, Francis I, king of France, was represented as Mercury, Mars, Diana, Amour and Mercury all conflated together into a single androgynous image (Fig. 12.10). In the present context, the significance of these portrayals is the way in which individuals identified themselves not through the expression of personal temperament but by association with *classical precedents*, which conferred magnificence and divinity on them, and *ideas*, to be interpreted in keeping with an external code. Towards the end of the seventeenth century, the use of allegorical imagery began to decline in favour of more direct, literal modes of representation. Even Louis XIV, who used the rhetorical power of allegory to mythologise himself throughout his reign (Fig. 12.11), contributed towards this

THE PORTRAYAL OF THE SELF 237

FIGURE 12.10: Attributed to Nicolo dell'Abbate, *Mythological image of François I combining the attributes of Minerva, Mars, Mercury and Diana*. Parchment pasted on panel, around 1545. Bibliothèque nationale de France.

change. The king had originally wanted the ceiling of the Hall of Mirrors at Versailles, painted by Charles Le Brun between 1678 and 1684, to be decorated with allegorical representations of himself – first as the sun-god Apollo, and later as Hercules – but he eventually opted for a scheme that depicted his actual historical triumphs; that is to say, a scheme that showed him *as himself*, in a more personal, but no less glorious, capacity, albeit surrounded by personifications of peace and abundance (Fig. 12.12). In this respect, he began to embody the qualities that were traditionally appropriated from external sources *in and as himself*. Moreover, as we have seen, during the final phase of building at the palace, which began in 1699, he famously requested that the menagerie be built in a more 'youthful' style, clearly condoning a movement away from the formal, impressive style that characterises the rest of the building towards a style that was more relaxed, intimate and *felt*.[3]

This relaxation of the dependence on classical precedents, upheld as an external, objective source of value, was directly related to the legitimisation of personal feeling

FIGURE 12.11: Charles Poerson (attributed to), *Louis XIV as Jupiter, defeating the Fronde*, 1648–67. Palais de Versailles. Photo © RMN-Grand Palais (Château de Versailles)/Gérard Blot.

as an internal, subjective one. The conflict between these two agendas was initially an academic issue, originating at the French Academy in the late 1650s. Were classical precedents always superior to modern developments, or could innovations also be of value? The chief concerns of the Academy were to promote the dignity of the French language over Latin – should inscriptions on public monuments be in Latin or French? – and to improve the quality of contemporary French literature. Eminent writers, including Racine, Molière and La Fontaine, extolled the virtues of classical literature, advocating that contemporary writers subject themselves to ancient precedents which, they claimed, represented the pinnacle of good taste. This view was challenged by a group of writers, including Charles Perrault and Bernard de Fontanelle, who were keen to become free of subservience to traditional authority, which in their view had become formulaic and pretentious, and to celebrate the independent virtues of contemporary French culture. Thus began the famous 'Quarrel between the Ancients and the Moderns' in which writers from the past and

FIGURE 12.12: Charles Le Brun, *Louis XIV rules alone*, 1661, Château de Versailles. Photo © Château de Versailles, Dist. RMN-Grand Palais/Jean-Marc Manaï.

present were pitted against each other in a battle of words which lasted for over three decades. While the supporters of the ancients maintained that the likes of Plato, Aristotle, Homer and Cicero could not be surpassed, the modernists claimed that, although ancient literature was indeed great, the accumulation of scientific knowledge and philosophical understanding over the previous two millennia had advanced human culture to an even higher level of achievement, worthy of the gracious rule of Louis XIV. Indeed, Perrault claimed that the moderns understood more about the human mind and passions than the ancients, thereby paving the way for a time in which the expression of feeling would no longer depend on the legitimising narratives of classical mythology (and, as we have seen, Pierre Daniel Huet had reservations about the gods' manners). In his *Parallel between the Ancients and Moderns regarding the arts and sciences* (1693), Perrault wrote: 'In the tragedies of Corneille alone there are more delicate thoughts on ambition, vengeance and jealousy than there are in all the books of antiquity.'[4]

With these words, Perrault was reflecting the impact of Descartes' treatise *The Passions of the Soul* (1649), in which the philosopher attempted to explain how the passions – today's 'emotions' – are merely physiological functions of the soul, unconnected to any pre-existent religious principle. In contrast to his predecessors – for instance, Thomas Wright, whose *Passions of the Minde* was thoroughly moralising – Descartes made a point of stating that he was writing as a detached 'physicist' (*physicien*) rather than a 'moral philosopher'. He claimed that corporeal perceptions and sensations were registered in the body, which he conceived as a mechanical automaton, and transmitted via 'animal spirits' in the blood to the immaterial soul that was linked to the body via the pineal gland in the brain. The soul received the animal spirits passively and involuntarily (just as the medieval soul had been menaced by demons), and responded by transmitting signals to the muscles. The 'actions' of the soul, which complemented its 'passions', were manifest as the will, which Descartes considered to be its most noble and rational function. The importance of *The Passions of the Soul* lies in the way it liberated the realm of feeling from the preconceived contexts of classical and Christian meaning, and the vested interests of those who controlled them, and re-identified it as an independent function of the self which Descartes himself had taken such pains to identify as an autonomous principle. Significantly, he opened the treatise by dissociating from the classical tradition:

> The defectiveness of the sciences we inherit from the ancients is nowhere more apparent than in what they wrote about the Passions. For even though this is a topic about which knowledge has always been vigorously sought, and though it does not seem to be one of the most difficult – because as everyone feels them in himself, one need not borrow any observation from elsewhere to discover their nature – nevertheless what the Ancients taught about them is so little, and for the most part so little believable, that I cannot hope to approach the truth unless I forsake the paths they followed. For this reason I shall be obliged to write here as though I were treating a topic which no one before me had ever described.[5]

As he said himself, Descartes' originality lay in the fact that he ceased to rely on classical sources for insights into the nature of the passions but began to look into experience itself, developing an understanding of how the passions worked that was entirely based on evidence. Having presented a general consideration of the way in which the body and soul interact with each other and how the passions, stimulated by bodily impressions, are excited in the soul, *The Passions of the Soul* outlines what Descartes considered to be the six basic 'primitive' passions – wonder, love, hatred, desire, joy and sadness – and their external signs, principally 'actions of the eyes and face, changes in colour, trembling, languor, fainting, laughing, tears, groans and sighs'.[6] In the final section of the treatise, Descartes enumerated the secondary passions, which are variations and mixtures of the six primitive passions; these include hope, scorn, humility, pride, respect, jealousy, fear, anger and many others.

The Passions of the Soul analysed the various passions, describing their constituent parts and relationships, and established a vocabulary with which to realise and describe the entire realm of emotional experience. The subtle shades of difference that it articulated are significant; for instance the word 'passion', signifying the soul's passivity to external agency, was increasingly supplemented by 'emotion', reflecting the active 'moving outwards' or *ex*-pression of the soul, especially as registered in the body; the soul became the *seat* or *source*, rather than *victim*, of feeling. But of equal, if not greater, significance is the fact that it contributed towards the creation of a discourse in which the independent experience of emotion could be realised at all, without being subjected to a preconceived system of values or moral code. With regard to painting, the inadequacy of classical precedents made it newly important to study the physiology of human expression on its own terms and thereby to understand the laws that determined the way people appeared when they were feeling emotions. Although several earlier painters had made detailed observations of expressions of emotion (e.g. van Eyck, van der Weyden) and some had made studies of facial types (Dürer, Leonardo), no one had attempted a comprehensive systematisation of the way in which the passions were directly linked to a range of physiological responses. This task fell to Charles Le Brun, 'First Painter' to Louis XIV, who created a 'vocabulary of facial expressions', specifically for the benefit of artists; it remained a key resource for French masters of dramatic painting well into the eighteenth century.

Le Brun, who became director of Royal Academy of Painting and Sculpture in 1664, was a staunch classicist. However, although he promoted the ideal of history painting over all other genres (portraiture, landscape and still life) and espoused a grand rhetorical manner, as in the ceiling of the Hall of Mirrors at Versailles, he also stressed the importance of emotional realism (albeit in the context of history painting) and spent much time researching the effect of emotional experience on facial expression with a view to depicting it convincingly. Characteristically, his research was rooted in observations of classical portrait busts and the classical sentiments they seemed to convey, as well as the resemblance of human expressions to the apparent expressions of animals which were traditionally associated with their perceived dispositions – for instance, lions with courage and oxen with bullishness (Fig. 12.13). But Le Brun also studied the human face and eyes 'from nature', describing their various contortions, and the passions that corresponded to them, in the minutest detail. Led to believe, by Descartes' *Passions of the Soul*, that the soul was located in the pineal gland, he reasoned that the face and especially the eyebrows (the facial features closest to the brain) were the first, and most revealing, part of the body to react to the passions that were excited there (Fig. 12.14). In the case of gentle passions, the eyebrows would rise up 'towards' the brain; in the case of violent ones, they would 'descend' towards the heart (Fig. 12.15). Le Brun presented the conclusions to his research, undertaken over many years, at a lecture at the Academy in 1668. Numerous drawings of individual facial expressions, and systematic tables of studies of the eyes and eyebrows of men and animals in a variety of expressive states, were produced for the occasion (Fig. 12.16).

Although it offered many insights, Le Brun's system was criticised from the outset for being too simplistic and formulaic. It failed to take into account how, despite its apparently rational and physiological basis, the expression of emotion is subject to infinite circumstantial conditions such as age, facial type and social background, and is therefore impossible to classify definitively. Even so, partly because his lecture was published more widely than any of the arguments that challenged it, it remained influential in France for over a hundred years. Its importance lay, above all, in the fact that it generated a discourse in which the physiological expression of emotion

FIGURE 12.13: *Three perspectives on the head of an ox and three on the head of an ox-like man, showing the physiognomical relations between certain of the species.* Etching, around 1820, after Charles Le Brun. Wellcome Collection.

came to be discussed not only as a means for serving the ideals of history painting but for its own sake; and, in this respect, it made a fundamental contribution towards the provision of an independent language of emotion, and towards the formation of the self-sense that this language accommodated.

Although it was not fully theorised until the middle of the seventeenth century, the expression of personal feeling – and the spontaneity it presupposes – was first included in portraits *for its own sake* at the end of the sixteenth century. This development was evident in Italy (for instance in the portraits of Annibale Carracci) but it was especially widespread in the northern Netherlands where confederate, rather than courtly, patterns of patronage emerged at a relatively early date. This unique and precocious state of affairs took root in 1581 when Protestants, reacting against persecution from the Catholic Hapsburgs who ruled over them, formed an independent 'Republic of United Provinces' – at a time when other European domains were ruled by centralised monarchies. The absence of a royal court and the diminished power of the ecclesiastical hierarchy (resulting from the qualified value that Protestants ascribed to the Eucharist) were reflected in a lack of high cultural patronage by the state and the Church in this region. This gap was filled by a professional, secular elite which, like traditional elites,

THE PORTRAYAL OF THE SELF 243

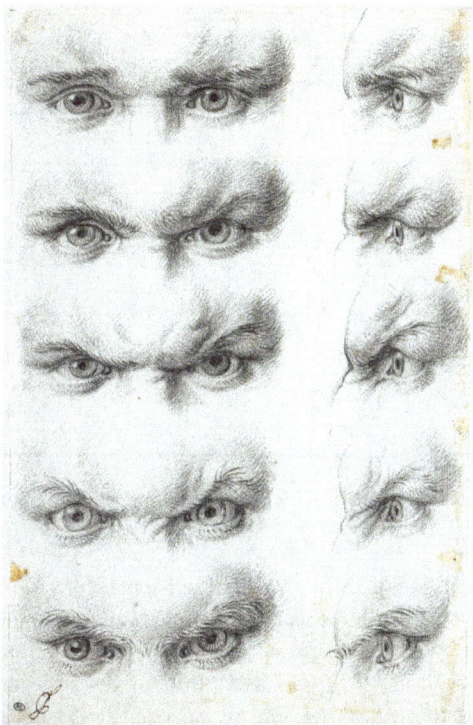

FIGURE 12.14: Charles Le Brun, *Studies of Human Eyes*, around 1690. Musée du Louvre, Paris. Photo © RMN-Grand Palais (Musée du Louvre)/Michel Urtado.

FIGURE 12.15: Bernard Picart, Two faces, one expressing extreme despair (left), the other expressing anger mixed with rage (right). Etching after Charles Le Brun, 1713. Wellcome Collection.

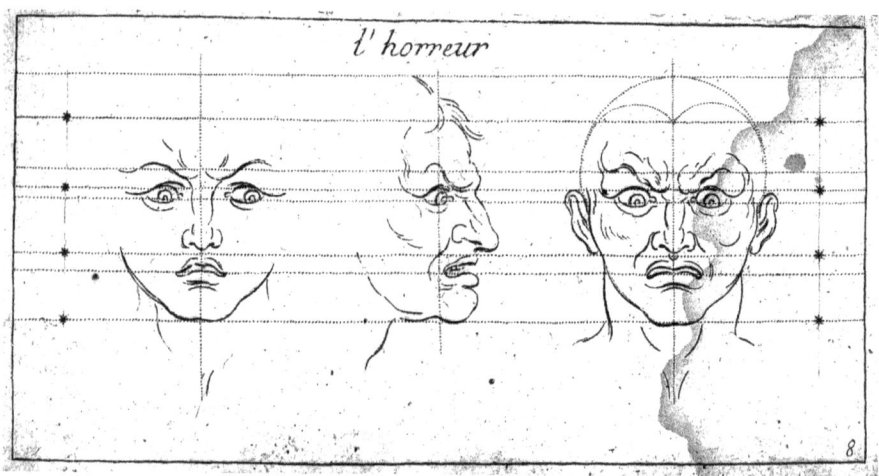

FIGURE 12.16: Charles Le Brun, a plate (horror) from a study of human emotions. Wellcome Collection.

sought to consolidate its status through acts of self-representation – though, unlike the Church and court, it aimed to do this more on the basis of personal integrity than of ritual compliance or inherited status. The Protestants' reaction against what they believed to be the Catholic Church's ascription of a quasi-magical power to the Eucharist, enabling it to cleanse the soul of sin regardless of the individual's actual moral orientation, led them to highlight the moral rather than sacramental significance of daily life and work, and to attach moral value to the fruits of honest industry. In line with this way of thinking, many Christian holy days had been abolished at the time of the Reformation on the grounds that they were not only superstitious but reduced the work time of the faithful, thereby diminishing their productivity, profits and well-being. This change of attitude towards commercial activity not only inspired people to work hard, increase their earnings and raise their standard of living. It also invested professional affluence with moral value that legitimised both the political power associated with it, and the associated process of self-substantiation through art patronage.

The shift of legitimacy away from inherited authority towards a more personal and meritocratic embodiment of identity is reflected in contemporary portraiture which, because it was often patronised by self-made merchants and dignitaries rather than aristocrats, became increasingly focused around the personality of the sitter, in tacit recognition of their individual 'selfhood', rather than the impersonal, formal communication of status which had been the priority of Renaissance patrons. What had previously been seen as a pioneering sign of individuality – the mere act of depicting an individual – now seemed remarkably *impersonal*. As a result, the formal and contrived poses of traditional portraits – which had the effect of homogenising them – were frequently abandoned, increasing the impression of sitters' spontaneous and relaxed engagement with the viewer. Characteristically, the Dutch painter Peter Lely (who spent most of his career in England) was especially respected for his ability to capture the 'minde' of his sitters without having to resort to crude signifiers of personal qualities, such as tears, and 'hieroglyphic' symbols. As the English poet Richard Lovelace said of him, in around 1647:

> Not as of old, when a rough hand did speake
> A strong Aspect, and a faire face, a weake;
> When only a black beard cried Villaine, and
> By *Hieroglyphicks* we could understand;
> When Crystall typified in a white spot,
> And the bright Ruby was but one red blot;
> Thou [Lely] dost the things *Orientally* the same,
> Not only paintst its colour, but its *Flame*:
> Thou sorrow canst designe without a teare,
> And with the Man his very *Hope* or Feare;
> So that th'amazed world shall henceforth finde
> None but my *Lilly* [Lely] ever drew a *Minde*.[7]

Because expressions of emotion are fleeting, painters of portraits that aimed to capture them maximised the sense of *momentariness* in their work by using a number of secondary devices, apart from the actual facial expressions of their sitters. In some cases (for instance, the work of Godfried Schalcken) a single candle was used as a light source not only because it intensifies the contrast between light and shade, but because it is highly mobile – such that the scenes it lights can only be moment-specific (Fig. 12.17) –

FIGURE 12.17: Godfried Schalcken, *Willem III, Prince of Orange, King of England and Stadtholder*, around 1692–7, oil on canvas, 76.5 × 65 cm. Rijksmuseum, Amsterdam.

in contrast to the even, diffused and enduring light of most Renaissance portraits (Fig. 12.9). For the same reason, sitters were frequently shown in poses that cannot be sustained over time – exuberantly gesticulating, drinking or making music, or tipping their chair back on its back legs. In this way, the amount of time that the sitter was seen to occupy was reduced to an instant. The conceit is present in innumerable portraits of the period. In Jan de Bray's group portrait of *Regents of the Children's Almshouse in Haarlem* (1663), the six regents are thoroughly respectable but they are shown without airs and graces (Fig. 12.18). Despite being established and authoritative, the fact that two of the regents are gesticulating with their hands, that one of them appears to have looked up from his writing and that two of them have turned round, somewhat uncomfortably, to look at the viewer over the backs of their chairs – as if interrupting themselves briefly for a quick photograph – gives a strong impression of the transience of the moment; this in turn conveys a sense of the spontaneity and authenticity of the sentiments (and sense of identity) that are expressed in it. Moreover, each of the regents makes eye contact with the viewer, entering into a contract of mutual recognition and acknowledgement with him – an impression that is intensified by the absence of background distractions. There is no respite for the viewer; in each face, he sees himself instantly but momentarily reflected and necessitated.

While portraits of elite Republican patrons became increasingly relaxed and spontaneous, showing little concern for titles and coats of arms, they continued to be at least slightly flattering, discreetly taking pains to preserve the composure and dignity of their sitters. It was only with lowly, insignificant people, such as musicians,

FIGURE 12.18: Jan Salomonsz de Bray, *The Regents of the Children's Almshouse in Haarlem*, 1663, oil on canvas, 186 × 250 cm. Frans Hals Museum, Haarlem. Photo: Tom Haartsen.

drinkers and buffoons, who had little dignity or status to lose, that the impulse to capture and validate the experience of momentary feeling, regardless of the loss of composure that it might involve, became totally unrestrained (Fig. 12.19). In such carefree circumstances, sitters were frequently shown smiling and even laughing. The transient experience of laughter, which is notoriously difficult to capture in painting without being made to resemble a grimace, was traditionally associated with loss of rational self-restraint and dignity. Indeed, courtesy books frequently stated that laughter should be strictly controlled, if not eliminated altogether from honourable behaviour. During the Middle Ages, it was debated whether Christ himself could have *ever* laughed, reflecting concern for his dignity.

In order to explore the look and language of personal presence in even more depth, many artists used themselves as models for painting, capitalising on the growing availability of mirrors. This was not only cost-free and time-efficient; as with unimportant models, artists that painted themselves were also free from any obligation to flatter or dignify the sitter, allowing them to experiment with facial expressions. Rembrandt, for instance, painted over sixty portraits of himself, not to mention prints and drawings, in a variety of emotional states (Fig. 12.20). Reflecting the potential use of self-portraits as studies for the expression of emotion in history

FIGURE 12.19: Judith Leyster, *The Jolly Drinker*, 1629, oil on canvas, 89 × 85 cm. Rijksmuseum, Amsterdam.

FIGURE 12.20: Rembrandt Harmenszoon van Rijn, *Self-portrait with beret, wide-eyed*, 1630, etching, 50 × 45 mm. Rijksmuseum, Amsterdam.

painting, one of Rembrandt's students, Samuel van Hoogstraten – probably under the influence of his master – recommended to his own students that they imagine and express the feelings of the historical characters under consideration while observing themselves in the mirror: 'If one wants to gain honour in this noblest area of art [history painting], one must transform oneself wholly into an actor . . . [you will] benefit from acting out the passions you have in mind, chiefly in front of a mirror, so as to be actor and spectator at the same time.'[8]

The shift in the focus of portraiture in the seventeenth century was significant because it gave rise to a convention in which *spontaneous feeling* came to be seen as culturally legitimate, both in principle and in experience. On the one hand, by representing the experience of emotion in works of art, artists elevated the subject of emotion to the level of cultural currency, investing it, in a general sense, with cultural value. On the other hand, by engaging with such works, viewers were invited to enter into an experience that presupposed and legitimised their *own* emotional involvement – not in a generally idealised and timeless capacity, as with formal Renaissance portraits which aimed to 'transcend time' – but only in the very moment in which the encounter with the sitter was presumed to be happening – that is to say, in the very moment in which the viewer's glance meets the fleeting glance of the sitter. Contemporary awareness of the significance of this experience is reflected in the fact that Hoogstraten felt the need both to coin a new word for it – *oogenblikkig* ('eye-glancing') – and to discuss it in his *Introduction to the Academy of Painting* (1678).[9] The logic of such works – their pretension to capture a moment and *only* a moment – required the viewer to experience them in a very particular way, manoeuvring him or her into a state of *instantaneous presence*. It only makes sense to see such works in passing (again and again if necessary); under sustained scrutiny, they can easily seem artificial and unrealistic. By adapting to this new way of engaging with a picture, the viewer was tacitly enabled, expected and empowered to become a spontaneous and 'feeling' being, in the present moment, without having to account for himself in relation to a preconceived legitimising standard. Moreover, it is surely no accident that the new ability to find cultural value in the experience of a fleeting moment evolved at exactly the same period as the balance-spring and pendulum – new devices in watches and clocks that enabled the temporal unit of the 'moment', or 'second', to be accurately measured, and therefore meaningful, for the first time. The significance of this new valorisation of the 'moment' was that it focused attention on the fractional unit of time which a spontaneous feeling needs in order to arise in consciousness and be experienced completely. As such it is rooted in *present consciousness*, and presupposes a self-sense that is realised in the experience of present consciousness – in contrast to an unchanging 'persona', represented by an enduring image, mask or pose that is only known by memory and expectation in extended time.

Self-portraits did not only provide artists with a medium through which to experiment with new experiences and expressions of feeling. They also became a means through which viewers of art could process their own capacity for self-awareness, as if the experience of looking at a self-portrait – that is to say, 'looking at a person who is looking at themselves' – could become a template for looking at oneself and becoming conscious of oneself. In Johannes Gumpp's *Self-Portrait* of 1646 (Fig. 12.21), the equation of the 'artist seeing himself' with the 'viewer seeing herself' is explicit, to the point at which their self-awareness becomes one (rather as God's vision of man and man's vision of God become one in Nicholas of Cusa's *Vision of God*, discussed in chapter 5). Most self-portraits can only be *known* to be 'of the artist' on the basis of secondary information we have about them; without documentary evidence, suggestive attributes or knowledge of the artist's appearance, it is impossible to tell whether a given portrait is 'of the artist' or 'of another person'. The status of Gumpp's self-portrait, however, is explicit, and the identification of the artist's self-awareness with that of the viewer is therefore self-evident; for, firstly, the viewer can *see* that the sitter, seen in the painting on the right, is the artist (who has his back to us); and, secondly, she can *see* that what that sitter sees, *even when he is 'seen to be seeing himself'*, is the viewer, because he is *looking at the viewer*; he is looking at himself and at the viewer in the same act of looking. Conversely because the viewer is *explicitly* seeing the artist 'as he (the artist) sees himself', it is as if she – by virtue of the act of seeing him in this way – *becomes* the artist, and is made to participate in, and identify with, his state of self-awareness. Not only, therefore, is the

FIGURE 12.21: Johannes Gumpp, *Self-portrait*, 1646, oil on canvas, 88.5 × 89.0 cm. Uffizi Gallery, Florence.

presence of the viewer necessitated by the image, because a figure in the picture makes eye contact with the viewer; but, her *self-awareness* is necessitated by it too, because it explicitly shows a person who is looking at '*a person looking at themselves*'. Indeed to the extent that the *act* of seeing the picture becomes an expression of the self-awareness of the viewer, it is also a kind of *self-portrait of the viewer*.

Gumpp's *Self-Portrait* forms part of the pioneering collection of self-portraits (from the fifteenth century until his own day) that Cardinal Leopoldo de Medici began to assemble in 1664 and which is still housed in the Uffizi Gallery in Florence (Fig. 12.22). Leopoldo had already assembled a *kunstkammer* which subjected the contents of the world – represented by the encyclopaedic range of his collection – to the capacity of his own understanding, by classifying his collection according to a principle of his own devising. In this way, he turned his possessions into the constituent parts of a self-portrait, typically – by virtue of the rarity and diversity of the objects, and the rationality of the relationships between them – reflecting his own perceived universality and rationality. But by forming a collection of self-portraits, Leopoldo reconfigured the self-awareness of *other* individuals into an expression of his *own* interests and experience (clearly communicated through the sculpted portrait of himself that he had placed at the centre of the display). Rather than simply seeking the universal rationality of his own mind in his collection,

FIGURE 12.22: Giuseppe Sacconi, *Cardinal Leopoldo de Medici's collection of self-portraits installed in the Uffizi Galleries*, 1753–65. Austrian National Library, Vienna.

Leopoldo also sought (and reflected) his *capacity for self-awareness*. Indeed by adding a new dimension of awareness to the self-awareness that is already present in self-portraits, his collection instituted the moment of self-reference even more absolutely than an individual self-portrait or private collection, because it conflated the two; it reflected not just his self-awareness but his *awareness of his self-awareness*. Whereas painted self-portraits, on the one hand, and private collections, on the other, represent independent manifestations of self-consciousness, on the part of the particular artists or collectors behind them, Leopoldo's collection of self-portraits amounted to the 'best of both worlds'. Like Gumpp's *Self-Portrait*, it constituted a self-conscious meditation on the state of self-consciousness, realising it explicitly and making it available therefore to all who engaged with it. As Descartes had proclaimed: the conditions of identity were no longer set by external circumstances; they were set by personal self-awareness.

CHAPTER THIRTEEN

The Enjoyment of the Self: Sexuality and the Valorisation of Meaningless Pleasure

Despite Descartes' declaration that personal identity is a self-evident function of consciousness, it was not until the mid-eighteenth century that the notion of the 'autonomous self' became established as a convention, independent of extraneous meanings and moral obligations. This liberation coincided with the development of a new source of value that resided not only in the subject of experience (the mind, where Descartes found it) but also in the texture of experience. Its outward sign, and apparent proof, was cultural forms that accommodated the *enjoyment* of experience – or *pleasure* – for its own sake.

The commodification of pleasure was most clearly reflected in new attitudes towards sexuality. Believing the body to be innately corrupt, medieval authorities had been highly suspicious of sexuality. Sexual intercourse for any reason other than procreation was considered to be sinful – especially if it occurred outside marriage. Masturbation was one of the devil's tools; demons fashioned their bodies from wasted semen.[1] Even within marriage, sexual pleasure was dangerous. According to one thirteenth-century source, sex with one's own spouse was adulterous if one enjoyed it too much.[2] But at the beginning of the sixteenth century, attitudes towards sexuality began to change, and signs of an interest in sex as a source of pleasure began to appear. While the identification and characterisation of erotic passions, such as lust, lasciviousness and cupidity, were achieved through symbolism and allegory (Fig. 13.1), the actual *expression* of these feelings was achieved through dramatisation. These first steps were taken with some hesitation. Until the self-sense was sufficiently evolved to realise the experience of passion as its own, it projected it outside of itself – firstly, into images of saints in religious ecstasy, and secondly, into prescribed narratives, through which viewers could experience it vicariously and rehearse their anxiety about it. In the sixteenth and seventeenth centuries, these prescribed narratives were derived from Christianity, history and pagan mythology, in which the structures of dramatic experience already existed and which were already legitimised by their religious or intellectual associations.

FIGURE 13.1: Cesare Ripa, *Lussuria* (lust), *Iconologia*, 1625.

It is ironic that although the Church policed the morality of contemporary culture – insisting, for instance, in 1563 that the genitals of the numerous nudes in Michelangelo's monumental *Last Judgement* in the Sistine Chapel be painted over – its imagery also provided considerable scope for the processing of erotic fantasy. This ironic situation was to some extent a continuation of the medieval tradition in which highly exaggerated images of Christ's suffering were produced to induce responses of contrition in their viewers; but it was intensified after the Reformation, when the Catholic Church lost large numbers of its fold to Protestantism. Following this crisis, both religious persuasions acknowledged a greater sense of individuality among their members; but whereas the Protestants appealed to the individual's capacity for thinking, promoting a rationalised approach to Christianity and dismissing relics and sacred images as superstitious cult objects, the Catholic Church appealed to the individual's capacity for feeling, encouraging him or her to visualise the lives of Christ, the Virgin and the saints and to respond to them with 'real' emotion. To this end, it positively promoted the use of images as aids to meditation, specifically developing and exploiting their affective potential.

Of all the texts that advised readers to make use of images in their visualisations of Christ's suffering, the most widely read was the *Spiritual Exercises* of Ignatius Loyola, written in 1522–4 and printed in 1548. Reacting against humanist rationalism by reviving the pious practices of the late Middle Ages, this devotional manual encouraged its readers to rehearse the minutest physical details of the daily life of Christ in their imaginations to ensure the maximum authenticity in their responses. Especially in Catholic Spain and Italy, highly dramatic pictures of saints in states of ecstatic response to visions of Christ became common – albeit painted in the newly illusionistic styles of the time. These paintings operate on two levels. Firstly, they provide the viewer with an image of a sacred event – for instance, a vision of Christ – to which to respond; and secondly, by including an image of an ecstatic and emotional saint, or soul, in the picture, they strongly suggest to the viewer how he or she should respond to it. In Velázquez's *Flagellated Christ Contemplated by a Christian Soul* (1628–9), the instructive aspect of the picture is emphasised by the presence of an angel who is clearly guiding the contrite soul (and implicitly, the viewer) in his or her devotions, somewhat at the expense of its own attentiveness to Christ's suffering (Fig. 13.2). Excruciating paintings of the martyrdom of saints also proliferated. However, although such pictures were conceived to inspire zeal and contrition in their viewers, some of them show saints in heightened states of exhaustion that surely stimulated masochistic and erotic fantasies. Saint Sebastian, whose martyrdom offered more scope for representing an almost naked man in a state of rapture than any other Christian figure apart from the wounded Christ, was especially popular from the end of the fifteenth century onwards (Fig. 13.3). The saint was typically shown in a state of ecstatic absorption in God while being pierced by the arrows of his torturers. A painting of the scene by Fra Bartolommeo (1472–1517) was allegedly removed from its original place in the chapel of a convent because it inspired corrupt thoughts in those who saw it. In the seventeenth century, the potential of devotional art to function as a medium for the expression of erotic feeling continued unabated. Louis Cousin's *St Catherine of Siena Drinking from the Wound in Christ's Side* of around 1648 is a case in point (Fig. 13.4). Bernini's famous sculptures of *St Theresa in Ecstasy* (1652) and *The Blessed Ludovica Albertoni* (1671–4) are equally suggestive (Fig. 13.5). All of these images show a woman in a state of blissful fusion with the divine that borders on orgasmic abandon. Bernini's *St Theresa*, in Santa Maria della Vittoria in Rome, is based on a passage from the autobiography of St Theresa of Avila (1515–82), in which the saint, like St Sebastian, is ecstatically pierced by an arrow, albeit in a rather different circumstance (which, in this case, invites the viewer to identify with the Annunciate Virgin and Crucified Christ simultaneously). Referring to an angel of God that materialised to her:

> I saw in his hand a long spear of gold, and at the iron's point there seemed to be a little fire. He appeared to me to be thrusting it at times into my heart, and to pierce my very entrails; when he drew it out, he seemed to draw them out also,

FIGURE 13.2: Diego Velázquez, *The Flagellated Christ Contemplated by a Christian Soul*, around 1630, oil on canvas, 165 × 206 cm. National Gallery, London.

and to leave me all on fire with a great love of God. The pain was so great, that it made me moan; and yet so surpassing was the sweetness of this excessive pain, that I could not wish to be rid of it.[3]

Even when the monopoly that Christianity held over the medieval imagination began to weaken, and secular values became more accepted, the tendency to use preconceived narratives as media through which to experience and express erotic feeling continued to prevail. In the sixteenth century, Christian narratives were increasingly supplemented by narratives from classical mythology, vastly increasing the range of experiences available to viewers. But for many years, even these mythological narratives were justified on the basis of their Christian potential. In the fourteenth century, for instance, Ovid's *Metamorphoses* – the key source of classical myths throughout the Middle Ages and Renaissance – was rewritten as a moralising allegory of Christian doctrine, despite the fact that it consists largely of amatory tales of the classical gods which pre-date Christianity. In the following century, however, as humanist philosophers endeavoured to consolidate the status of antiquity as a golden age, classical myths were increasingly allegorised on their own terms, without a Christian explanation. For instance, Botticelli's famous *Birth of Venus* (1486) is widely held to present an elaborate allegory of the progress of the soul, symbolised

FIGURE 13.3: Follower of Sodoma, *Saint Sebastian*, early–mid sixteenth century, pen and brown ink with brown wash over black chalk, 26.4 × 18.4 cm. Metropolitan Museum of Art, New York, Robert Lehman Collection.

by Venus, the goddess of love, through the mundane realm of life on earth (Fig. 13.6). Its uncompromising presentation of nudity on such a large scale was unprecedented and, had it not been hidden from public view in a private bedchamber, would have been highly controversial; indeed, in 1497 Botticelli himself was said to have been roused by the reactionary preacher Savonarola to burn some of his earlier pagan works on the grounds that they were immoral. Having said this, despite its suggestive allure, the *Birth of Venus* is – like the Christian art of the period – a moralising, doctrinal image, probably representing a neo-Platonic theory inspired by the humanist philosopher Marsilio Ficino, who was tutor to Lorenzo de Medici when Lorenzo commissioned the painting. Thus, although it undoubtedly adds to her charm, the nakedness of Venus is not primarily intended to be erotic; on the contrary, it is symbolic of the goddess's purity.[4] Significantly, in the same artist's *Calumny of Apelles* (1495) which, broadly speaking, depicts a conflict between

THE ENJOYMENT OF THE SELF 257

FIGURE 13.4: Louis Cousin (called Il Primo, or Il Gentile), *St Catherine of Siena Drinking from Christ's Wound*, around 1648, oil on lapis lazuli, 23 × 27.3 cm. Private Collection.

FIGURE 13.5: Gian Lorenzo Bernini, *Ecstasy of Saint Theresa*, 1647–52, marble, life-size. Santa Maria della Vittoria, Rome.

FIGURE 13.6: Sandro Botticelli, *The Birth of Venus*, 1484–6, tempera on canvas, 172 × 278 cm. Uffizi Gallery, Florence.

virtue and vice, only the personifications of virtue (Innocence and Truth) are shown naked; the same association was surely to be seen in the precocious sculptor Donatello's naked *David*, from around 1450. In the sixteenth century, the association of nakedness with innocence and purity, rather than sexuality, was sufficiently strong to inspire several elite women to have themselves portrayed naked. The mistress of Henry II of France, Diane of Poitiers (1499–1556), was frequently depicted as Diana, goddess of hunting and chastity, to show her prowess and honour; but she was sometimes shown naked (hunting or bathing like Diana) to indicate these additional virtues. Similarly, Gabrielle d'Estrées (1573–99), mistress of Henry IV of France, was depicted bare-breasted in her bath (sometimes with one of her sisters). Pregnant with the child of the king, her nakedness was a sign of her nubility, fecundity and honourable maternity.

In the sixteenth century, the role of classical imagery began to change. As secular knowledge and experience became more acceptable, people became more conscious of their feelings, expressing them in the cultural language of the time, which they adapted to their own needs. Just as the increased devotion to Christ's Passion had enabled late medieval society to process its own suffering by projecting it on to Christ and experiencing it through him, so the amorous and violent adventures of the classical gods provided sixteenth-century viewers of art with a range of increasingly legitimised cultural forms, justified on account of their intellectual associations, through which to experience secular emotions. Above all, nudity became more explicitly charged with erotic potential. Venus, the goddess of love, provided the most obvious excuse for representations of nudity and she was often painted at her *toilette*, by Cranach, Giorgione, Titian, Rubens and Velázquez among others; but she was not alone. The vice of Vanity, for instance, was often personified as a naked woman (looking at herself seductively in a mirror, sometimes accompanied by a skeleton); this image was justified on the grounds that it was teaching a moral lesson.[5] In 1545, Cardinal Alessandro Farnese commissioned Titian to paint a picture of the mythological figure Danae in the throngs of being seduced, giving her the facial features of his mistress (Fig. 13.7).[6] According to various classical sources, the childless Danae was imprisoned in a cave by her father, who had been told by an oracle that he would be killed by his grandson. She was left with nothing but a crack for light and air, whereupon Jupiter transformed himself into golden rain and impregnated her; the rain is sometimes represented as golden coins, as in this case. The painting is erotic by the standards of the time and was clearly commissioned for this reason, but it was only justifiable on the grounds of the potential moral and symbolic significance of its classical subject-matter. In the Middle Ages, Danae had been compared to the Virgin Mary, and her impregnation to the Annunciation, but her seduction could equally well be used to focus on the difference between spiritual and worldly communion (especial relevant for a cardinal). This need to legitimise emotion and passion by placing it in an ennobling mythological context persisted throughout the seventeenth century. Bernini's highly sensuous sculpture of *Apollo and Daphne*, commissioned by Cardinal Barberini (later Pope Urban VIII) in 1622, typifies the trend. Despite showing Apollo grasping at the soft and sensuous flesh of

FIGURE 13.7: Titian, *Danae*, 1553–4, oil on canvas, 120 × 172 cm. Museo di Capodimonte, Naples.

Daphne as she turns into a laurel tree to escape him, the base of the sculpture was inscribed with the moralising words: 'Whoever, being in love, pursues the delight of fleeting appearance, finds his hands full of foliage or plucks only bitter berries.' Ironically, the sculpture itself epitomises 'the delight of fleeting appearance'.[7]

Ambivalence about the legitimacy of producing erotic images and – more importantly – of experiencing the feelings that they stimulated, was not only *reflected* in the mythologisation of such feelings. It was also *built into* the very narratives that provided artists with opportunities to depict nudity. For instance, the image of the *Judgement of Paris*, painted by numerous artists from Cranach to Rubens, revolves around the attempt by Paris, a mortal, to judge which of the three goddesses – Hera (Juno), Athena (Minerva) or Aphrodite (Venus) – was the most beautiful. Each goddess bribed Paris to favour them, with Venus, goddess of love, offering him the most beautiful woman in the world as a reward for choosing her, which he duly did (thereby provoking the Trojan War). In his *Judgement* of 1632–5, Rubens took the opportunity to show a naked woman from the front, back and side (Fig. 13.8). But the figure of Paris is equally important. For while the story provides a legitimate opportunity to depict nudity, it is the presence of Paris that legitimises the act of *looking* at it. By implicitly putting the viewer in Paris's position, the subject allows, and even requires, him to gaze at the women and judge them.

In the same way, the image of *Diana and Actaeon*, popular throughout the sixteenth and seventeenth centuries, shows Actaeon out hunting in the woods with

FIGURE 13.8: Peter Paul Rubens, *The Judgement of Paris*, 1632–5, oil on oak, 144.8 × 193.7 cm. National Gallery, London.

his dogs when he accidentally stumbles across Diana and her friends bathing naked in a pond. Diana is so incensed by Actaeon's indiscretion that she transforms him into a stag and has him attacked by his own hounds. Again, the subject provided plenty of scope for painting naked women but, this time, it construes the sighting of them as an accidental, semi-voyeuristic act rather than a beauty contest. The viewer of the painting is made to identify with Actaeon merely by seeing the women, and is therefore cast as a voyeur. While the picture may seem to confront him with a dilemma surrounding the nature of sexual desire, and expose him to the disturbing ambivalence of his own thoughts and feelings, most important is the fact that it 'licensed' him to experience them at all. Significantly, when Orsino, in Shakespeare's *Twelfth Night* (1601), first sees Olivia, he compares himself to a stag chased by his own hounds, dogged by desire for her.

Feelings of ambivalence around the expression of erotic desire were not only reflected by classical precedents. They were also suggested by images from the Old Testament. The encounters of David and Bathsheba (2 Samuel 11), and Susanna and the Elders (Daniel 13) both involve illicit gazing at naked women, resulting in punishment. In the former case, King David is usually shown looking down from his house at the beautiful Bathsheba who is bathing below, and lusting after her (Fig. 13.9, 16.5). In subsequent scenes from the story, which are less commonly represented, David summons Bathsheba to his house, despite the fact that she is married – to Uriah, a soldier in David's army, currently away at war – and makes her pregnant. He then attempts to conceal the evidence of his adultery by inviting Uriah back from the war and encouraging him to make love to Bathsheba in order to (seemingly) impregnate her, which Uriah refuses to do, as it is his duty to abstain from sexual intercourse during battle and to sleep in the company of his soldiers; getting him drunk does not help. In order to avoid the ultimate confrontation, David then orders that Uriah be placed at the most dangerous place in the battle line before suddenly ordering the surrounding troops to withdraw, leaving him exposed to the enemy, who kill him. He then marries Bathsheba, but is punished by God, who causes the death of their child – though following his repentance, his second child with Bathsheba, Solomon, succeeds him as king of Israel. While the act of God's punishment construed the voyeuristic David's lust as a sin, thereby investing the viewers' equivalent experience of seeing paintings of Bathsheba with its own moral ambiguity, David's repentance provided the scene with a degree of morally uplifting potential that ultimately legitimised contemplating it. At the Palazzo Tè in Mantua, painted by Giulio Romano and assistants from 1525 to 1535, there is an open loggia decorated with scenes from the life of David, including his spying on Bathsheba; because the loggia actually overlooks a number of ponds, it enabled its patron, Federico II of Gonzaga (whose favoured mistress's husband was murdered in mysterious circumstances) to both admire and perform the voyeuristic role of David.

This capacity of pre-legitimised narratives to accommodate eroticism by seeming to bring a high-minded pedigree to it was most explicitly indulged in relation to a rare set of sixteen drawings of lovers in a variety of sexual positions by Giulio Romano (a student of Raphael) in the early 1520s. The drawings, called *I Modi* (*The Ways* or *The Positions*), were engraved in 1524 by Marcantonio Raimondi, Raphael's engraver, who was imprisoned for publicising them, and printed by Baviero de' Carrocci (called

FIGURE 13.9: In the style of Robinet Testard, *David and Bathsheba*, from a Book of Hours, around 1500, France, Kings 7, f.54. British Library, London. © The British Library Board.

Baviera), who also worked for Raphael. Today, the images are only known through anonymous woodcut copies of the engravings, as Giulio Romano's drawings are lost and the original engravings were destroyed on moral grounds (Fig. 13.10). Their significance lies in the fact that, shortly after their first scandalous appearance, a new set of engravings – also produced by Baviera and almost certainly inspired by those of Marcantonio – was printed;[8] but this time the images of the lovers were supplemented with the attributes of Jupiter (his eagle and thunderbolt, held by a cupid) and presented as the classical *Loves of the Gods*, whereupon they were deemed acceptable. In some cases, the form into which Jupiter metamorphosed in order to seduce his victim is also shown. To seduce Io, for instance, the god was transformed into a cloud of mist, just as he had been transformed into golden rain for Danae (Fig. 13.11).

The point here is that the experience of eroticism was only legitimised to the extent that it was mediated in the safe and meaningful language of mythological iconography. Like Jupiter himself, the viewer of such images had to assume an artificial persona to have access to the object of his desire. It is arguable moreover

FIGURE 13.10: Anonymous woodcut after Marcantonio Raimondi, after Giulio Romano, from *I Modi* (*The Positions*), sixteenth century. Private Collection, Geneva.

FIGURE 13.11: Jacopo Caraglio, *Jupiter and Io*, engraving after Perino del Vaga, early-mid sixteenth century. Istituto Nazionale per la Grafica, Rome.

that, even without the figure of Jupiter, Giulio's original drawings retained a degree of legitimising propriety on the grounds that that they were academic exercises in Renaissance antiquarianism. They were clearly inspired by images of copulation that Giulio must have seen on ancient objects, such as coins and ceramic lamps, votive jewellery and amulets, where phalluses served as agents of protection, healing, fertility and good luck. Even the fact that Giulio produced a series of *sixteen* images may have been inspired by a Roman precedent. From the middle of the second century until the middle of the third century, the Roman *denarius* was divisible into sixteen (rather than ten) units, called *asses*. A number of imitation *as* coins, adorned with scenes of copulation in a variety of different positions, were also produced, and were numbered on their backs from I to XVI (Fig. 13.12). While the original function of these coins (called *spintriae*) is unclear, they are thought by some to have been made for use in brothels, as it was illegal, on pain of death, to use coins decorated with the head of the emperor for this purpose.[9] It seems likely that Giulio based his designs for *I Modi* on examples of such coins, some of which are known to have belonged to Federico Gonzaga, for whom Giulio worked. As a knowledgeable collector of antique coins and medals in his own right (according to Vasari), Giulio may have owned examples himself.

Giulio's initiative received positive as well as negative responses. In 1526, the poet Pietro Aretino was inspired by the designs to write a series of erotic sonnets – the

FIGURE 13.12: Roman *spintriae*, first century AD. © The Hunterian, University of Glasgow 2018. Photo: John Faithfull.

Sonetti Lussuriosi ('Lustful Sonnets') – to accompany them, partly in defiant response to the imprisonment of Raimondi, who produced the original engravings for them. The verses, which are even more explicit than the designs – fixating on the genitals and referring to them in shockingly coarse language – are often considered to represent the origins of pornography. In his introduction, Aretino makes a direct case for enjoying sex for its own sake, maintaining that the genitals have caused less harm to the world than the hands or mouth which remain uncovered, while also pointing out that even the saints would not have existed without copulation. Having said this, although the verses make little actual reference to classical mythology, they were also broadly antiquarian, rooted in a classical tradition that did something to qualify their blatant obscenity. Besides justifying his work by comparing it explicitly to classical love poetry (such as Ovid's *Ars Amatoria*), Aretino developed a second line of defence by citing classical writers who also justified the production of erotic art or poetry as a form of relaxation or pleasure.[10]

While taking an extremely hedonistic attitude towards sexuality, Aretino's works tacitly acknowledge an ambivalence surrounding the legitimacy of sexual pleasure (or pretend to) by presenting it as transgressive. His *Ragionamenti* ('Dialogues') of 1536, for instance, is one of his most explicit works but he self-consciously distances the dangers of sexual licence that he describes in it from the safe realm of 'normal morality' by associating it with the 'easily corruptible' nature of women – the lascivious promiscuity of nuns, the adulterous deception of wives or the manipulative self-interest of whores. In this way, he casts an unbridled appetite for sex in a negative light – as a weakness bequeathed to humanity by Eve – and thereby *appears* to claim a degree of moral distance from it. Using a format that deliberately parodies Castiglione's virtuous *Courtier*, Aretino has his revelations of sexual detail divulged by an experienced courtesan, Nanna, in a series of discussions about the best way for a woman to lead a fulfilling life – given the available options: nun, wife or whore? His conclusion, voiced by Nanna, was that, while the life of a prostitute was dissolute, it was also the least dishonest and, as result, he has Nanna recommend it for her daughter. Following Aretino's example, the format of an experienced prostitute sharing her experiences with a novice became one of the most common genres of erotic literature, giving rise to a tradition of 'whore dialogues' (from which the word 'pornography' derives) that thrived, initially in Italy and France, until the mid-eighteenth century.[11]

Although Aretino indulged sexual licence because it is pleasurable, this pleasure was not purely sensuous for him; a part of the pleasure lay in the fact that licentiousness was controversial, exposing moral hypocrisy – especially that of the Church, which he considered to be a bastion of sexual perversion and duplicity. By accusing the Church of gross indecency, he was not only venting his spleen against it; he was also artfully deflecting criticism away from the 'indecencies' themselves, thereby creating a degree of 'psychological space' for sexual licence by allowing it to be momentarily overlooked. The fact that Nanna had been initiated into her sexuality when she was a nun was presented as a routine example of the Church's double standards. Real occurrences of this kind were not unusual, especially as it was conventional for aristocratic young women to be educated in convents. In 1668, for instance, a group of Franciscan monks was accused of infusing the education of the nuns in their charge with 'a spirit of wantonness and libertinism'; one commentator stated that the typical transgressions of such monks involved circulating the nuns' confessions amongst themselves in order to 'favour their design upon those whom they had a mind to seduce' and furnishing them with romances and other suggestive literature in order to 'insensibly ingage them in vitious inclinations'.[12]

Such occasions were common enough to underpin a second tradition of erotic writing, parallel to that of the 'whore dialogues', in which the process of sexual awakening assumed the guise of religious instruction, offered by an experienced member of the Church to a novice. A late sixteenth-century painting by Cornelis Cornelisz van Haarlem that shows a monk touching the exposed breast of a nun, as if to become more sensitive to her feelings, captures the situation perfectly (Fig. 13.13). One writer, Ferrante Pallavicino, who worked in the satirical style of Aretino, maintained in his *Retorica della puttane* (*The Whore's Rhetoric*) of 1642 that the persuasive rhetoric of the Jesuits was no different to the seductive charms of prostitutes. Indeed, he recommended that prostitutes become familiar with cultural

FIGURE 13.13: Cornelis Cornelisz of Haarlem, *The Monk and the Nun*, 1591, oil on canvas, 116 × 103 cm. Frans Hals Museum, Haarlem. Photo: Tom Haartsen.

conventions, such as elegance in architecture, in order to be able to ingratiate themselves with their clients 'like Jesuits' (who used their knowledge of technology, for instance, to impress potential converts in China).

In France, which supplanted Italy as the centre of libertine culture in the seventeenth century, erotic literature adapted several mainstream literary conventions to its own needs, blurring the boundary between the polite and the provocative. Most obviously, it retained the sociable format of the instructive conversation (popularised by Castiglione's *Courtier*), justifying itself on the grounds that it offered a means to self-improvement. The misleading impression of such dissembling is reflected in *L'Escole des filles* (1655), which Samuel Pepys picked up in 1668, thinking it was a book of etiquette that his wife could translate into English, only to discover to his horror that it was in fact 'the most bawdy, lewd book that I ever saw' (though this did not stop him from returning to the bookseller three weeks later, buying the book, reading it, masturbating and destroying it, 'that it might not be among my books, to my shame').[13] Despite Pepys' reaction, the considerate tone of the book, which consists of two conversations between two respectable women (the innocent Fanchon and her more experienced cousin Suzanne), indicates that it was not primarily intended to shock or offend. Indeed, although it is extremely explicit, its narrative is frequently reduced to detached descriptions of sexual techniques – from Suzanne's opening introduction to the very notion of sex, to passages (in the second conversation, following implementation by Fanchon of some of the ideas discussed in the first) in which technical information is shared. As a result, while clearly offering itself as fodder for sexual fantasy, the book's claim to be educational (outlined in its preface, and title) is superficially plausible. Certainly, although the text describes the pleasures of sex in detail, the twelve illustrations to the English edition in 1680 are arguably more informative than arousing; they provide an instructive series of postures but make no attempt to transmit the lovers' experience of feeling or pleasure (Fig. 13.14).

The same cannot be said of the notorious *Venus dans le cloître*, in which an equivalent series of conversations about sexual experience is put into the mouths of two nuns. The book, which was written by a French cleric, abbé Jean Barrin, in 1680, opens with the older of the two nuns, Sister Angelica, entering the room of the younger nun, Sister Agnes, and catching her unawares, with reason to be embarrassed. Their warm greetings and expressions of mutual trust lead to affectionate kisses, and then to caresses, causing Agnes to fear that 'in the excess of that satisfaction which I have tasted, there may be [something] intermixed, that may give me cause to reflect upon my conscience'.[14] Angelica then takes pains, in the manner of a confessor, to relieve Agnes of her dilemma by explaining the difference between the original inner religion of God, which is pure, direct and free, and the later outer religion of man which gave rise to the masochistic rituals of self-mortification, self-denial and self-isolation. In her own case, Angelica rejected the latter so that she could 'without scruple, lengthen her chains, embellish her solitude and, giving herself a gay air in all things, make herself familiar with the world'. She explains that man, with his scheming 'policies', has corrupted the monastic vocation to such an extent that governments now use monasteries as dead-end institutions ('like sewers for their superfluities') in which to place weak and useless members of society in the hope that

FIGURE 13.14: Michel Millot, *The School of Venus, or the Ladies Delight, Reduced into Rules of Practice* (translation of *L'Escole des filles*, 1655), 1680.

they will destroy themselves by excessive self-deprivation. Agnes is instantly relieved of her belief in the beneficial effect of her ritual devotions, which include self-flagellation, realising that the urges that she had been aiming to destroy were natural, innocent feelings, and not demonic impulses. When Angelica sees the self-inflicted wounds on Agnes's thighs, she kisses them – somewhat to Agnes's surprise – as if to heal them and, while doing so, notices the beauty and whiteness of Agnes's skin, touching her where there might 'blow up a fire not easily to be extinguished'.[15] Dismissing the suggestion that there might be anything sinful in their shows of affection, she anticipates the various instructive encounters that Agnes might have with male members of the monastic community – now that the simple virtue of nature's gifts has been explained to her – thereby restoring the original and natural harmony between religious devotion and sexual pleasure. The rest of the book consists of a string of discussions about episodes in their convent of a more or less sexual nature, interspersed with moments of sexual contact between the women. In this way, Agnes's assessment of pleasure as diverging from preconceived moral standards, and therefore deserving of guilt and self-punishment, was painstakingly dismantled, and a rationale for the enjoyment of pleasure for its own sake was constructed in her – and the reader's – mind.

Despite its directness, *Venus dans le cloître* claimed a degree of moral responsibility by exposing the cynicism of the Church – like several of its predecessors. The first pornographic text that was written *purely* for pleasure – without apology or political agenda – was a novel. Significantly, it was not only the content of the work that was conceived to stimulate pleasure; it was also its epistolary form which, as we have seen, was inherently conducive to the stimulation of intimate, interior fantasies. *Fanny Hill, or Memoirs of a Woman of Pleasure*, written by John Cleland in 1748, tells the story – not just as a sequence of anecdotes, but as a narrative – of a poor, uneducated young woman, following the death of her parents, who moves from her village near Liverpool to London. Her first accommodation turns out to be a brothel and her first sexual encounter is with another woman. During the course of the book, she has a wide range of sexual experiences, both as participant and voyeur. As in sixteenth- and seventeenth-century paintings of voyeurs, her role as a voyeur tacitly accommodates the presence of the reader in the narrative. Fanny loses her virginity to a young man called Charles, with whom she falls in love but who, after several months of passion – all described in vivid detail – is suddenly exiled to the South Seas without warning, by his father. Having become used to the separation, Fanny begins to have sex with other men, despite remaining in love with Charles, taking every opportunity to share her pleasures, which form the core content of the book, with the reader. At the end of the book, she meets up with Charles again by chance, and marries him; they have several children. The significance of the book lies in the fact that Fanny celebrates extreme pleasure for its own sake, giving it precedence over 'vulgar prejudices in favour of titles, dignities, honours, and the like' – the traditional attributes of cultural value – while eventually managing to reconcile it with the conventional model of a respectable marriage and life. As such, despite the fact that Cleland was prosecuted for corruption, the book set a powerful and inspiring precedent for its readers, in its principle if not in its details.

In exactly the year in which *Fanny Hill* was published in London – 1748 – a parallel demonstration of the unmitigated enjoyment of pleasure was offered to French readers in the form of *Thérèse Philosophe*, an exercise in 'philosophical pornography', probably written by the Marquis d'Argens. In this work, descriptions of sexual episodes are interspersed with philosophical reflections on the sensory basis of pleasure and knowledge, the non-existence of free will in human beings and the pervasive presence of God which transcends the prejudicial manipulations of human religions. The work consists of a series of memoirs in which Thérèse recalls a number of key moments in her sexual and intellectual education, culminating in her meeting, and retreat to the countryside, with the Count to whom the memoirs are addressed. The opening episode provides a classic example of a confessor-as-seducer, maximising the erotic potential of religious instruction and experience, while also exposing the openness of confessional vulnerability to clerical abuse. It tells of a fervently pious young woman, Mademoiselle Eradice, who is intent on sanctifying herself, by self-mortification if necessary, and her confessor Father Dirrag, who is intent on helping her achieve her aim. He does this during a confessional session, voyeuristically witnessed by Thérèse from a hidden closet, first of all by flagellating Eradice as she kneels at her prayer stool, in order to help her dissociate from the banality of the flesh, like a saint or martyr, and then by 'purging her of all her impurities' with a relic of the 'venerable cord of St Francis' which he happens to have on his person. Eradice, who is a paragon of innocence and inexperience, later tells Thérèse that she has 'seen

Paradise unveiled' and has 'experienced angelic bliss': 'so much pleasure, my friend, for only a moment of pain! By virtue of the holy cord my soul was almost freed from matter ... Make no mistake: one degree more of excitement and I would have passed over forever into the realm of heavenly contentment.'[16] In the second section of the book, Thérèse, who had been confined to a convent until she was twenty-three years old, is instructed by her own confessor to relieve herself of various discomforts, and rejuvenate herself, by masturbating. Besides stating that this remedy would improve her health (contrary to contemporary medical and moral advice on the subject), her confessor justified the practice on the all-important grounds that it did no harm to society, one of the crucial conditions that enabled the pleasures of non-procreative sex to become socially acceptable and eventually conventional. Besides highlighting the purely pleasurable potential of sex, masturbation was important to Thérèse because she was afraid both of getting pregnant through penetrative sex and of the very real dangers of childbirth, which had almost killed her mother. Indeed, because it was harmless and safe in these ways, and had no direct impact on the well-being of society (for instance by resulting in unwanted children), it epitomised the experience of isolated self-oriented pleasure which formed the basis of her philosophy.[17] At the end of the book, Thérèse meets the Count and falls in love with him, grafting the sexual exploits of her past on to the stock of a respectable relationship in the present, as in *Fanny Hill*.

Frustrated by being confined to mutual masturbation with Thérèse, the Count proposes a wager: he lends her his collection of erotic literature and pictures, promising her that she can keep the collection for a year if she can resist masturbating for two weeks, but insists that she will have to yield to him and allow him to penetrate her (but withdrawing before ejaculating to avoid pregnancy) if she fails (Fig. 13.15). She accepts the wager, but fails in her resolve and pays the price, which she continues to do thereafter for ten years 'without a problem, without a worry, without children'.[18] Thérèse's description of her inability to resist the temptation to pleasure herself is significant, partly because of the way it creates a precedent for the reader to do the same, as in so many novels of the period. For the first four days she 'devoured' erotic books, only putting them down 'in order to examine the pictures avidly, where the most lascivious poses were rendered with a colouring and an expressiveness that sent fire coursing through my veins'.[19] On the fifth day, after an hour of reading, she fell into a kind of ecstasy. Seeing some pictures, she describes how her 'imagination began to be ignited by the attitudes represented in them' and how she prepared to imitate all the positions she saw – demonstrating exactly how engagement with new cultural forms can precipitate new experiences in their consumers. Responding to an image of *The Feast of Priapus* (typically couched in the legitimising context of classical mythology), she relates how her right hand 'travelled to the spot where the man's hand [in the picture] was placed'. Of an image of *The Love Affair of Venus and Mars*, she wrote: 'What sensuality in Venus' stance! Like her, I stretched out lazily. With my thighs slightly apart and my arms spread open voluptuously, I admired the striking attitude of the god Mars. The fire with which his eyes, and especially his lance, seemed to be animated passed directly into my heart. I slipped under the sheets ...', eventually crying out: 'Ah! dear lover! I can resist no longer. Come forward, Count, I am no longer afraid of your dart. You may pierce your lover ...'[20] The similarity

FIGURE 13.15: Attributed to Jean-Baptiste de Boyer, Marquis d'Argens, *Thérèse Philosophe*, 1748, Montigny (though made to seem to have been printed in The Hague). Private Collection.

between this passage and the famous description, by Thérèse's namesake St Theresa of Avila, of the mystical experience in which an angel appeared to thrust a long spear of gold 'into my heart, and to pierce my very entrails' leaving her 'all on fire with a great love of God' reflects the way in which traditional expressions of religious ecstasy also set a precedent, and provided a vocabulary of postures and gestures, for the free expression of sexual pleasure in its viewers.

The contribution that erotic novels made to the naturalisation of pleasure in the eighteenth century was complemented by a proliferation of images of sexual acts – as Thérèse herself demonstrated – and by the development of sensuous and sympathetic environments in which to perform them. Especially in France, depictions of sexual pleasure, enjoyed for its own sake, became conventional at this period. Such images rarely focused on the act of intercourse itself, which left little to the imagination and therefore excluded the viewer; they tended to concentrate on moments of anticipation or reflection, documenting every stage of the process of seduction, and frequently accommodating the viewer in the narrative as a voyeur. The role of mythological iconography was also downplayed, to make space for easier identification on the viewer's part. Where it did occur – for instance, in images of Leda and the Swan, or Venus and Cupid (who replaced the Virgin and Christ in

FIGURE 13.16: Attributed to François Boucher, *Leda and the Swan*, around 1740, oil on canvas. Private Collection.

the elite imagination) – it was entirely tokenistic and carried no moralising associations (Fig. 13.16). A number of François Boucher's paintings of women, splayed out in voluptuous poses, tangled up in ruffled and tousled bedcovers or sunk into banks of luxuriant plump cushions, involve actual named women (including the painter's own wife) rather than remote goddesses, lending an air of real possibility to the fantasies they are designed to stimulate. His paintings of *Marie-Louise O'Murphy* and *L'Odalisque* are the most celebrated examples but others were circulated in print form (Fig. 13.17).[21] In the 1760s, Pierre-Antoine Baudouin, a pupil and son-in-law of Boucher, became notorious for his representations of libertine scenes, which he normalised by painting in an innocuously fashionable style and openly offering for public appreciation at 'salon' exhibitions. In *La Lecture* (*Reading*) of about 1765, a young woman is shown lying back in a richly upholstered chair, lost in her thoughts (Fig. 13.18). The image recalls representations of saints in states of mystical experience and, at first glance, bears an uncanny resemblance to Bernini's *St Theresa in Ecstasy* (Fig. 13.5). On closer inspection, however, it becomes clear that a comparison with *Thérèse Philosophe* would be more appropriate. For like Thérèse, at the moment of her lapse, the source of the depicted woman's reverie is a book that she has just let slip, though her fingers continue to mingle suggestively with its open pages. The stretched expanse of her voluptuous blue dress indicates that her legs are apart and its rich textures evoke the softness and openness of what it conceals. Her right hand is clearly lost in its silk folds, inviting the viewer to

FIGURE 13.17: Jean Edme Nochez, *Study of a Reclining Nude* (after Boucher), around 1760–70, etching and engraving, 24.7 × 30.2 cm. Metropolitan Museum of Art, New York, The Elisha Whittelsey Collection, The Elisha Whittelsey Fund.

complete the analogy between the open book that she seems to finger with her left hand, and her crotch. The title of the book is indecipherable but it is surely the kind of amorous novel that Rousseau said was to be read 'with one hand'. This is certainly the case in Jean-Baptiste Greuze's *Lady Reading the Letters of Heloise and Abelard* (1758–9), in which a woman swoons as the words of the famous lovers (refashioned into a romantic drama for seventeenth- and eighteenth-century readers) inflame her own desires, prompted by the intimate letter on her side table. In François Hubert's *Honi Soit Qui Mal Y Pense* (*Shame on Him who Thinks Evil of This*), the incriminating book is clearly identifiable as *L'Art d'Aimer – The Art of Love*, a translation of Ovid's *Ars Amatoria*, published in French in 1775. In this instance, the open book languishes in the lap of its reader where it serves as a surrogate object of fascination for the viewer just as it had done for the reader before she slipped one of her hands beneath the sumptuous folds of her dress. Her heavy eyelids, limpid eyes and slightly parted lips, together with the angle of her head, tilted very slightly backwards, all indicate that she has slipped into a state of erotic reverie (Fig. 13.19).

As the eighteenth century gathered momentum, images of this kind were circulated widely in elegant, discreet engravings, especially but not exclusively among the aristocracy. The quality of the prints raises them above the level of their English equivalents, which used a cruder style to serve their more satirical and moralising ends, and contextualises them as refined and collectable works of art. The affluent

FIGURE 13.18: Pierre Antoine Baudouin, *La Lecture*, around 1765, gouache, 29 × 22.5 cm. Musée des Arts Décoratifs, Paris.

interiors and gardens in which most of the scenes take place give some impression of the social level of the audience expected to identify with them; but they also indicate how the visual language of the domestic interior had become suffused with agendas – not only of civility, as demonstrated in chapter 11 – but also of pleasure-seeking. This trend is immediately evident in the way the ornamental language of the interiors of the mid-eighteenth century becomes sensuous and curvaceous, implicitly incorporating the movements of the body into its vocabulary – thereby approving

FIGURE 13.19: François Hubert, *Honi Soit Qui Mal Y Pense* (*Shame on Him who Thinks Evil of This*), 1776, engraving, 44 × 31 cm. Galerie l'Horizon Chimérique, Bordeaux.

and encouraging them – rather than referring to an objective code of classical values (implicit in the earlier baroque style), which are alien to the sensory appetites of the individual. It is nowhere more explicitly reflected than in a novel of the period, *La Petite Maison* (*The Little House*), in which the protagonist, the Marquis de Trémicour, strategically uses the aesthetic appeal of his home as an instrument of seduction; indeed the decorative scheme of his house was specifically conceived for this purpose, 'artfully contrived for love'.[22]

La Petite Maison, written by Jean-François de Bastide in 1758, tells the tale of a beautiful, intelligent and virtuous virgin, Mélite, who has always succeeded in resisting the advances of her suitors, whose motives she perpetually suspects.

Time that other women [had] squandered in love and deception, [she had] spent in instruction, acquiring true taste and knowledge. She had learned to recognise the works of the best artists at a glance. She looked on their masterpieces with respect and awe, while their true value was lost to most other women, who were capable only of whimsical love for trifles and triviality.[23]

The Marquis, who is not used to having his advances rejected, is piqued by her resistance and proposes a wager to her, just as the Count had done with Thérèse in *Thérèse Philosophe*. He claims that if Mélite would accompany him on a guided tour of his house, she would surely succumb to his charms; and she, confident of her resolve not to, agrees. Little does she know that his house was designed to seduce, making use of the greatest artists and designers of the day – Hallé, Pineau, Dandrillon, Cafieri, Huet, Boucher, Germain, the Martin Brothers, Falconet and others. Indeed, the book itself gives such a detailed account of the layout and decoration of a typically lavish Parisian *hôtel* in the 1750s that it has also been seen as an architectural treatise. Mélite is duly guided round the house, delighting in its contents, which are carefully ascribed to specific makers and designers. At one point, Trémicour takes Mélite into a salon that opens on to the garden: 'so voluptuous was this salon that it inspired the tenderest feelings, feelings that one believes that one could have only for its owner.'[24] Mélite's resistance is gradually worn down: '"I cannot take this any longer," she says. "This house is too beautiful. There is nothing comparable on earth . . ."';[25] and eventually, at the very end of the book, she 'shuddered, faltered, sighed and lost the wager'.[26]

Just as the Count had used his pornographic books and images to seduce Thérèse, so Trémicour had used the ravishing impression of the decorative interiors of his house to seduce Mélite. The story is exaggerated and slight but it does reflect – in an absurdly caricatured way, but one that is entirely in keeping with the frivolous spirit of the age – how the possibilities of experience (in this case, the possibility of meaningless pleasure) are determined by the language of the environment, both material and psychological, in which they occur. Indeed, to the extent that Trémicour uses his house as an extension and embodiment of himself – generating a pleasurable environment in order to find his pleasure-seeking self reflected in it – the very principle or subject of experience is also determined in this way.

In the middle of the eighteenth century, several more serious architectural treatises also testify to the new interest in the sensuous, physiological potential of decorative forms. For instance, in his *Livre d'Architecture* (*Book of Architecture*), initiated in 1734 but only published in 1745, the French architect Germain Boffrand compared the decorative use of curved and straight lines in buildings to musical notes, maintaining that, purely on the basis of their visual impact, they are capable of expressing feelings of joy, sadness, love, hate, grace or terror. For this reason, he added, they should not be selected abstractly and mechanically, in keeping with an imagined principle, nor randomly, as was too often the case in the architecture of his contemporaries; on the contrary, while honouring classical propriety, they should be selected according to the specific function and character of the building in question – whether a theatre, mausoleum or private residence.[27] Moreover, especially in relation to domestic interiors, where the obligation to observe public principles of propriety was less absolute, there was also scope to use decorative schemes to reflect the personal character of the patron. Indeed, a degree of causal connection between the disposition of the owner and the environment he created for himself was almost inevitable:

> If the master has petty notions, he will build to suit them; his house will be composed and ornamented with gewgaws [trifles]. If the master's character is modest and sublime, his house will be distinguished more by elegant proportions than by rich materials. If the master's character is wayward and eccentric, his house will be full of disparities and parts out of agreement. In short, judge the character of the master for whom the house was built by the way in which it was planned, decorated and furnished.[28]

The surviving interior designed by Boffrand that most eloquently manifests his attunement of design to character is his 'Salon de la Princesse' in the Hôtel de Soubise (Fig. 11.4). As a consummate example of the rococo style, the room refuses to support the frame of mind that identifies itself in relation to meaningful references to abstractions that it can 'understand'; on the contrary, it presumes the presence of one who is identified by their feelings and whose feelings change spontaneously in relation to their sensations. It was in this spirit that, from the 1750s, 'boudoirs' became common as small rooms in which women could (according to a description from 1770) 'retire to think, or read, or work or, in a word, be alone'.[29] The boudoir was one of the first cultural conventions in which the possibility of solitude and privacy for women was deliberately institutionalised in an enduring form. That it was specifically conceived to embody and accommodate a particular mood is suggested by the derivation of the word 'boudoir' from the word *bouder*, meaning 'to sulk' in French. This association highlights the capacity of the room to support the experience of reflective solitude that had already been coded into the more masculine space of the study, though it was also used for conversation and romance to the extent that it became loaded with innuendo – as, for instance, exploited by the Marquis de Sade in his meta-erotic and sadistic novel, *La Philosophie dans le boudoir* of 1795 (Fig. 13.20).

A firm footing for the appreciation of the symbiotic relationship between sensation and architectural form was further established in a treatise by the architect Nicolas Le Camus de Mézières, published in 1780, called *Le génie de l'architecture; ou, L'analogie de cet art avec nos sensations* (*The Genius of Architecture; or, the Analogy of that Art with our Sensations*). At the very beginning of this work, Le Camus established that architects have hitherto been using the five orders of antiquity 'mechanically', without appreciating their ability to produce sensations in their viewers and without relating their proportions to the passions of the soul. He then sets out to convince the viewer that 'every object possesses a character, proper to it alone, and that often a single line, a plain contour, will suffice to express it'. Inspired by Charles Le Brun's attempt to create a language of human emotion from a vocabulary of facial expressions, and ever inclined to find precedents in nature, he observes that

> the faces of the lion, the tiger, and the leopard are composed of lines that make them terrible and strike fear into the boldest hearts. In the face of the cat, we discern the character of treachery; meekness and goodness are written on the features of a lamb; the fox has a mask of cunning and guile; a single feature conveys their character.[30]

FIGURE 13.20: Donatien Alphonse François, *Marquis de Sade*, a plate from *La Philosophie dans le boudoir*, volume I, page 42, London, 1795.

The fact that Le Camus completely ignores the ways in which knowledge of the behaviour of these creatures might inform people's interpretations of their appearances is naïve, but when he applies his principle to inanimate objects, and even abstract forms, it becomes more pertinent: 'a structure catches the eye by virtue of its mass; its general outline attracts or repels us.'[31] Indeed, a wide spectrum of feelings can be expressed and evoked by judicious use of the vocabulary of architectural features. Sadness and gaiety, for instance, arise from the greater or lesser compactness of the masses; you must either circumscribe the soul or give it the free rein that nature dictates. We are so constituted that in moments of joy our heart expands and loses itself in space. An open place, abundant daylight, great harmony, great consonance, little shadow and therefore less contrast, will evoke the spirit of gaiety that accords so well with health. If you wish to see gaiety unconfined, contrive to have as much daylight as possible and masses that are not too strong, so that nothing seems to engage the mind and that enjoyment may be unreflective. There must be nothing to break the mood. To render a place sad, the rules are more or less the opposite: the daylight must be sombre and restricted and must create half-tones; there must be simple and unified masses, and therefore less liveliness in the whole; impose monotony, that the eye may not stray and be distracted by variety . . .[32]

Resonating with the intentions of the Marquis de Trémicour in *La Petite Maison*, Le Camus continues: 'If you wish to inspire a dainty passion, then avoid straight lines in the plan; or, at least combine them with curves; these forms are sacred to Venus. The light must not be too brilliant or all her mystery will be lost. Gallantry and delicacy must prevail. Dainty ornaments are fitting here; bestow them with taste.'[33] And reflecting altogether on the ingenious efficacy of this art, he addresses the generality of great French designers who have raised it to such a level. Speaking to them of the refined 'man of sensibility' who finds himself in an exquisitely contrived environment of luxury and comfort, he says: 'One step more, and his soul will take wing; he is transported by the harmony and rapport of architectural proportions wisely employed. You govern the motions of his heart, and by a kind of magic you excite all manner of sensations at will.'[34]

The significance of Boffrand and Le Camus lies in the way that, despite their respect for propriety, they contributed towards the formulation of a language of visual culture in which the experience of meaningless pleasure was validated. In the visual arts, this sensibility is typically associated with the whimsical rococo style, which flourished in the middle decades of the eighteenth century. The style was hugely criticised by conservative contemporaries for its apparently self-indulgent randomness and triviality, which seemed to show little regard for public principles of decorum, and it is still often seen as a precedent for all that is garish and kitsch. But to evaluate it in this way is to limit its significance unfairly; though it may have been *meaning*less, it was not *worth*less. In its individual manifestations, it surely did respond to an impulse towards immediate self-gratification; but, on a larger scale, it embodied a new paradigm in which an individual's sense of identity was no longer determined by preconceived ideas, validated by external structures of conformity and belief, but was free to determine itself on the basis of its own experience. As such, it also embodied (albeit indirectly) an immensely courageous and liberating impulse towards personal 'awakening', as individuals jettisoned the legendary scaffolding of history and religion, provided by hearsay, in favour of a simple, but real and personal, experience of pleasure. While rococo interiors set the stage, legitimising the possibility of unrestrained pleasure by writing it into the domestic

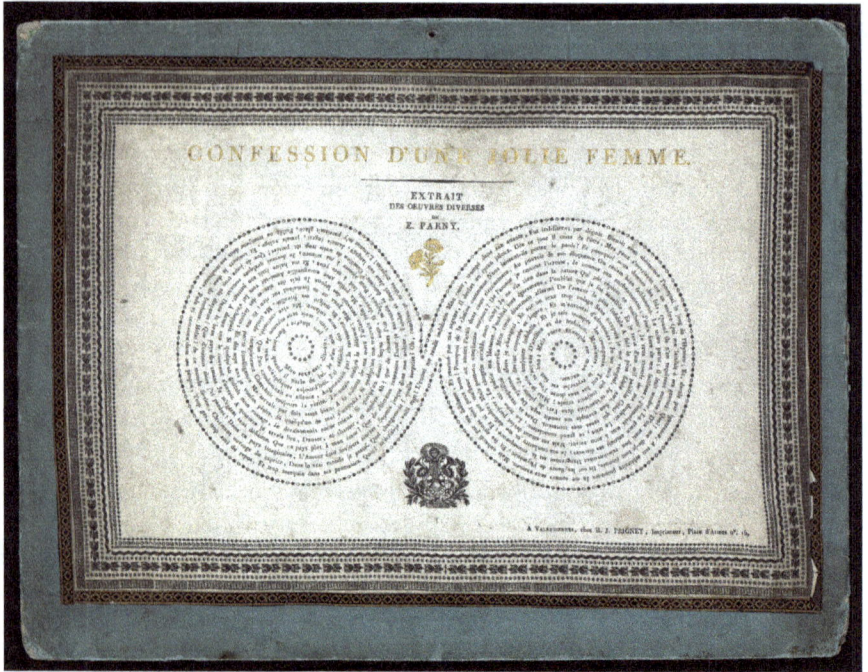

FIGURE 13.21: A silk handkerchief printed with a description of an erotic encounter with the words in the form of breasts. Mixed media, 1802, after Evariste Parny. Wellcome Collection.

environment, textual and visual representations of libidinous sex record that the script was increasingly performed – as described by one witness who presented her confession of descent from innocent principle to cynical duplicity in the form of two breasts (printed on a handkerchief), to be perused in the greatest detail by the dizzy reader (Fig. 13.21).

CHAPTER FOURTEEN

The Embodiment of the Self: the Awakening to Sensation

We saw in the previous chapter how the parameters of identity were seen to shift from the realm of *moral rectitude*, where it positioned itself in relation to authorised, 'objective' ideas, towards the subjectivity of *pleasure*. The criterion against which a phenomenon was judged was internalised to the point at which the process of evaluation seemed to become a natural function of a 'self', manifest as the apparently self-evident experience of pleasure (or pain). This inclination to 'autonomise' the self-sense through pleasure, and the corresponding disregard for the external determinants of cultural value, was paralleled by changes to the way in which the experience of *sensation* was newly valorised – for the experience of sensation, which precedes judgement, was also increasingly seen to be independent of meaning.

In the Middle Ages, the senses had been regarded as carnal and corrupt. To yield to the pleasures of the flesh was to cede influence to a source of authority other than God or the Church and over which the devil held sway. Mortification of the flesh was just one way to ensure that the soul remained dissociated from the body – as practised by flagellants, and parodied in *Thérèse Philosophe*. In the sixteenth and seventeenth centuries, efforts were made to rationalise perceptions of the senses by classifying them 'objectively'. The senses came to be represented allegorically, as a set of five female personifications identified by symbolic attributes – birds or musical instruments for hearing, flowers or dogs for smell, mirrors or texts for sight etc. (Fig. 14.1). Towards the end of the seventeenth century, this rationalisation was superseded by a more experiential approach. The value of vision, for instance, was re-evaluated in a series of debates that took place at the French Academy concerning the value of *colour* in painting. The question here was whether colour was a fundamental part of painting, informed by an ennobling intelligible principle, or whether it was subjective and changeable, and therefore of secondary importance. The relative values of design and colour had been pitted against each other since the sixteenth century when the status of painting as a liberal art was first being articulated. The Florentines, who prioritised design (*disegno*), claimed that it was in the drawing that the iconography of a painting – and therefore the meaning – was invested; the fact that drawing presupposed some understanding of intellectual disciplines, such as perspective, geometry and anatomy, also meant that it could be taught and was therefore worthy of dissemination in an academy. Colour (*colore*),

FIGURE 14.1: Isack Elyas, *Merry Company (The Five Senses)*, 1629, oil on panel, 47.1 × 63.2 cm. Rijksmuseum, Amsterdam. Smell is symbolised by the woman with a dog; sight, by the man with a piece of paper; touch, by the amorous couple; taste, by the man with a glass of wine; sound, by the lutenist. The couple to the right are patrons.

they maintained, was a mere embellishment, requiring manual skill rather than intellectual understanding, and it appealed to the senses rather than the mind. In keeping with this position, Florentine paintings tended to be calculated in advance through preparatory drawings. The Venetians, by contrast, prioritised colour and light (as also reflected in their mastery of glass- and mirror-making), working more spontaneously 'from nature'. They maintained that drawing provided only the 'body' of a painting, and that it was colour that gave it a 'soul' and brought it to life. According to Vasari, Venetian painters such as Giorgione and Titian drew with paint straight on to their canvases, improvising their compositions without recourse to preliminary drawings; hence their weakness. Underlining the association of drawing with the intellectual dimension of painting, he claimed that

> the use of drawings furnishes the artist's mind with beautiful conceptions and helps him to depict everything in the natural world from memory; he has no need to keep his subject in front of him all the time or to conceal under the charm of his colouring the lack of knowledge of how to draw, as was the case for many years with the Venetian painters Giorgione, Palma, Pordenone and the rest.[1]

As a Tuscan, Vasari surely exaggerated his case; nevertheless, the authority of his *Lives* put Venetian 'colourism' on the defensive for the next hundred years.

FIGURE 14.2: Titian, *Madonna with St John the Baptist and St Agnes*, around 1535, oil on canvas. Musée des Beaux-Arts, Dijon. Photo © RMN-Grand Palais/Agence Bulloz.

The debate was revived in the French Academy in 1671 when the painter Philippe de Champaigne (1602–74) gave a lecture on a painting by Titian – *The Virgin and Child with St John* – in which he criticised the artist's excessive dependence on colour to create effect (Fig. 14.2). By way of contrast he mentioned Nicolas Poussin (1594–1665), who began his career as a colourist but who soon 'corrected his ways' and converted to a design-led process that revolved around academic knowledge of the rules of human proportion and anatomy. Six months later, Champaigne's argument was challenged by Louis Gabriel Blanchard (1630–1704), who attempted to raise the status of colour to the same level as design. In its defence, Blanchard claimed that colour was an indispensable part of painting, uniquely differentiating it from other arts, and that it enabled artists to imitate nature in a way that no other art could achieve. The fact that it was held in high esteem by the 'ancients' also substantiated its reputation. In addition to the Venetian colourists (Giorgione, Titian, Tintoretto, Veronese), Rubens (1577–1640) was mentioned. That Rubens was perceived to have prioritised sensuality over structure (see Fig. 13.8) led to a polarisation of views between *Poussinistes*, who prioritised design, and *Rubenistes* who defended colour (despite the fact that both Poussin and Rubens were long since dead, both of them were masters of design *and* colour, and neither of them had taken sides in this debate). The following year, Le Brun himself gave a lecture in support of design, presenting a number of reasons for its superiority (principally that drawing can exist without colour but that colour cannot exist without drawing). His argument culminated in the proposal that design appeals to the intellect whereas colour only appeals to the eyes. In 1673, Le Brun's argument, which represented the formal position of the Academy, was in turn refuted by the theorist Roger de Piles (1635–1709), one of the critics who had already challenged his excessively formulaic approach to the classification of facial expressions. De Piles, who was not a member of the Academy, made an important new contribution to the debate by proposing that the reason drawing is traditionally held in higher esteem than colour is not that it is inherently more valuable but that it is informed by rules (proportion and anatomy) and that its quality can therefore be measured against an academic standard. In contrast to previous defenders of colour, he maintained that colour also has rules but that they are 'not very much known' because the 'books' in which they are written are the works of the very few artists – especially Rubens – who have understood them.[2] Significantly, it was at precisely this date that a scientific understanding of colour was indeed being developed for the first time and that the appreciation of colour was being invested with intellectual significance, and therefore status. Sir Isaac Newton's research into the nature of light was presented in his *Opticks*, which analysed the refraction of light into a regular sequence of colours. His observations of the structure of rainbows seemed to reveal a natural 'scale of colours' that could be equated to the laws of musical harmony, thereby acquiring a mathematical rationale. Although not published until 1704, this pioneering work recounted experiments first explained and circulated in 1672.

The importance of De Piles' challenge to the *Poussinistes* lies in the way it extended value to the role of colour in painting despite the fact that the hypothetical 'rules' that govern it seem to elude the intellect and appeal to a more subjective capacity in the viewer. In supporting this view, he was acknowledging an alternative non-cerebral frame of reference in which paintings could acquire cultural value and, as such, he was validating the experience of a purely emotional 'feeling-response' to art, unsupported by an intellectual agenda; indeed he also advocated the practice of landscape painting precisely because, having no subject-matter from which to derive morals and meanings, it enabled a painter to focus on the expression of feeling. Significantly, the one experience that even Le Brun conceded could not be represented without colour was blushing, an experience that epitomised the delicate sensibilities of the following century and everything that stemmed from them and depended on the acceptance of colour as a primary dimension of art. With the ascent of the colourists, the status of emotional experience was raised to a new level of cultural dignity and legitimacy, at the expense of academic principle. This move towards a greater acceptance of the subjective and unquantifiable component in painting was reflected in the fact that when Le Brun died in 1690, he was replaced as 'First Painter to the King' by a *Rubeniste*, Pierre Mignard I (1612–95); in 1699, De Piles was also elected to the Academy. By slow degrees, the obligation to legitimise art by clothing it in high-minded iconography and subjecting it to classical principles of design began to weaken in favour of more spontaneous and sensuous forms of culture. Indeed, this shift became evident in all realms of sensation. As the abbé Dubos proposed, in 1719, with regard to the sense of taste:

> Do we ever reason, in order to know whether a ragoo [ragout] be good or bad; and has it ever entered into any body's head, after having settled the geometrical

principles of taste, and defined the qualities of each ingredient that enters into the composition of those messes, to examine into the proportion observed in their mixture, in order to decide whether it be good or bad? No, this is never practised. We have a sense given us by nature to distinguish whether the cook acted according to the rules of his art. People taste the ragoo, and tho' unacquainted with those rules, they are able to tell whether it be good or no. The same may be said in some respect of the productions of the mind, and of pictures made to please and move us.[3]

Although Dubos was describing the experience of tasting food, the principle of 'evaluating without a principle' could also – as he said himself – be applied to other forms of experience. Indeed it was for this very reason – the lack of principle – that the emerging rococo style was criticised by its detractors. As if to compensate for the loss of meaning that the spontaneous enjoyment of sensation implied, commentators began to explore the nature of sensation from within itself, seeking to discover whether it had its own laws. On the grounds that there might be an overall 'common sense', with its own rationale, they sought correspondences – scientific or otherwise – between the five senses. Indeed, several individuals also made conscious attempts to synthesise the newly appreciated capacities of the senses into a consummate experience of art. For instance, as early as 1650, the Jesuit polymath Athanasius Kircher (c.1602–1680) stated: 'If, when a musical instrument sounds, someone would perceive the finest movements of the air, he certainly would see nothing but a painting with an extraordinary variety of colours.' Conversely, 'colours also have their harmony, which pleases no less than music, and this analogous harmony even has a very strong power to excite the affects of the mind.'[4] In 1736, the abbé Marsy asked:

> Might it be possible, at least to suit a poetic imagination, to combine the colour tones as we do sounds; to join them into a sort of concert, a kind of mute symphony, a sort of instrument without pipes, harmonious though lacking sound, that surprises and delights the eyes; in short, an ocular music that charms the senses of the spectators?[5]

In the 1720s, the Jesuit mathematician Louis-Bertrand Castel (1688–1757) speculated that sensations of sound could be translated into sensations of colour on the grounds that both media could be reduced to vibrations. Intrigued by the apparent equivalence between the musical scale of seven notes and Newton's spectrum of seven colours, he spent the rest of his life developing an 'ocular harpsichord' with which to demonstrate his theory (parodied in Fig. 14.3). The first of his many versions of the instrument was completed in 1734. It was contrived to ensure that whenever a note was sounded, a piece of coloured glass, horn, fabric or paper, illuminated by a lantern or candle, would also be exposed. According to the composer Georg Philipp Telemann, who saw some form of the contraption in 1739, it was fitted with 'silken threads or iron wires or wooden levers, which by push or pull uncover a coloured box, or a ditto panel, or a painting, or a painted lantern, such that at the same moment when a tone is heard, a colour is seen'.[6] Believing the ultimate source of all pleasure to be the harmonious proportions of the ratios latent

FIGURE 14.3: Charles-Germain de Saint-Aubin, *Que n'ont ils tous Employés leurs tems à la même Machine* (*If only they'd all spent their time on this machine*), 1740–57, watercolour, ink and graphite on paper, 18.7 × 13.2 cm. The Rothschild Collection, Waddesdon Manor.

in sensations, Castel also speculated about a possible music of textures, tastes and smells.[7] One hundred years before Septimus Piesse created the musical nomenclature of perfume that is still in use today (consisting of 'chords' of high, middle and base 'notes' that fade successively, offering a layered sequence of sensations), Castel imagined a keyboard of scents, in which the keys would lift the lids of forty scent bottles, each filled with a different scent, releasing a melodious series of fragrances. His suggestion of a music of tastes was expanded by Polycarp Poncelet, whose *Chimie de gout et d'odorat* (1755) proposed a harmony of flavours, using a scale of sour, bland, sweet, bitter, sweet-and-sour, tart and hot notes.[8]

While some of these notions may seem far-fetched today (as they did, to many people, in their own day), they do accurately reflect the growing impulse in the mid-eighteenth century to create a homogenous 'discourse of sensation' that was independent of extraneous sources of meaning – and which therefore invoked an innately sentient dimension of selfhood in its users. The contemporary French philosopher, Denis Diderot, made a direct link between the relative meaninglessness of pure sensation, especially as manifest in instrumental music, and the inclination of the individual self to respond and propagate itself: 'How is it possible that out of the three arts imitating nature [poetry, painting and music], the most arbitrary and the least precise speaks the most forcefully to our soul? Would it be that [instrumental music], by showing the objects [i.e. subject-matter] to a lesser degree, leaves more room for our imagination?'[9]

Diderot was instrumental in the ascription of cultural value to the experience of sensation, drawing attention to the particular characteristics of the various senses, and analysing the possibilities of experience, knowledge and identity that they determined. He tested his insights against the experience of blind and deaf-mute people, whom he observed and questioned on several occasions, and he published his findings. His *Lettre sur les Aveugles a l'usage de ceux qui voient* (*Letter on the Blind for the use of those who see*), published in 1749, is largely based on reports of first-hand encounters with blind people, including many of his own. Much of the book is epistemological, attempting to grasp what blind people are able to understand by abstract notions such as 'God', 'beauty', 'geometry' and 'virtue', and by vision-based phenomena, such as facial expression, eyes and mirrors – without the experience of vision, and without access to analogies based on the experience of vision. He was especially fascinated by the English mathematician Nicholas Saunderson (1682–1739), who became professor of Newtonian physics, astronomy, acoustics and optics at Christ's College, Cambridge in 1711 despite having been blind since the age of twelve months. While Saunderson was immensely capable of understanding and remembering complex principles of algebra and geometry, how did the limitations on his sensory faculties determine the way he was able to articulate, conceptualise and even experience the notion of God? While speculating on the kinds of experience and knowledge that are possible for blind people, Diderot also marvelled at the compensatory sensitivity of their other senses, drawing attention to their extraordinary subtlety and delicacy. By commenting on the ability of one blind young woman to 'tell from the sound of the liquid as it fell, when her glass was full' and to 'measure space by the sounds of footsteps or the echo of voices', he was not only appreciating *her* sensitivity to the richness and depth of her sensations; he was also showing his own appreciation of that sensitivity – and thereby introducing this quality to his readers as a new 'possibility of experience' for them too. As also demonstrated by his responses to contemporary painting and sculpture (documented in detail in his reviews of art salons from 1759 to 1781), Diderot was especially sensitive to the way the self-sense could not only receive and assess impressions but could be moulded and even created by them.

Diderot's approach to hearing was equally pragmatic. His positive attitude towards Castel's ocular keyboard was partly shaped by the revealing response of a deaf man that he took with him when he went to see the instrument – an episode that he recorded in his *Lettre sur les sourds et muets* (*Letter on Deaf-mutes*) in 1751. Having no concept of sound, the deaf man was unable to understand the experience in any way other than by analogy with his experience of the other four senses. In this instance, he sought an analogy in his understanding of reading, concluding that the instrument must be 'used to communicate with other people . . .; that each colour shade on the keyboard had the value of one of the letters of the alphabet; and that by way of the keys and the agility of his fingers, [Castel] combined these letters and formed words, phrases, indeed a whole conversation in colours.'[10]

Diderot's appreciation of the experience of sensation for its own sake was corroborated by the contemporary philosophy of 'sensationism', which maintained that all human knowledge and ideas are determined, *not* by pre-existent truths, but by the capacity of the brain to process the information it receives through the senses. This line of enquiry gave rise to all manner of questions: what mental state, if any, exists prior to the experience of sensation and the formation of knowledge? Is it possible to know anything without recourse to images, sounds, smells, tastes and textures and, if so, what and how? Could human beings have more than five senses and, if they did, how might the world seem different? According to mainstream 'sensationism', there are no such things as 'innate ideas' – knowledge or ideas that are present in individuals from birth. On the contrary, at the moment of birth, a child is a *tabula rasa*, a clean slate; *all* the ideas that he or she develops in life are derived from experience. This radical philosophy was first developed by the English philosopher John Locke, whose *Essay Concerning Human Understanding* (1690) challenged both the medieval doctrine of original sin (the notion that man is born into a state of moral debt) and the Cartesian belief in the *a priori* presence of fundamental ideas (such as that of 'God') in the mind. The Puritan economist Nicholas If-Christ-had-not-died-for-thee-thou-hadst-been-damned Barbon (1640–98) was born just too early to benefit from this initiative.

Locke's influence on 'sensationism' was largely focused around his response to the so-called 'Molyneux problem', which he published in the second edition of his *Essay* in 1694. In 1688, William Molyneux, an Irish philosopher and politician, had written to Locke, asking him the following question: would a man who had been born blind, and who had learned to distinguish between a sphere and a cube by touch, be able to correctly identify the two objects by sight alone, if he were to have his sight restored? Both Molyneux and Locke speculated that he would not be able to, as he would not yet be familiar with the conventions of perception that would enable him to identify and interpret the relevant visual information. Locke used this argument to confirm his notion that knowledge is not innate but derives from experience and reflection on experience. But concrete evidence was urgently needed. At a cataract operation in England in 1709, one 'gentleman, particularly curious' was keen not to waste a unique opportunity to observe the reaction of a mature man to his first experience of vision, and requested 'the whole company [of spectators] to keep secret, and let the patient make his own observations, without the direction of anything he had received by his other senses'; but it yielded little relevant information.[11] Locke's argument did, however, gain weight in 1728 when an eminent surgeon, Dr William Cheselden, published an account of a successful cataract operation on a thirteen- or fourteen-year-old boy 'who was born blind, or lost his sight so early that he had no remembrance of ever having seen'. Among his various observations (which were discussed by Diderot), Cheselden noted that

> when [the boy] first saw, he was so far from making any judgement about distances, that he thought all objects whatever touched his eyes (as he expressed

it) [just] as what he felt did his skin, [he] thought no objects so agreeable as those which were smooth and regular, though he could form no judgement of their shape, or guess what it was in any object that was pleasing to him: He knew not the shape of any thing, nor any one thing from another, however different in shape or magnitude; but upon being told what things were, whose form he before knew from feeling, he would carefully observe, that he might know them again; but having too many objects to learn at once, he forgot many of them; and (as he said) at first he learned to know, and again forgot a thousand things a day.[12]

Locke's speculations, increasingly reinforced by practical experiments of this kind, were hugely influential on the empirical, rationalist philosophies of the eighteenth century. They were especially significant for the French philosopher, Etienne Bonnot de Condillac, who adopted his notion of the origin of knowledge in experience and took it to its logical conclusion. Locke had maintained that knowledge was created both from primary sensations and from the natural 'operations of our mind' which transform these sensations into ideas; he called this process 'reflection', referring to it as a kind of 'internal sense' which included the functions of 'perception, thinking, doubting, believing, reasoning, knowing, willing'.[13] It was by these 'operations of the mind' that Cheselden's boy was eventually able to transform his initial perceptions into knowledge. However, while Condillac adopted the experiential approach of Locke, he considered himself to be taking Locke's theories a necessary step further by relegating 'reflections' to a secondary stage in the process of knowing, on the grounds that even the ability to evaluate the positive or negative charge of a sensation, which requires a degree of cognition, is not innate but is acquired from the experience of comparing sensations. He explained this notion, in his *Treatise on the Sensations* (1754), by imagining a marble statue that is conscious but has no senses and therefore, because it cannot perceive objects and has no language, has been unable to substantiate any ideas, including the idea of identity which, like all ideas, was not innate for him. He then imagined giving the statue one sense at a time, in order to assess what knowledge it would be able to develop on the basis of the evidence provided by each faculty.

By examining the early stages of the process of knowledge-acquisition in this way, Condillac aimed to establish a principle according to which all ideas can be seen to be based on evidence derived from complex combinations of sensations and on conclusions drawn from these combinations. He began with smell because smell is the sense that contributes least to the acquisition of human knowledge. Presented with a rose, the statue experiences the smell of a rose. Because it has no other experience and therefore has no evidence on the basis of which to differentiate between experiences, it is unable to circumscribe the smell of the rose; moreover, in this primitive state, 'it can no more have ideas of extension, shape or anything outside itself, or outside its sensations, than it can have ideas of colour, sound or taste';[14] nor can it differentiate between the smell of the rose and the very experience of selfhood – it is unable to differentiate between what 'is itself' and what 'is not itself'. As such the statue's identity is so completely invested in the experience of the smell of the rose that, from its own point of view, it *is* the smell of the rose, and is as indeterminate and uncircumscribed as the smell is; the experience of smell is nothing but the 'modification' or 'manner' of its being. When the smell of a rose is followed by the smell of another flower, the experience of the transience of the first smell activates the mental function of 'memory' in which past sensations are retained as 'ideas' (despite the fact that neither the past memory of the first smell nor the present sensation of the second one can yet be associated with objects). It is at this stage, when the statue becomes capable of relating different experiences to each other – in this case a sensation and a memory – that it becomes a unifying principle and acquires an identity:

> It seems that what we understand by this word ['me'] can only be applied to a being who notices in the present moment that he is no longer what he was. As long as he does not change, he exists without reflection on himself: but as soon as he changes he concludes that he is the same person as the one who was previously in such a state, and he says 'me'. This observation confirms that in the first moment of its existence, the statue could not form desires: for before being able to say 'I desire', it would have had to say 'me' or 'I' . . . Its 'me' is only the sum of sensations that it experiences or of those that memory recalls to it. In a word, it is at once the consciousness of what it is and the remembrance of what it has been.[15]

The relationship between the two smells also enables the statue to differentiate between relatively agreeable and disagreeable experiences, activating another mental function: that of 'judgement'. It is from this crucial function – the ability to differentiate between pain and pleasure – that 'desire' and 'volition' evolve.

Having analysed the potential of smell, Condillac moved on to the possibilities of hearing – first on its own and then in conjunction with smell – followed by taste and vision in various combinations, in each case confirming and elaborating the principles he had established in relation to smell. Exposed to hearing alone, for instance, the statue would simply *become* what it hears – 'a noise, a sound, a symphony'.[16] If first exposed to smell and hearing together, it would not be able to distinguish between the two sensations, but would experience them as a single modification of its being;[17] only when experienced successively would it be able to distinguish between them. Likewise, when first granted vision, the statue would be unable to differentiate between itself and the light and colours it was seeing. Indeed, the sensation of adjacent colours, perceived simultaneously, would expose it to the new experience of extension (not yielded by the senses it had so far experienced), and in such a case it would therefore be induced to experience itself as an uncircumscribed extension of colour. Condillac is keen to point out that this extension would not be 'a surface because the idea of surface presupposes the idea of a solid body, and [the statue] has not and could not have this idea [on the basis of evidence acquired from vision alone]. Nor has it any definite size, for a particular size is an extension enclosed within limits which circumscribe it.'[18] With regard to the sense of selfhood implied by such an indeterminate experience, he continues:

> The 'I' of the statue cannot feel itself circumscribed within limits. It is at one and the same time all the colours which modify it, and since it sees nothing beyond, it cannot perceive itself as circumscribed; since it is modified at one and the same

time by several colours, and since it feels that it exists equally in each, it feels itself extended, and since it perceives nothing which circumscribes it, it has only a vague feeling about its extension. For it, extension is unlimited. It seems to repeat itself indefinitely, and to know nothing outside the colours it believes itself to be. It is to itself immense, everywhere and everything.[19]

While the complexity of the knowledge and psychological functions that the statue would now be able to derive from its experience of sensation was immense, Condillac maintained that, with these four senses alone, it would still not be able to differentiate between itself and the outside world. Even vision, which provided evidence of extension, differentiation and variation, was unable to confirm that the sensation of seeing is not merely a function of the eye, as fantasies are a function of the mind, but that it actually involves a subject sensing objects that are not itself, for 'our cognitions are limited uniquely to the ideas we have learned to notice'.[20] The experience of otherness, by contrast, was only brought to it by the sensation of touch for, unlike the other senses, the organ of touch is knowingly able to sense both itself and objects that are not itself. If the statue were to touch itself – for instance by touching its chest with one of its fingers – it would experience *two* sensations (one in its finger and one in its chest); but if it were to touch something that was not itself it would have only *one* sensation (in its finger), from which it would be able to deduce that those objects that it could not feel as itself were not itself.[21] On the basis of this experience, it could eventually identify the sensing body as itself (because it could sense itself *as a sensing subject*) and everything else as a part of an outside world that exists independently of the body. In combination with the sense of sight it could then also begin to develop notions of shape, space, distance and movement, eventually managing to attain the 'conventional' fullness of human experience. Without the sense of touch a human being would merely 'see, smell, taste and hear without knowing that it has eyes, a nose, a mouth and ears. It [would] not even know that it has a body'; experiencing these four senses in a succession of combinations, it would think of itself as 'a colour which is successively odoriferous, savourous and sonorous' or as 'a savoury, sonorous and coloured odour'.[22]

Condillac's thought experiment was undertaken to demonstrate how all human knowledge can be deduced from the experience of sensation without recourse to innate ideas. His aim was to liberate his readers from submission to the tyranny of prejudicial beliefs, providing an argument that allowed the acquisition of knowledge to occur as a function of the body-mind. Significantly, in the main body of the *Treatise*, he was not especially preoccupied with the question of the statue's personal self-awareness or identity. Indeed, because the concept of an absolute personal identity is an abstraction, he largely passed over it. Having said that, although he did not believe in the existence of an absolute personal identity, he did repeatedly make allowances for the *feeling* or *experience* or *appearance* of identity, surmising for instance that 'it is the mode of being which [the statue] habitually *is* – that it must *experience* as the "I"; and this "I" must *appear* to it the subject of all the modifications of which it is susceptible';[23] that is to say, the statue's sense of itself is abstracted from its experience of sensation, as the apparent subject of that experience. It is not until the very end of the treatise, when Condillac allowed the statue to reflect on its experience of awakening, speaking for the first time as 'I', that he addresses this issue directly, albeit rather minimally and open-endedly. In the final chapter, called 'The memory of one who has been given the use of his senses in succession', the statue reflects: 'When I was only uniform feeling, I was, as it were, a point . . . At the first moment of my existence, I knew nothing of what was going on within me. I could not distinguish anything. I had no consciousness of myself.'

Following its first sensations, the statue noticed that 'what I feel is only myself', wondering if its sensations were 'only different modes of my own being'. As sensations came and went, it marvelled: 'I seem to alter at every moment. I seem to cease to be myself in order to become another.' Whereas it had originally felt 'without desires, without fear', it now came to feel that 'enjoying and suffering by turns make up my existence. The succession of my modifications makes me perceive that I endure. It is this variation from moment to moment, this change from pleasure to pain, and from pain to pleasure, from one state to its opposite, which was necessary to bring me to the knowledge of myself.' The first sensation of touch brought 'consistency to all my modes of being' but it also introduced the statue to a knowledge of its own body and to the experience of objects that seemed not to be itself: 'From the moment I realise this, it seems my modes of being cease to belong to me. I make them into collections outside me. I form them into objects of which I am aware.' It was not long, however, before this state became habitual; it 'formed certain habits of judgement that make me believe my sensations to be outside myself although they are not'; that is to say, sensible characteristics, such as hardness or softness, seem to be the innate properties of objects, rather than qualities of experience. Moreover as the world of apparently external objects began to expand beyond its reach, it began to feel that 'everything which I meet being formed at the expense of my own being, is made known to me only by restricting my modes of being within ever narrowing limits' (i.e. within its body, as a separate subject). Indeed, it eventually seemed to the statue that it had become the 'victim of an illusion': 'I now seem to owe all these modifications of myself to objects, for I have formed such a habit of perceiving them in objects that I have come to believe they are really there, and it is now difficult for me to believe otherwise.' That is to say, our perceptions are determined by our capacity to perceive (in the sense that the visible aspect of an object is only manifest to the extent that we can see it) and they are therefore as much manifestations of our capacity to experience – the definitive characteristic of our identities – as they are revelations of objective phenomena; not realising this, we project our 'capacity to experience' on to the objects themselves, unwittingly determining the manner in which they appear to us. Conversely, we fail to notice how the manner in which the objects of our perception seem to exist determines the manner in which we identify ourselves as perceiving subjects. As a result of this oversight, the illusion of identification seems to work. Nevertheless, Condillac is careful to have the statue acknowledge that, just as its knowledge of objects is ultimately imperfect, so is its ultimate knowledge of itself. He has it say:

> I perceive that I am formed of organs fitted to receive different impressions, I perceive that I am surrounded with objects all of which act upon me, and each acts in its own way . . . But, this 'I' which takes colour under my eyes, solidity under my hands, does it know itself any better because at the present moment it

regards all the parts of this body in which it is interested as belonging to it, and because it believes that it exists in this body? I know this body belongs to me, though how, I cannot understand. I see myself, I touch myself, I am conscious of myself, but I do not know what I am. If I believe myself to be sound, taste, colour, smell, I am no nearer the true knowledge of what I myself actually am.[24]

While Condillac used the image of the statue, progressively awakened to its senses, to demonstrate the *significance* of sensation – how sensation itself can *seem* to generate a sense of personal identity without *actually* doing so – it was also used, by several of his contemporaries, as a metaphor for the awakening of the self to the *pleasures* of sensation. Indeed, Condillac himself repeated throughout the treatise that the fundamental motive of the sentient statue was the attraction to pleasure and aversion to pain. He had the statue assert:

> It is to the consideration of pleasure and pain that I owe all my cognitions, and it is to ideas of pleasure and pain that I owe all that I am. My wants and desires and the different interests which are the motive force of my actions, arise from my ideas of pleasure and pain, so that I only observe things with a view to finding what is pleasurable in them or to discovering how to avoid them should they be painful. Pleasure and pain, then, are the light which illumines objects according to the relations in which they stand to me.[25]

In contrast to Condillac's detached and analytical reflection on the reactions of his statue, the fantasy of the French naturalist, the Comte de Buffon – of a full-grown man awakening to his senses for the first time – was a more illogical and romantic affair. Buffon's description formed part of his epic *Naturelle Histoire* (1750), in which human beings were controversially studied in the same context, and using the same methods, as other creatures in the natural world. In a section in which Buffon attempts to explain how human beings are superior to other sentient beings, he imagines their responses to their sensations of the world. Unlike Condillac's statue, his awakening man was able to recognise objects and revel in their beauty as soon as he opened his eyes. Like Condillac, on the other hand, Buffon ascribed special significance to the sense of touch, which he said was particularly developed in human beings (and apes) as reflected in the advanced development of their hands. In human beings touch was raised to a unique level of sensitivity due to its ability to induce *feeling* in them. Thus when his primitive man discovered a certain unfamiliar object beside him, he responded as follows:

> I ventured to lay my hand upon this new being; with rapture and astonishment I perceived that it was not myself, but something much more glorious and desirable; and I imagined that my existence was about to dissolve, and to be wholly transfused into this second part of my being. I perceived her to be animated by the touch of my hand: I saw her catch the expression in my eyes; and the lustre and vivacity of her own made a new source of life thrill in my veins. I ardently wished to transfer my whole being to her; and this wish completed my existence; for now I discovered a sixth sense.[26]

With regard to combinations of the senses, Buffon was again more interested in the potential for pleasure than the potential for knowledge. Remembering later how the sun set on the innocent lovers as they began to discover each other – throwing them into darkness – the awakened man recalled that though he could not see his beloved, he could still derive pleasure and identity from the sensation of touching her: 'I perceived with pain, that I lost the sense of seeing; [but] my [tactile] enjoyment was too exquisite to allow me [to] dread annihilation.'[27]

The image of the senseless body coming to life was further explored through the mythological figure of Pygmalion, who became a subject of fascination for writers and artists at the beginning of the eighteenth century. According to Ovid's *Metamorphoses*, Pygmalion was a Cypriot sculptor who carved the figure of a woman from a piece of ivory and, because the sculpture was more beautiful than any living woman, promptly fell in love with her. Responding to his prayer to Venus for a woman of equal beauty, the goddess took pity on him and contrived that, yielding to his touch and gathering warmth from his kisses, the statue should come alive and that they should marry. At the beginning of the eighteenth century, the scene (which retained a modicum of dignity on account of its classical source) was conceived in the manner of a gallant pastoral idyll but, as the century progressed, it became ever more loaded with philosophical and poetic associations. In his fable *Pigmalion, ou la Statue animée* of 1741, for instance, the philosopher Andre-François Boureau-Deslandes used the story to articulate a philosophy of universal materialism in opposition to Descartes' mind-and-body dualism. In conjunction with his rejection of the dualistic belief in abstractions, Boureau-Deslandes' insistence on the unity of existence led him to posit that the universe must consist of a single substance and, therefore, that all signs of change, including the apparent movement of thought and the cycle of life and death, are mere modifications of that one substance. Consciousness, therefore, is not a gift from 'above'; it is a natural property of matter, waxing and waning, as exemplified by the apparent 'awakening' of the sculpture. As with Condillac, whom he influenced, Boureau-Deslandes believed that all knowledge is derived from sensory experience and that the impression of personal identity is no more than a conflation of reminiscences, a 'joining together of ideas that follow each other, only interrupted by short intervals'.[28] As a result, Boureau-Deslandes relates that Pygmalion's sculpture (like Condillac's statue) knows nothing when she first comes to life, though (like Buffon's awakening man) she can formulate her first thoughts: 'Who am I, and what was I a moment ago? I do not understand myself. What is my destiny? Why have I been extracted from the nothingness?' Moreover, she soon becomes able to formulate ideas about her nature: 'The only thing I notice, the only thing I am permitted to know is that I exist and that I sense that I exist . . . I sense that if I exist I must exist with contentment, with satisfaction about myself.'[29] Pygmalion attempts to explain to her who she is, and eventually kisses her on the lips, introducing her to the experience of what he calls 'pleasure', whereupon she realises that it is not only sensation, but the *pleasure* of sensation that is the proof and principle of her identity: 'Now I cannot doubt that I live. What you call pleasure succeeds in convincing me of my being and persuading me of its reality.'[30]

While the transformation of Pygmalion's sculpture from an inert block of ivory into a beautiful, sensuous woman (called 'Galatea' from the middle of the eighteenth century) was put to good use by the advocates of sensationism and materialism, the *timing* of the revived interest in the image resonated with historical developments that were beyond the philosophers' immediate control. Just as Galatea awakened from an elevated state of unattainable perfection to the lively and affecting experience of sensation and relationship, so – in the mid-eighteenth century – the conventional experience of personal identity (among the privileged) slowly began to shift from a model of individuality that was oriented towards an objective ideal, to a model that was conceived around the self-centred pleasures of sensory experience. Galatea's moment of transformation was aptly captured in numerous paintings of the scene in which her legs are still made of stone (replacing the original ivory) but her torso, arms and head have become tinted with the colours of life, as if blood has begun to course through her veins, dispelling the pallor of numbness (Fig. 14.4). Etienne Falconet's marble sculpture of the subject (1763) captures this moment without recourse to colour (Fig. 14.5). Writing in *Le Mercure*, a contemporary critic of the work pointed out that Galatea's legs are carved to look like marble – a sculpture of a sculpture – whereas her torso, animated by Cupid's kiss, is carved to look like flesh – a sculpture of a body.[31] To achieve this effect it is arguable that Falconet has

FIGURE 14.4: Jean Raoux, *Pygmalion falling in love with his statue*, 1717, oil on canvas, 129.1 × 97.5 cm. Musée Fabre, Montpelier.

FIGURE 14.5: Etienne-Maurice Falconet, *Pygmalion and Galatea*, 1763, marble, 59.5 × 40 × 29 cm. Walters Art Gallery.

made Galatea's legs in an idealised classical style and her torso in a softer, more natural rococo manner, such that the narrative development and stylistic variation in the work become mutually enhancing functions of each other; in so doing, he demonstrated his conviction that the key challenge for a sculptor was not just to imitate the form of the human body but to infuse it with *feeling* – a skill with which he believed the Moderns to be more endowed than the Ancients.[32] All that remains is for the viewer to notice the shift – an act of perception that presupposes that, without his necessarily knowing it, he is also awakening to a new level of sensitivity, and is therefore coming alive. Indeed, in that moment of perception, the two awakenings become co-causal reflections of each other, such that the viewer's awakening to his own feelings, as a sentient and sensitive individual, is accomplished *by*, and reflected back to him *as*, his recognition of Galatea coming to life.

The self-reflective potential of the encounter between Pygmalion and Galatea was especially resonant in the middle of the eighteenth century. In Rousseau's lyrical dramatisation of the story, written in 1762, it is the profound longing of Pygmalion to perfect the realisation of his own artistic idea – and, by proxy, of his own identity – that brings Galatea to life. Indeed such is her dependence on his imagination that, when she touches him, she believes herself to be touching herself, whereupon he, in response, exclaims: 'I have given you all my being, I no longer live but by you.'[33] According to Diderot, this symbiotic mechanism is also implicit in Falconet's work, which he discussed in his Salon review of 1763. The fact that Falconet was sculpting an image of Galatea identifies him, by analogy, with the transformative figure of Pygmalion. By extension, the fact that he was carving an image of Pygmalion raises the possibility that *that image* might also magically come to life, and that he might therefore also be 'realising himself', creating his own awakening. Among the art-viewing public as a whole, it was a viewer's sensory capacities (newly valorised by the establishment of new cultural conventions) rather than his antiquarian or connoisseurial skills, that brought a work of art to life, as a vicarious realisation of his own identity as a sentient and sensitive individual.

CHAPTER FIFTEEN

The Autonomy of the Self: the Invention of Taste and Aesthetics

While the experience of sensation is, in itself, meaningless, philosophers argued that it could not be arbitrary. For if it was arbitrary, people would be randomly attracted to, and repelled by, objects of sensation – and this is not the case. Nor could the attractive aspect, or beauty, of a phenomenon be an objective property of that phenomenon because, if it was, everybody would observe it – which they clearly do not do. Therefore there must be some internal principle that informs the evaluation of the pleasurability of a sensation. This principle was loosely identified as 'taste'. Applied in all experiences of *pleasure* and *beauty*, and elevated to the level of a 'discipline' in *aesthetics*, the notion of taste developed as a direct function of the sense of personal identity, institutionalising it as a 'self-evident' social and psychological convention.

One of the first writers to address this question was the writer, politician and journalist Joseph Addison, who observed in 1712 that the word 'taste' 'arises very often in conversation'.[1] As a result of this observation, Addison took it upon himself to give some account of the word in *The Spectator* magazine, which he had co-founded in the previous year as a forum for the public discussion of current affairs and ideas. By generating debate around this topic – often in coffee houses, newly conceived for this newly informal mode of socialising – Addison was instrumental in establishing a 'discourse of taste' in which individuals were expected to become sensitive to their preferences, and to adapt the parameters of their identities accordingly.

At the time at which Addison was writing, classical or classicising literature was still considered to be the most elevated form of cultural expression and it is natural, therefore, that Addison himself should have formulated his notion of taste in relation to this conservative medium. Regardless of the areas in which it was applied, however, the notion itself was novel. Addison identified taste as 'the faculty of the soul which discerns the beauties of an author with pleasure, and the imperfections with dislike'. He explained that the reason why the discourse of taste makes use of the word used for sensing the flavour of food – not only in English, but in several languages – was the 'very great conformity' between the two phenomena: while 'mental taste' involves 'many degrees of refinement in the intellectual faculty', 'sensitive [sensory] taste . . . gives us a relish of every different flavour that affects the palate'. The expansion of the meaning of this word – from a form of sensing to a form of knowing – anticipated Condillac by highlighting how the possibility of human knowledge is determined by the experience of sensation, not least when it inherits the language used to articulate that experience and re-uses it metaphorically. Demonstrating how the semantic conventions associated with a sensation could help express and shape a new concept, Addison continued:

> I knew a Person who possessed [sensitive taste] in so great a Perfection, that after having tasted ten different Kinds of Tea, he would distinguish, without seeing the Colour of it, the particular Sort which was offered him; and not only so, but any two Sorts of them that were mixt together in an equal Proportion; nay he has carried the Experiment so far, as upon tasting the Composition of three different Sorts, to name the Parcels from whence the three several Ingredients were taken. A Man of a fine Taste in Writing will discern, after the same manner, not only the general Beauties and Imperfections of an Author, but discover the several Ways of thinking and expressing himself, which diversify him from all other Authors, with the several Foreign Infusions of Thought and Language, and the particular Authors from whom they were borrowed.[2]

Having identified that taste is not only a faculty of discernment but also of 'diversification' (or individuation), Addison goes on to consider how it is acquired, immediately coming face to face with the problem that remained a key focus of the debate throughout the eighteenth century – 'is taste naturally present in human beings or is it acquired?' – to which he answered, inconclusively, 'both': 'notwithstanding this Faculty must in some measure be born with us, there are several Methods for Cultivating and Improving it.' While he recommends studying the works of 'great authors' and the 'best critics, both ancient and modern', and keeping the company of 'men of polite genius' (without saying what makes them 'great' or 'genius'), he also says that, by becoming familiar with these sources, 'a Man who has any Relish for fine Writing . . . naturally wears himself into the same manner of Speaking and Thinking'; that is to say, beyond merely *imitating* his models, he appropriates the broader *condition* in which they are seen to function, as his own, and is then duly subject to it. Reflecting his originality, Addison concludes, somewhat wistfully, by acknowledging that contemporary writing continues to be evaluated according to its conformity to rules, which are prescribed and objective, rather than taste, which is conscious and subjective:

> I must confess that I could wish there were Authors of this kind, who beside the Mechanical Rules which a Man of very little Taste may discourse upon, would enter into the very Spirit and Soul of fine Writing, and shew us the several Sources of that Pleasure which rises in the Mind upon the Perusal of a noble Work.[3]

One philosopher who, inspired by Addison, attempted to 'shew us the sources of pleasure', was the Irish philosopher Francis Hutcheson. In his *Inquiry into the Original of our Ideas of Beauty and Virtue* of 1725, Hutcheson pointed out that, while recent rationalist philosophy had largely revolved around the 'understanding of [objective] truth' and the inclination of truth to make men happy or to give them 'the greatest and most lasting pleasure', it neglected to show 'how it is that knowledge or truth is pleasant to us' – that is to say, how an objective truth, identified by reason, is subjectively evaluated and enjoyed. The same was true of 'our sensible pleasures [which] are slightly pass'd over, and explained only by some instances in tastes, smells, sounds, or such-like, which men of any tolerable reflection [conservative rationalists] generally look upon as very trifling satisfactions'.[4] To correct this prejudice, he set out to show that the capacity to experience pleasure from objects did not simply follow on from a rational understanding of the significance or value of those objects, or even from their moral value, but that it was an independent and automatic function or 'internal sense', as natural to human beings as their five 'external' senses.

The attempt to identify this 'internal sense', spontaneously motivated by attraction to pleasure and aversion to pain, remained a preoccupation of philosophers throughout the eighteenth century. Although the exact manner of its working was constantly being refined, it was widely hypothesised that, in one way or another, the capacity to experience pleasure presupposed the existence of a subjective faculty of discernment, or taste. Indeed, the mechanism that underpinned the mutual dependency of pleasure and taste was gradually conventionalised to the point at which it seemed to be natural. It is arguable that the flourishing of the rococo style was a spontaneous expression of this faculty, showing no interest in its principles but only in its exercise. Whether one approved of the style or not was irrelevant; more significant was the fact that its very existence helped to weave the legitimacy and expectation of a self-image, constructed around the possibility of pleasure, into the fabric of the culture. For the first time, it became culturally acceptable for individuals to make artistic choices without having to rationalise or justify them. In some instances, the quality of artistic experience, approved by taste, was rated more highly than the conventional promises of religion salvation. In 1721, the painter Antoine Watteau was said to have rejected the crucifix held out to him on his deathbed by his confessor, on the grounds that it was not 'good art'.

Even so, while the concept of taste institutionalised and legitimised the experience (and, most significantly, the subject) of pleasure – answering charges of 'randomness' on the one hand, and 'objectivity' on the other – it was also problematic because it suggested that people were constitutionally, and therefore equally, endowed with the capacity to discern between pleasures, just as they are equally endowed with an ability to discern between colours. But, surely, if this were the case, all people would find the same sensations equally pleasurable – which they clearly do not do. Nor does the endowment of people with taste explain what it is that inclines them to prefer one sensation to another (without recourse to rational interpretation). Despite the impossibility of solving this problem, the attempt to define a faculty of taste coincided with the growing *abstraction* of the discourse, in the sense that it was not only associated with the socialised appreciation of literature and manners (chronically distorted by snobbery, despite pretensions to objectivity) but also, more fundamentally, with the exploration of pleasure as a primary form of human cognition. In Germany this shift was reflected in the evolution of the concept of 'aesthetics', based on an ancient Greek word that was adapted by the philosopher Alexander Baumgarten (1714–62) to refer to the experience of sensory perception as a direct means of knowing, distinct from the experience of conceptual understanding.[5] Baumgarten conceived the discipline of aesthetics as a principled 'science of sensory cognition' that aimed to expand the realm of the explorable world, beyond the limits of the measurable and comprehensible, to include complex, immeasurable and uncontainable objects of experience. His pioneering *Aesthetica* (conceived in 1735 but not published until 1750) was at least partly inspired by the efforts of his predecessor Christian Wolff (1679–1754) to develop an empirical and metaphysical 'science of the soul' in his *Psychologia Empirica* (1732) and *Psychologia Rationalis* (1734). By attempting to define subjective experience in terms of practical and theoretical principles – what *does* happen, and what *could* happen, in the mind – Wolff not only institutionalised an independent, autonomous identity for the self, but also provided a foundation – and eventually a name – for the incipient discipline of 'psychology'. Preceding psychometric testing by over a century, he was the first to think of *attention* – constituting the selective direction of subjective consciousness towards objects – as a function of individual minds that could be measured.

Especially in Britain, the notion and inclinations of personal identity were supported by the proto-psychological notion of 'associationism'. Advocates of this theory, spearheaded by the philosopher David Hartley (1705–57), proposed that an individual's capacity to evaluate his experience is determined not only by the objective (or at least impersonal) value of what he experiences, which is shared by others, but also by the particular associations which his experiences conjure up in him *personally*. Thus, an apple, for instance, could be experienced as food, a specimen of natural history or a symbol of religious meaning, but it might also carry unhappy associations with, for instance, an orchard that one had to walk through as a child on the way to an unpleasant school. In this way, it became possible for the world of 'rational meaning' to be supplemented, and even challenged by, a world of 'irrational meaning'. In the latter capacity, the value of the apple is completely subjective and has nothing to do with the apple as such; nor is it shared by other individuals. Moreover, an individual can become so habituated to these associations that they acquire the power of a natural truth. In the words of John Locke, who laid the foundations of associationism in 1700 when he added a new chapter, 'Of the Association of Ideas', to the fourth edition of his *Essay Concerning Human Understanding*:

> Some of our ideas have a natural [objective] correspondence and connexion one with another: it is the office and excellency of our reason to trace these, and hold them together in that union and correspondence which is founded in their peculiar beings. Besides this, there is another connexion of ideas wholly owing to chance or custom, ideas that in themselves are not all of kin, come to be so united in some men's minds, that 'tis very hard to separate them, they always keep in company, and the one no sooner at any time comes into the understanding, but its associate appears with it; and if they are more than two which are thus united, the whole gang always inseparable show themselves together. This strong combination of ideas, not allied by nature, the mind makes in itself either voluntarily or by chance, and hence it comes in different men to be very different, according to their different inclinations, education, interests, &c. Custom settles habits of thinking in the understanding, as well as of determining in the will, and

of motions in the body; all which seems to be but trains of motions in the animal spirits, which once set agoing continue in the same steps they have been used to; which, by often treading, are worn into a smooth path, and the motion in it becomes easy, and as it were natural.[6]

Although meanings conceived by association were originally subjective and experiential, they too could become established as conventions through usage – legitimising not only the individual fruits of subjectivity (e.g. highly subjective 'Romantic' works of art, which became common accordingly towards the end of the eighteenth century) but also the very principle of subjectivity as a ground for shared cultural values. In such cases, the sources of cultural values become so embedded in the mindset of the culture that they become invisible and untraceable, such that their effects become 'as it were natural'. Writing in 1754, the philosopher David Hume was intrigued by the fact that the contemporary poet Thomas Blacklock could have developed an appreciation of colour sufficiently accurately to use it in his work, despite the fact that he was totally blind. Blacklock explained that he had 'met so often both in [dictated] Books and conversation, with the terms expressing colors, [that] he had formed some false associations, which supported him when he read, wrote, or talk'd of colors: but that the associations were of the intellectual kind'. Using a kind of reverse engineering, he was able to derive meaning from the linguistic conventions themselves, regardless of their origins and without actually experiencing that to which they referred. By such means, Hume surmised, the conventions of language can become an autonomous source of meaning – simulating reality, independent of the outside world: "tis but too frequent to substitute Words in stead of Ideas.'[7] Indeed, as Condillac also suggested, even a sense of self can be elicited from language and cultural conventions.

In experiences in which the impact of associations is powerful, the 'determinant of value' is not only necessarily subjective, as in the experience of taste or beauty; it is also relatively random and idiosyncratic – deeply personal in fact – *unlike* the experience of taste or beauty which seemed to be shared by groups of people and was therefore presumed to be informed by a common principle (albeit an elusive one, as we have seen). Indeed, to the extent that such experiences are shaped by the personal memories of the individual that has them, they are entirely solipsistic, manifesting the disposition of the subject more than the properties of their objects per se. It is precisely in its tolerance of the arbitrariness of subjectivity that the importance of associationism lies: it articulated a rationale for personal identity that made no significant claims to objectivity, and thereby provided cultural legitimacy for a dimension of selfhood that could be substantiated entirely from within its own experience, no matter how irrational and idiosyncratic that experience might be. As such, it was to become integral to the practical discipline of psychology – seeking and finding a rationale for personal selfhood in the manifestations of its innermost mental activity, rather than in the notion of the self as a persona or social reality. The extent to which this uniquely personal dimension of selfhood was newly accommodated in contemporary culture is reflected, not only in the institutionalisation of the discipline of psychology itself, but also in the way in which extreme cases – that is, deranged individuals who were obsessively identified with the contents of their own minds – were accommodated by new social and medical organisations. Until the seventeenth century such cases had typically been classed as incurable and demonic lunatics, and were alienated in madhouses that resembled prisons. But, in the eighteenth century, the first therapeutic asylums were founded, reflecting how even the most exaggerated and anti-social experiences of subjectivity could now be accommodated within the fabric of cultural life.

Despite the fact that a sense of personal self had been realised in western culture since Descartes, and increasingly manifest in the material culture of the time, it had always succeeded in evading *direct* observation. At the same time, although it was variously seen to be immaterial, insubstantial, provisional, or even entirely fantasised, such was the force of its self-reflexivity that it was – *from its own perspective* – impossible to deny. As soon as Descartes announced the self-evident existence of the self, on the grounds of its self-awareness – a turning point in the history of European experience and culture, of inestimable significance – philosophers began to contemplate it. Descartes himself had suggested that the essence of the human individual (variously referred to as the 'soul' or 'self' or 'mind') was an immaterial substance, independent of, but organically related to, the material body. Even though he was ultimately, and paradoxically, unable to relinquish the notion of God, his rejection of the notion of belief was of paramount importance because it made way for a genuinely empirical investigation of the phenomenon of consciousness which the paradigm of belief had previously rendered both unnecessary (because the notion of 'God' answered all the difficult questions) and fruitless (because the notion of God was beyond the possibility of understanding). Similarly, by discrediting the 'innate idea' of original sin, Locke removed a powerful emotional constraint that militated against any attempt at a disinterested investigation into the nature of human experience. But, like Descartes, he could not relinquish the idea of God (on moral grounds). Indeed, it was partly in response to the implications of his philosophy for Christianity that he felt compelled to explore the issue of personal identity (adding a chapter on the subject to the 1694 edition of his *Essay*): what part of the human individual will be resurrected at the end of time, as promised to the blessed by the Church – the body, the soul, the 'person'? On what grounds could the one God be said to be three 'persons'? Out of these theological questions came the more radical question: what is it exactly that constitutes the individual 'person' or 'self'?

Although both Descartes and Locke affirmed the existence of God – as a matter of principle – their views prepared the ground for a self-sense that was not predicated on religious belief; indeed the possibility of atheism, hitherto inconceivable, was emerging in their time. By slow degrees, the word 'soul' – referring to the ethereal essence of an individual, traditionally considered to be an immortal 'part of God' – was eclipsed by the word 'mind' – referring to the non-substantial consciousness of personal identity as an autonomous semi-technical function of individuality, unencumbered by metaphysical speculations. Ironically, significant contributions to the development of the discourse of independent identity were also made by Locke's Puritan detractors, in spite of themselves. It was partly through their verbose diatribes against any attribute that reflected a sense of independent 'self', as opposed to a dependent 'soul' – both in themselves and others – that 'self'-oriented words such as 'self-interest', 'self-indulgence' and 'self-confidence' were introduced to the

English vocabulary. Some of these concepts were developed in the context of individuals' written 'reflections' on their inner life which, in Protestant Britain, replaced the Catholic practice of confessing to a priest. Although such reflections were initially self-deprecatory – following the example of St Augustine's *Confessions* – they also established the self-sense as both author and authority, paving the way for the 'memoire' as a primary medium for the cultivation of personal identity.

Significantly, it was precisely at this time that thinkers began to articulate the notions of 'consciousness' and 'self-consciousness' as phenomena in their own right (regardless of the concept of God) and to develop a vocabulary that both facilitated and shaped their exploration. Based on the Latin *con* and *scire*, meaning 'to know ... with ...', the Latin word *conscius* originally signified 'shared knowledge', especially knowledge shared by an exclusive group – 'knowing something *with* another'. Because such knowledge was held in secret, it became a form of power, rooted in trust, and it acquired moral implications. It could for instance be used against another person (e.g. in blackmail). By the Middle Ages, awareness of the moral potential of shared knowledge had been internalised as moral knowledge of one's *own* actions, or 'conscience' (as we saw in chapter 2). But in the seventeenth century, the word was developed in such a way that it could also refer to a purely metaphysical awareness of subjectivity. In Britain, the words 'consciousness' and 'self-perception' developed to refer to this new meaning. Reflecting the emergence of a new mode of experience and a new model of personal identity, they were first used (without any moralising association with the more ancient English word 'conscience') by Ralph Cudworth in 1678.[8] Conflating the two terms, the notion of 'self-consciousness' appears to have developed in around 1690. This word was popularised by Locke, who was accused by one English critic of having 'stocked our language with such a spawn of new words that one will need a new dictionary to understand English'.[9] In France, by contrast, academics were highly conservative in their efforts to preserve the purity of the French language and were painstaking in their attempts to find appropriate vocabulary, often already current, for new concepts. As a result, in France the word *conscience* was extended to cover 'consciousness' (as well as the English 'conscience'). A French–English dictionary of 1611 captured the word in a transitional state, in which the two meanings are strongly inter-related, rendering it as 'the testimony of our own knowledge, the witness of our own thoughts, a remorse or remorseful remembrance of', as if independent self-awareness, distinct from God's knowledge of oneself, was itself a cause for remorse; indeed, throughout the seventeenth century, French moralists – most notably Blaise Pascal – were anxious that excessive scrutiny of oneself would lead to *amour-propre* or self-love.[10] The broadening of the meaning of the French word *conscience* was sealed by the desire to translate Locke's *Essay*, through which the new term 'self-consciousness' (rendered in French as *conscience*) became currency.

The adaptation of old words to new ends, and the development of entirely new words, was significant for several reasons: firstly, it made it possible to articulate new ideas, furnishing the embryonic discipline of psychology with a vocabulary; secondly, it enriched the vernacular languages, promoting their use in place of Latin, which had been universal among scholars for centuries but which was now seen to be archaic and socially exclusive; and thirdly, it institutionalised new possibilities of experience, rooted in the perception of an independent self-sense, both in the present and for the future.

The conceptualisation of self-consciousness had a momentous impact on the notion of personal identity, consummating it – by rendering it self-reflexive – while also seeming to dissolve it. In his *Essay*, Locke rejected Descartes' polarised notion of selfhood (between the soul and the body) on the grounds that it turned the sense of self into a theoretical abstraction or object. He maintained that the self is neither a material nor an immaterial substance. On the one hand, the fact that the material particles of the body are perpetually changing, and that the sense of personal identity is not diminished by the amputation of a limb, is enough to demonstrate that the self is not identified with the material substance of the body; on the other hand, that our sense of self changes during the course of our lives demonstrates that it is not an independent abstraction, disengaged from our material circumstances. On the contrary, confronting the subject on its own terms for the first time, Locke proposed that personal identity is not so much an entity as a form of consciousness – that it exists as a function in experience that is conscious of itself:

> To find wherein personal identity consists, we must consider what 'person' stands for; which, I think, is a thinking intelligent being, that has reason and reflection, and can consider itself as itself, the same thinking thing, in different times and places; which it does only by that consciousness which is inseparable from thinking, and, as it seems to me, essential to it: it being impossible for any one to perceive without perceiving that he does perceive. When we see, hear, smell, taste, feel, meditate, or will anything, we know that we do so. Thus it is always as to our present sensations and perceptions: and by this every one is to himself that which he calls 'self' . . . Since consciousness always accompanies thinking, and it is that which makes every one to be what he calls 'self', and thereby distinguishes himself from all other thinking things, in this alone consists personal identity, i.e. the sameness of a rational being.[11]

Besides being conscious and self-reflective, Locke also maintained that personal identity is continuous, remaining the same over time; indeed, the word 'identity' comes from the Latin word for 'the same', *idem*, indicating that identity is that which remains the same as itself – the same as, or 'identical' to, what it was. Despite the fact that the same perceptions are not always 'consciously present' to the mind, personal identity remains coherent over time by virtue of memory and expectation. This is due to the fact that

> any intelligent being can repeat the idea of any past action with the same consciousness it had of it at first, and with the same consciousness it has of any present action; so far, it is the same personal self. For it is by the consciousness it has of its present thoughts and actions, that it is self to itself now, and so will be the same self, as far as the same consciousness can extend to actions past or to come.

Indeed, the self is no more fragmented by the coming and going of experiences 'than a man be two men by wearing other clothes to-day than he did yesterday, with a long or a short sleep between'. On the contrary, it would be 'the same consciousness uniting those distant actions into the same person, whatever substances contributed to their production'.[12]

Many conservatives reacted against Locke's views of personal identity – on theological and moral grounds – for they seemed to undermine the notion of a soul capable of salvation by God and the possibility of taking personal responsibility for one's actions. But they were also hugely influential on progressive thinkers both in England and in France. Following Locke, the French philosopher Henri de Boulainvilliers maintained in his *Essai de métaphysique* of 1712 that the self – 'the present me' (*le moi présent*) – was not the independent and autonomous *subject* of its perceptions but that it was a transitory mental construct abstracted from its perceptions:

> My self is neither a faculty that thinks or has ideas, nor is it a simple or composite idea; but rather it is a succession or continuity of ideas which are born from my perceptions, in so far as the organic constitution of my body renders it capable of feeling; perceptions are the basis and the proper matter of my self (*mon esprit*).[13]

Elsewhere he stated: 'The human soul (*l'âme humaine*) has no other reality than that which it draws from the ideas with which it is successively occupied.'[14] Thus, the self does not exist as an autonomous phenomenon; it only exists to the extent that it is aware of itself; in fact it is the *activity of self-reflection* (arising in selfless consciousness) that creates and indeed constitutes it. Thirty years later, David Hume was addressing the same issue and, on the basis of empirical research, ended up questioning the existence of the personal self altogether. In his *Treatise of Human Nature* (1739–40), he wrote:

> There are some philosophers who imagine we are every moment intimately conscious of what we call our *self*; that we feel its existence and its continuance in existence; and are certain, beyond the evidence of a demonstration, both of its perfect identity and simplicity. The strongest sensation, the most violent passion, say they, instead of distracting us from this view, only fix it the more intensely, and make us consider their influence on self either by their pain or pleasure.

But, Hume argues, because such impressions are fleeting and transient, it is impossible for them to embody a continuous sense of selfhood:

> But, self or person is not any one impression, but that to which our several impressions and ideas are supposed to have a reference. If any impression gives rise to the idea of self, that impression must continue invariably the same, through the whole course of our lives; since self is supposed to exist after that manner. But, there is no impression constant and invariable. Pain and pleasure, grief and joy, passions and sensations succeed each other, and never all exist at the same time. It cannot, therefore, be from any of these impressions, or from any other, that the idea of self is derived; and consequently there is no such idea.

Speaking for himself, he adds:

> For my part, when I enter most intimately into what I call myself, I always stumble on some particular perception or other, of heat or cold, light or shade, love or

hatred, pain or pleasure. I never can catch myself at any time without a perception, and never can observe any thing but the perception. When my perceptions are removed for any time, as by sound sleep; so long am I insensible of myself, and may truly be said not to exist. And were all my perceptions removed by death, and could I neither think, nor feel, nor see, nor love, nor hate after the dissolution of my body, I should be entirely annihilated.

Therefore, despite our great 'propension to ascribe an identity to these successive perceptions, and to suppose ourselves possest of an invariable and uninterrupted existence through the whole course of our lives', personal identity is

nothing but a bundle or collection of different perceptions, which succeed each other with an inconceivable rapidity, and are in a perpetual flux and movement. Our eyes cannot turn in their sockets without varying our perceptions. Our thought is still more variable than our sight; and all our other senses and faculties contribute to this change; nor is there any single power of the soul, which remains unalterably the same, perhaps for one moment. The mind is a kind of theatre, where several perceptions successively make their appearance; pass, re-pass, glide away, and mingle in an infinite variety of postures and situations. There is properly no simplicity in it at one time, nor identity in different, whatever natural propension we may have to imagine that simplicity and identity. The comparison of the theatre must not mislead us. They are the successive perceptions only, that constitute the mind; nor have we the most distant notion of the place, where these scenes are represented, or of the materials, of which it is composed.[15]

While it would be too much to expect Hume's realisation of the indeterminacy of the mind to be reflected in formless art, as it was in the twentieth century, it was entirely consistent with Hogarth's contemporary observation (published in his *Analysis of Beauty*, Fig. 11.6) that our visual experience consists, not of homogenous apprehensions of static objects, extended in time, but of rapid sequences of perceptions, synthesised into mental abstractions. Indeed it is arguable that Hume's indeterminacy was subliminally dispersed into the culture by, and as, taste for the amorphous rococo style that Hogarth's observation justified. Perhaps the most direct near-contemporary visualisation of this formlessness of the mind is to be found in Laurence Sterne's novel *The Life and Opinions of Tristram Shandy, Gentleman* (1759–67), in which the narrator endeavours to tell his life story but fails, on account of the numerous digressions he is unable to resist making. In an unprecedented gesture, Sterne/Shandy self-consciously illustrated the way he was failing to achieve his aim with a page of marbling that he inserted into the middle of the text (Fig. 15.1). It was surely the fact that the marbled page (unique in each copy of the book) was both indeterminate and created by random and accidental processes that he called it a 'motly emblem of my work', referring to his doomed effort to 'realise himself' as a coherent self.

Hume's refusal to find an abiding principle where he did not experience one was criticised for exactly the reasons the contemporary rococo style was criticised. While both phenomena were empirical – indeed *because* both phenomena were empirical, embracing the vagaries of personal psychology – they seemed to lack an objective

FIGURE 15.1: The marbled page from Laurence Sterne's *Tristram Shandy*, London, 1795 edition. Private collection.

principle. And just as the formlessness of the 'indulgent' rococo style was superseded by the 'responsible' neo-classical style which constituted a revival of interest in classical principle, so the formlessness of subjective psychology was superseded by an insistence that the self-sense *must* exist – not on the grounds of experience but *as a matter of principle*. Kant, for instance, reacted against both Hume and Baumgarten. Not unlike a neo-classical critic of the rococo style, he criticised Hume for questioning the possibility of absolute knowledge, and the threat to morality that his 'scepticism' seemed to pose; and he criticised Baumgarten's 'aesthetic principle' on the grounds that it was entirely dependent on empirical evidence and was therefore impossible to objectify: it should only be used, he maintained, in relation to the equally conditional context of 'psychological' meaning (though he did also concede that, although psychology was not a science, it was worthy of study as a discipline at university level).[16] As he wrote in his *Critique of Pure Reason*, in 1781:

> The Germans are the only people who currently make use of the word 'aesthetic' in order to signify what others call the critique of taste. This usage originated in the abortive attempt made by Baumgarten, that admirable analytical thinker, to bring the critical treatment of the beautiful under rational principles, and so to raise its rules to the rank of a science. But, such endeavours are fruitless. The said rules or criteria are, as regards their chief sources, merely empirical, and consequently can never serve as determinate *a priori* laws by which our judgment of taste must be directed.[17]

It was, however, with Kant that the paradoxical problem of taste – and, above all, the self-sense it presumes – came to a head. Frustrated by not being able to objectify a principle of aesthetic appreciation empirically, Kant was determined to push the discourse of taste to its logical conclusion by establishing an absolute *a priori* principle of beauty that need not, and could not, be modified on theoretical grounds. To achieve this, he elevated beauty to the level of a 'universal', observing that, unlike a simple experience of pleasure which can easily be ascribed to a subjective whim, an experience of beauty *seems* to be objective. Moreover, he hypothesised that, for an experience of beauty to feel authentic, its cause must at least *seem* to be a property of the object under consideration; hence the inevitable impression that its appeal must be universal. Having said this, because the faculty of taste that discerns beauty is necessarily subjective, the experience of 'objective beauty' must also involve the fulfilment of an innate potential for objective knowledge within the subject. Indeed, to the extent that the capacity to experience objective beauty presupposes a degree of objectivity within the subject, conferring absolute autonomy on a sense of selfhood that had only been *implicit* in the earlier discourse of taste, it concretises, and seems to prove, the existence of the subjective self; once established, the object and the subject (seem to) necessitate each other.

It is arguable that the possibility of experiencing objective beauty was constructed at this time as the consummate 'form' of the personal self-sense. Precisely because the experience of beauty was perceived to be absolutely independent of the need for an external rationale, it provided the self-sense with a frame of reference in which it could also experience *itself* as independent of the need for an external rationale, and therefore as self-authenticating. As such, the 'experience of beauty' – elevated to the level of an objective truth by Kant's highly influential philosophy of aesthetics – amounts to a sacralisation, and even an apotheosis, of subjectivity.

Although, in practice, beauty was constantly found to be falling short of the ideal of objectivity, the *discourse* of aesthetics provided an ever-flexible frame of reference in which the spontaneous faculty of taste, and the pleasure-seeking sense of self that exercised it, could thrive. Indeed, it is arguable that, once it became established as a convention – and regardless of its contents – the discourse of taste and aesthetics became one of the most pervasive and effective sources of personal identity in the westernised world (especially, but by no means exclusively, as institutionalised in the convention of 'art'). But because it was ultimately impossible for Kant to prove the existence of 'pure subjectivity' (because it only *seemed* to be absolute), it became a theoretical and linguistic construct – an *idea*. To the extent that his hypothesis was accepted, it became a *belief*. Motivated by the same resistance as Kant to the indeterminacy and non-existence of personal identity (advocated by Locke and Hume respectively), some philosophers proposed that the self must exist on the basis of *common sense*, rendering it even more deeply embedded in the mind than belief, and scarcely worthy of attention. Overlooking the circularity of his argument, concealed by the solipsistic nature of language, but anticipating the pragmatism of psychology, Thomas Reid asserted in 1764 that a sense of self was so obviously suggested by experience that knowledge of it was quasi-instinctive.[18] Subsequently, because it *seemed* to be self-evident *to itself*, manifestations of personal selfhood (words, concepts, objects, institutions) continued to be generated as cultural conventions, *as if* it existed. Indeed, as the cultural conventions that seemed to accommodate it became accessible to an ever larger proportion of the population, so the sense of identity that seemed to be implicit in them became the inheritance of an increasingly large number of people, to the point at which it became the very principle of life experience.

CHAPTER SIXTEEN

The Naturalness of the Self: the Picturesque Transformation of Nature into a Mirror of Personal Sublimity

While the evolution of personal identity generated the discourse of aesthetics – enabling the self-sense to realise its own autonomy through it – it also led to changing attitudes towards nature. This shift enabled the self-sense to project itself into the natural world and to experience itself there, as if it was 'innate' (literally 'inborn') and transrational, rather than constructed. Nowadays, it is widely felt that the natural environment is one of the richest and most universally appreciated sources of beauty, but this has not always been the case. On the contrary, it is arguable that not only is the inclination to invest nature with aesthetic power a culturally constructed phenomenon, but it is a relatively recent one, dating back, broadly speaking, to the early eighteenth century. Indeed there is a case for saying that the aesthetic and affective potential of nature was developed into a phenomenon at this time precisely in order to facilitate newly *aestheticised* modes of experience in the European psyche, and to consolidate and naturalise the sense of autonomous selfhood on which they are predicated.

The first person to have enjoyed being 'in nature' for its own sake is frequently said to have been Petrarch who, in 1336, ascended Mont Ventoux in Provence simply to enjoy the view. Prior to this time, it would have made little sense to do this. Treacherous to cross, and difficult to cultivate, mountains were only of interest to the extent that they expressed moral or spiritual meaning. Travelling through them was one of the ordeals northerners had to endure if they wanted to make a pilgrimage to Rome or Santiago de Compostela. Monasteries were located in scenic locations not because of their 'beauty' but because of the physical resources they offered and their remoteness from the worldly comfort of towns. Even Petrarch was slightly ambivalent about the experience. While at the top of Mont Ventoux, he consulted a copy of St Augustine's *Confessions* which he happened to have with him, opening the book by chance at a passage in which the saint states that such journeys in the material world are insignificant compared to the interior journey of the soul. Revising his first impression of wonder, Petrarch reflected that in themselves such views have nothing to offer. According to the *Très Riches Heures* of Jean Duc de Berry (from around 1410), there were no mountains in paradise; mountains characterised the barren realm into which Adam and Eve were expelled (Fig. 16.1). In the fifteenth and sixteenth centuries, when writers were able to take a more secular approach to nature, descriptions of mountains continued to depend on tradition – usually classical and biblical precedents. When they began to be based on experience rather than ideas, as they did in the seventeenth century, they were usually negative, seeing their subjects as chaotic, ugly and threatening. In one case, a Welsh traveller, James Howell, returning from Italy in 1621, wrote:

> I am now got over the Alps and return'd to France; I had crossed and clambered up the Pyreneans to Spain before; they are not so high and hideous as the Alps; but for our mountains in Wales . . . they are but molehills in comparison of these; they are but pigmies compar'd to giants, but blisters to imposthumes, or pimples to warts. Besides, our mountains in Wales bear always something useful to man or beast, some grass at least; but these uncouth, huge, monstrous excrescences of Nature bear nothing (most of them) but craggy stones.[1]

FIGURE 16.1: The Limbourg Brothers, *The Expulsion of Adam and Eve from Paradise*, from the *Très Riches Heures* of Jean Duc de Berry, folio 25v, around 1410. Musée Condé, Chantilly. Photo © RMN-Grand Palais (domaine de Chantilly)/René-Gabriel Ojéda.

Similarly, in Joshua Poole's *English Parnassus; or, A Help to English Poesie* (1657), written to provide aspiring poets with a range of appropriate words, phrases and metaphors to use in their works, the author considered it fitting to describe mountains as Earth's 'dugs, risings, tumours, blisters and warts'; his suggestions for adjectives are dominated by such unappealing qualities as 'insolent, surly, ambitious, barren, supercilious, inhospitable, freezing, infruitful, crump-shouldered, unfrequented, forsaken, melancholy, pathless'.[2] In making this selection, he was not only reflecting current attitudes towards mountains but was also subtly determining the possibilities of experience that they were likely and expected to stimulate in their readers. His attitude reflects the extent to which the sight of mountains was *not* being used as a catalyst for the expanded experience of aesthetic feeling at this period.

A generation later, the theologian Thomas Burnet explained that the reason these 'heaps of stones and rubbish' look so 'unnatural', 'ruined' and 'confused' is that God created them as a sign of his anger with mankind, at the time of the great flood. His book, *The Sacred Theory of the Earth*, first published in 1681, represents an earnest attempt to reconcile the infallibility of biblical revelation with the ever more persuasive arguments of observation and reason, which increasingly seemed to contradict the Bible. In this work, Burnet tried to account for the astute observation that, although the book of Genesis clearly states that the earth was completely submerged by the great deluge, there is not enough water on the earth to have covered it in this way. Therefore, how could the biblical account of the flood be true? After carefully examining every conceivable aspect of this thought-provoking subject, Burnet proposed that the earth was originally a perfectly smooth, seasonless orb – a rational and pleasing form – and that it was only in this pure and mountainless state that the water of the deluge could have completely covered it (Fig. 16.2). The flood waters were made up of the forty days' rain that are described in the book of Genesis, but they also came from a watery abyss at the centre of the earth which, Burnet suggested, issued forth on to its surface 'at a time appointed by all-wise Providence for the punishment of a sinful world'. At that moment, 'the whole fabric brake, and the frame of the earth was torn in pieces, as by an earthquake; and those great portions or fragments, into which it was divided, fell down into the abyss, some in one posture, some in another' – giving rise to the mountains and the deep ravines into which the oceans settled.[3]

Burnet's attempt to subject religious belief to the criteria of rationalism was itself the reflection of an emergent sense of personal identity, for it enabled that identity to exercise its sense of its own rationality and coherence. However, as we have seen, towards the end of the seventeenth century, changing attitudes towards what constituted 'value' in an experience – expanding beyond order (presupposing rationality) towards beauty (presupposing feeling) – put fewer demands on the objects of experience to be rational and coherent. By slow degrees, therefore, it ceased to be necessary for God to seem to be perfectly rational in order to be venerable; he could also be incomprehensible and overwhelming. As a result, it also ceased to be necessary for erratic mountains to be signs of God's displeasure; they could become signs of his 'incomprehensible and overwhelming' nature. Thus, despite calling the earth 'a little dirty planet', Burnet could also be moved by his experience of the natural world. More significantly, it ceased to be necessary for an

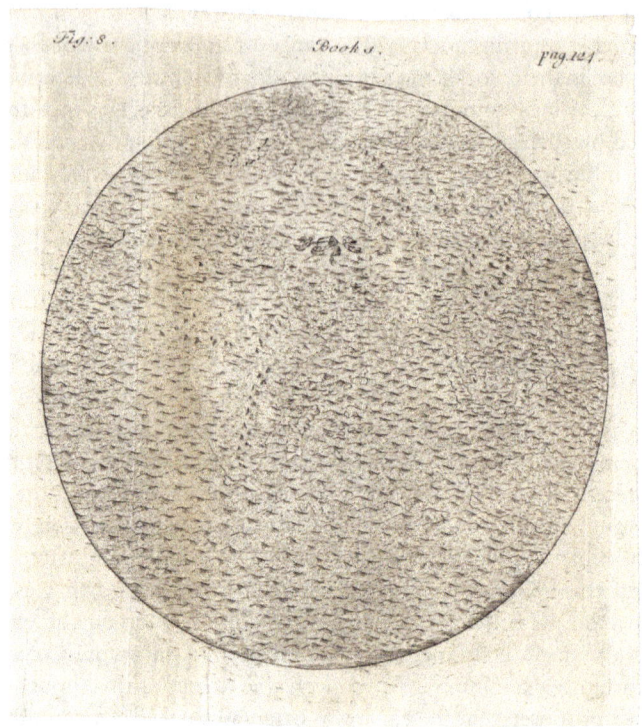

FIGURE 16.2: Thomas Burnet, the flooded earth with Noah's Ark and two angels, from *Sacred Theory of the Earth* (originally 1681), 1759 edition. Cornell University Library.

indeterminate feeling-oriented self-sense to be seen as inconsistent with a relationship to God; a degree of indeterminacy was possible in both. Thus although Burnet attributes the wonders of nature to 'God and his greatness' in the conventional pious way, he also allows them to provide form for an imaginative mental space that exists beyond human comprehension but in which an irrational mode of personal experience (and therefore identity) could nevertheless be accommodated:

> The greatest objects of Nature are, methinks, the most pleasing to behold; and next to the great concave of the heavens, and those boundless regions where the stars inhabit, there is nothing that I look upon with more pleasure than the wide sea and the mountains of the earth. There is something august and stately in the air of these things, that inspires the mind with great thoughts and passions; We do naturally, upon such occasions, think of God and his greatness: and whatsoever hath but the shadow and appearance of INFINITE, as all things have that are too big for our comprehension, they fill and over-bear the mind with their excess, and cast it into a pleasing kind of stupor and admiration.[4]

Despite Burnet's attempt to process his mixed perception of the natural world as an object of admiration, his overall approach was from a fundamentally religious point of view, and the second half of *Sacred Theory* is dedicated to the natural history of the Apocalypse, which he was convinced was destined to bring about the end of the world. Nevertheless, his book does reflect the beginnings of a sensitivity to the irregularity of nature and his perception did enable him to give incipient form to a personal experience – not just an idea – that confounded the rationalising tendencies of the mind. In the ensuing years, the capacity of the perceived wildness of nature to accommodate a growing impulse towards transrational experience slowly began to establish itself as a cultural convention. In 1709, for instance, such a shift was clearly reflected in the words of the Third Earl of Shaftesbury, who described how an appreciation of the immensity and power of nature corresponded directly with the growth of a passion within himself – though, unlike Burnet, he felt no compulsion to reconcile his experience with the dictates of Christian doctrine:

> I shall no longer resist the passion growing in me for things of a natural kind; where neither art, nor the conceit or caprice of man has spoil'd that genuine order, by breaking in upon that primitive state. Even the rude rocks, the mossy caverns, the irregular unwrought grotto's, and broken falls of waters, with all the horrid graces of the wilderness itself, as representing Nature more, will be the more engaging and appear with a magnificence beyond the mockery of princely gardens.[5]

Although Shaftesbury pitched the rugged truth of natural wildness against the pretentious artifice of formal gardens, he did not intend to dismiss the designing of gardens altogether. On the contrary, he believed that the correct planning of gardens could reveal the 'genuine order' that nature manifests when left to its own devices. Indeed, it was through the creation and appreciation of informal gardens that individuals first became able to engage the magnificent wildness of nature as a surrogate form of experience, and not merely as a distinctive *object* of experience – a dangerous and threatening 'other', according to the seventeenth-century commentators cited above. It is arguable that, for the apprehension of the 'wildness of nature' to function as a medium of transrational experience, it had to be appropriated by the individual and recreated as his own imaginative activity; it had to be reconceived as a projection of his own disposition. It was to this end that, in 1720, the poet Alexander Pope created a rustic grotto, conducive to contemplation, in the garden of his new Palladian villa in Twickenham, near London.[6] More generally, it was to give cultural form to this imaginative process that the informal 'English' landscape garden, designed to look undesigned, first evolved.

Although the new appreciation of the wildness of nature (and its transformation into a taste for informal gardens) may have evolved in conjunction with a growing inclination towards transrational experience, it acquired its legibility and legitimacy as a cultural convention by association with two key precedents whose cultural value had already been established. On the one hand, there were the fashionable images of Chinese landscapes which showed apparently random, asymmetrical views of 'natural', unmanicured scenery in which human interference seemed to be minimal (Fig. 16.3); these images, which presented a stark contrast to the formal parterre gardens that had been popular in Europe since the Renaissance, had been known to western Europeans from books and decorated porcelain since the beginning of the

FIGURE 16.3: Sheng Mou, *Recluse Fisherman, Autumn Trees*, Yuan Dynsaty, 1349, fan mounted as an album leaf, ink and colour on silk, 26.7 × 33.7 cm. Metropolitan Museum of Art, New York, ex coll. C. C. Wang Family, Purchase, Florence Waterbury Bequest and Gift of Mr and Mrs Nathan Cummings, by exchange.

seventeenth century, and they brought an appealing element of exoticism to the concept of 'naturalness'. On the other hand, there were classical sources, especially Pliny the Younger's descriptions of his villas at Tuscum and Laurentinum near Rome, in which formally designed gardens were juxtaposed with areas of natural untouched land and, more importantly, with areas of garden that were contrived to *look* like natural untouched land (Fig. 16.4). As in so many other areas of contemporary culture, such classical precedents were cited to confer intellectual dignity and political authority on the new conventions that they were made to anticipate. Despite their associations with antiquity, they complemented the impression of exoticism given by their Chinese equivalents. According to Robert Castell, who presented them to the public in his *Villas of the Ancients Illustrated* in 1728, classical gardens resembled Chinese gardens whose beauty consisted in a close imitation of nature; where, tho' the parts are disposed with the greatest art, the irregularity is still preserved; so that their manner may not improperly be said to be an artful confusion, where there is no appearance of that skill which is made use of, their rocks, cascades and trees, bearing their natural forms.[7]

Besides introducing elements of irregularity into their designs, many early eighteenth-century landscape gardeners attempted to capture the spirit of antique landscape by including classical monuments (antique or modern sculptures of classical figures, funerary urns, columns, grottoes, temples, mausolea etc.) in their designs. These monuments, and striking views of them across a lake or vale, were located at specific points along the route around the landscape to help the viewer interpret his experience of the view before him. Some of these evocative aids were

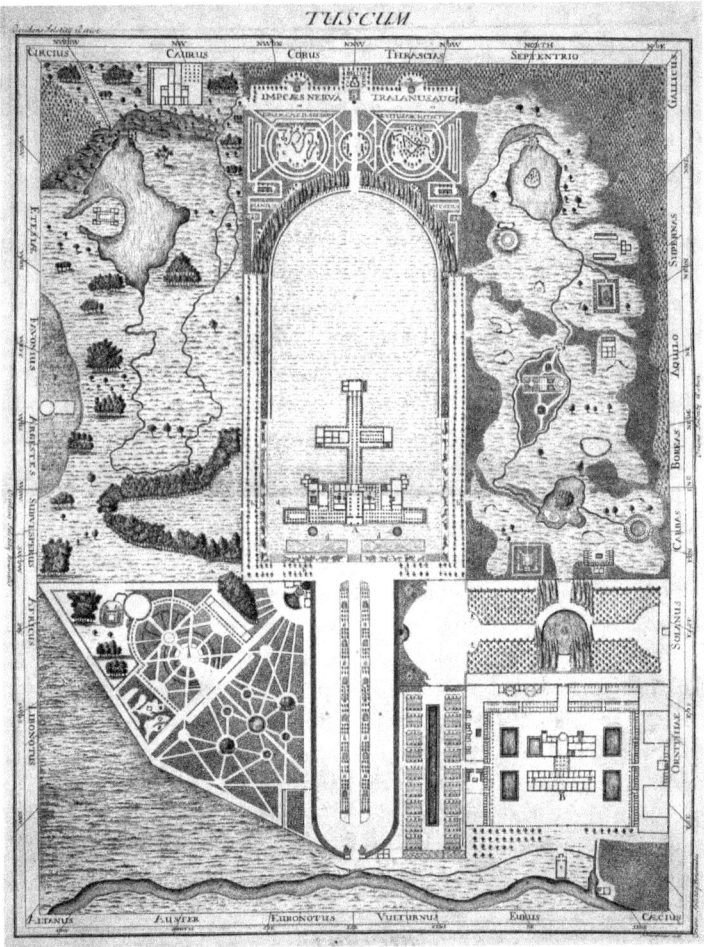

FIGURE 16.4: Plan of Tuscum from Robert Castell's *The Villas of the Ancients*, 1728, London, between pages 126 and 127.

strategically arranged in sequences that amounted to programmes of moral instruction. Landscape gardens of this kind were created not as beautifications of the external environment for its own sake but as forms of experience to be appropriated by their witnesses as psychological dispositions. This intention was reflected in a number of gardens in which staged viewpoints were accompanied by monuments and inscriptions that characterised the frame of mind that they were supposed to induce – for instance, The Leasowes in the West Midlands, designed by the poet William Shenstone between 1743 and 1763. The moralising conceit was taken to an extreme by the playwright Aaron Hill, who developed a design for a rock-work garden that also functioned as a moral maze.[8] The garden, conceived in 1734 but never realised, was to revolve around a 'Temple of Happiness' on a hill at its centre, with a smaller 'Cave of Content' in a less exposed position nearby. This central area was to be enclosed by a wall, beyond which extended a wood. Winding through the wood were to be four walled passages and eight smaller 'bye-paths', each one appearing to lead to the Temple. However, although the statue of Happiness on the dome of the Temple was visible from all over the garden, 'holding out an elevated torch in an attitude of invitation', only one of the twelve paths actually led to it. Each of the four walled passages, conceived as a grotto, represented an aim in life – Power, Riches, Honour or Learning – 'distinguished each by its statue, placed over the entrance'. The exteriors of these passages were 'rugged and irregular, adorned with shells of the largest kind'; the interiors were decorated with shell-work imagery and ornament, relating to the overall theme of the passage. The interior of the 'riches' passage, for instance, was 'chiefly composed of glass-house clinkers', enlivened by samples and simulations of precious metals and ores; the interior of the 'power' passage was to be hung with 'chrystals of salt-petre, the foundation of that friend of power, gunpowder'. Openings in the sides of each of the passages (three to the left, three to the right) gave views of thematically related statues, strategically placed at the ends of long vistas. These represented the negative consequences of the four aims; from the 'riches' passage, distant statues of Danger, Deafness, Blindness, Vanity, Indolence and Luxury could be seen. Further personifications – this time depicting the positive consequences of each of the four aims – were placed at the entrances to the eight smaller 'bye-paths'. Each of these bye-paths led to its own independent grotto of virtue – such as Munificence, Patriotism, Pleasure, Love – before progressing to a further destination. However, in every case but one, this further destination was a dead end (Ingratitude, Folly, Envy or Despair); the 'Grotto of Pleasure', for instance, led on to the 'Temple of Death'. It was only the 'Grotto of Independence', reached from the path of Reason and Innocence, that led to the 'Temple of Happiness'. Above all, the garden was conceived as a psychological environment, embodying a sequence of frames of mind that provided a form for the experience of moral purification. It demonstrated, albeit in a highly artificial way, how nature was progressively being reconfigured and reinterpreted to serve as a medium through which to realise new experiences of life and new modes of self-identification.

Although Hill's garden bears some resemblance to Madamoiselle de Scudéry's *Carte de Tendre* (Fig. 10.10) and John Bunyan's *Pilgrim's Progress* (1678), the moral potential of topography was no longer purely allegorical by his time. On the contrary, from the early eighteenth century onwards, it was increasingly being projected into actual landscapes that were conceived to affect the viewer *experientially* – on the basis of their aesthetic and physiological impact rather than their symbolic meaning. The consummate example of this trend is to be found at Stowe in Buckinghamshire, where the gardens were almost continuously being 'improved' in the latest fashion from around 1715 onwards. By 1748, by which time the gardens had been furnished with a wide range of classicising enhancements (for instance, William Kent's 'Temple of Ancient Virtue', designed in the same year as Aaron Hill's rock garden), the moral implications of aesthetic sensitivity were so developed that it was possible for one visitor to Stowe, William Gilpin, who wrote a *Dialogue* on its gardens, to comment:

> I must own there appears a very visible Connection between an *improved* Taste for Pleasure, and a Taste for Virtue: When I sit ravished at an Oratorio, or stand astonished before the Cartoons, or enjoy myself in these happy Walks, I can feel my Mind expand itself, my Notions enlarge, and my Heart better disposed either for a religious Thought, or a benevolent Action: In a Word, I cannot help imagining [that] a Taste for these exalted Pleasures contributes towards making me a better Man.[9]

The original garden at Stowe, created at the end of the seventeenth century, had been a formal parterre garden composed of regular, geometrical beds divided by straight paths, in the widely imitated Versailles manner. Decorated gardens of this kind had become popular throughout Europe in the Renaissance and were designed as much to be admired from an upper floor in the house as to be walked in; thus when King

FIGURE 16.5: Herri met de Bles, *The Story of David and Bathsheba*, around 1535–40, oil on panel, 46.2 × 69.2 cm. Isabella Stewart Gardner Museum, Boston.

David is shown watching Bathsheba bathing in a garden, sometimes in a fountain, he is often shown doing so from an elevated balcony (Fig. 13.9, 16.5 with King David in the top right hand corner and Bathseba bathing in the bottom left hand corner). Moreover, in England, the 'long galleries' that graced the grandest houses of the period were designed not only to provide a large interior space in which to take exercise (partly owing to misgivings about the healthiness of air, commonly believed to transmit diseases) but also to give a good view of the garden through prestigious expanses of newly glazed windows.[10] From 1714, the gardens at Stowe were extended by the landscape gardener Charles Bridgeman (1690–1738), who added a number of traditional features, such as straight avenues, clipped hedges and geometrically shaped ponds, but who also introduced a range of novel atmospheric elements. These more evocative features, which included classical sculptures and urns, mock temples and pavilions, tended to be one-offs and were distributed throughout the gardens asymmetrically. Their irregularity enabled visitors to discover them as if by accident, making room for an element of surprise in an experience that would have otherwise been a ritual performance of a known and approved convention. Bridgeman also made early use of the ha-ha, a sunken ditch, derived from military defences, that was placed at the perimeter of a garden to conceal the point at which it borders the wild land beyond it, as seen from the house, without allowing the livestock grazing there to approach the house (Fig. 16.6). The connoisseur Horace Walpole, who wrote a *History of Modern Taste in Gardening* in 1770, maintained that it was this removal of the visible boundary between the designed, principled garden and the unpredictable

FIGURE 16.6: Ha-ha at Hopetoun House, 1725, by William Adam (father of Robert Adam). Image: Andrew Shiva.

FIGURE 16.7: View of a formal garden, from Stoke Edith, Herefordshire, around 1710–20, embroidered linen canvas with silk and wool, and appliqué, 714.0 × 335.0 cm. Victoria and Albert Museum, London.

wildness of nature that was the 'capital stroke, leading to all that followed' in landscape gardening; it allowed the garden 'to be set free from its prim regularity, that it might assort with the wilder country without' (as recorded, for instance, in the embroideries of the formal gardens of Stoke Edith House in Herefordshire, now at the Victoria and Albert Museum, Fig. 16.7).[11] By ascribing a degree of cultural value to the uncontrollable waywardness of nature in this way, the advent of the ha-ha reflected a growing openness to the possibility of experience beyond the safety of rational understanding.

According to Walpole, it was the painter, architect and landscape gardener William Kent (1685–1748) who 'leaped the fence, and saw that all nature was a garden', enabling the vast expanses of natural land to be included within the realm of the 'aesthetic' for the first time. Significantly, it was Kent's early years of experience as a painter in Rome, where he became familiar with the idyllic classicising landscape paintings of Claude Lorrain and Nicolas Poussin, that had taught him to do this (Fig. 16.8). Indeed, it was precisely his ability to appreciate and develop the painterly and pictorial potential of landscape that has assured Kent such a central place in the history of garden design; for it was largely by being submitted to the conventions of art appreciation that the enjoyment of natural wildness – and the corresponding shifts in the experience of identity that it facilitated – acquired value and became culturally legitimate.

Following his return from Rome to England in 1719, Kent was commissioned to work on a number of gardens that had already been 'improved' in the moderately progressive style of Charles Bridgeman. Chief among these were Chiswick House near London (from 1726), Stowe (from around 1730) and Rousham in Oxfordshire (from 1737). In each of these cases, Kent softened the structured compositions of Bridgeman (who was the son of a gardener and trained as a gardener, not a painter),

FIGURE 16.8: Claude Lorrain, *View of La Crescenza*, 1648–50, oil on canvas, 38.7 × 58.1 cm. Metropolitan Museum of Art, New York, Purchase, The Annenberg Fund Inc. Gift.

subjecting them to a more integrated vision of the landscape as a whole by allowing the land itself, and not only its staged 'features', to be invested with mood and value. While he continued to put the fullest importance on evocative classicising monuments which he placed throughout his landscapes, he was also newly sensitive to the effects of light and shade, shape and texture, savouring the 'delicious contrast of hill and valley changing imperceptibly into each other' and 'the beauty of the gentle swell, or concave scoop'.[12] Drawing on his training as a painter, he used the 'pencil of his imagination' to 'bestow all the arts of landscape [painting] on the scenes he handled' and, in so doing, to create compositions worthy of the greatest landscape painters. Whether Kent's landscaped gardens were directly inspired by individual paintings (or parts of paintings) by Claude, Poussin and others – as Henry Hoare's gardens at Stourhead (from 1743) appear to have been – is debatable. Certainly the fundamentally pictorial nature of his designs was reflected in the ease and frequency with which they were translated back into the medium of painting and hung, self-reflectively, in the houses associated with them. More to the point is the fact that landscape gardens were increasingly being *discussed* in terms of painting, to the extent that a distinctive discourse – that of the *picturesque*, referring to views of landscape that *look* like pictures – evolved to express their potential as works of art. Indeed, Walpole himself frequently used comparison with the work of a well-known painter or print-maker as a means of praising a landscape; for, by applying the conventions of art appreciation to a view of nature, he was investing it with the cultural value that was usually associated with that frame of reference. By 1770, the application of pictorial values to landscape gardening had become so pervasive that, for one visitor to Britain, 'every journey is made through a succession of pictures'.[13]

The association of landscape gardening with painting eventually became so established in Britain that appreciation of the natural world soon came to be justified on the basis of its aesthetic appeal alone, without recourse to the monumental 'prompts' (its classical statuary etc.) that had previously articulated its cultural value. These monuments now came to seem heavy-handed and superfluous and, largely due to the influence of the best-known and most prolific of all English landscape gardeners – Lancelot 'Capability' Brown (1716–83) – their popularity eventually declined. From 1741, Brown was head gardener at Stowe, where he was clearly influenced by the 'naturalising' innovations of William Kent, which he developed. Throughout the 1740s, he opened the views at Stowe, transforming undeveloped farmland to the north-east of the house into the Grecian Valley, softening the shapes of water features and planting swathes of trees. Although Brown's landscapes were the products of sophisticated and ambitious planning, he eschewed all outward signs of artistry, as if such traces of human contrivance might prevent the viewer from being drawn beyond the possibilities of human reason towards an experience of the garden as a direct, unmediated manifestation of nature. Reacting against the cerebral classicising features typically used in gardens, one commentator, Thomas Whately, said:

> All these devices are rather *emblematical* than expressive; they may be ingenious contrivances, and recall absent ideas to the recollection; but they make no immediate impression, for they must be examined, compared, perhaps explained, before the whole design of them is well understood; and though an allusion to a favourite or well-known subject of history, of poetry, or of tradition, may now and then animate or dignify a scene, yet as the subject does not naturally belong to a garden, the allusion should not be principal; it should seem to have been suggested by the scene: a transitory image, which irresistibly occurred; not sought for, not laboured; and have the force of a metaphor, free from the detail of an allegory.[14]

Thinking along the same lines, Brown dispensed with any vestiges of formality that had survived in the immediate vicinity of country houses, typically extending the simulated naturalness of the landscape that surrounded them right up to their windows. In place of classical terraces, sculptures and fountains, his repertoire of features consisted of rolling expanses of grassland, serpentine lakes and clumps or belts of trees. He used these features like paint – to activate relationships between the forms, colours and textures of his compositions – and to create an aesthetic impression. When the plantations in the Grecian Valley at Stowe were mature (in 1770), Whately described their effect as if he was looking at a painting:

> Lovely woods and groves hang all the way on the declivities; and the open space is broken by detached trees, which near the park are cautiously and sparingly introduced, lest the breadth should be contracted by them; but as the valley sinks, they advance more boldly down the sides, stretch across or along the bottom, and cluster at times into groups or forms, which multiply the varieties of the larger plantations; those are sometimes close coverts, and sometimes open groves; the trees rise in one upon high stems, and feather down to the bottom in another; and between them are short openings into the park or the gardens.[15]

Brown's gardens were clearly designed to evoke experiences of beauty in their viewers on the basis of the pleasurable sensations that they offered. In this respect they were consistent with the sensuality of rococo art. Although Brown himself did not explicitly describe his ideal of beauty, his gardens conform, in many respects, to the description proposed by his contemporary, the philosopher and statesman Edmund Burke (1729–97) who, observing that the appreciation of beauty does not depend on a subjective whim or a deliberate act of will or reason, proposed (despite the theory of taste) that it must, therefore, be a property that belongs to objects. In his *Philosophical Enquiry into the Origin of Our Ideas into the Sublime and Beautiful* (1757), Burke considered the definitive characteristics of beautiful objects to include smoothness, variety, delicacy, gradual variation, absence of abrupt angularity and parts that 'melt as it were into each other' without any unexpected appearances of force or power. Making a case for smoothness, he cited the beautiful surfaces of nature in a way that recalls the undulating flow of one of Brown's creations: 'In trees and flowers, smooth leaves are beautiful; smooth slopes of earth in gardens; smooth streams in the landscape.' Or, in another context:

> The smoothness; the softness; the easy and insensible swell; the variety of the surface, which is never for the smallest space the same; the deceitful maze, through which the unsteady eye slides giddily, without knowing where to fix or whither it is carried. Is not this a demonstration of that change of surface, continual, and yet hardly perceptible at any point, which forms one of the great constituents of beauty?[16]

The fact that, in this latter instance, Burke was in fact reflecting on 'that part of a beautiful woman where she is perhaps the most beautiful, about the neck and breasts' draws attention to the newly perceived resonance between natural and erotic beauty, and highlights the extent to which gardens were conceived to induce sensuous pleasure. In around 1760, Sir Francis Dashwood made this connection explicit in his poetic garden at West Wycombe, part of which was said to have been 'laid out by a curious arrangement of streams, bushes and plantations to represent the female form'. A Temple to Venus is raised on a mound which can still be entered via an oval archway, described by one contemporary witness as 'the same entrance by which we all come into the world' (Fig. 16.9).[17]

Although Brown's gardens could certainly induce extreme experiences of beauty, they were never intended to disturb the pleasurable balance between man and nature, or reason and feeling. On the contrary, the fact that they were commissioned by aristocratic patrons as demonstrations of wealth, status and power through ostentatious land-ownership reflects how they were, in fact, intended to reinforce, beautify and deepen the pleasurable feeling of social and psychological stability by associating it with the immense and serene majesty of nature. As such, they also embodied the personal identities of their patrons, who saw their magnified sense of well-being reflected in them. Observing this symbiotic relationship between identity and its projections, Whately described William Shenstone's garden at The Leasowes as 'a perfect picture of his [Shenstone's] mind, simple, elegant, amiable'.[18]

FIGURE 16.9: The Temple of Venus, West Wycombe Park, removed in 1796, reinstated in the 1980s.

The Leasowes inspired a French aristocrat, the Marquis René-Louis de Girardin, to develop his own *jardin anglais*, punctuated with thought-provoking monuments, at his estate in Ermenonville, north east of Paris. Girardin was also inspired by the philosopher Jean-Jacques Rousseau, who raised the concept of naturalness to the level of an ideal, applying it not only to gardening but to all aspects of life. Rousseau became a friend of Girardin and spent the last months of his life at Ermenonville, savouring its 'natural' retreats, which included a deserted island in the middle of a lake and a deliberately dilapidated peasant's cottage. Following his death in 1778, Rousseau's body was laid to rest in a sarcophagus on the island, where it became a philosophical monument worthy of contemplation on its own account (Fig. 16.10). Shortly before he died, he wrote his *Reveries of the Solitary Walker*, in which he offered a final reflection on his experiences of life and nature. In the fifth of these reflections or 'walks', he recalled a period of two months that he had spent on a little-known island (St Peter's Island) in the middle of Lake Bienne in Switzerland, conveying how its naturalness was conducive to the ideal experience of selfhood. The location provided him with a relaxed and harmonious setting in which to feel divinely suffused beyond thought in peace. Although he felt able, with difficulty, to experience such feelings in prison if necessary, they were most powerfully induced in him in remote natural surroundings. Reflecting on the state in which he found himself 'during my solitary reveries on St Peter's Island, either lying in my boat as I let it drift with the water or seated on the banks of the tossing lake;

FIGURE 16.10: The tomb of J. J. Rousseau on an island in the gardens of Ermenonville, 1779, engraving, 9.2 × 14.7 cm. Wellcome Collection.

or elsewhere, at the edge of a beautiful river or of a brook murmuring over pebbles', he mused:

> If there is a state in which the soul finds a solid enough base to rest itself on entirely and to gather its whole being into, without needing to recall the past or encroach upon the future; in which time is nothing for it; in which the present lasts forever without, however, making its duration noticed and without any trace of time's passage; without any other sentiment of deprivation or of enjoyment, pleasure or pain, desire or fear, except that alone of our existence, and having this sentiment alone fill it completely; as long as this state lasts, he who finds himself in it can call himself happy, not with an imperfect, poor and relative happiness such as one finds in the pleasures of life, but with a sufficient, perfect and full happiness which leaves in the soul no emptiness it might feel a need to fill. What do we enjoy in such a situation? Nothing external to ourselves, nothing if not ourselves and our own existence. As long as this state lasts, we are sufficient unto ourselves, like God.[19]

Rousseau's sensitivity to the way in which natural scenery could induce and sacralise a sense of autonomous self made its way back across the English Channel. Sir Brooke Boothby, a friend and translator of the philosopher, used both a secluded grove and a book by Rousseau as personal attributes with which to define himself as a quasi-melancholy 'man of nature and truth' in the celebrated portrait that he commissioned Joseph Wright of Derby to paint of him in 1781 (Fig. 16.11).

FIGURE 16.11: Joseph Wright of Derby, *Sir Brooke Boothby*, 1781, oil on canvas, 148.6 × 207.6 cm. Tate, London. © Tate, London.

Parallel to Rousseau's idealisation of nature (though far more artificial), Brown's transformation of wild and working land into visions of serenity changed the appearance of the English countryside. Capitalising on the new 'Acts of Inclosure', which entitled the nobility to appropriate land that had hitherto been common property, his services were required up and down the country. By the time of his death in 1783, he had developed up to two hundred gardens into natural 'Edens'. By the end of the century, however, his formula for 'improving' nature had become so conventional that it ceased to function as a source of wonder; it had become too comfortable to be intensely beautiful. Some detractors claimed ironically that his landscapes were so 'natural' that they scarcely qualified as gardens; others complained that they were repetitive, bland, stifling and *un*natural. For such individuals, Brown's gardens no longer mediated the spontaneity of the natural world, giving access to unprecedented realms of feeling; on the contrary, they had become an obstruction, subjecting the formless powers of nature to the limited, self-identifying capacities of the human mind.

Some artists, therefore, felt compelled to enhance and intensify the effect of the picturesque by depicting exceptional aspects of the landscape – dramatic waterfalls, avalanches, erupting volcanoes – in which nature was not merely conceived as wayward and whimsical, but was positively mysterious and unpredictable, to the point of being dangerous. At its most intriguing extremes, exposure to these aspects

FIGURE 16.12: Pietro Fabris, *Lava emerging from Mount Vesuvius at night and running towards Resina*, 11 May 1771, from Sir William Hamilton's *Campi phlegraei*, Naples 1776, vol. 1, plate XXXVIII, coloured etching after a drawing made (by Fabris) in 1771, 21.2 × 39.1 cm.

of the natural world could induce awe, excitement and ecstasy (Fig. 16.12). Such states were newly promoted in relation to natural features that had hitherto been regarded as chaotic and ugly: rough surfaces, sharp angles, abrupt contrasts, contorted forms, obscure atmosphere. These characteristics addressed not a rational and self-contained model of the self but one that was constantly found to be unstable and unresolved.

One contemporary commentator, Uvedale Price, demonstrated how such ugliness could be made to seem beautiful – by a change of mind. In 1801, he wrote a dialogue in which two gentlemen, 'remarkably fond of pictures', explain in detail to a friend of theirs, ignorant of pictures, how an ugly and impoverished scene of a 'ruinous hovel on the outskirts of a heathy common' – that the three men had accidentally encountered while walking in the countryside – could be of positive picturesque value. In a dark corner of the hovel,

> some gypsies were sitting over a half-extinguished fire, which every now and then, as one of them stooped down to blow it, feebly blazed up for an instant, and shewed their sooty faces, and black tangled locks. An old male gypsey stood at the entrance, with a countenance that well-expressed his three-fold occupation, of beggar, thief and fortune-teller; and by him a few worn out asses: one loaded with rusty panniers, the others with tattered cloaths and furniture. The hovel was propt and overhung by a blighted oak; its bare roots staring through the crumbling bank on which it stood. A gleam of light from under a dark cloud, glanced on the most prominent parts: the rest was buried in deep shadow; except where the dying embers 'taught light to counterfeit a gloom.[20]

The 'ignorant' friend was disgusted by the scene, seeing no more than

> the old gypsey's wrinkles... I see that his beard is not only grizzle, but rough and stubbed, and, in my mind, very ugly. I see that the hovel is rough and uneven, as well as brown and dingy: and I cannot get these things out of my mind by any endeavours: in short, what I see and feel to be ugly, I cannot think, or call beautiful, whatever lovers of painting may do.

By contrast, the two connoisseurs 'talked in raptures of every part: the catching lights, the deep shadows, the rich mellow tints, the grouping, the composition, the effect of the whole'. They had been initiated into the mindset of picturesque aestheticism, and they evaluated the world, not in relation to health, morality or comfort but in relation to the incomprehensible vitality of nature and, above all, the potential of that vitality to reflect and activate the uncontainable dynamics of the mind; in this way, they were engaging in, and legitimising, a process of identity-formation that straddled the boundary between the known and the unknown. The extent to which appreciation of the 'incorrect' irregularities of nature was perceived to take place beyond the rational coherence of the mind was described by the Reverend William Gilpin (1724–1804) in his essay *On Picturesque Travel* (1792):

> We are most delighted, when some grand scene, tho perhaps of incorrect composition, rising before the eye, strikes us beyond the power of thought – when the *vox faucibus haeret* [the voice sticks in the throat]; and every mental operation is suspended. In this pause of intellect; this *deliquium* [the melting away or swooning] of the soul, an enthusiastic sensation of pleasure overspreads it, previous to any examination by the rules of art. The general idea of the scene makes an impression, before any appeal is made to the judgment. We rather *feel*, than *survey* it.[21]

On the surface, images of the dangerous aspects of nature appeared to represent threats to the rational integrity of the individual self, thereby causing it to intensify its sense of itself through fearful recoil. But they also presented it with the fascinating possibility of its dissolution *beyond itself* into the irrational – or transrational – forces of nature. As such, they embodied Edmund Burke's newly popularised notion of the 'sublime' – the feeling of compulsive attraction to natural sources of terror that are known, in a general sense, to be able to consume and destroy the viewer, but which are also known, in the moment of experience, not to be able to do so imminently or in this particular instance; that is to say, they magnify knowledge of the possibility of death and dissolution without actually or presently realising it. In his *Philosophical Enquiry*, Burke had identified the characteristics of objects that induce this feeling as 'powerful' and 'terrifying', 'vast' and 'obscure' (in contrast to the mild characteristics of 'beautiful' objects, outlined above). Above all, such phenomena – tempests, mountains, misty gorges etc. – were too dangerous and uncontainable to be reduced to distinct controllable objects and they thereby resisted the impulse of the self to find itself reflected coherently in them. On one level, therefore, the cult of the sublime seemed to undermine the sense of personal self by presenting it with visions of incomprehensible phenomena. On another level, however, it can be seen to have challenged the ability of the self to control and protect itself *rationally*, precisely in order to concentrate and essentialise its experience of itself at a more fundamental and existential level: what such experiences denied to the self – rational self-determination – they replaced with intensity, taking its sense of itself to the point at which its very existence seemed to be in danger and was therefore experienced *beyond mental clarity*, with the utmost immediacy and power. Of course, in order to function as the causes of sublime experience, such scenarios (which were fundamentally contrived, and therefore necessarily concealed a degree of rational self-awareness) could never be *actually* life-threatening. If they had been, they would have induced genuine fear rather than the 'astonishment' and 'delight' that accompanied the self-conscious experience of sublimity. Although they clearly communicated a sense of the force and magnitude of nature (inducing astonishment) and dramatically confronted the observer with a sense of the overwhelming inevitability of death (inducing terror), they also highlighted his awareness of his present distance from any immediate cause of death (inducing delight). It was precisely in order to create and furnish this imaginary psychological space, in which a sense of identity could exist beyond the parameters of rational coherence – but without actually being annihilated – that the discourses of the picturesque and the sublime evolved.

The significance of the picturesque and sublime lies in the way they transformed the natural environment from a barren place of exile, in which the Christian soul was alienated from God, into a language of feeling in which entirely new modes of experience and identity were possible. Prior to this development, cultural value had tended to be vested in preconceived meanings that were abstracted from the natural environment and accessed through symbolic objects; the sublime, for instance, was experienced by imagining the Last Judgement or dramatic moments in history, rather than by engaging with the overwhelming vastness of nature. The natural environment was either condemned as forsaken and corrupt, or transformed into symbol and allegory. The notion of the picturesque, however, constituted a frame of reference in which the aesthetic experience of nature acquired a value of its own – without recourse to meaning – by virtue of its perceived equivalence to art appreciation. Indeed, it ultimately provided a psychological device with which *any* experience could be translated into an aesthetic experience – thereby exercising the self-sense that generated the notion of the picturesque in the first place. In this way, it contributed towards the creation of a discourse – the discourse of aesthetics, consummated in *art* – in which cultural value is ascribed to objects on the basis of its own ever more independent and self-referential criteria. In so doing, it bypassed the structures of authority that traditionally controlled the creation of meaning (principally the Church, State and aristocracy) and, by further legitimising the independent experiences of sensation and pleasure, conventionalised a new source of cultural value – the personal self. Gilpin himself observed that, although he was inclined to interpret the picturesque beauties of Nature in a 'moral style', reflecting that 'Nature is but a name for an effect, whose cause is God', not everyone would follow him. On the contrary, the whole point of the picturesque, which he was, ironically, so instrumental in developing, was that the criteria of beauty were autonomous and independent of any preconceived index of values. Indeed, anticipating a shift that would have a vast impact on the subsequent development of the history of art, there was no reason why the perception of beauty should necessarily be associated with virtue or morality at all:

> We might observe, that a search after beauty would naturally lead the mind to the great origin of all beauty; to the first good, first perfect, and first fair. But, tho in theory this seems a natural climax, we insist the less upon it, as in fact we have scarce ground to hope, that every admirer of picturesque beauty, is an admirer also of the beauty of virtue.[22]

William Gilpin's own paintings capture something of the challenging grandeur of nature (Fig. 16.13). The oval shape and sepia tones of many of his works reflect the fact that he composed them with the help of a 'Claude glass', a dark, oval, convex mirror (unknown to the much-admired French landscape painter, Claude Lorrain, after whom they were named) in which to see reflections of views, framed in keeping with picturesque principles, rather as we might use the viewfinder of a camera to compose a photograph today (Fig. 16.14). This device was specifically invented to help translate the incomprehensible arbitrariness of nature into cultural currency by submitting it to the conventions of art appreciation and, as such, it embodied the essence of the picturesque.

It was particularly with regard to composition, according to Gilpin, that nature needed artistic assistance. While accepting that nature is an 'admirable colourist', harmonising tints 'with infinite variety and beauty', he felt that 'she is seldom so correct in composition, as to produce an harmonious whole. Either the foreground,

FIGURE 16.13: William Gilpin, *Tintern Abbey*, 1782, aquatint, 10 × 17 cm. By courtesy of the Department of Special Collections, Memorial Library, University of Wisconsin-Madison.

FIGURE 16.14: 'Claude' glass (a convex blackened mirror glass in a leather case), 1775–80, width 14 cm. Victoria and Albert Museum, London.

or the background, is disproportioned: or some awkward line runs across the piece: or a tree is ill-placed: or a bank is formal: or something or other is not exactly what it should be.' He attributes this to the fact that

> the immensity of nature is beyond human comprehension. She works on a vast scale; and, no doubt, harmoniously, if her schemes could be comprehended. The artist, in the mean time, is confined to a span; and lays down his little rules, which he calls the principles of picturesque beauty, *merely to adapt such diminutive parts of nature's surfaces to his own eye, as come within its scope.*[23]

That is to say, the notion of the picturesque submits the infinite, indeterminate and incomprehensible experience of nature to the capacity of the human mind; it translates it into a medium – a language, evolved by human beings to serve as a means of communication and self-understanding – in which individuals can experience it *as a function of themselves*. It would eventually become an entirely self-sufficient and autonomous 'mode of perception', conferring cultural value on any object it was used to frame.

Gilpin popularised his notion of the picturesque in a number of publications. It was through his *Essay on Prints containing Remarks upon the Principles of Picturesque*

Beauty (1768), in which he described the picturesque as the 'kind of beauty which is agreeable in a picture', that the term entered common parlance. In his various books of *Observations* – of the Wye Valley and South Wales (1782), the Lake District (1786) and the Highlands (1789) – he celebrated the picturesque scenery of the British landscape, describing the features that make it beautiful, and explaining exactly how to 'read' them. Capitalising on the improvement of the quality of roads (a key outcome of the Industrial Revolution) and on war with France (which prevented young aristocrats from undertaking the Grand Tour to Rome between 1793 and 1815), such books were instrumental in the development of 'picturesque tourism' in Britain. Gilpin's publications encouraged people – not just the land-owning nobility – to take walks in the countryside for pleasure, and to become amateur artists, making sketches in order to 'fix and communicate' their impressions. Indeed, Gilpin maintained that such sketches could communicate the picturesque impact of the landscape more effectively than the landscape itself for, by translating it from the enigmatic language of God into the human language of art, they transformed it into a function of the personal self, rendering it more palatable, digestible and comprehensible:

> There may be more pleasure in recollecting, and recording, from a few transient lines, the scenes we have admired, than in the present [actual] enjoyment of them. If the scenes indeed have peculiar greatness, this secondary pleasure cannot be attended with those enthusiastic feelings, which accompanied the real exhibition. But, in general, tho it may be a calmer species of pleasure, it is more uniform, and uninterrupted. *It flatters us too with the idea of a sort of creation of our own.*

Although nature was abundantly rich with unadorned scenes of picturesque beauty, Gilpin also included 'elegant relics of ancient architecture – the ruined tower, the Gothic arch, the remains of castles, and abbeys' in his lexicon of picturesque features. 'These are the richest legacies of art. They are consecrated by time; and almost deserve the veneration we pay to the works of nature itself.'[24] However these 'venerable vestiges of the past' were much more necessary in painted landscapes than in natural ones – again because they *humanised* the language of nature, making it easier to identify with it. Although they

> often give animation and contrast to these [natural] scenes; yet still they are not necessary [in the landscape]. We can be amused without them. But, when we introduce a scene on canvas – when the eye is to be confined within the frame of a picture, and can no longer range among the varieties of nature; the aids of art become more necessary; and we want the castle, or the abbey, to give consequence to the scene. Indeed, the landscape-painter seldom thinks his view perfect, without characterising it by some object of this kind.[25]

As with extreme manifestations of natural power, architectural ruins were also re-contextualised by painters (and poets) of the picturesque and sublime as metaphors for the irrational, transpersonal dimensions of experience. In Britain, the ruins of medieval abbeys had hitherto signified the corruption and superstition of the Catholic Church, abolished under Henry VIII, and the violent dissolution of the monasteries in 1536–40. Moreover, especially during the heyday of Renaissance classicism and its aftermath, the architectural styles of the Middle Ages were considered to be primitive and barbaric. Hence the naming of the 'Gothic' style after barbarian tribes (the Goths) that invaded Europe between the third and sixth centuries, leading to the fall of the Roman Empire. But, in the eighteenth century, the associations of Gothic ruins changed, in keeping with the notion of the picturesque. Besides highlighting stimulating memories of the ancient past (especially the ancient *national* past), the ruins of Gothic buildings became potent evocations of the relentless inclination of nature to re-appropriate the monuments of human endeavour over time, stimulating observers to reflect on the transience of the world and the sublimities of nature and history. They also mimicked the fragmentary nature of human memory, evoking a powerful sense of what has been lost and forgotten (what exists beyond the boundaries of rationality) and thus clouding the origins of knowledge and the ground of personal identity on which they are built (Fig. 16.15).

While the notion of personal identity could not be proven to exist as a rational entity, it could be sustained in transrational forms of feeling and imagination. To this

FIGURE 16.15: Philip James (Jacques) de Loutherbourg, *Visitor to a Moonlit Churchyard*, 1790, oil on canvas, 86.4 × 68.6 cm. Yale Center for British Art, Paul Mellon Collection.

end, the concept of nature was reconfigured through picturesque art to serve as the perfect, but incomprehensible, object of beauty, thereby enabling the self-sense to see itself reflected in it as an autonomous transcendental subject. Historic monastic ruins were sometimes included to suggest that the truth to which they stood witness was ancient, religious and lost beyond knowledge and memory, inviting the self-sense to objectify itself accordingly – as *timeless*, *sacred* and *unknowable*. Although the experience of personal identity was indeterminate to the point at which its very existence was debatable, the self-sense that it seemed to imply became so embedded in conventional interpretations of nature, history and memory – and so pervasive in the culture as a whole – that it acquired the felt-status of an absolute truth.

CHAPTER SEVENTEEN

The Consummation of the Self: the Sanctification of Art

The growth of interest in monastic ruins in the late eighteenth century formed part of a reconceiving of personal identity in relation to the relentless forces of nature and history. Besides bringing 'consequence' and 'character' to the unfathomable mystery of nature in a general sense, ruins also evoked feelings of Christian religiosity. Christianity had been threatened by the rationalising influences of Descartes and Locke, and it was challenged by Enlightenment philosophers throughout the eighteenth century. Atheism was on the rise and, especially after the French Revolution, anti-clericalism became common. However, towards the end of the century, the romantic attraction to non-rational modes of knowledge and experience also gave rise to an interest in the value and history of religion. Christianity was fundamentally reviewed, but other religions – especially the religious cultures of India – also attracted attention. It is no accident, for instance, that the *Bhagavad Gita* and the *Upanishads* were first translated into European languages at this time – in 1785 and 1801 respectively. Because these Sanskrit scriptures offered possibilities of metaphysical experience that were untouched by the sentimental credulity of popular Christianity and the worldliness of Enlightenment rationalism, they had no distracting political or social associations. Moreover, because they taught that the world of appearances, including the appearance of a personal self, are illusory modifications of one divine substance, they were perfectly placed to influence the transcendentalist idealists of the early nineteenth century who sought new depths of spiritual awareness. In the nineteenth century, the exploration of Buddhism – largely neglected by Europeans until this time – paralleled the evolution of scientific psychology and seemed to provide a model for the 'atheistic religion' that that rational age seemed to crave.

Above all, Christianity was revitalised, partly in reaction to the crude materialism of some atheists – for instance Julien Offray de La Mettrie (1709–51), whose *L'homme machine* (*Man Machine*) of 1748 denied the existence of the soul, thereby reducing human beings and all forms of life to mechanical configurations of matter. While La Mettrie's thoroughly rationalised 'non-existence of the soul' parallels Hume's denial of the existence of a personal self, his failure to account for self-consciousness and free will left his philosophy fatally unsatisfying. It is arguable, in this context, that the subsequent revival of interest in Christianity was not so much a sign of renewed belief in Christian doctrine as the appearance of yet another cultural convention – albeit with its own unique background and associations – through which it was socially acceptable to process the irrational feeling-dimension of experience. At the end of the eighteenth century, the revival also reflected a desire to restore a principle of moral authority, which was seen to have been lacking during the French Revolution (especially in the 'Terror' of 1793–4) and the decades of 'libertinism' and 'indifferent toleration' that had preceded it. Paradoxically, the ruling that desecration of the Eucharist should be punishable by death was reintroduced in France in 1825.[1] This desire for moral rectitude was an impulse that Christian conservatives were eager to appropriate and monopolise, casting it as an innately Christian quality. Significantly, this impulse was also used to reinstate an *absolute* sense of selfhood that was able to take full responsibility for its decisions. Rejecting the 'imputed' self of Condillac's sensationism, Victor Cousin (1792–1867), a leading philosopher in post-Revolutionary France, developed a reactionary philosophy that revolved around an objectively real sense of *moi*. Inspired by the evidence of the new 'empirical' psychology, he introduced techniques of self-oriented introspection to the syllabus of French schools in order to mould a generation of confident, motivated individuals.[2]

Changing attitudes towards Christianity were reflected in changing attitudes towards Christian art. As the discipline of art history took shape, reflected in the historical orientation of new public museums, so connoisseurs became interested in works of art from the point of view of their sources of inspiration. In the past, the greatest painters – Raphael, Titian, Reni, the Carracci brothers – had been celebrated by the Academy of Painting for their understanding of colour and composition and their grandeur of effect; now, however, the fact that they painted pictures of *Christian* subjects also had to be taken into consideration. Some credit for the quality of their art was surely due to its subject-matter. In fact, in his immensely popular *Génie du christianisme* of 1802 – a detailed exposition of the legitimacy of Christianity – the writer and politician François-René de Chateaubriand maintained that the quality of the art of these artists was itself a testimony to the truth and excellence of the Christian religion which informed it.

Even in Britain, where Protestant antipathy to religious imagery had prevailed for almost three hundred years, there was a revival of interest in the visual culture of Christianity. As we have seen, the Gothic style was newly invested with positive associations. The style was initially revived in the middle of the eighteenth century as a whimsical parallel to the rococo and chinoiserie styles, which were seen as alternatives to the ponderous, rational classicism of the baroque; significantly, the project that popularised it (Horace Walpole's villa at Strawberry Hill, started in 1749) was secular (Fig. 17.1). Towards the end of the century, the capacity of the style to signify irrationality was pushed to the point at which it seemed mysterious and sublime – partly because of the perceived obscurity and superstition of monastic devotions and partly because so much Gothic architecture lay in ruins (Figs 16.13, 16.15); but it was not yet religious per se. A taste of things to come can be seen at Audley End House in Essex, where Gothic features were used for the chapel, built between 1768 and 1772. Although this space was conceived as a kind of mini-cathedral with aisles and transepts, its delicacy and grace are still highly reminiscent

FIGURE 17.1: The Library at Strawberry Hill, Twickenham, London, from 1749.

of the mild and genteel neo-classicism used by Robert Adam elsewhere in the house (Fig. 17.2). Indeed, the Gothic style was mostly seen to be fit for libraries and studies at this time – as at Lee Priory near Canterbury, started in 1783 – rather than social or even religious spaces. It was not until the beginning of the nineteenth century that it was made to acquire specifically Christian associations, on historical grounds; that is to say, it was seen to be innately religious due to its Christian origins. As part of the same process of moral re-evaluation, the perceived dependence of medieval art on *craftsmanship* also enabled it to be contrasted with the moral and social ills of the Industrial Revolution at this time.

This reintroduction of Christian values to art and architecture came to head with the Gothic revivalist architect, A. W. N. Pugin (1812–52), whose observation that the Gothic style was originally an expression of Catholic rather than Protestant culture was so strong that he felt compelled, in 1834, to convert to Roman Catholicism. It was as if religious conversion was the natural and necessary outcome of his appreciation of the style. In doing this, he was participating in the rehabilitation of Catholicism, which had been de-stigmatised or 'emancipated' in Britain five years earlier – three hundred years after its suppression at the Reformation. Conversely because, in Protestant Britain, Catholicism was specifically associated with the *past* (as it was *not* in France and Italy), it seemed entirely natural to Pugin, and even morally obligatory, to revive a *historical* style in order to promote it. Religiosity, the Gothic style and historicity seemed to require each other. Significantly, following the foundation of the Oxford

FIGURE 17.2: The Chapel at Audley End, Essex, 1768–72. © Photo SCALA, Florence.

Movement (1833) and the Cambridge Camden Society (1839), which attempted to revitalise the somewhat depressed Anglican Church, the Gothic style also became increasingly acceptable to Protestants – though, reflecting ever growing levels of knowledge and interest in the subject, many considered the English Gothic style to be less tainted with 'popery' than French Gothic. Indeed, the Gothic style eventually became so associated with traditional British values that, after a century of intense re-contextualisation, it could be used for the most establishmentarian institution in the land – the Houses of Parliament, part-designed by Pugin – from 1835.

It is no surprise that the revival of interest in Christianity should have coincided with the demise of Enlightenment rationalism. Indeed, where many seventeenth-century theologians had attempted to demonstrate the compatibility of Christianity and rational philosophy, many late eighteenth-century reactionaries used the transrational dimension of Christianity to *undermine* the 'cult of reason' (just as many Enlightenment philosophers had, conversely, used reason to discredit Christianity). It is also unsurprising that, on purely historical grounds, the demise of Enlightenment rationalism should have raised questions about the stability and rationality of classical ideals altogether. Thus it was only at this time, after three centuries of striving to define and imitate the supreme achievements of the ancient world, that historians began to ponder: if the Roman Empire was so exemplary, how and why did it come to an end? Why could it not perpetuate itself? This was precisely the question that Edward Gibbon attempted to answer in his six-volume *History of the Decline and Fall of the Roman Empire*, published between 1776 and 1789.³ Of the many reasons that he proposed for this calamity, the debilitating impact of Christian other-worldliness on rational Roman virtue was the most controversial. Little did Gibbon, a staunch classicist, know that the forces at work in antiquity, leading to the 'irrational' Christian eclipse of the classical world, were at work again in his own time, leading to the Romantic eclipse of Enlightenment values. Indeed, his own mentality – the very fact that he *noticed* that the classical world came to an end, and that he was disturbed by the observation – was a reflection of these forces, accidentally realising the decline and fall of commitment to classical rationalism for the second time.

In the early nineteenth century, the new interest in the demise of the Roman Empire was reflected in the proliferation of works of art (operas and novels, as well as paintings) that addressed the 'last day' of Pompeii. Pompeii was a thriving city in the south of Italy that, together with nearby Herculaneum, was obliterated in AD 79 by the eruption of Mount Vesuvius. Both cities were very suddenly and entirely covered in thick layers of volcanic ash, killing several thousand people, many of them instantly. When they were discovered (Herculaneum in 1738, Pompeii in 1748), many of the inhabitants were found exactly as they were when the eruption occurred. Partly because the two sites revealed so much about the domestic interiors of ancient Roman houses (unlike most of the already known remnants of Roman civilisation, which were funerary or public monuments made of stone), they became important sources of inspiration for the neo-classical style which thrived in the second half of the eighteenth century; as such, they were seen to promote the neo-classical ideal. Indeed, Duke Leopold III of Anhalt-Dessau was so smitten by the sight of Mount Vesuvius, which he experienced on his Grand Tour in 1766, that he had a working artificial volcano created in his otherwise 'English' garden near Dessau.⁴ However, the unexpected amount of erotica decorating the walls of some of the buildings at Pompeii caused some disillusionment, among conservatives, with the morals of ancient Rome (and delight among libertines). Moreover, as we have seen, the taste for the sublime had altered the associations of volcanoes by the end of the century, affording them a certain amount of quasi-mystical power. By the time, therefore, that the Russian artist Karl Briullov came to paint his epic picture *The Last Day of Pompeii* in 1830–3, it had become fashionable to interpret the destruction of Pompeii not as a tragedy signifying the end of the classical civilisation but as a positive act of the Christian God, implementing Christianity (Fig. 17.3). In this work, which was painted in Rome, the downfall of the Roman Empire is symbolised by the falling of pagan idols from the roof of the temple (on the right) and by the fleeing priest (centre, background), while the ascent of Christianity is symbolised by the cross-wearing Christian (on the far left) advancing conscientiously towards the light. Just as the subject represents the superseding of classical paganism by Christianity, so the painting itself represents the superseding of the cool order of neo-classicism by the dynamic feeling-oriented spirit of Romanticism.

This demise of Enlightenment values was also directly reflected in changing attitudes towards classical works of art. Ever since the Renaissance, antique sculptures, mostly of the human form, had been highly prized and collected by

FIGURE 17.3: Karl Briullov, *The Last Day of Pompeii*, 1830–3, oil on canvas, 456.5 × 651 cm. Russian Museum, St Petersburg. © Photo SCALA, Florence.

aristocratic patrons. They were seen to reflect the dignity of mankind in ways that were completely unknown to the Christian Middle Ages and they therefore came to represent one of the key aspects of antiquity that contemporary observers sought to revive. The sculptures themselves had been largely overlooked since the fall of the Roman Empire on the grounds that they were pagan and idolatrous; and, over the centuries, most of them were lost or damaged. The process of rediscovering and restoring them, which began in the fifteenth century, reflected the re-assessment of the identity of mankind that constituted the humanist Renaissance. Indeed, the process of returning them to their original state of pristine perfection (sometimes rather fancifully) paralleled and embodied the effort to revitalise the ideals that they represented. Especially in the eighteenth century, many restored works were acquired by aristocratic 'Grand Tourists' seeking to appropriate their associations of rationality, dignity and power, and sometimes to add poetry and meaning to their newly landscaped gardens. To satisfy the market, a veritable industry of restoration and fabrication developed in Rome, producing a wide range of modifications, replicas, casts and forgeries, as well as modern equivalents inspired by classical models. For instance, when, in 1795, the Roman sculptor Giovanni Pierantoni restored a fragmentary second-century marble sculpture of Antinous, a lover of the Emperor Hadrian, he replaced the missing arms and a leg, and gave the figure an honorific cup and ewer, before selling the work as Ganymede to the British collector Thomas Hope.[5] It was important to collectors that the sculptures were – or appeared to be – intact, to ensure that their associations of 'rationality, dignity and power' should seem timeless and complete, and therefore able to support the self-image of 'rationality, dignity and power' that their owners sought to find reflected in them.

At the very end of the century, however, this attitude began to change. As connoisseurs began to consider works of art from the point of view of their historical significance as well as their decorative and status-related value, they also became more interested in their authenticity. Especially in the new public museums, in which the historical approach to collections of art was first enshrined, efforts were made to preserve the physical fabric of antique sculptures in the condition in which they were found – damaged and incomplete if necessary. This principle appears to have been applied for the first time at the Museo Chiaramonti in the Vatican in Rome, conceived by Pope Pius VII in 1802 to house newly excavated finds; but it only developed into a trend when Antonio Canova, the celebrated neo-classical sculptor and General Inspector of Antiquities at the Vatican, declined Lord Elgin's invitation to restore the ancient Parthenon sculptures which Elgin had begun transporting from Athens to London in 1801. Canova saw drawings of the marbles in 1803 when Lord Elgin consulted him about their conservation in Rome, and he saw the sculptures themselves in London in 1815, subsequently prompting the British Museum to buy them. Reflecting on their condition, he commented that

> however greatly it was to be lamented that these sculptures should have suffered so much from time and barbarism, yet it was undeniable that they had never been retouched, that they were the work of the ablest artists that the world [has] ever seen ... It would be sacrilege [for] him[self], or any man, to presume to touch them with a chisel.[6]

Canova's respect both for the artistic quality of the works and for their historical authenticity was symptomatic of a general shift in attitudes towards antique sculpture; for instance, the British Museum published prints of ruined fragments from the ancient Greek site of Bassae in 1820 (Fig. 17.4). It is, however, ironic that, although Canova's personal aim had been to protect the physical integrity of the surviving remnants, the new acceptance of fragmentary works that his purist approach necessitated (in contrast to the eighteenth-century ideal of completeness) corresponded to an erosion of belief in the coherent integrity of the classical world, as both explained by, and reflected in, Gibbon's *Decline and Fall*. It also tacitly reflected a capacity and willingness to engage with that which was incomplete, fragmentary, ruined and forgotten in human experience, constituting a challenge to the rational model of personal identity that the classical world had hitherto been required to accommodate.

In less than a century, the associations of the Gothic and classical styles had undergone radical change. Where medieval culture had been allowed to decay for centuries on the grounds that it was backward and uncivilised but was now being reconstituted as the reflector of a new moral and spiritual truth, so classical civilisation, which had been perfected in the imagination for three hundred years in the name of rationality, was now being allowed to remain in the ruined state in which it was found. As with the parallel change in attitudes towards mountains,

FIGURE 17.4: Battle between the Greeks and Amazons (from the Bassae frieze, fifth century BC), *Engravings from the Ancient Marbles in the British Museum*, London, 1820, Part IV, Plate XVII. Private Collection.

these shifts facilitated, and were facilitated by, the evolution of an unprecedented mode of subjectivity, rooted in the legitimacy of personal psychology and processed through the appreciation of the picturesque in nature and art. As a result, the conventions of art appreciation, both psychological and social, became a primary means through which viewers had access to the privileged domain of 'autonomous identity'.

It is arguable that it was partly to facilitate this process that the archetype of 'the artist' evolved. As we have seen, the first step in the creation of the archetype was taken in the sixteenth century when efforts were made by painters to elevate their status above that of other craftsmen on the grounds that their art was more poetic and intellectual. It was not, however, until the early nineteenth century that the archetype of the artist, embodying the possibility of autonomous identity and creative individuality, became more widely established as a defining principle of European culture. This was partly due to the changing nature of its audience. Whereas the earliest consumers of art had tended to be elite patrons, including the Church, and, increasingly in the seventeenth century, private collectors, the privilege of art consumption and appreciation was now extended to the growing 'public'. But while members of the public became increasingly enfranchised to participate in the process of identity-formation – in public exhibitions of art but also, more generally, through the consumption of the cheaper, more abundant commodities generated by the Industrial Revolution – their impulse to do so was also frustrated by their vast numbers. With the exception of the relatively few individuals who for one reason or another became distinguished, the possibility of an intensely experienced and acknowledged sense of personal identity was consistently being lost in the overall sense of the community as a whole. In order to compensate for this situation, the individual self was impelled to imaginatively project its sense of itself outside of itself, into some form of external agency. It is arguable that the role of the artist was elevated to the level of an objective archetype at this time expressly for this purpose – to serve as a surrogate medium of individual selfhood for the growing numbers of aspirational individuals who were otherwise unable to 'express' themselves fully. While the notion of the informed 'public' offered a greater number of individuals the possibility of involvement in the cultural process, albeit anonymously, the romanticised archetype of the artist – and indeed the glorified notion of art as a whole – enabled members of the public to articulate a sense of their personal distinctiveness and selfhood – albeit vicariously – as a fantasy. Public galleries and museums evolved to accommodate and institutionalise this possibility.

The quintessential attribute of the artist was his unique power and insight into the depths of human experience, based on his unique understanding of, and mastery over, nature. This reputation originated in his apparently superhuman ability, respected since ancient times, to imitate the creativity of the gods and to reproduce nature so perfectly that 'she confused herself'. In antiquity, which by the fifteenth century had become a quasi-mythical ideal, images were judged on their verisimilitude; paintings of fruit were praised for being so realistic that 'birds tried to peck at them'. At the same time, makers of cult images were revered on account of their mysterious and powerful – but magical and dangerous – ability to embody invisible spirits in material form (though the latter skill could not be credited to individuals personally, as only devils and demons claimed to possess the divine powers that passed through them). In the Middle Ages, by which time the heritage of antiquity had faded, fear of idols and a mistrust of image-makers is reflected both in the avoidance of monumental sculpture (until the twelfth century) and in the commitment of craftsmen to *copying* images rather than *originating* them; moreover, whereas God created matter from nothing, images were merely old matter refashioned into new forms. Representations of image-makers from this early period are rare, and those that survive are mostly negative, associated with idolatry. It was not until the fifteenth century, when the art of painting was raised to the level of a liberal art, that the role of the *creative* artist first came to be idealised. Even at this time, however, the privilege was extended to a relatively few celebrated individuals and was not extended to painting as a whole which, for the most part, continued to be seen as a humble craft. Artists were empowered to bring a degree of personal 'freedom' to their commissions but they continued, broadly speaking, to be the instruments of their patrons or the Academy and, in many cases, they were placed on the same social level as servants.

Whereas traditional artists had been regarded as inspired *mediators* and *interpreters* of the world around them (albeit with unique insights), at the end of the eighteenth century they came to be seen as *sources* of inspiration; they became less directly dependent on commissions, co-conceived with their patrons, and more inclined to work from their own imaginations. Their clients were expected to respect and admire their inspired choices; indeed they were increasingly required to fulfil this role, for just as members of the public needed artists through whom to express themselves, so artists needed their audience through which to be received, and conducted, into the world. Having said this, the relationship was by no means stable. On the contrary, the struggles that some artists suffered in developing cultural forms to effectively capture and communicate their experience was seen to account for their 'melancholy' frame of mind. This disposition was easily exacerbated by viewers' resistance to artistic innovation, which often cast progressive artists into the roles of 'rebels' or 'outcasts' – roles that artists often appropriated and dramatised, willingly or otherwise. Conversely, by bringing the depths of human experience to the surface where they could be realised by their viewers, artists also came to be seen as 'prophets' or 'visionaries' and, if they suffered for the cause, 'martyrs', conflating the Romantic notion of visionary subjectivity with the neo-classical ideal of heroic self-sacrifice. Either way, the two roles – artist and viewer – were functions of each other. Their mutual dependency established a mechanism of self-reference at the heart of the culture.

By the end of the eighteenth century, the significance of artists' contributions to the well-being of society was so highly esteemed that their lives became the subject-matter of neo-classical history painting. This genre had traditionally focused on scenes from classical history, on account of their elevated significance, and on politicised battle and treaty scenes. It had originally been used allegorically to glorify the self-sense of patrons but, towards the end of the century, its centre of gravity shifted towards scenes in which heroic acts of self-sacrifice were performed – for instance, Jacques-Louis David's *Oath of the Horatii* (1784) – partly as a reaction against the self-indulgence of the rococo sensibility and partly to promote the ideal of public virtue. The depiction of episodes from the lives of *artists* constituted a significant modification of the genre. It developed as an aspect of nationalistic history painting in which scenes from the medieval and later history of modern nation states were depicted at the expense of classical subjects, which seemed to border on mythology by comparison. Thus, some of the very earliest pictures of this type – for instance, François-Guillaume Ménageot's *Death of Leonardo da Vinci in the arms of Francis I* (1781) or Pierre-Nolasque Bergeret's *Emperor Charles V picking up the paintbrush of Titian* (1808) – reflect as much on the virtues of the monarchs depicted (respecting the genius of artists, despite their own superior status) as on the heroism of the artists (Fig. 17.5). In due course, as the role of the artist came to epitomise the aspirations of the romantic spirit ever more closely, it became unnecessary to contextualise it in relation to his munificent patrons – a shift that corresponds to artists' growing independence of commissions. Paintings of scenes from the lives of Raphael, Leonardo, Michelangelo, Titian, Rubens and many others – especially their beginnings, inspirations, loves and deaths – became common. Classicising artists such as Ingres tended to identify with Raphael, seeking to appropriate his grace and composure, while more romantic, painterly artists such as Delacroix identified with the solitary, turbulent and persecuted genius of Michelangelo. Although this tradition continued to flourish until the end of the nineteenth century, it reached a head in

FIGURE 17.5: François-Guillaume Ménageot, *The Death of Leonardo*, 1781, oil on canvas, 278 × 357 cm. Musée de l'Hôtel de Ville, Amboise. © Ville d'Amboise.

1855 when Gustave Courbet (1819–77) applied the scale and conventions of monumental history painting to a picture of himself at work on a landscape painting in his studio, surrounded by friends and commoners (*The Painter's Studio*, 1854–5). In one fell swoop, he ridiculed and debased the pompous affectations of academic history painting, while using its rhetoric to elevate himself *as an artist* to a level of historical significance and grandeur (Fig. 17.6).

At the beginning of the nineteenth century, attempts were made to objectify the archetype of the artist – to turn it into a 'natural truth' – by identifying 'typical' physiological features in the physical body that predetermined it. Practitioners of the new science of phrenology, which aspired to read personality traits from the shape of the skull, claimed to be able to identify an 'artistic' skull-type (Fig. 17.7). Using portraits and sculptures of famous artists, they even claimed to be able to differentiate between skulls that would be pre-disposed towards colour and portraiture (Titian, Rubens) and those that would be inclined towards line and history painting (Poussin), perpetuating the colour–line debates of the sixteenth and seventeenth centuries.[7] One phrenologist, Joseph Vimont, went so far as to say that the shape of Raphael's skull (Fig. 17.8) – known from portraits and casts of his death mask – determined that he would have been a great painter even if he had had no arms. To lend weight

FIGURE 17.6: Gustave Courbet, *The Painter's Studio*, oil on canvas, 361 × 598 cm. Musée d'Orsay, Paris. Photo © Musée d'Orsay, Dist. RMN-Grand Palais/Patrice Schmidt.

to his argument, he compared the artist to the handicapped painter Louis-Joseph-César Ducornet, a contemporary painter who was indeed born without arms and who painted with his feet (Fig. 17.9).[8]

Above all, regardless of the various signs that were created or found to 'prove' the existence of artistic genius, it was because artists created the cultural language in which viewers became able to bring the hidden depths of their own otherwise unattainable experience into consciousness that the role of the artist was transformed into an alter ego, or archetype, of the self. For while viewers *used* the language of their time to perform their identities (which were therefore tacitly determined by the capacities of that language to embody identity), artists *created* new language, realising experiences that the current language of the day was otherwise incapable of expressing, and thereby increasing the possibilities of experience both for themselves and for their viewers. Needless to say, the prophetic revelations of artists were often so profound and precocious that their viewers could not understand them. Beethoven (1770–1827), who epitomised the 'prophetic' artist, provided many examples. The string quartets that he composed for Count Razumovsky, the Russian ambassador in Vienna, in 1805–6 were so ahead of their time that the musicians commissioned to perform them were baffled. In response to their incomprehension, Beethoven commented: 'They are for a later age.' To this day, many people would agree that some of their most significant feelings are experienced in relation to works of art – which is indeed why we engage with art. This does not necessarily imply that such works of art *transmit* such feelings, as if their audience is a detached receptacle for feelings that are pre-invested in independent works of art; it may just as well be that such works of art provide their audience with the formal language with which to

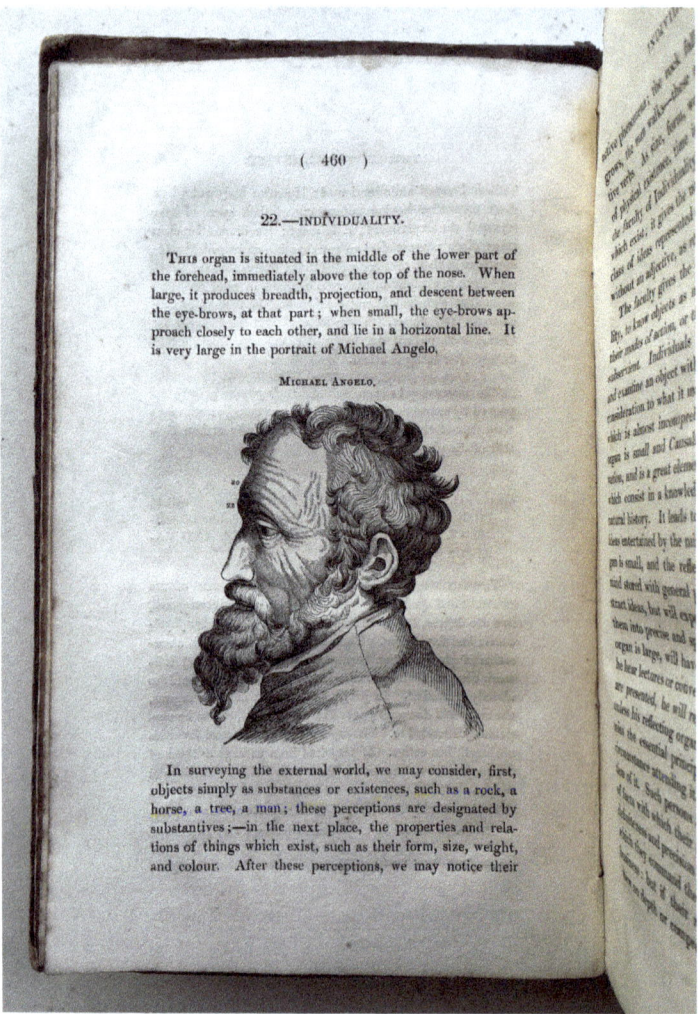

FIGURE 17.7: Head of Michelangelo from George Combe, *System of Phrenology*, fourth edition, vol. II, p. 460, Edinburgh, 1836. Private collection.

express or realise a dimension of feeling that *already* exists within them in a latent, unmanifest state – as a *possibility* of self-awareness or personal identity – but which lacks a form in which to rise into consciousness and thereby acquire a character. It was to this end – providing their audience with the forms of their *own* experience, which they were unable to articulate or express for themselves – that the role of the artist came be constructed as an archetype of the self, offering 'prophetic' insight into the nature of human experience.

One of the artists in whom the archetype of the 'artist as surrogate self' was most fully realised was the German painter, Caspar David Friedrich (1774–1840), whose work revolves around the sanctity of nature and the sacrificial insignificance of

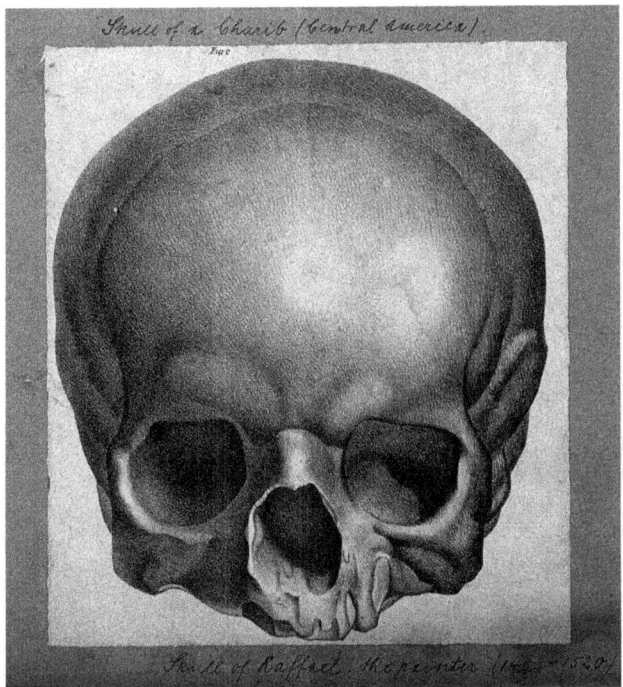

FIGURE 17.8: Raphael's skull, plate from Joseph Vimont, *Traité de phrenologie humaine et comparée*, Brussels, Établissement encyclographique, 1835. Wellcome Collection.

human beings sublimated within it. What makes Friedrich unique is the way he framed the appearance of nature as a spiritual vision, thereby transforming painting – especially landscape painting – into a form of contemplation and elevating it to the level of a religion. This religious capacity in his work was explicit in his first mature oil painting, *The Cross in the Mountains* (1807–8), conceived as an altarpiece for a private chapel in Tetschen, Bohemia (Fig. 17.10). This work is picturesque in its approach to rugged natural scenery, showing a dramatic outcrop of rock surmounted by a scattering of fir trees rising up to a diminutive crucifix, but it is nevertheless a sacramental object, decorated with images of wheat and grapes symbolising the bread and wine of the communion service. Moreover, in a rare moment of self-explanation, Friedrich compared the rays of the setting sun in the work to the radiant light of God. In the rest of the artist's works, the possibility of a religious function is only ever implicit. Even when signs of religiosity, such as Christian crosses or monks, are included, they tend to be minimal (as they are in *The Cross in the Mountains*), serving not so much to impose a religious narrative of the work as to suffuse the whole with an aroma of sanctity.

The iconography of Friedrich's works is extremely limited, mostly comprising expansive views of nature, leading over a threshold towards a distant horizon. Despite their various settings (harbours, mountains, woods), the evocation of silence, stillness and space is universal. Although they were often worked up from memory,

FIGURE 17.9: Louis-Joseph-Cesar Ducornet, *Self-portrait*, about 1840, oil on canvas, 82 × 65 cm. Palais des Beaux-Arts, Lille. Photo © RMN-Grand Palais/Jacques Quecq d'Henripret.

they were based on the visible world and were therefore associated with the objectivity of sensory experience. Indeed, their subject-matter was always 'possible'; it was never supernatural. Moreover, while his work was rarely symbolic, it was replete with associations. References to Christianity, for instance, are associated not only with piety and self-sacrifice but also with transcendental divinity; medieval ruins evoke the intensity of ancient devotions, the vastness of time and the inevitable decay of all things, but also the merciless angularity and harshness of the material world; graves and cemeteries refer to mortality but also suggest the surrender and re-integration of the human body into the body of the earth; ships sailing towards the horizon and fading into the distance are thick with the flavour of life as a journey into the unknown; gnarled and wintery trees evoke the urgent, uncompromising forces of nature, starkly set against the peaceful immensity of skies at dawn or dusk. Friedrich repeatedly returned to these potent images. Although many of them are ancient, classic symbols, inviting interpretation, they were primarily intended to

FIGURE 17.10: Caspar David Friedrich, *The Tetschen Altar*, or *The Cross in the Mountains*, 1807, oil on canvas, 115 × 110.5 cm. Galerie Neue Meister, Dresden. Photo: bpk/Staatliche Kunstsammlungen Dresden/Elke Estel/Hans-Peter Klut.

communicate by association, rather than through meaning. Indeed, Friedrich clearly intended the resemblances between his motifs – treetops, spires, masts and crosses – to create resonance, each one saturating the others with associations that reverberated throughout his work. As a result, his trees became sacred, and his churches rooted in natural law; his crosses became symbolic of the will to engage with destiny, while a sea voyage became an act of self-sacrifice.

Despite their rich associations, the essence of Friedrich's paintings does not lie in the 'sanctity of nature'; it lies in the 'sanctity of art'. This revolutionary shift is reflected in the presence of a further motif – the *Rückenfigur* (back-figure) or 'figure seen from the back' – that recurs throughout Friedrich's work, differentiating it fundamentally from that of other painters of sublime and picturesque landscapes. The back-figure, or -figures, features in Friedrich's work in various ways. In some cases, they are tiny presences appearing in the far distance, and are scarcely noticeable. In other cases, however, they appear, in groups of two or three, in the middle distance, sharing their view with the viewer of the paintings. Finally, they stand alone in the foreground of the picture, obscuring the view they are contemplating and thereby replacing it as the main subject-matter of the picture (Fig. 17.11). It is the latter examples that are the most radical (establishing the associations that are nevertheless latent in all his back-figures regardless of their size).

The significance of the *Rückenfigur* is twofold. Firstly, the fact that the figures have their backs turned to the viewer suggests not that they have simply not noticed the viewer but that the viewer does not exist for them, that the *self* of the viewer does not exist for them. The figures in question are invariably in peaceful states of mind, completely absorbed in the awesome objects of their contemplation (in so far as it is possible to tell from their graceful and relaxed postures). To introduce the possibility that they might be surprised by the sudden appearance of the viewer from behind them would be alien to the self-contained, meditative spirit of the works. Moreover, particularly in *The Wanderer above a Sea of Fog* and *The Woman before*

FIGURE 17.11: Caspar David Friedrich, *The Wanderer*, 1819, oil on canvas, 98.4 × 74.8 cm. Hamburger Kunsthalle. Photo: bpk/Hamburger Kunsthalle/Elke Walford.

the Setting Sun (both of around 1818), the figures are so large and centralised that they positively obscure the view beyond them. Thus, not only does the figure seem to be oblivious to the existence of the viewer but the painter appears to be so too, completely transgressing the conventions of the picturesque which, as we have seen, seeks the 'kind of beauty which is agreeable in a picture' and translates it into the language of human experience by subjecting it to the parameters of art appreciation; indeed, in his back-figure works, Friedrich deliberately impedes that experience.

Secondly, because Friedrich has, in some examples, placed more attention on the figures looking at the landscapes than on the landscapes themselves, it is arguable that it is their *act of looking* that constitutes the real subject-matter of the painting and not the view that they seem to be contemplating. If this is the case, then it must also be allowed that it is in the act of looking at the painting rather than in the painting itself that the value of the painting lies. If this is so, then – contradicting what was suggested above – the identity of the viewer *is* tacitly acknowledged by the painting, but only in so far as he identifies with the figure in the painting, through the shared act of looking. That is to say, the existence of the viewer is *not* acknowledged to the extent that he *observes* the figure in the painting (for whom he is non-existent and whose experience he cannot share), but *is* acknowledged to the extent that he *identifies* with that figure. For this paradox to be resolved, the viewer's experience of seeing the painting must be conflated with the back-figure's experience of seeing the sanctity of nature; indeed, the experience of seeing the painting must *become* an experience of seeing the sanctity of nature. Only in this way can the sublimity of the back-figure's vision, which is otherwise blocked by his body, be transmitted to the viewer. For this to happen – and therefore for the internal logic of the painting to work – the painting itself must be raised to the level of a sacred and natural object – equal to nature itself – and the experience of viewing it must become a sacred and natural activity.

Friedrich's importance lies precisely in the way that he sanctified the concept of art, raising it to the level of an absolute. In so doing, he also sanctified the role of the artist, thereby perfecting a model of subjective identity that functioned as an archetype for the general public, and which continued to function as the mainspring and principle of western European culture throughout the nineteenth and twentieth centuries. The extent to which Friedrich regarded artists as facilitators or agents of public self-awareness, providing his viewers with the cultural forms of their own experience, is reflected in his advice to artists to 'close your bodily eye so you may see your picture first with the spiritual eye. Then bring to the light of day that which you have seen in the darkness so that it may *act upon others from the outside inwards*'[9] – as it were, manoeuvring the viewer into the visionary space or disposition that the artist was in when he was painting it.

Friedrich's work demonstrates how the archetype of the artist was established to transmit uniquely creative personal insights – by means of art – to society as a whole; it represents the consummation of art, epitomising the way in which the convention of art appreciation was established as a medium of spiritual insight. It is, however, ironic that, as soon as the archetype of subjective identity was institutionalised in the 'temple' of art and made accessible to the public in this form, it began to unravel. For, as Friedrich himself demonstrated with his back-figures, the identity of the viewer is only recognised to the extent that it *loses itself* in visions of sublimity; that is to say – paradoxically – that the self is only consummated by experiencing the *selfless* sanctity of God. As Carl Gustav Carus, an amateur follower of Friedrich, remarked in one of his *Nine Letters on Landscape Painting*, written in the early 1820s:

> Climb to the topmost mountain peak, gaze out across long chains of hills, and observe the rivers in their courses and all the magnificence that offers itself to your eye – what feeling takes hold of you? There is a silent reverence within you; you lose yourself in infinite space; silently, your whole being is purified and cleansed; your ego disappears. You are nothing; God is all.[10]

It is in this context – in anticipation of the vanishing of the self – that Friedrich includes so many thresholds in his paintings (windows, gates, church portals, symmetrical screens of trees, open graves, beaches etc.), repeatedly placing himself, and the viewer, on the verge of an imaginative journey into the selfless unknown. In his *Abbey in the Oak Forest* (1809–10), for instance, the viewer is not only presented with a series of graves in the foreground (prompting him to reflect on his own mortality), but also with the portal of a ruined abbey (suggesting entrance into the uncontainable formlessness of God) and a 'natural' portal of symmetrical trees, towards which a group of shrouded monks are solemnly proceeding. Likewise, in *My Burial* (an early sepia drawing of 1803–4, now only known from contemporary descriptions), Friedrich depicted an open grave, surrounded by mourners, with the ruins of a Gothic church in the background. On a cross near the grave were inscribed the words *Hier ruht in Gott C. D. Friedrich* (*Here rests C. D Friedrich in God*). These words clearly refer to Friedrich's visualisation of his own death; but they also reflect his contemplative, self-forgetting immersion in the sanctity of God that his painted visions express and evoke. Indeed, the inscription suggests that the work did not simply *represent* his grave, reminding him of his own mortality and encouraging him to direct his life journey accordingly; it also *was* his grave, inviting him to die into it (through the practice of self-transcending art) and to be psychologically buried in it. In the same way, his major works (of landscapes, harbours etc.) do not simply *depict* thresholds; they *are* thresholds, not only offering imaginative journeys into mysterious landscapes but actually becoming artistic visions of the unknown.

The fact that Friedrich's works were intended to work not just on a symbolic level, depending on the associations of their iconography, but also on a visionary level is also strongly supported by their compositions. In many cases, these were designed to have an immediate physiological effect on their viewers, inducing contemplative states in them, rather than to ease them into a picturesque or poetic narrative. Thus, unlike Claude and his eighteenth-century followers whose artfully asymmetrical compositions, often framed by prominent features at their edges, invite the viewer to wind their way easefully into the pictorial space, zigzagging from one side of the image to the other (Fig. 16.8), Friedrich typically confronts his viewer with a starkly centralised composition, allowing for no waywardness on the viewer's part, in which the dominant element of iconography (often a strong vertical – a tree, a figure, a ruin) is placed at the very centre of the work. Rigorous symmetrical frontality is rare in historic paintings other than cult images designed for contemplation, and in Friedrich's work this device is repeatedly used to create iconic intensity. To the left and right of the central feature, the landscape frequently extends to the edges of the painting, without being framed by visual features that help the viewer 'contain' his experience within it. In several examples, the composition is dominated by the relationship between the earth and the sky, represented as two horizontal bands that not only establish a dramatic contrast between the this-worldly foreground and the otherworldly background but also reduce the painting, at a purely formal level, to two principle elements, one above the other. The relationships between vertical elements, which are placed against this fundamental structure, tend to take a secondary place. In images of the sea, in which the horizon is perfectly flat, the contrast between the upper and lower sections is especially stark and strong, even when its intensity is relieved by the delicate masts of ships. In the most extreme examples – for instance, *Monk by the Sea* (1809–10) – the flatness of the distant horizon is both entirely unbroken and uncontained (Fig. 17.12). This work consists of nothing more than a broad band of sky, a narrow band of deep blue sea and a narrow stretch of rock on which the scarcely visible figure of a monk stands in contemplation. In fact, the subject-matter of the painting is so reduced, providing the viewer with so little visual information, that its potential for any form of narrative fantasy is minimal, almost non-existent. Furthermore, the composition of the painting is so simple that the viewer (like the monk) has little choice but to experience it *physiologically*; that is to say, not as a representation *of something*, but as a purely optical and even abstract experience. It is, ultimately, through the optical experience it affords that the truly visionary significance of the painting is realised, anticipating the evolution of abstract painting. *The Monk by the Sea* certainly can be read as a conventionally symbolic image, for it nominally represents a monk (the renunciate painter or viewer of the image) looking across the sea (meditating on the passage through life) towards the distant horizon (the formless infinity of God). But this reference to the formless infinity of God is only translated from an *idea*, indicated by symbols, into a *reality* to the extent that it is experienced as an indeterminate and undifferentiated object. The viewer's preoccupation with iconography, therefore – with meaningful objects, needing to be interpreted – must be complemented, and even challenged and superseded, by his absorption in the immediate experience of objectless sensation. For it is only by surrendering the sense of coherent objectivity – in relation to which the viewer coordinates his own sense of subjective identity – that the coherent identity of the viewer is itself truly surrendered into the formless infinity of God. And it is only in this way – by seeming to surrender its own coherence as an object – that the purpose of the work of art is fully consummated, 'acting [on the viewer] from the outside inwards'.

Friedrich's significance lies in the way he both embodied the archetype of the artist as a primary source of inspiration, serving as a surrogate model of creative individuality for the public, and produced works of art that functioned as iconic instruments or catalysts of cultural and psychological change. He was one of many progressive 'romanticising' artists, composers and poets into whose work ordinary individuals could project their appetite and potential for personal identity. In this way, the conventions that developed around the production and consumption of 'artistic culture' became surrogate mechanisms through which the personal identities

FIGURE 17.12: Caspar David Friedrich, *A Monk by the Sea*, 1809, oil on canvas, 110 × 171.5 cm. Alte Nationalgalerie, Berlin. Photo: bpk/Nationalgalerie, SMB/Jörg P. Anders.

and individuality of 'ordinary' people could be experienced and expressed. The medium of art became the language of the self.

Once established, the process of art appreciation could also be applied retrospectively. As the discourses of art and aesthetics gathered momentum, so the appreciation of historic objects and images was increasingly seen to be an aesthetic experience, a matter of 'taste'; it became perfectly legitimate to enjoy an ancient artefact 'aesthetically' without necessarily understanding its original function or iconography. The fact that we may find cave paintings or medieval imagery 'beautiful' does not imply that they were created on the basis of a self-conscious awareness of beauty as an independent phenomenon (any more than a spider is conscious of, or motivated by, a sense of beauty when it creates a cobweb), though we may equally well bring our inclination to aestheticise our experiences to it. To think of prehistoric or medieval objects as 'art' is to project an anachronistic frame of reference on to them that reflects *our* requirement and need (for the sake of *our* own identities) that they accommodate the possibility of self-gratification, rather than the agendas of their actual makers (which we can only surmise). To withhold the labels of 'beauty' or 'art' from such creations is not to denigrate them; to suppose that it is is to simply perpetuate the post-eighteenth-century presumption that the key index of legitimate identity and cultural value is aesthetic self-awareness and self-expression. It is arguable that, prior to this development, beauty was not experienced as a function of subjectivity; to the extent that it was objectified at all, it was associated with exterior criteria – for instance, conformity to preconceived principles of proportion, or religious and symbolic meaning.

While the impulse to 'individuate' was gratified through the cult of art and the paraphernalia of art appreciation, it was also – throughout the nineteenth century – enshrined in monuments and institutions that elevated individuality to the level of a sacred ideal. In Germany, a temple to memorable and inspiring individuals of Germanic origin was conceived in 1807 by King Ludwig I of Bavaria; based on the Parthenon and consisting mostly of marble portrait busts, it opened to the public as the Walhalla 'Hall of Fame' outside Regensburg in 1842 (Fig. 17.13). In France, Napoleon's Edict of Saint-Cloud (1804) showed new respect for the individual by outlawing mass graves but it also decreed that cemeteries should be moved away from city centres towards the outskirts, on grounds of hygiene, and that graves should be 'democratically' regular and of a prescribed size. The cemetery of Père Lachaise in Paris, then to the east of the city centre, is only the best known of several cemeteries built at the time. But the prescriptive nature of the decree was also perceived by some to limit the scope for honouring the memory of deceased individuals and admiring their noble deeds, and a reaction set in accordingly.[11] In Italy, where the decree was introduced in 1806, the poet Ugo Foscolo's *Dei Sepolcri* (*The Sepulchres*), published the following year specifically to highlight the inspirational potential of tombs, led to the transformation of Santa Croce in Florence into a national (Tuscan) mausoleum. Efforts were made to repatriate the remains of Dante from Ravenna, to no avail; Florence had to make do with a cenotaph. In 1841, Florence also saw the creation of the 'Tribune of Galileo' – a neo-classical shrine to

FIGURE 17.13: Walhalla Hall of Fame, Regensburg, 1830–42. Photo: Christine Geth.

the long-maligned astronomer, decorated with biographical frescos and bas-reliefs. Some of the tomb sculptures in the monumental cemeteries in Italy, developed later in the nineteenth century (for instance, in Milan and Genoa), pushed dignified respect for the individual to the brink of intensely emotional subjectivity; in some cases, the devastation of mourners adorning the tombs resembles erotic abandon. In Britain, the archetype of the heroic individual was historicised by the writer Thomas Carlyle, whose 'Great Man Theory' was expounded in his *On Heroes, Hero Worship and the Hero in History* (1841). Reflecting his conviction that history is not the outcome of impersonal spiritual or cultural forces (as it was, for instance, for Hegel) but 'is nothing but the biography of great men', Carlyle was instrumental in the foundation of the National Portrait Gallery in London, which opened in 1856 to celebrate the role of 'the individual' in history. The artist George Frederic Watts (1817–1904) shared Carlyle's belief in the power of portraits to inspire viewers to respect and emulate great individuals and, over a fifty-year period starting in the late 1840s, he painted a series of intimate portraits of eminent contemporaries (including Carlyle), many of which he donated to the gallery at the end of his life. He was also one of many artists who contributed towards the series of thirty-five monumental mosaics of historical artists and craftsmen, from Phidias and Apelles to his own day, that were produced, from 1865, to decorate the South Court of the South Kensington Museum (now the Victoria and Albert Museum). Known as the 'Kensington Valhalla',

FIGURE 17.14: *Memorial to Heroic Self-Sacrifice*, conceived by George Frederic Watts for Postman's Park, St Paul's, London, 1900.

the mosaics identified and honoured key protagonists in the history of art and design. Other schemes that monumentalised not only individuals but individual *artists* were Paul Delaroche's *Hemicycle* of seventy-five artists in the Ecole de Beaux Arts in Paris (1841) and Nicaise de Keyser's *Fame of the Antwerp School* in the Museum of Fine Art in Antwerp (1861–72). Monuments that telescoped history into a timeless grouping of national heroes were also erected in Novgorod (the Millennium monument of 1862) and Vienna (the Maria Theresa monument of 1865).

Extending his belief in the sacred potential of individuality beyond 'the great and the good', in 1898 Watts conceived a public monument to commemorate recent acts of personal heroism by ordinary people who died saving others. The memorial – an open loggia of ceramic plaques, inscribed with details of the circumstances in which the individuals lost their lives – was unveiled in a public park near St Paul's Cathedral in 1900 (Fig. 17.14). By this time, the possibility of 'consummate, redemptive individuality' was no longer reserved for geniuses and their admirers; it was deeply woven into the cultural, linguistic and psychological conventions of the culture, and was extended to everybody.

CHAPTER EIGHTEEN

The Seamless Garment of the Self

The Invention of the Self has aimed to demonstrate the symbiotic relationship between the history of culture – especially the notion of 'art' – and 'personal identity'. It has attempted to show that, although images have been created since the origins of human history, the concept and discourse of '*art*' evolved in the Renaissance, as an instrument of self-consciousness, and came to a head at the turn of the nineteenth century, when it became the consummate medium for the realisation of a sense of personal self. During the eighteenth century, the notion of 'art' ceased to be a 'secondary' convention that was dependent on 'primary' sources of legitimacy – such as social status, religious belief and moral obligation – and became *self*-authenticating; that is to say, it was constructed – as a new cultural convention – such that the source of its legitimacy seemed to lie *within itself*. In the cultural sphere, this 'mechanism of self-reference' materialised as the freedom and power of the 'artist' (or, at least, the *ideal* 'artist') to source his ideas from within himself, and increasingly to 'express' himself. It was made accessible to ordinary people – increasingly identified as 'the public' – by means of works of art which were made to function as instruments of imaginative access to a realm of insight, feeling and depth that would otherwise be inaccessible to them. In order to fulfil this role, works of art were implicitly invested (via the empowered 'artist') with qualities that seemed to be objective and innate; they were conceived as discrete repositories of meaning, depth, beauty, authenticity and originality which could then be harvested by their viewers and experienced by them, vicariously, as their own.

But this is not the whole story for, although individual artists created the works of art that promised to actualise the experience of personal identity both in themselves and in their viewers, they did not create the *parameters* within which the experience of personal identity became possible or valuable. These parameters also unfolded in time, and also need to be accounted for. During the Renaissance, painters became free to originate their own ideas. Indeed it was on account of this freedom that they came to be regarded as liberal 'artists' and that the archetype of 'artist' first evolved. The artist was free, and empowered, to make certain choices, and the artistic choices he made were an expression or manifestation of his personal freedom and creativity – which was thereby transmitted to his viewers. But although artists (and their viewers) were free in this way, they were only free *within* the parameters of their time; they were not free to go beyond them. So, for instance, although Raphael was increasingly free to paint an infinite number of different pictures in a style that was characteristic of his period, he was not free to paint in the Cubist style of Picasso; although there was nothing, theoretically and physically, to stop him from placing the brushstrokes in the positions in which Picasso placed them, it would have been culturally and psychologically impossible for him to do so. This raises the question: while actual works of art are subject to the conditions that prevail at the time at which they are made, what is it that *determines those conditions*? Why was it *impossible* for Raphael to paint in the style of Picasso? One of the factors was obviously external constraints; on many different fronts, the historical, cultural and material circumstances of his time simply did not support such a style. But there were surely internal constraints too; that is to say, Cubism was *inconceivable* to Raphael. Not only did Raphael not experience the cultural contexts that generated the style and in which it arose, but – precisely *because* he did not have that experience – he did not have the *mental infrastructure* with which to even imagine it or relate to it; this infrastructure had not evolved in him.

Exactly the same could be said of our own capacity for experience: because our sensory faculties are limited to sight, sound, smell, taste and touch, we are unable to perceive the world other than by seeing, hearing, smelling, tasting or touching it. This is not necessarily because the world is only visible, audible, smellable, tastable and tangible; it is because these are the only aspects of the world that we are able to experience on the basis of the faculties at our disposal. The world may have other dimensions that exist beyond our capacity to know them; indeed it may have *many* other dimensions that exist beyond our capacity to know them. In the light of this possibility, it becomes clear that our experience of the world is as much a reflection of our own 'capacity to experience' it, as it is of the world itself; and indeed it could therefore be said to be an *embodiment of the subject* in which the 'capacity to experience' implicitly inheres. In the same way, it is arguable that, while Raphael was incapable of painting in the style of Picasso because he did not have the mental infrastructure to do so, the work that he *did* produce is a reflection of the mental infrastructure that he *did* have. As such, his work was not only a voluntary expression of his feelings and ideas, in relation to which he was empowered, as an artist, to exercise personal freedom, but it was also an *involuntary manifestation* of his *capacity for experience* – and, therefore, of the 'parameters of his self-sense', over which he will have had relatively little direct personal control. While an individual is free to act as he pleases, subject to the possibilities that are available to him, he is not free to act beyond those possibilities; and although those possibilities may change in the course of time, he is subject to them while they prevail and it is difficult and often impossible for him to actively change them. For instance, although we are free to *say* whatever we like, we are limited by the capacity of language to be expressive, and hugely restricted in our ability to alter that capacity (or even to be conscious of it); even the introduction of a new word to the lexicon is almost impossible for us. The capacity of language – the *range* of meanings that are possible for us at any given time – remains the inheritance of society as a whole and co-evolves with it, in keeping with its more collective tendencies.

Of course, the possibilities of experience are determined by innumerable different factors. On the one hand, there must be consciousness; without consciousness, there is no experience. On the other hand, there are objects – that which is experienced.

What differentiates human beings from other species is our ability to *abstract* from our experience, and accommodate our abstractions in mental and cultural conventions, including language, that hold their users together as a self-conscious community of communicants. As we have seen, while these conventions express the values of a society, they also manifest its capacity for experience, which is implicitly suggestive of a subject of experience, to the point at which they constitute an embodiment of that subject. Indeed, what *The Invention of the Self* has attempted to show is precisely how the concept and discourse of personal identity emerged, in conjunction with the swathe of cultural conventions that co-evolved with it – *implicitly* in the late Middle Ages, *explicitly* (if exclusively) in the Renaissance, and ever more widely thereafter, until it was realised as a self-evident, and apparently *autonomous*, phenomenon, pervading society, in the eighteenth century.

The process was a symbiotic 'chicken-and-egg' one. While the burgeoning self-sense was evoked, shaped and affected by the cultural conventions it encountered, so these cultural conventions were themselves generated *by* the evolving self-sense. This is because, on one level – the most immediate level – the world is appearing to us; we are passive to it (we see it, hear it etc.). But on another level, we are *creating* it, in the sense that, although we do not create the substance of which the world is composed, its apparent nature is determined by our capacity to realise it. Thus, an object (like a rose) or a sound (even a word) has no *inherent* meaning; nor indeed does it even have its own absolute discreteness as an object. On the contrary, its meaning and discreteness are ascribed to it by a subject, or self – whether that self seems to *make* the object in question (like a work of art), or whether it simply *abstracts* it from the pre-existent field of indeterminate consciousness (i.e. anything that it identifies as an object). That is to say, the self objectifies and structures its experience – which would otherwise be infinite and amorphous – according to the potential of its perceived objects and structures to embody pertinent meaning, coherence, integrity and value. The principle according to which the self makes these spontaneous judgements is its own existence, or capacity for identity, for it cannot exist – or know itself to exist – without generating reflectors in the world, in which it 'finds' itself reflected. Thus, in an inconceivable act of self-creation, *it makes or identifies objects in order to see itself reflected in them*. There are two important implications here. On the one hand, the self is inherently dualistic, bringing itself into existence, as a discrete subject, by knowing itself *through its objects* (whereupon it can also be conceived, by analogy, to be an object); all the objects it identifies innately reflect it to itself, appearing to *prove* it to itself, precisely because they are 'objects'. On the other hand, it is impossible for the self to know the state of selflessness which precedes the division of consciousness into subject and object, without ceasing to be a distinctive subject and without, therefore, surrendering the possibility of knowledge (which presupposes a subject) in the process. That is to say, the self cannot know itself *absolutely*, untrammelled by conditional forms of language and culture, precisely because, in surrendering those forms of language and culture, it surrenders the medium that makes knowledge – including knowledge of itself – possible and in which its own distinctive identity resides; it would cease to be itself. It cannot be otherwise, for the subject and the object are causally dependent on each other; they are functions of each other, implicitly bringing each other into existence (as argued by Nicholas of Cusa in his *De Visione Dei*, described in chapter 5).

This mutual inter-dependence of subject – the conscious 'I' – and object – that which is 'not I' ('it', 'her', 'him', 'them' etc.) – is fundamental to the experience of personal identity; indeed it is arguably the definitive, constitutive characteristic of personal identity. The two notions necessitate each other in exactly the way that, when I see myself in a mirror, my reflection always seems to be looking at me. This is not because it *is*, independently, looking at me; it is because I am looking at it. Indeed (owing to the technical properties of mirrors) the impression that it is looking at me is an inevitable *function* of the fact that I am looking at it. Moreover, not only can I not look in a mirror without seeing myself, but I cannot see myself without looking in a mirror. In exactly the same way, the subject of experience can *only* see itself in, and as, its objects, and its objects can *only* be seen to be reflecting the subject. That is to say, I can only see myself looking at myself – I cannot see myself *not* looking at myself; moreover, because phenomena can only be objectified (or seen as objects) in keeping with my capacity, as a subject, to objectify them, then everything that I see is a realisation of my capacity to experience in the world, and is therefore, in a certain sense, a solipsism, a *vision of myself*. The apparent nature of the world and my less apparent 'capacity to see the world' unfold together, as one.

Precisely because the objects that a subject sees are determined by the subject's capacity to objectify phenomena, the creation or recognition of cultural objects is tacitly, and tautologically, an affirmation of subjective identity. That sense of subjectivity will rise to the surface and be reflected in cultural conventions to the extent that the cultural language of the time is able to accommodate and process it. In the Middle Ages, it could only be realised in relation to the *collectivised* identity of the Church – whether in line with Christian belief (for instance, as private devotion) or against it (as heresy). In the early Renaissance, the concept and practice of 'art' provided a new range of cultural conventions through which subjectivity could be experienced and expressed *personally*; for just as the act of conceiving 'objects' co-conceives the notion of the 'subject', so the act of conceiving 'art' co-conceived the notion of the personal 'self', conferring a uniquely charged cultural, social and psychological value on it. It was this necessary, but hidden, co-dependency that made the relationship between the self and its cultural objects (including art) such a compelling and effective one from the early 'Renaissance', when the modern sense of the self first emerged, until the end of the eighteenth century, when it became *autonomous*. In the fifteenth and sixteenth centuries, signs of subjectivity began to proliferate, albeit within a Christian frame of reference. In the middle of the seventeenth century, Descartes wrested the soul from the Church, enabling the experience of existence to become self-authenticating for the first time; towards the end of that century, Locke dislocated personal identity from the substance of the soul, which Descartes located in the pineal gland in the brain, in favour of a more immaterial consciousness; and one hundred years later, Kant established the 'logical necessity' of autonomous subjectivity. Although he could not, significantly, prove his theory (which therefore shared some of the characteristics of a religious belief), the concept acquired the status of a 'fundamental truth'. Most significantly, the value of subjectivity was no longer subject to moral justification. Indeed, for Kant, the opposite formula was true: the possibility of morality was based on the realisation of autonomy.

The realisation of psychological autonomy was important because it represented the point at which the sense of a personal self became so spontaneous and even automatic, that it became unconscious and unnoticeable; it became an innate and inalienable property of experience. In the practical realm, the experience of autonomy was institutionalised in the elevated discourses of art and aesthetics, and the cultification of beauty, which conferred unprecedented cultural value on it. Although beauty came to be experienced as a self-sufficient attribute in objects (independent of extraneous factors), it is arguable that its deeper source was the resonant self-sufficiency of the *subject* – projected on to, and seen in and as, the objective world – and that the autonomous discourse of aesthetics was generated, not merely in relation to historical trends, but precisely in order to facilitate the realisation of the autonomous self. At the other end of the scale, the autonomy of the self also informed the transient conventions of 'ordinary' everyday thinking, feeling and behaviour that left nothing but incidental traces in the material and psychological environments in which they occurred. From the middle of the eighteenth century, these environments became so attuned to the dynamics and discourse of personal identity (which they shaped in return) that they came to be pervaded by them. Indeed, the *dynamics* of personal identity became so profoundly coded into the fabric of the culture that they seemed to be *natural*. It was precisely at this point – when the autonomy of the self-sense came to seem natural rather than constructed – that the existence and legitimacy of personal identity became a fundamental and pervasive principle of western culture and the invisible lens through which we continue to see the world. Like a seamless garment, it seemed to have no source or origin.

Of course, as the effects of the self-sense became manifest, so alternative dynamics also developed – as a counter-sign of its prevalence. Firstly, the personal identities of consumers of culture were subsumed in the new identity of the 'public'. While the infrastructure of art appreciation (for instance, art museums and galleries, and illustrated art books) increased the access of ordinary people to works of art, it was inevitably oriented toward a relatively homogenous experience that instituted the generalised identity of a public at the expense of individual sensitivities. Thus, at the very moment at which the experience of cultural depth was becoming disseminated throughout society, it was also being de-personalised in public institutions; indeed, it was partly in order to compensate for this associated loss of individuality that members of the 'public' were encouraged to project their capacity for creative insight on to individual 'artists'. Secondly, the role of the individual in history was hugely undermined by the theory of evolution which, from its origins at the end of the eighteenth century, ascribed causality to forces of nature, with or without divine guidance, at the expense of the individual will; as study of the mind grew into the new science of psychology, even the notion of 'genius' – the essence of individuality – was subjected to scrutiny as if it was a function of nature, associated with a rare physiological condition, rather than a quasi-mystical 'personal' gift. And thirdly, the existence of personal identity was questioned altogether. As early as 1738, David Hume expressed his practical inability to confirm the existence of a self-sense on the basis of experience.

As such he anticipated postmodernist rejections of coherent 'selfhood' as an artificial and ideologically charged concept. Moreover, although the notion of the self was perpetuated as a cultural convention throughout the nineteenth century (despite these challenges), it also underwent its own process of disintegration, subsumed both in the history of psychology, which splintered it into myriad combinations of conscious and unconscious parts, and the subsequent history of culture. While art continued to be cultivated as a medium of self-expression, it was, according to some determinists, also subjected to a depersonalising process of 'purification' that led to the realisation of abstract and non-objective art at the beginning of the twentieth century – and eventually to the death of art and the concomitant death of the self. Some radicals, especially in Russia, claimed that the medium of art – once used by privileged artists to deliver the 'depth of reality' to the public – had evaporated because, like a crutch, it was no longer necessary: partly due to the development of psychology, the 'depth of reality' could now communicate itself to people directly, or im-mediately. These radicals maintained that creative endeavour should no longer be invested in 'artistic' initiatives, which were monopolised by a minority of 'aestheticist' individuals to disenfranchise the uninitiated masses, but that it should be invested in the design of utilitarian projects that made such endeavour accessible and useful to the whole of society. At the other end of the scale, Marcel Duchamp inaugurated a tradition that attempted to replace the redundant mediatory function of art with a new rationale that justified it purely on its own terms, to the extent that anything that was said *by an artist* to be art could become art, purely by virtue of being identified as such. The notion of 'art for art's sake' had first been mooted at the beginning of the nineteenth century, in relation to the autonomous authority of the artist and his 'licence' to find cultural value in the depth of his own experience, albeit within the parameters of the time. But now, even those parameters ceased to apply, and art could be *anything*; it had become 'pure idea', a figment of the imagination, an act of the mind. Thus, what was at stake here was not so much the 'existence of art' as the *existence of the self-sense* which had come to co-depend on art, and which, as we have seen throughout this book, generated the discourse of art, over many centuries, as a means with which to propagate itself and thrive. While the notion of art had originally developed as a medium of expression for, and of, the self, there was now a danger that it had also become a device with which the self could protect itself against knowledge of its own non-existence. As Nietzsche said: 'We need art lest we perish of the truth.' This statement is as pertinent now as it was when it was first made in the 1880s. Because the 'I' only exists to the extent that it sees itself, it generates circumstances that seem to reflect it, to this day.

NOTES

PREFACE AND ACKNOWLEDGEMENTS

1. Arthur Guirdham, *The Cathars and Reincarnation*, Spearman, 1970.

2. THE EMERGENCE OF THE SELF

1. The Gospel of John, chapter 5, verse 30.
2. Miri Rubin, *Corpus Christi: the Eucharist in Late Medieval Culture*, Cambridge University Press, 1991, p. 82.
3. Ibid., pp. 65–6.
4. For instance, Santa Maria del Naranco, Oviedo, Spain (9th century); the Church of St Margaret of Antioch, Kopcany, Slovakia (9th–10th century); the Saxon church in Escomb, County Durham (founded in the 7th century); St Laurence in Bradford, Wiltshire (from around 1000); Sanfins de Fiestas, Portugal (11th century).
5. Timothy C. Potts, *Conscience in Medieval Philosophy*, Cambridge University Press, 1980, p. 107.
6. Peter Abelard, *Ethical Writings*, translated by Paul Vincent Spade, Hackett, 1995, p. 29, section 131.
7. Meister Eckhart in Old German, Hadewijch in Middle Dutch, Marjorie Porete in Old French.
8. Meister Eckhart, *German Sermons and Treatises*, edited and translated by M. O'C Walshe, Vol. 1, Watkins, 1979, p. 143.

3. THE RESURRECTION OF THE SELF

1. Cited in Barbara Catherine Raw, *Trinity and Incarnation in Anglo-Saxon Art and Thought*, Cambridge University Press, 1997, p. 58.
2. Morgan Library, New York, MS M.917/945.
3. Transcribed from the Middle English, in Ellen M. Ross, *The Grief of God: Images of the Suffering Jesus in Late Medieval England*, Oxford University Press, 1997, p. 24. The original manuscript, containing various devotional treatises and sermons, is British Library MS Harley 2398 (f. 186b).
4. Netherlandish woodcut, c.1495–1505, in the British Museum, 1856,0209.81.

NOTES 367

5. Steven E. Plank, '*Wrapped all in woe*: Passion Music in Late Medieval England' in A. A. MacDonald, H. N. B. Ridderbos and R. M. Schlusemann, *The Broken Body, Passion Devotion in Late Medieval Culture*, Egbert Forsten, 1998, p. 94.
6. Ross, *The Grief of God*, p. 75.
7. Almuth Seebohm, 'The Crucified Monk', in *Journal of the Warburg and Courtauld Institutes*, vol. 59, 1996, pp. 69–70.
8. Julian of Norwich, *Revelations of Divine Love*, translated by Clifton Wolter, Penguin Classics, 1980, chapter 60, page 169.
9. Ross, *The Grief of God*, p. 18.
10. The thought was voiced by Prince Myshkin in *The Idiot*, and elsewhere. See Erika Michael, *Hans Holbein the Younger: A Guide to Research*, Garland, 1997, pp. 50–3.

5. THE NECESSITATION OF THE SELF

1. The Lippi painting is now in the Gemäldegalerie, Berlin.
2. The first explicit association of the image with Christ occurred in 1637 in a painting of *Christ and the Woman taken in Adultery* (Bayerische Staatsgemaldesammlung, Munich) by Georg Vischer, in which the image of Christ is clearly based on Dürer's Self-Portrait. Joseph L. Koerner, *The Moment of Self-Portraiture in German Renaissance Art*, University of Chicago Press, 1993, pp. 71–2.
3. It is not inconceivable that the *Salvator Mundi*, attributed to Leonardo da Vinci in 2011 and painted at around the same time as Dürer's work, is also a self-portrait. Apart from the fact that the figure is making eye contact with the viewer – typical both of self-portraits and of cult images of Christ – the *Salvator Mundi* bears a striking resemblance both to a portrait drawing of Leonardo by his pupil Francesco Melzi (of around 1510) and Leonardo's red chalk drawing of an old man (from around 1512–15, now in Turin) which is also considered by many to be a self-portrait. Notwithstanding the age difference of the sitters in these images (Leonardo would have been 48 years old in 1500 and would therefore have had to make himself younger in order to use himself as a model for Christ, who died aged 33), their eyes, nose, lips and hair – not to mention their overall demeanour – are remarkably similar. Certainly Leonardo, who considered the art of painting to be more noble than both sculpture and poetry (reflected, for instance, in its unique ability to represent crystal, as demonstrated in the *Salvator Mundi*), regarded the gifts of the artist as divine.
4. The copy of the tapestry, produced before 1461, is currently in the Bern Historical Museum. See Koerner, *The Moment of Self-Portraiture*, p. 128.
5. Nicholas of Cusa, *De Visione Dei*, translated by Jasper Hopkins, A. J. Banning Press, 1985, chapter 5, section 15.
6. Ibid., chapter 6, section 20. Conversely, God's creation of the world is also a kind of self-portrait: 'You, Oh Lord, who work all things for Your own sake, created this whole world on account of the intellectual nature. [You created] as if you were a Painter who mixes different colors in order, at length, to be able to paint Himself – to

the end that He may have an image of Himself wherein He himself may take delight and His artistry may find rest'. Chapter 25, section 111.
7. Academies of Art did not become conventional elsewhere in Europe until the seventeenth and eighteenth centuries: Paris in 1648, St Petersburg in 1755 and London in 1768.
8. Koerner, *The Moment of Self-Portraiture*, pp. 168–9. The relief, carved by Hans Daucher of Augsburg, is in the Bode Museum, Berlin, inventory no. 804.

6. THE ABSTRACTION OF THE SELF

1. *Summa Theologica*, Part 1, Question 1, Article 3: 'Is sacred doctrine a single science?'
2. For a full transcription of the interrogation, see Robert Klein and Henri Zerner (eds.), *Italian Art: Sources and Documents 1500–1600*, Northwestern University Press, pp. 129–32.
3. Leah Knight, *Of Books and Botany in Early Modern England*, Ashgate, 2009, p. 57.

7. THE IMAGINARY ENVIRONMENTS OF THE SELF

1. Terrence G. Kardong, *The Life of St Benedict, by Gregory the Great*, Liturgical Press, 2009, p. 2.
2. Guglielmo Cavallo and Roger Chartier (eds), *A History of Reading in the West*, University of Massachusetts Press, 2003, p.75.
3. Ibid., pp. 73–4.
4. St Augustine, *Confessions*, translated by Maria Boulding, Book VI, chapter 3, New City Press, 1997.
5. Malcolm Beckwith Parkes, *Pause and Effect: An Introduction to the History of Punctuation in the West*, Scolar Press, 1992, chapter 4.
6. *The Rites of Durham*, ed. Surtees Soc. 1844, p. 70, cited in John Willis Clark, *The Care of Books*, Cambridge University Press, 1901, p. 90.
7. 'The Testimony of Brother Stephen' in 'The Process of Canonization at Bologna' (1233), section 38, in Simon Tugwell, *Early Dominicans: Selected Writings*, Paulist Press, 1982, p. 80.
8. See Bernard Ridderbos, *Saint and Symbol: Images of Saint Jerome in Early Italian Art*, Bouma's Boekhuis, 1984. An earlier suggestion is that of P. H. Jolly, 'Antonello da Messina's "St Jerome in His Study": a disguised portrait?' *Burlington Magazine*, 124 (1982), 27–9.
9. A second example is at the Ringling Museum, Sarasota, Florida.
10. Urbino: 360 × 335 cm. Gubbio: 510 × 380 cm.
11. Robert Kirkbride, *Architecture and Memory, The Renaissance Studioli of Federico da Montefeltro*, Columbia University Press, 2008, page/section 37.

12. For instance, logic (Plato), mathematics and music (Boethius), astronomy (Ptolemy), geometry (Euclid), rhetoric (Cicero), law (Solon), medicine (Hippocrates). The churchmen include Sts Gregory, Augustine, Ambrose and Jerome, Thomas Aquinas and Albert Magnus.
13. William N. West, 'Reading Rooms: Architecture and Agency in the Houses of Michel de Montaigne and Nicholas Bacon', *Comparative Literature*, Vol. 56, No. 2 (Spring), 2004, p. 112.
14. *Essaies* II, 18. My translation, and my italics. See West, 'Reading Rooms' and Richard L. Regosin, *The Matter of My Book: Montaigne's 'Essaies' as the Book of the Self*, University of California Press, 1977, pp. 190–2.
15. Frances A. Yates, *The Art of Memory*, Pimlico, 2008, p. 131.
16. Ibid., p. 27.
17. Mary Carruthers, *The Book of Memory: A Study of Memory in Medieval Culture*, Cambridge University Press, 2008, pp. 10, 117.
18. Ibid., p. 99.
19. Ibid., p. 53. My italics.
20. *Ordo Universi et humanarum scientiarum prima monumenta.*
21. *Anatomia Magistri Nicolai Physici*, quoted and translated by Corner in George W. Corner, *Anatomical Texts of the Earlier Middle Ages*, Washington, 1927, p. 72; cited in Plinio Prioreschi, *A History of Medicine: Medieval Medicine*, Horatius Press, 2003, p. 254.
22. Frederique Lachaud, 'Dress and Social Status in England before the Sumptuary Laws', in Peter Coss and Maurice Keen (ed.), *Heraldry, Pageantry and Social Display in Medieval England*, Boydell Press, 2008, pp. 107–8.
23. Letter from Viglius Zuichemus to Erasmus in 1532, published in Susan Pearce and Kenneth Arnold, *The Collector's Voice*, Volume 2: *Early Voices*, Ashgate, 2000, pp. 4–5.
24. Oliver Impey and Arthur Macgregor (eds), *The Origins of Museums: The Cabinet of Curiosities in Sixteenth and Seventeenth Century Europe*, House of Stratus, 2001, p. 9.
25. In some gallery paintings, each of the miniature paintings was painted by a different artist – constituting a copy of a painting on the one hand and an original painting on the other, such that the gallery painting became not only a representation of a gallery but also a miniature gallery in itself. For instance, *Interior with Figures in a Picture Gallery* 1667–72 and 1706, by Gonzalez Coques and many others, in the Mauritshuis, The Hague, museum number 238. See Ariane van Suchtelen, 'Collecting within the Picture Frame: Collaborative Gallery Paintings' in Ariane van Suchtelen and Ben van Beneden (eds), *Room for Art in Seventeenth Century Antwerp*, Waanders, 2009, pp. 99–117. In 1660, Teniers also produced a catalogue of the Archduke's collection, *Theatrum Pictorium*, illustrated with engravings.

8. THE PRIVATISATION OF THE SELF

1. Bede, *Ecclesiastical History*, Book 2, chapter 13.
2. Margaret Wood, *The English Medieval House*, Ferndale, 1981, p. 23

3. Text B, Passus X, cited (slightly modernised) in Mark Girouard, *Life in the English Country House*, Yale University Press, 1978, p. 30.
4. Conversely, in the summertime precedence was reflected in proximity to 'aire' (doors and windows). The quote is from *Youth's Behaviour*, a late sixteenth-century French text, as translated by Francis Hawkins (aged ten) in 1661, quoted in Anna Bryson, *From Courtesy to Civility: Changing Codes of Conduct in Early Modern England*, Clarendon Press, 1998, p. 90.
5. Kate Robinson, *A Search for the Source of the Whirlpool of Artifice: The Cosmology of Giulio Camillo*, Dunedin Academic Press, 2006, p. 47.
6. Robin Middleton, 'Enfilade – the Spatial Sequence in French Hotels of the 17th and 18th centuries', *Daidalos*, no. 42, 1991, p.164. See also Nicolas Le Camus de Mézières, *The Genius of Architecture, or the Analogy of that Art with our sensations*, with introduction by Robin Middleton, Getty Center, 1992, p. 33.
7. Sabine Melchior-Bonnet, *The Mirror: A History*, Routledge, 2002, p. 189.
8. Vincent Ilardi, *Renaissance Vision from Spectacles to Telescopes*, American Philosophical Society, 2007, pp. 43ff.
9. Melchior-Bonnet, *The Mirror*, pp. 28–9.

9. THE AUTOMATION OF THE SELF

1. The system was conceived by the Jesuit polymath Athanasius Kircher. Examples survive in the cloister of the convent of the Trinita dei Monti in Rome, designed by Emmanuel Maignan in 1637, and in the stairwell of the former Jesuit College in Grenoble, designed by Jean Bonfa in 1673.
2. Peter Rolfe Monks, *The Brussels Horloge de Sapience*, Brill, 1990, pp. 53–8.

10. THE SENSIBILITIES OF THE SELF

1. A customary for the convent of Syon, dating to the early 1430s, describes the space at the middle of the high table reserved for the abbess, with the other sisters sitting at side tables 'in ther order as they be professyd' (entered the convent). Jonathan W. Nicholls, *The Matter of Courtesy: Medieval Courtesy Books and the Gawain-Poet*, Brewer, 1985, p. 33.
2. The fourteenth-century poem, *Cleanness*, probably written by the writer of Sir Gawain and the Green Knight, cited in Nicholls, *The Matter of Courtesy*, p. 9.
3. Boyd Taylor Coolman, *The Theology of Hugh of St Victor: An Interpretation*, Cambridge Univesity Press, 2010, p.199. For other sets of instructions for novices, see Nicholls, *The Matter of Courtesy*, p. 36, n. 39.
4. Frederick J. Furnivall, *The Babees Book*, Early English Text Society, 1868, pp. 328–31.
5. Nicholls, *The Matter of Courtesy*, pp. 20–1.
6. Furnivall, *The Babees Book*, p. ix.

7. Ibid., p. xviii. Nicholas Orme, *From Childhood to Chivalry: The Education of the English Kings and Aristocracy 1066–1530*, Methuen, 1984, p. 62.
8. John Gillingham, 'From Civilitas to Civility: Codes of Manners in Medieval and Early Modern England', *Transactions of the Royal Historical Society*, 6th series, XII, Cambridge University Press, 2002, p. 281.
9. Maurice Keen, *Chivalry*, Yale University Press, 2005, p. 91.
10. Ibid., pp. 116–17. Robert Bartlett, *England Under the Norman and Angevin Kings, 1075–1225*, Clarendon Press, 2000, p. 561.
11. Furnivall, *The Babees Book*, p. 16.
12. The gospel of Luke I, 29.
13. A later courtesy book, *Il Galateo*, written by Giovanni della Casa and published in Venice in 1558, reiterates this precept, advising the reader not to 'inspect your handkerchief, after blowing your nose, as if pearls or rubies have fallen from your skull'.
14. Alessandro Olivieri, *Portrait of a Young Man*, around 1510, National Gallery of Ireland.
15. Nicholas Breton, *The Court and Country, or, A Brief Discourse between a Courtier and a Country-man*, London, 1618.
16. C. Stephen Jaeger, *The Origins of Courtliness: Civilizing Trends and the Formation of Courtly Ideals – 939–1210*, University of Pennsylvania Press, 1985.
17. Ludovico Ariosto, *Orlando Furioso*, XI, 26, cited in Giovanni della Casa, *Il Galateo*, translated by R. S. Pine-Coffin, Penguin, 1958, p. 107.
18. Baldassare Castiglione, *The Book of the Courtier*, translated by George Bull, Penguin Classics, 1976, p. 256.
19. Ibid., p. 40.
20. Ibid., p. 125.
21. Ibid., pp. 125–6.
22. Ibid., p. 132.
23. Ibid., p. 131.
24. Ibid., p. 322.
25. Ibid., p. 319.
26. Ibid., p. 114.
27. Ibid., p. 124. One participant in the conversations, signor Morello da Ortona, says that he learned this skill from friars at confession when he was a child, p. 115.
28. Ibid., p. 114.
29. Ibid., p. 115.
30. Ibid., p. 116.
31. Ibid., p. 136.
32. Ibid., p. 67.

33. In his *Civil Conversation*, first published in Italian in 1574, Stefan Guazzo criticises those that 'seeme to doo all thynges of his owne mother witte as it were: not considering how we deserve no prayse for that, which God or nature hath bestowed upon us, but only for that, which we purchase by our owne industry'. Translated by George Pettie in 1581, edited by Sir Edward Sullivan, Constable, 1925, vol. I, p. 8.

34. The concept of *sprezzatura* was first used in relation to art theory by the Venetian art theorist Ludovico Dolce in his dialogue *L'Aretino* of 1557. See Peter Burke, *The Fortunes of the Courtier: The European Reception of Castiglione's 'Cortegiano'*, Polity Press, 1995, p. 53.

35. Thomas Wright, *Passions of the Minde* (facsimile), Georg Olms Verlag, 1973, p. 45. Also quoted in Anna Bryson, *From Courtesy to Civility: Changing Codes of Conduct in Early Modern England*, Clarendon Press, 1998, p. 90.

36. Castiglione's *Il Cortegiano* was first translated into English, as *The Courtyer*, by Thomas Hoby in 1561; *Il Galateo* was translated by Robert Peterson in 1576; and Books 1–3 of Stefano Guazzo's *Il Civile Conversazione* were first translated into English, as *The Civil Conversation*, by George Pettie in 1581; Book 4 was translated by Bartholomew Yonge in 1586.

37. The poet and novelist, Jean Regnault de Segrais. See Benedetta Craveri, *The Age of Conversation*, New York Review of Books, 2005, p. 41.

38. The Abbé de Pure, around 1660. Even in 1724, Eliza Haywood, a prolific novelist, could explain and justify her predilection for romantic fiction by writing: 'But, as I am a Woman, and consequently depriv'd of those Advantages of Education which the other Sex enjoy, I cannot so flatter my Desires, as to imagine it in my Power to soar to any Subject higher than that which Nature is not negligent to teach us'. Cited in Robert A. Day, *Told in Letters: Epistolary Fiction before Richardson*, University of Michigan Press, 1966, p. 81.

39. Jane Rather Thiebaud, 'Madame de Rambouillet's Chambre Bleue (Blue Room): Birthplace of Salon Culture', PhD dissertation for the University of Maine, 2007, p. 55, citing the first-hand description of the room by the contemporary historian Henri Sauval.

40. Gédéon Tallemant des Réaux, *Historiettes*, Paris, 1834, vol. I, p. 443, cited in Craveri, *The Age of Conversation*, p. 27.

41. Ibid.

42. Du Plaisir, in his 'Sentiments sur les lettres et sur l'histoire' (1683). Cited in Elizabeth Goldsmith, *Exclusive Conversations*, University of Pennsylvania Press, 1988, p. 34.

43. Tallemant des Réaux, *Historiettes*, ed. Antoine Adam, 2 vols., Paris, Pléiade, 1960–1, vol. 1, pp. 330–1, cited in Jonathan Dewald, *Aristocratic Experience and the Origins of Modern Culture*, University of California Press, 1993, p. 175.

44. See, for instance, Gary Schneider, *The Culture of Epistolarity: Vernacular Letters and Letter-Writing in Early Modern England, 1500–1700*, University of Delaware Press, 2005, pp. 235ff.

45. Goldsmith, *Exclusive Conversations*, p. 25.

NOTES 373

46. From Part 4, Book 2 of a 1678 translation of *Clélie, Histoire romaine* by George Havers, in *Women Critics 1660–1820: An Anthology*, edited by the Folger Collective on Early Women Critics, Indiana University Press, 1995, p. 6.
47. Pierre Daniel Huet, *The History of Romances*, translated by Stephen Lewis, London, 1715, pp. 3–4.
48. Ibid., pp. 127–9.
49. Ibid., pp. 139–41.
50. Ibid., p. 144.
51. Ibid., pp. 143–4.
52. François de la Rochefoucauld, Maxim no. 136: 'Il y a des gens qui n'auraient jamais été amoureux s'ils n'avaient jamais entendu parler de l'amour.'
53. Samuel Richardson, *Selected Letters*, edited by John Carroll, Clarendon Press, 1964, p. 41.
54. Ibid., p. 34.
55. Anthony Stafford, *The Guide of Honour*, 1634, quoted in Bryson, *From Courtesy to Civility*, p. 236.

11. THE BEHAVIOUR OF THE SELF

1. Edmund Spenser, 'A View of the Present State of Ireland', Corpus of Electronic Texts (http://celt.ucc.ie). Partly cited in Ann Rosalind Jones and Peter Stallybrass, *Renaissance Clothing and the Materials of Memory*, Cambridge University Press, 2000, p. 4.
2. See Reed Benhamou, 'Parallel Walls, Parallel Worlds: The Places of Masters and Servants in the Maisons de plaisance of Jacques-François Blondel', *Journal of Design History*, 1994, vol. 7, no. 1; Andrew Ayers, *The Architecture of Paris*, Edition Axel Menges, 2004, p. 362.
3. John Morley, *The History of Furniture: Twenty-five Centuries of Style and Design in the Western Tradition*, Little, Brown and Company, 1999, p. 168.
4. Mimi Hellman, 'Furniture, Sociability and the Work of Leisure in Eighteenth-Century France', *Eighteenth-Century Studies*, 1999, vol. 32, no. 4, pp. 415–45.
5. Randall Cotgrave, *Dictionarie of the French and English Tongues*, cited in Marta Straznicky, *Privacy, Playreading and Closet Drama, 1550–1700*, Cambridge University Press, 2004, p. 115.
6. The double meaning of the word 'secret' – to 'keep separate' and to 'keep private' – is reflected in the two words 'discrete' and 'discreet', which originated as one word and share a root with 'secret': a prefix + *cretus*, the past participle of *cernere*, to 'separate'. To 'dis-cern' and 'be con-cerned with' belong to the same group.
7. See Richard Collins' *Family Drinking Tea*, oil on canvas, c.1727, Victoria & Albert Museum, London, P.9-1934.

12. THE PORTRAYAL OF THE SELF

1. The horoscope appeared in Cardano's 'Commentary on Ptolemy's *Tetrabiblos*'. In the second edition (1557), the publisher replaced the horoscope with a description of the new clock in Strasburg Cathedral. Anthony Grafton, *Cardano's Cosmos: The Worlds and Works of a Renaissance Astrologer*, Harvard University Press, 2001, pp. 151–5.
2. Margaret J. Kidnie (ed.), 'A Critical Edition of "The Anatomie of Abuses" by Philip Stubbes', PhD thesis, University of Birmingham, 1996, p. 121.
3. Jennifer Spinks, 'Louis XIV's Youthful Spirit: The 1699 Redecoration of the Versailles Menagerie', master's research, University of Tasmania, 2000.
4. Charles Perrault, *Parallel between the Ancients and Moderns regarding the arts and sciences*, 2nd edition, II, 29–31, cited in Arthur A. Tilley, *The Decline of the Age of Louis XIV*, Barnes & Noble, 1968, p. 338.
5. René Descartes, *The Passions of the Soul*, translated by Stephen Voss, Hackett Publishing Co. 1989, pp.18–19.
6. Ibid., Article 112, p. 79.
7. Richard Lovelace, 'To my Worthy Friend Mr. Peter Lilly', 1647, in Jonathan F. S. Post, *English Lyric Poetry: The Early Seventeenth Century*, Psychology Press, 2002, pp. 126–7.
8. Cited in Thijs Weststeijn, *The Visible World: Samuel van Hoogstraten's Art Theory and the Legitimation of Painting in the Dutch Golden Age*, Amsterdam University Press, 2008, p. 183.
9. Ibid., p. 185.

13. THE ENJOYMENT OF THE SELF

1. Dyan Elliot, *Fallen Bodies: Pollution, Sexuality, and Demonology in the Middle Ages*, University of Pennsylvania Press, 1999, p. 33.
2. Thomas of Chobham, in Robert Bartlett, *England Under the Norman and Angevin Kings, 1075–1225*, Clarendon Press, 2000, p. 569. The belief was attributed to St Jerome: Bette Talvacchia, *Taking Positions: On the Erotic in Renaissance Culture*, Princeton University Press, 1999, p. 116.
3. *The Life of St Teresa of Avila*, translated by David Lewis, Cosimo Classics, 2011, Chapter 29, part 17, p. 226.
4. That both of the Virgin Mary's breasts are fully exposed in the Nativity scene on the fourteenth-century altarpiece from Castle Tyrol in the Landesmuseum Innsbruck (Plate 10.8) is unique, unambiguously referring to her nurturing of Christ.
5. For instance, Hans Memling's 'Luxury' (or 'Vanity') in the Musée des Beaux-Arts, Strasbourg, reproduced in 'Le Bain et le Miroir: Soins du corps et cosmétiques de l'Antiquité à la Renaissance', Gallimard, 2009, p. 66.
6. Talvacchia, *Taking Positions*, p. 46. Roberto Zapperi, 'Alessandro Farnese, Giovanni della Casa and Titian's 'Danae' in Naples', *Journal of the Warburg and Courtauld Institutes*, vol. 54, 1991, pp. 159–71.

7. Jean Seznec, *The Survival of the Pagan Gods: The Mythological Tradition and its Place in Renaissance Humanism and Art*, Princeton University Press, 1972, p. 271.
8. Engraved by Jacopo Caraglio, after designs by Perino del Vaga.
9. Talvacchia, *Taking Positions*, pp. 59–62.
10. Ibid., p. 86.
11. *L'Escole des Filles* (1655) by Michel Millot, *Satyra sotadica* (1660) by Nicolas Chorier and *Venus dans la cloitre* (1680) by Jean Barrin (1680) – translated into English as *The School of Venus* (1680), *A Dialogue between a Married Lady and a Maid* (1740) and *Venus in the Cloister* (1725).
12. James Grantham Turner, *Schooling Sex: Libertine Literature and Erotic Education in Italy, France and England, 1534–1685*, Oxford University Press, 2003, p. 112.
13. Entries for January and February 1668, in Robert Latham and William Matthews (eds.), *The Diary of Samuel Pepys*, vol IX, 1668–9, HarperCollins, 2000, pp. 21–2 and 59.
14. Ian McCormick (ed.), *Secret Sexualities: A Sourcebook of 17th and 18th Century Writing*, Routledge, 1997, p. 191.
15. Ibid., p. 196.
16. Robert Darnton, *The Forbidden Best-Sellers of Pre-Revolutionary France*, Harper Collins, 1996, p. 262.
17. Interestingly, Kant also identified masturbation with unadulterated pleasure, but he evaluated it very differently. Because it seemed to reduce human beings to the level of impulsive animals, beneath the level of moral actions, he considered it to be more unnatural than suicide. Rousseau, on the other hand, disapproved of it because it was a-social; as he elaborated in his *Confessions*, he preferred to be spanked.
18. Darnton, *The Forbidden Best-Sellers of Pre-Revolutionary France*, p. 298.
19. Ibid., p. 296.
20. Ibid., p. 297.
21. A second painting of Marie-Louise O'Murphy is in the collection of the Alte Pinakothek in Munich. The *Odalisque* is in the Museum of Fine Art, Reims.
22. Jean-François de Bastide, *La Petite Maison: An Architectural Seduction*, translated with introduction by Rodolphe El-Khoury, Princeton Architectural Press, 1996, p. 58.
23. Ibid., pp. 72–3.
24. Ibid., p. 67.
25. Ibid., p. 83.
26. Ibid., p. 110.
27. Germain Boffrand, *Book of Architecture*, translated by David Britt, introduction by Caroline van Eck, Ashgate, 2002, p. 6.
28. Ibid., p. 6.
29. *Dictionnaire d'architecture*, 1770, cited in Nicolas Le Camus de Mézières, *The Genius of Architecture, or the Analogy of that Art with our sensations*, with introduction by Robin Middleton, Getty Center, 1992, p. 191.

30. Ibid., p. 70.
31. Ibid..
32. Ibid., p. 96.
33. Ibid., p. 97.
34. Ibid., p. 104.

14. THE EMBODIMENT OF THE SELF

1. Giorgio Vasari, *The Lives of the Artists*, translated by George Bull, Penguin, 1965, pp. 443–4.
2. 'For near Three Hundred Years since Painting was reviv'd, we can hardly reckon six Painters that have been good Colourists' in Charles Harrison, Paul Wood and Jason Gaiger (eds), *Art in Theory 1648–1815*, Blackwell, 2001, p. 190.
3. Jean-Baptiste Dubos, *Réflexions critiques sur la peinture et sur la poesie*, Paris, 1719, p. 342, as translated in Thomas Nugent, *Critical Reflections on Painting, Poetry and Music*, London, 1748, vol. II, pp. 238–9.
4. Athanasius Kircher, *Musurgia*, vol. 2, p. 240 resp. 223, cited in Maarten Franssen, 'The Ocular Harpsichord of Louis-Bertrand Castel: The Science and Aesthetics of an Eighteenth-Century Cause Célèbre', *Tractrix*, vol. 3, 1991, pp. 19–20.
5. Franssen, 'Ocular Harpsichord', p. 47.
6. Ibid., p. 28.
7. Ibid., p. 22.
8. Hogarth and Prévost also contemplated a 'concert of flavours'. Franssen, 'Ocular Harpsichord', p. 48.
9. Ibid., p. 57.
10. Ibid., p. 49.
11. Jessica Riskin, *Science in the Age of Sensibility: The Sentimental Empiricists of the French Enlightenment*, University of Chicago Press, 2002, p. 31.
12. William Cheselden, *The Anatomy of the Human Body*, London, 1763, p. 301.
13. John Locke, *An Essay Concerning Human Understanding*, Book II, chapter 1, sections 2–4 (abridged and edited by Kenneth P. Winkler, Hackett, 1996, pp. 33–4).
14. Etienne Bonnot de Condillac, *Treatise on the Sensations*, translated by Geraldine Carr, University of Southern California, 1930, p. 3.
15. Condillac, *Treatise on the Sensations*, trans. Carr, p. 43; see also *Philosophical Writings of Etienne Bonnot, Abbe de Condillac*, translated by Franklin Philip, Psychology Press, 2014, p. 200.
16. Condillac, *Treatise on the Sensations*, trans. Carr, p. 47.
17. Ibid., p. 53.
18. Ibid., p. 67.
19. Ibid., p. 67; see also *Philosophical Writings*, 2014, p. 217.

20. Condillac, *Treatise on the Sensations*, trans. Carr, p. 69.
21. Ibid., p. 87.
22. Ibid., pp. 71–2.
23. Ibid., my italics.
24. Ibid., pp. 235–6; see also *Philosophical Writings*, p. 336.
25. Condillac, *Treatise on the Sensations*, trans. Carr, pp. 233–4.
26. Julia V. Douthwaite, *The Wild Girl, Natural Man and the Monster: Dangerous Experiments in the Age of Enlightenment*, University of Chicago Press, 2002, p. 75.
27. Ibid.
28. Condillac, *Treatise on the Sensations*, trans. Carr, p. 253.
29. Ibid.
30. Mary D. Sheriff, *Moved by Love: Inspired Artists and Deviant Women in Eighteenth-Century France*, University of Chicago Press, 2004, p. 114.
31. *Le Mercure*, November 1763.
32. Sheriff, *Moved by Love*, p. 172.
33. Ibid., p. 182; Condillac, *Treatise on the Sensations*, trans Carr, p. 242. Also Jean-Jacques Rousseau, *Oeuvres Completes*, edited by Bernard Gagnebin and Marcel Raymond, Gallimard, 1959, 2: 1231, cited in Brad Prager, *Aesthetic Vision and German Romanticism: Writing Images*, Boydell and Brewer, 2007, p.207 [I have translated it differently to Prager, putting 'by you' for 'par toi', instead of his 'for you'].

15. THE AUTONOMY OF THE SELF

1. Joseph Addison, *The Spectator*, No. 409, Thursday 19 June 1712.
2. Ibid.
3. Ibid.
4. Peter Kivy (ed.), *Francis Hutcheson: An Enquiry Concerning Beauty, Order, Harmony, Design*, Martinus Nijhoff, 1973, p. 23.
5. Alexander Baumgarten, *Meditationes philosophicae de nonnullis ad poema pertinentibus* (*Philosophical meditations pertaining to some matters concerning poetry*), doctoral thesis, University of Halle, 1735.
6. John Locke, *An Essay Concerning Human Understanding* (abridged and edited by Kenneth P. Winkler), Hackett, 1996, Book 2, Chapter 33, Sections 5 & 6, p. 173.
7. David Hume to Joseph Spence, 15 October 1754; in Spence, *Anecdotes: Observations, and Characters, of Books and Men*, edited by Samuel W. Singer, W. H. Carpenter, 1820, pp. 448–53. While Hume was full of admiration for Blacklock's sensitivity, he was gratified to learn that the poet did not leave it to the imagination when it came to matters of love and that 'girls of my [Blacklock's] acquaintance indulge me on account of my blindness, with the liberty of running over them with my hand'.

8. Ralph Cudworth, *The True Intellectual System of the Universe*, London, 1678, chapter V, section IV. See Udo Thiel, *The Early Modern Subject*, Oxford University Press, 2011, pp. 5–18.
9. Cited in Catherine Glyn Davies, *Conscience as Consciousness: The Idea of Self-Awareness in French Philosophical Writing from Descartes to Diderot*, Voltaire Foundation, 1990, p. 25.
10. Ibid., p. 5.
11. Locke, *Essay Concerning Human Understanding*, Book 2, Chapter 27 (Of Identity and Diversity), section 9: Personal Identity, p. 138.
12. Ibid., section 12: Consciousness Makes Personal Identity, p. 139.
13. The *Essai* was written from 1704 to 1712 and was immediately circulated in manuscript form, though it was not published until 1731. Cited in Roberto Festa, 'An eighteenth-century interpretation of the Ethica: Henri de Boulainvilliers' Essai de métaphysique', in Silvia Berti, Françoise Charles-Daubert and Richard Henry Popkin (eds), *Heterodoxy, Spinozism, and Free Thought in Early-eighteenth-century Europe*, Kluwer Academic Publishers, 1996, p. 324. The quote is also partly cited in Davies, *Conscience as Consciousness*, p. 79.
14. Davies, *Conscience as Consciousness*, p. 79.
15. David Hume, *A Treatise of Human Nature*, edited by David Fate Norton and Mary J. Norton, Clarendon Press, 2007, Part 4, section 6 ('Of Personal Identity').
16. Fernando Vidal, *The Sciences of the Soul: The Early Modern Origins of Psychology*, University of Chicago Press, 2011, pp. 98, 114.
17. Immanuel Kant, *Critique of Pure Reason*, translated by Norman Kemp Smith, Macmillan, London, 1929, p. 66.
18. Thomas Reid, *An Inquiry into the Human Mind on the Principles of Common Sense*, Dublin, 1764, chapter 2, section 7.

16. THE NATURALNESS OF THE SELF

1. James Howell, *Epistolae Ho-Elianae: Familiar Letters, Domestic and Foreign, Historical, Political, Philosophical*, London, 10th edition, 1787, p. 78, partly cited in Marjorie Hope Nicolson, *Mountain Gloom and Mountain Glory: The Development of the Aesthetics of the Infinite*, University of Washington Press, 1997, p. 61.
2. Nicolson, *Mountain Gloom and Mountain Glory*, p. 35
3. Thomas Burnet, *Sacred Theory of the Earth*, London, 1681, Book I, Chapter VI.
4. Ibid., Book I, Chapter XI.
5. Anthony Ashley Cooper, Earl of Shaftesbury, *The Moralists: A Philosophical Rhapsody, Being a Recital of Certain Conversations Upon Natural and Moral Subjects*, London, 1709, Part III, Section 2, p. 205.
6. The moment is captured in a rare sketch, attributed to the architect-designer William Kent, in which Pope appears to be using the grotto as an inspirational site for writing. Collection of the Duke of Devonshire, Chatsworth House.

NOTES 379

7. Cited in John Dixon Hunt and Peter Willis (eds), *The Genius of the Place: The English Landscape Garden, 1620–1820*, MIT Press, 2000, p. 189.
8. Described in a letter to Lady Walpole on 8 June 1734, *The Works of the Late Aaron Hill*, London, 1753, pp. 199–210.
9. William Gilpin, *A Dialogue upon the Gardens of the Right Honourable the Lord Viscount Cobham at Stow in Buckinghamshire*, London, 1748.
10. Rosalys Coope, 'The "Long Gallery": Its Origins, Development, Use and Decoration', *Architectural History*, vol. 29, (1986), pp. 43–84.
11. Hunt and Willis, *The Genius of the Place*, p. 313. Also Peter Willis, 'From Desert to Eden: Charles Bridgeman's "Capital Stroke"', *The Burlington Magazine*, vol. 115, no. 840, (March), 1973, p. 153.
12. Jeremy Black, *Culture in Eighteenth-Century England: A Subject for Taste*, Hambledon and London, 2005, p. 61.
13. David Watkin, *The English Vision: The Picturesque in Architecture, Landscape and Garden Design*, Harper and Row, 1982, p. vii.
14. Thomas Whately, *Observations on Modern Gardening*, London, 1771, p. 151. Stephanie Ross, *What Gardens Mean*, University of Chicago Press, 2001, p. 61.
15. Whately, *Observations on Modern Gardening*, p. 224.
16. Edmund Burke, *A Philosophical Enquiry into the Origin of Our Ideas of the Sublime and Beautiful* (1757), edited by Adam Phillips, Oxford World's Classics, 1998, Part III, section 15, p. 105.
17. John Wilkes MP (1725–98). See Christopher Thacker, *The History of Gardens*, University of California Press, 1979, p. 204, and Wendy Frith, 'Sexuality and Politics in the Gardens at West Wycombe and Medmenham Abbey', in Michael Conan (ed.), *Bourgeois and Aristocratic Cultural Encounters in Garden Art, 1550–1850*, Dumbarton Oaks, 2002, p. 301. Also Ross, *What Gardens Mean*, pp. 66ff.
18. Whately, *Observations on Modern Gardening*, p. 162.
19. From the Fifth Walk in Jean-Jacques Rousseau, *Reveries of a Solitary Walker*, translated by Charles Butterworth, Hackett, 1992, pp. 68–9.
20. Uvedale Price, 'A Dialogue on the Distinct Characters of the Picturesque and the Beautiful', London, 1801, in Charles Harrison, Paul Wood and Jason Gaiger (eds), *Art in Theory 1648–1815*, Blackwell, 2001, pp. 878–9.
21. Essay II in William Gilpin, *Three Essays: On Picturesque Travel*, London, 1792, p. 49.
22. William Gilpin, *On Picturesque Travel* from *Three Essays* (second edition), London, 1794, pp. 46–7.
23. William Gilpin, *Observations on the River Wye* (second edition), London, 1789, p. 31.
24. Gilpin, *On Picturesque Travel*, p. 46.
25. Gilpin, *Observations on the River Wye*, pp. 25–6.

17. THE CONSUMMATION OF THE SELF

1. Sheryl Kroen, *Politics and Theater: The Crisis of Legitimacy in Restoration France, 1815–1830*, University of California Press, 2000, p. 113.
2. Jan Goldstein, *The Post-Revolutionary Self: Politics and Psyche in France, 1750–1850*, Harvard University Press, 2005.
3. For exceptional precedents to Gibbon, see Peter Burke, 'Tradition and Experience: The Idea of Decline from Bruni to Gibbon', in G. W. Bowersock, John Clive and Stephen R. Graubard (eds), *Edward Gibbon and the Fall of the Roman Empire*, Harvard University Press, 1977.
4. Gillian Darley, *Vesuvius: The Most Famous Volcano in the World*, Profile Books, 2011, pp. 125–6. The garden also featured a 'Rousseau island', like Ermenonville.
5. Lady Lever Art Gallery, National Museums Liverpool, inv. no. LL208.
6. Orietta Rossi Pinelli, 'From the Need for Completion to the Cult of the Fragment', in Janet Burnett Grossman, Jerry Podany and Marion True (eds) *History of Restoration of Ancient Stone Sculptures, Papers from a Symposium*, J. Paul Getty Museum, 2001, p. 68.
7. Henri Scoutetten, *Leçons de Phrénologie*, S. Lamont, 1834, cited in Alain Bonnet and Hélène Jagot, *L'Artiste en Représentation*, Fage, 2012, p. 83; also p. 88.
8. The phrenological potential of Raphael's skull is discussed in *The Phrenological Journal and Miscellany*, vol. 9, Edinburgh, Sept 1834 – March 1836, pp. 92–4.
9. William Vaughan, *German Romantic Painting*, Yale University Press, 1984, p. 68.
10. Letter II in Carl Gustav Carus, *Nine Letters on Landscape Painting, Written in the Years 1815–1824; with a Letter from Goethe by Way of Introduction*, translated by Oskar Bätschmann, Getty Publications, 2002, p. 87.
11. The Edict of Saint-Cloud, passed in France in 1804, was extended to Italy in 1806. James D. Garrison, *A Dangerous Liberty: Translating Gray's 'Elegy'*, University of Delaware Press, 2009, p. 76.

BIBLIOGRAPHY

Abelard, Peter, *Ethical Writings: his Ethics or 'Know Yourself' and his Dialogue between a Philosopher, a Jew, and a Christian*, translated by Paul Vincent Spade, Hackett, 1995.
Ames-Lewis, Francis, *The Intellectual Life of the Early Renaissance Artist*, Yale University Press, 2007.
App, Urs, *The Birth of Orientalism*, University of Pennsylvania Press, 2010.
Arditi, Jorge, *A Genealogy of Manners: Transformations in Social Relations in France and England from the Fourteenth to the Eighteenth Century*, University of Chicago Press, 1998.
Arikha, Noga, *Passions and Tempers: A History of the Humours*, Harper, 2007.
Arlès, Philippe and Duby, Georges (eds), *A History of Private Life* (4 vols), Belknap Press, 1992–98.
Ayers, Andrew, *The Architecture of Paris*, Edition Axel Menges, 2004.
Ayres-Bennett, Wendy, *Sociolinguistic Variation in Seventeenth-Century France: Methodology and Case Studies*, Cambridge University Press, 2004.
Bartlett, Robert, *England Under the Norman and Angevin Kings, 1075–1225*, Clarendon Press, 2000.
Bastide, Jean-François de, *La Petite Maison: An Architectural Seduction*, translated with introduction by Rodolphe El-Khoury, Princeton Architectural Press, 1996.
Beckwith, Sarah, *Christ's Body: Identity, Culture and Society in Late Medieval Writings*, Routledge, 1996.
Belting, Hans, *Likeness and Presence: A History of the Image before the Era of Art*, University of Chicago Press, 1994.
Benhamou, Reed, 'Parallel Walls, Parallel Worlds: The Places of Masters and Servants in the Maisons de plaisance of Jacques-François Blondel', *Journal of Design History*, vol. 7, no. 1, 1994.
Berg, Maxine and Eger, Elizabeth (eds), *Luxury in the Eighteenth Century*, Palgrave, 2003.
Berger, Peter and Luckmann, Thomas, *The Social Construction of Reality: a Treatise in the Sociology of Knowledge*, Anchor Books, 1967.
Biller, Peter and Hudson, Anne, *Heresy and Literacy, 1000–1530*, Cambridge University Press, 1996.
Bimbenet-Privat, Michèle, *Le Bain et le Miroir: Soins du corps et cosmétiques de l'Antiquité à la Renaissance* (exhibition catalogue), Gallimard, 2009.
Black, Jeremy, *Culture in Eighteenth-Century England: A Subject for Taste*, Hambledon and London, 2005.
Blanning, T. C. W., *The Culture of Power and the Power of Culture*, Oxford University Press, 2004.
Boffrand, Germain, *Book of Architecture*, translated by David Britt, introduction by Caroline van Eck, Ashgate, 2002.
Bonnet, Alain and Jagot, Hélène, *L'Artiste en Représentation*, Fage, 2012.

Bony, Jean, *French Gothic Architecture of the 12th and 13th Centuries*, University of California Press, 1983.
Borst, Arno, *Les Cathares*, Payot, 1978.
Bowie, Andrew, *Aesthetics and Subjectivity: From Kant to Nietzsche*, Manchester University Press, 2003.
Breton, Nicholas, *The Court and Country, or, A Brief Discourse between a Courtier and a Country-man*, London, 1618.
Bruno, Giuliana, *Atlas of Emotion: Journeys in Art, Architecture and Film*, Verso, 2007.
Bryan, Jennifer, *Looking Inward: Devotional Reading and the Private Self in Late Medieval England*, University of Pennsylvania Press, 2008.
Bryson, Anna, *From Courtesy to Civility: Changing Codes of Conduct in Early Modern England*, Clarendon Press, 1998.
Brown, Jonathon D., *The Self*, McGraw-Hill, 1998.
Burke, Edmund, *A Philosophical Enquiry into the Origin of Our Ideas of the Sublime and Beautiful*, 1757, edited by Adam Phillips, Oxford World's Classics, 1998.
Burlingame, Anne E., *The Battle of the Books in its Historical Setting*, Biblo & Tannen, 1969.
Burton, Robert, *The Anatomy of Melancholy*, with an introduction by William H. Gass, New York Review of Books, 2001.
Bynum, Caroline Walker, *The Resurrection of the Body in Western Christianity, 200–1336*, Columbia University Press, 1995.
Burke, Peter, 'Tradition and Experience: The Idea of Decline from Bruni to Gibbon', in G. W. Bowersock, John Clive and Stephen R. Graubard (eds), *Edward Gibbon and the Fall of the Roman Empire*, Harvard University Press, 1977.
Burke, Peter, *The Fortunes of the Courtier: The European Reception of Castiglione's 'Cortegiano'*, Polity Press, 1995.
Burke, Peter, *The Art of Conversation*, Polity Press, 2007.
Burnet, Thomas, *Sacred Theory of the Earth*, London, 1681.
Camille, Michael, *The Gothic Idol: Ideology and Image-Making in Medieval Art*, Cambridge University Press, 1995.
Cardano, Girolamo, *The Book of my Life*, with an introduction by Anthony Grafton, New York Review of Books, 2002.
Carruthers, Mary, *The Book of Memory: A Study of Memory in Medieval Culture*, Cambridge University Press, 2008.
Carruthers, Peter and Chamberlain, Andrew (eds), *Evolution and the Human Mind: Modularity, Language and Meta-Cognition*, Cambridge University Press, 2000.
Carus, Carl Gustav, *Nine Letters on Landscape Painting, Written in the Years 1815–1824; with a Letter from Goethe by Way of Introduction*, translated by Oskar Bätschmann, Getty Publications, 2002.
Cary, Philip, *Augustine's Invention of the Inner Self: The Largely of a Christian Platonist*, Oxford University Press, 2000.
Casa, Giovanni della, *Il Galateo*, translated by R. S. Pine-Coffin, Penguin, 1958.
Castiglione, Baldassare, *The Book of the Courtier*, translated by George Bull, Penguin Classics, 1976.
Cavallo, Guglielmo and Chartier, Roger (eds), *A History of Reading in the West*, University of Massachusetts Press, 2003.

Cheselden, William, *The Anatomy of the Human Body*, London, 1763.
Clark, John Willis, *The Care of Books*, Cambridge University Press, 1901.
Cohn, Norman, *Noah's Flood: The Genesis Story in Western Thought*, Yale University Press, 1999.
Condillac, Etienne Bonnot de, *Treatise on the Sensations*, translated by Geraldine Carr, University of Southern California, 1930.
Condillac, Etienne Bonnot de, *Philosophical Writings of Etienne Bonnot, Abbe de Condillac*, translated by Franklin Philip, Psychology Press, 2014.
Conley, John J., *The Suspicion of Virtue: Women Philosophers in Neoclassical France*, Cornell University Press, 2002.
Coolman, Boyd Taylor, *The Theology of Hugh of St Victor: An Interpretation*, Cambridge University Press, 2010.
Coope, Rosalys, 'The "Long Gallery": Its Origins, Development, Use and Decoration', *Architectural History*, vol. 29, 1986.
Cooper, Anthony Ashley, Earl of Shaftesbury, *The Moralists: A Philosophical Rhapsody, Being a Recital of Certain Conversations Upon Natural and Moral Subjects*, London, 1709.
Corner, George W., *Anatomical Texts of the Earlier Middle Ages*, Washington, 1927.
Correll, Barbara, *The End of Conduct: Grobianus and the Renaissance Text of the Subject*, Cornell University Press, 1996.
Coss, Peter and Keen, Maurice (eds), *Heraldry, Pageantry and Social Display in Medieval England*, Boydell Press, 2008.
Costelloe, Timothy M., *The British Aesthetic Tradition: From Shaftesbury to Wittgenstein*, Cambridge University Press, 2013.
Craveri, Benedetta, *The Age of Conversation*, New York Review of Books, 2005.
Crowley, John E., *The Invention of Comfort: Sensibilities and Design in Early Modern Britain and Early America*, Johns Hopkins University Press, 2001.
Cusa, Nicholas of, *The Layman about Mind (Idiota Mente)*, translated by Clyde Lee Miller, Abaris Books, 1979.
Cusa, Nicholas of, *De Visione Dei*, translated by Jasper Hopkins, A. J. Banning Press, 1985.
Darley, Gillian, *Vesuvius: The Most Famous Volcano in the World*, Profile Books, 2011.
Darnton, Robert, *The Great Cat Massacre, and Other Episodes in French Cultural History*, Basic Books, 1984.
Darnton, Robert, *The Forbidden Best-Sellers of Pre-Revolutionary France*, HarperCollins, 1996.
Davies, Catherine Glyn, *Conscience as Consciousness: The Idea of Self-Awareness in French Philosophical Writing from Descartes to Diderot*, Voltaire Foundation, 1990.
Day, Robert A., *Told in Letters: Epistolary Fiction before Richardson*, University of Michigan Press, 1966.
Dejean, Joan, *Tender Geographies: Women and the Origins of the Novel in France*, Columbia University Press, 1991.
Derbes, Anne, *Picturing the Passion in Late Medieval Italy: Narrative Painting, Franciscan Ideologies and the Levant*, Cambridge University Press, 1996.
Descartes, René., *The Passions of the Soul*, translated by Stephen Voss, Hackett Publishing Co., 1989.

Dewald, Jonathan, *Aristocratic Experience and the Origins of Modern Culture*, University of California Press, 1993.
Dixon, Thomas, *From Passion to Emotions: The Creation of a Secular Psychological Category*, Cambridge University Press, 2005.
Dohrn-van Rossum, Gerhard, *History of the Hour: Clocks and Modern Temporal Orders*, University of Chicago Press, 1996.
Donawerth, Jane and Strongson, Julie (eds), *Madeleine de Scudéry: Selected Letters, Orations and Rhetorical Dialogues*, University of Chicago Press, 2004.
Douthwaite, Julia V., *The Wild Girl, Natural Man and the Monster: Dangerous Experiments in the Age of Enlightenment*, University of Chicago Press, 2002.
Dubos, Jean-Baptiste, *Réflexions critiques sur la peinture et sur la poésie*, Paris, 1719, translated in Thomas Nugent, *Critical Reflections on Painting, Poetry and Music*, London, 1748.
Duffy, Eamon, *The Stripping of the Altars: Traditional Religion in England 1400–1580*, Yale University Press, 1992.
Ebner, Dean, *Autobiography in Seventeenth-Century England*, Mouton, 1971.
Eckhart, Meister, *German Sermons and Treatises*, vol. 1, edited and translated by M. O'C. Walshe, Watkins, 1979.
Eco, Umberto, *Serendipities: Language and Lunacy*, Columbia University Press, 1998.
Elias, Norbert, *The Court Society*, Pantheon Books, 1983.
Elias, Norbert, *The Civilising Process*, Blackwell, 2004.
Elliot, Dyan, *Fallen Bodies: Pollution, Sexuality, and Demonology in the Middle Ages*, University of Pennsylvania Press, 1999.
Erasmus, *A Handbook on Good Manners for Children*, translated by Eleanor Merchant, Preface Publishing, 2008.
Farmer, Norman K., *Poets and the Visual Arts in Renaissance England*, University of Texas Press, 1984.
Ferry, Luc, *Homo Aestheticus: The Invention of Taste in the Democratic Age*, University of Chicago Press, 1993.
Fischer, Stephen R., *A History of Reading*, Reaktion Books, 2005.
Folger Collective on Early Women Critics (eds), *Women Critics 1660–1820: An Anthology*, Indiana University Press, 1995.
Fontanelle, Bernard de, *A Discovery of New Worlds*, translated by Aphra Behn (originally in 1686), Hesperus Press, 2012.
Foxon, David, *Libertine Literature in England 1660–1745*, University Books, New York, 1965.
Franssen, Maarten, 'The Ocular Harpsichord of Louis-Bertrand Castel: The Science and Aesthetics of an Eighteenth-Century Cause Célèbre', *Tractrix*, vol. 3, 1991.
Freedberg, David, *The Power of Images: Studies in the History and Theory of Response*, University of Chicago Press, 1991.
Fried, Michael, *Absorption and Theatricality: Painting and Beholder in the Age of Diderot*, University of Chicago Press, 1988.
Frith, Wendy, 'Sexuality and Politics in the Gardens at West Wycombe and Medmenham Abbey', in Michael Conan (ed.), *Bourgeois and Aristocratic Cultural Encounters in Garden Art, 1550–1850*, Dumbarton Oaks, 2002.
Furnivall, Frederick J. (ed.), *The Babees Book*, Early English Text Society, 1868.

Gallagher, Shaun (ed.), *The Oxford Handbook of the Self*, Oxford University Press, 2013.
Gallagher, Shaun and Shear, Jonathan (eds), *Models of the Self*, Imprint Academic, 2002.
Gillingham, John, 'From Civilitas to Civility: Codes of Manners in Medieval and Early Modern England', *Transactions of the Royal Historical Society*, 6th series, XII, Cambridge University Press, 2002.
Gilpin, William, *Observations on the River Wye* (second edition), London, 1789.
Gilpin, William, *Three Essays: On Picturesque Travel*, London, 1792.
Girouard, Mark, *Life in the English Country House*, Yale University Press, 1978.
Goldie, Peter, *The Emotions: A Philosophical Exploration*, Oxford University Press, 2002.
Goldsmith, Elizabeth, *Exclusive Conversations: The Art of Interaction in Seventeenth-Century France*, University of Pennsylvania Press, 1988.
Goldsmith, Elizabeth and Goodman, Dena (eds), *Going Public: Women and Publishing in Early Modern France*, Cornell University Press, 1995.
Goldstein, Jan, *The Post-Revolutionary Self: Politics and Psyche in France, 1750–1850*, Harvard University Press, 2005.
Goodman, Dena, *Becoming a Woman in the Age of Letters*, Cornell University Press, 2009.
Grafton, Anthony, *Cardano's Cosmos: The Worlds and Works of a Renaissance Astrologer*, Harvard University Press, 2001.
Greenblatt, Stephen, *Renaissance Self-Fashioning from More to Shakespeare*, University of Chicago Press, 2005.
Guazzo, Stefano, *The Civile Conversation*, translated by George Pettie in 1581, edited by Sir Edward Sullivan, Constable, 1925.
Hall, James, *The Self-Portrait: A Cultural History*, Thames and Hudson, 2014.
Harré, Rom and Parrott, W. Gerrod, *The Emotions: Social, Cultural and Biological Dimensions*, Sage Publications, 1996.
Harrison, Charles, Wood, Paul and Gaiger, Jason (eds), *Art in Theory 1648–1815*, Blackwell, 2001.
Harth, Erica, *Cartesian Women: Versions and Subversions of Radical Discourse in the Old Regime*, Cornell University Press, 1992.
Heller, Thomas C. (ed.), *Reconstructing Individualism: Autonomy Individuality and the Self in Western Thought*, Stanford University Press, 1986.
Hellman, Mimi, 'Furniture, Sociability and the Work of Leisure in Eighteenth-Century France', *Eighteenth-Century Studies*, vol. 32, no. 4, 1999.
Hofstadter, Douglas, *I am a Strange Loop*, Basic Books, 2007.
Huet, Pierre Daniel, *The History of Romances*, translated by Stephen Lewis, London, 1715.
Humboldt, Wilhelm von, *On Language: The Diversity of Human Language-Structure and its Influence on the Mental Development of Mankind*, translated by Peter Heath, Cambridge University Press, 1988.
Hunt John Dixon and Willis, Peter (eds), *The Genius of the Place: The English Landscape Garden, 1620–1820*, MIT Press, 2000.
Hunt, Lynn (ed.), *The Invention of Pornography: Obscenity and the Origins of Modernity 1500–1800*, Zone Books, 1996.
Ilardi, Vincent, *Renaissance Vision from Spectacles to Telescopes*, American Philosophical Society, 2007.

Impey, Oliver and Macgregor, Arthur (eds), *The Origins of Museums: The Cabinet of Curiosities in Sixteenth and Seventeenth Century Europe*, House of Stratus, 2001.
Jaeger, C. Stephen, *The Origins of Courtliness: Civilizing Trends and the Formation of Courtly Ideals, 939–1210*, University of Pennsylvania Press, 1985.
Jensen, Katharine A., *Writing Love: Letters, Women and the Novel in France, 1605–1776*, Southern Illinois University Press, 1995.
Jeremiah, Edward T., *The Emergence of Reflexivity in Greek Language and Thought*, Brill, 2012.
Jolly, Penny H., 'Antonello da Messina's "St. Jerome in His Study": a disguised portrait?', *Burlington Magazine*, 124, 1982.
Jones, Ann Rosalind and Stallybrass, Peter, *Renaissance Clothing and the Materials of Memory*, Cambridge University Press, 2000.
Julian of Norwich, *Revelations of Divine Love*, translated by Clifton Wolter, Penguin Classics, 1980.
Kant, Immanuel, *Critique of Pure Reason*, translated by Norman Kemp Smith, Macmillan, 1929.
Kardong, Terrence G., *The Life of St Benedict, by Gregory the Great*, Liturgical Press, 2009.
Kavanagh, Thomas M., *Enlightened Pleasures: Eighteenth Century France and the New Epicureanism*, Yale University Press, 2010.
Keen, Maurice, *Chivalry*, Yale University Press, 2005.
Kelley, Carl Franklin, *Meister Eckhart on Divine Knowledge*, Yale University Press, 1977.
Kelley, Donald R. and Popkin, Richard H., *The Shapes of Knowledge from the Renaissance to the Enlightenment*, Kluwer Academic Publishers, 1991.
Kidnie, Margaret J. (ed.), 'A Critical Edition of "The Anatomie of Abuses" by Philip Stubbes', PhD thesis, University of Birmingham, 1996.
Kirkbride, Robert, *Architecture and Memory: The Renaissance Studioli of Federico da Montefeltro*, Columbia University Press, 2008.
Kitayama, Shinobu and Markus, Hazel Rose, *Emotion and Culture: Empirical Studies of Mutual Influence*, American Psychological Association, 1997.
Kivy, Peter (ed.), *Francis Hutcheson: An Enquiry Concerning Beauty, Order, Harmony, Design*, Martinus Nijhoff, 1973.
Klein, Robert and Zerner, Henri (eds), *Italian Art: Sources and Documents 1500–1600*, Northwestern University Press, 1990.
Knight, Leah, *Of Books and Botany in Early Modern England: Sixteenth-century Plants and Print Culture*, Ashgate, 2009.
Koerner, Joseph Leo, *The Moment of Self-Portraiture in German Renaissance Art*, University of Chicago Press, 1993.
Kroen, Sheryl, *Politics and Theater: The Crisis of Legitimacy in Restoration France, 1815–1830*, University of California Press, 2000.
Kuryluk, Ewa, *Veronica and her Cloth*, Blackwell, 1991.
Lakoff, George and Johnson, Mark, *Philosophy in the Flesh: The Embodied Mind and its Challenge to Western Thought*, Basic Books, 1999.
Lambert, Malcolm, *Medieval Heresy: Popular Movements from the Gregorian Reform to the Reformation*, Blackwell, 1997.
Latham, Robert, and Matthews, William (eds), *The Diary of Samuel Pepys*, vol IX, 1668–9, Harper Collins, 2000.

Leff, Gordon, *Heresy in the Later Middle Ages: The Relation of Heterodoxy to Dissent, c.1250–c.1450*, Manchester University Press, 1999.
Lewis, C. S., *Studies in Words*, Cambridge University Press, 2000.
Lewis, Suzanne, *Reading Images: Narrative Discourse and Reception in the Thirteenth Century Illuminated Apocalypse*, Cambridge University Press, 1995.
Locke, John, *An Essay Concerning Human Understanding*, Book II, chapter 1, sections 2–4 (abridged and edited by Kenneth P. Winkler), Hackett, 1996.
Luhmann, Niklas, *Love as Passion: The Codification of Intimacy*, Stanford University Press, 1998.
Macdonald, A. A. (ed.), *The Broken Body: Passion Devotion in Late Medieval Culture*, Groningen, 1998.
Manguel, Alberto, *A History of Reading*, Penguin, 1997.
Marshall, Peter, *The Magic Circle of Rudolph II: Alchemy and Astrology in Renaissance Prague*, Walker and Co., 2006.
Martin, Luther H. and Gutman, Huck (eds), *Technologies of the Self: A Seminar with Michel Foucault*, Tavistock, 1988.
Martin, Raymond and Barresi, John, *Naturalization of the Soul: Self and Personal Identity in the Eighteenth Century*, Routledge, 2004.
Martin, Raymond and Barresi, John, *An Intellectual History of Personal Identity*, Columbia University Press, 2006.
McCormick, Ian (ed.), *Secret Sexualities: A Sourcebook of 17th and 18th Century Writing*, Routledge, 1997.
McKeon, Michael, *The Secret History of Domesticity: Public, Private and the Division of Knowledge*, Johns Hopkins University Press, 2005.
Melchior-Bonnet, Sabine, *The Mirror: A History*, Routledge, 2002.
Mézières, Nicolas Le Camus de, *The Genius of Architecture, or the Analogy of that Art with our Sensations*, with introduction by Robin Middleton, Getty Center, 1992.
Michael, Erika, *Hans Holbein the Younger: A Guide to Research*, Garland, 1997.
Middleton, Robin, 'Enfilade – The Spatial Sequence in French Hotels of the 17th and 18th centuries', *Daidalos*, no. 42, 1991.
Millot, Michel, *Lesson in Seduction*, Ophir Books, 2007.
Monks, Peter Rolfe, *The Brussels Horloge de Sapience*, Brill, 1990.
Montaigne, *The Complete Essays*, translated by M. A. Screech, Penguin, 2003.
Morley, John, *The History of Furniture: Twenty-five Centuries of Style and Design in the Western Tradition*, Little, Brown and Company, 1999.
Mudge, Bradford K., *When Flesh Became Word: An Anthology of Early Eighteenth-Century Libertine Literature*, Oxford University Press, 2004.
Munro, James S., *Mademoiselle de Scudéry and the Carte de Tendre*, University of Durham Press, 1986.
Neri, Janice, *The Insect and the Image: Visualising Nature in Early Modern Europe, 1500–1700*, University of Minnesota Press, 2011.
Nicholls, Jonathan W., *The Matter of Courtesy: Medieval Courtesy Books and the Gawain-Poet*, Brewer, 1985.
Nicolson, Marjorie Hope, *Mountain Gloom and Mountain Glory: The Development of the Aesthetics of the Infinite*, University of Washington Press, 1997.

O'Neal, John C., *The Authority of Experience: Sensationist Theory in the French Enlightenment*, University of Pennsylvania Press, 1996.

Orme, Nicholas, *From Childhood to Chivalry: The Education of the English Kings and Aristocracy 1066–1530*, Methuen, 1984.

Pardailhé-Galabrun, Annik, *The Birth of Intimacy*, Polity Press, 1991.

Parkes, Malcolm Beckwith, *Pause and Effect: An Introduction to the History of Punctuation in the West*, Scolar Press, 1992.

Paster, Gail Kern (ed.), *Reading the Early Modern Passions: Essays in the Cultural History of Emotion*, University of Pennsylvania Press, 2004.

Pearce, Susan, and Arnold, Kenneth, *The Collector's Voice*, Volume 2: *Early Voices*, Ashgate, 2000.

Pelletier, Louise, *Architecture in Words: Theatre, Language and the Sensuous Space of Architecture*, Routledge, 2006.

Perkins, Jean A., *The Concept of the Self in the French Enlightenment*, Librairie Droz, 1969.

Peters, Jeffrey N., *Mapping Discord: Allegorical Cartography in Early Modern French Writing*, University of Delaware Press, 2004.

Plank, Steven E., 'Wrapped all in woe: Passion Music in Late Medieval England', in MacDonald, A. A., Ridderbos, H. N. B. and Schlusemann, R. M. (eds), *The Broken Body, Passion and Devotion in Late Medieval Culture*, Egbert Forsten, 1998.

Pomian, Krzysztof, *Collectors and Curiosities*, Polity Press, 1990.

Porter, Roy (ed.), *Rewriting the Self: Histories from the Renaissance to the Present*, Routledge, 1997.

Porter, Roy, *Flesh in the Age of Reason: The Modern Foundations of Body and Soul*, Norton, 2003.

Potts, Timothy C., *Conscience in Medieval Philosophy*, Cambridge University Press, 1980.

Prager, Brad, *Aesthetic Vision and German Romanticism: Writing Images*, Boydell and Brewer, 2007.

Prioreschi, Plinio, *A History of Medicine: Medieval Medicine*, Horatius Press, 2003.

Radden, Jennifer (ed.), *The Nature of Melancholy: From Aristotle to Kristeva*, Oxford University Press, 2000.

Raw, Barbara Catherine, *Trinity and Incarnation in Anglo-Saxon Art and Thought*, Cambridge University Press, 1997.

Rée, Jonathan, *I See a Voice: Language, Deafness and the Senses, a Philosophical History*, HarperCollins, 1999.

Regosin, Richard L., *The Matter of My Book: Montaigne's 'Essaies' as the Book of the Self*, University of California Press, 1977.

Reid, Thomas, *An Inquiry into the Human Mind on the Principles of Common Sense*, Dublin, 1764.

Renaut, Alain, *The Era of the Individual: A Contribution to a History of Subjectivity*, Princeton University Press, 1997.

Rice, Eugene F., *Saint Jerome in the Renaissance*, Johns Hopkins University Press, 1988.

Richardson, Samuel, *Selected Letters*, edited by John Carroll, Clarendon Press, 1964.

Ridderbos, Bernhard, *Saint and Symbol: Images of Saint Jerome in Early Italian Art*, Bouma's Boekhuis, 1984.

Rider, Frederick, *The Dialectic of Selfhood in Montaigne*, Stanford University Press, 1973.

Ringbom, Sixten, *Icon to Narrative: The Rise of the Dramatic Close-Up in Fifteenth-Century Devotional Painting*, Davaco, 1984.

Riskin, Jessica, *Science in the Age of Sensibility: The Sentimental Empiricists of the French Enlightenment*, University of Chicago Press, 2002.
Riskin, Jessica, *Genesis Redux: Essays in the History and Philosophy of Artificial Life*, University of Chicago Press, 2007.
Robinson, Kate, *A Search for the Source of the Whirlpool of Artifice: The Cosmology of Giulio Camillo*, Dunedin Academic Press, 2006.
Ross, Ellen, *The Grief of God: Images of the Suffering Jesus in Late Medieval England*, Oxford University Press, 1997.
Ross, Stephanie, *What Gardens Mean*, University of Chicago Press, 2001.
Rossi, Paolo, *Logic and the Art of Memory: The Quest for a Universal Language*, Continuum, 2000.
Rossi Pinelli, Orietta, 'From the Need for Completion to the Cult of the Fragment: How Tastes, Scholarship, and Museum Curators' Choices Changed Our View of Ancient Sculpture', in Grossman, Janet Burnett, Podany, Jerry and True, Marion (eds), *History of Restoration of Ancient Stone Sculptures, Papers from a Symposium*, J. Paul Getty Museum, 2001.
Rousseau, Jean-Jacques, *The Reveries of a Solitary Walker*, translated by Charles Butterworth, Hackett, 1992.
Rubin, Miri, *Corpus Christi: The Eucharist in Late Medieval Culture*, Cambridge University Press, 1991.
Rubin, Miri, *Gentile Tales: The Narrative Assault on Late Medieval Jews*, Yale University Press, 1999.
Sabean, David W. and Stefanovska, Malina (eds), *Space and Self in Early Modern European Cultures*, University of Toronto Press, 2012.
Saenger, Paul, *Space Between Words: The Origins of Silent Reading*, Stanford University Press, 1997.
Schneider, Gary, *The Culture of Epistolarity: Vernacular Letters and Letter Writing in Early Modern England, 1500–1700*, University of Delaware Press, 2005.
Scott, James W., *Madame de Lafayette: La Princesse de Clèves*, Grant and Cutler, 1997.
Seebohm, Almuth, 'The Crucified Monk', *Journal of the Warburg and Courtauld Institutes*, vol. 59, 1996.
Seigel, Jerrold, *The Idea of the Self: Thought and Experience in Western Experience since the Seventeenth Century*, Cambridge University Press, 2005.
Seznec, Jean, *The Survival of the Pagan Gods: The Mythological Tradition and its Place in Renaissance Humanism and Art*, Princeton University Press, 1972.
Sheriff, Mary D., *Moved by Love: Inspired Artists and Deviant Women in Eighteenth-Century France*, University of Chicago Press, 2004.
Shiner, Larry, *The Invention of Art: A Cultural History*, University of Chicago Press, 2001.
Simson, Otto von, *The Gothic Cathedral*, Pantheon Books, 1962.
Sinisgalli, Rocco, *Perspective in the Visual Culture of Classical Antiquity*, Cambridge University Press, 2012.
Sorabji, Richard, *Self: Ancient and Modern Insights about Individuality, Life and Death*, Oxford University Press, 2006.
Spacks, Patricia M., *Privacy: Concealing the Eighteenth-Century Self*, University of Chicago Press, 2003.
Spinks, Jennifer, 'Louis XIV's Youthful Spirit: The 1699 Redecoration of the Versailles Menagerie', master's research, University of Tasmania, 2000.

Spira, Andrew, *Simulated Selves: The Undoing of Personal Identity in the Modern World*, Bloomsbury, 2020.
Strawson, Galen, *The Evident Connexion: Hume on Personal Identity*, Oxford, 2011.
Strawson, Galen, *Locke on Personal Identity: Consciousness and Concernment*, Princeton University Press, 2011.
Straznicky, Marta, *Privacy, Playreading and Closet Drama, 1550–1700*, Cambridge University Press, 2004.
Suchtelen, Ariane van and Beneden, Ben van (eds), *Room for Art in Seventeenth-Century Antwerp*, Waanders, 2009.
Swann, Marjorie, *Curiosities and Texts: The Culture of Collecting in Early Modern England*, University of Pennsylvania Press, 2001.
Talvacchia, Bette, *Taking Positions: On the Erotic in Renaissance Culture*, Princeton University Press, 1999.
Tapié, Alain, *Portraits de la Pensée*, Chaudun, 2011.
Tarnas, Richard, *The Passion of the Western Mind: Understanding the Ideas that have Shaped our World View*, Pimlico, 1991.
Taylor, Charles, *Sources of the Self: The Making of the Modern Identity*, Harvard University Press, 1989.
Teresa of Avila, St, *The Life of St Teresa of Avila*, translated by David Lewis, Cosimo Classics, 2011.
Thacker, Christopher, *The History of Gardens*, University of California Press, 1979.
Thiebaud, Jane Rather, 'Madame de Rambouillet's Chambre Bleue (Blue Room): Birthplace of Salon Culture', PhD dissertation, University of Maine, 2007.
Thiel, Udo, *The Early Modern Subject*, Oxford University Press, 2011.
Thomas, Keith, *The Ends of Life: Roads to Fulfilment in Early Modern England*, Oxford University Press, 2009.
Tierney, Brian, *Origins of Papal Infallibility, 1150–1350: A Study on the Concepts of Infallibility, Sovereignty and Tradition in the Middle Ages*, Brill, 1972.
Tierney, Brian and Linehan, Peter (eds), *Authority and Power: Studies on Medieval Law and Government*, Cambridge University Press, 1980.
Tierney-Hynes, Rebecca, *Novel Minds: Philosophers and Romance Readers, 1680–1740*, Palgrave, 2012.
Tilley, Arthur A., *The Decline of the Age of Louis XIV*, Barnes & Noble, 1968.
Toohey, Peter, *Melancholy, Love and Time: Boundaries of the Self in Ancient Literature*, University of Michigan Press, 2004.
Tugwell, Simon, *Early Dominicans: Selected Writings*, Paulist Press, 1982.
Turner, James Grantham, *Schooling Sex: Libertine Literature and Erotic Education in Italy, France and England, 1534–1685*, Oxford University Press, 2003.
Vaneigem, Raoul, *The Movement of the Free Spirit*, Zone Books, 1994.
Vasari, Giorgio, *The Lives of the Artists*, translated by George Bull, Penguin, 1965.
Vaughan, William, *German Romantic Painting*, Yale University Press, 1984.
Vidal, Fernando, *The Sciences of the Soul: The Early Modern Origins of Psychology*, University of Chicago Press, 2011.
Vigarello, Georges, *Le propre et le sale: l'hygiène du corps depuis le Moyen Age*, Seuil, 2013.
Wagner, Peter, *Eros Revived: Erotica of the Enlightenment in England and America*, Paladin, 1988.

Wahrman, Dror, *The Making of the Modern Self: Identity and Culture in Eighteenth-Century England*, Yale University Press, 2004.
Wandel, Lee Palmer, *Voracious Idols and Violent Hands*, Cambridge University Press, 1995.
Watkin, David, *The English Vision: The Picturesque in Architecture, Landscape and Garden Design*, Harper and Row, 1982.
Watts, Pauline M., *Nicolaus Cusanus: A Fifteenth-Century Vision of Man*, Brill, 1982.
Webb, Diana, *Privacy and Solitude*, Hambledon Continuum, 2007.
Webber, Joan, *The Eloquent 'I' Style and Self in Seventeenth-Century Prose*, Wisconsin University Press, 1968.
Wegener, Charles, *The Discipline of Taste and Feeling*, University of Chicago Press, 1992.
West, William N., 'Reading Rooms: Architecture and Agency in the Houses of Michel de Montaigne and Nicholas Bacon', *Comparative Literature*, vol. 56, no. 2 (Spring), 2004.
Weston-Lewis, Aidan, *The Age of Titian: Venetian Renaissance Art from Scottish Collections*, National Galleries of Scotland, 2004.
Weststeijn, Thijs, *The Visible World: Samuel van Hoogstraten's Art Theory and the Legitimation of Painting in the Dutch Golden Age*, Amsterdam University Press, 2008.
Weygand, Zina, *The Blind in French Society from the Middle Ages to the Century of Louis Braille*, Stanford University Press, 2009.
Whately, Thomas, *Observations on Modern Gardening*, London, 1771.
Whyman, Susan E., *The Pen and the People*, Oxford University Press, 2009.
Wierzbicka, Anna, *Emotions Across Languages and Cultures: Diversity and Universals*, Cambridge University Press, 1999.
Willis, Peter, 'From Desert to Eden: Charles Bridgeman's "Capital Stroke"', *The Burlington Magazine*, vol. 115, no. 840, (March) 1973, p. 153.
Wind, Edgar, *Pagan Mysteries in the Renaissance*, Oxford University Press, 1980.
Winston-Allen, Anne, *Stories of the Rose: The Making of the Rosary in the Middle Ages*, Pennsylvania State University Press, 1997.
Wood, Margaret, *The English Medieval House*, Ferndale, 1981.
Wright, Lawrence, *Clean and Decent: The History of the Bathroom and the W.C.*, Routledge & Kegan Paul, 1984.
Wright, Lawrence, *Warm and Snug: The History of the Bed*, Sutton, 2004.
Wright, Rosemary M., *Art and Antichrist in Medieval Europe*, Manchester University Press, 1995.
Wright, Thomas, *Passions of the Minde* (facsimile), Georg Olms Verlag, 1973.
Wurzbach, Natasha (ed.), *The Novel in Letters*, University of Miami Press, 1969.
Yates, Frances A., *The Art of Memory*, Pimlico, 2008.
Young, Paul J., *Seducing the Eighteenth-Century Reader: Reading, Writing and the Question of Pleasure*, Ashgate, 2008.
Zapperi, Roberto, 'Alessandro Farnese, Giovanni della Casa and Titian's Danae in Naples', *Journal of the Warburg and Courtauld Institutes*, vol. 54, 1991.
Zöller, Günther, *Fichte's Transcendental Philosophy: The Original Duplicity of Intelligence and Will*, Cambridge University Press, 1998.

INDEX

The letter *f* following an entry indicates a page that includes a figure.

Abbey in the Oak Forest (Friedrich, Caspar David) 354
Abelard, Peter 29
  Ethics 30
  Historia Calamitatum (*History of My Calamities*) 29
  Sic et Non (*Yes and No*) 29, 129
Abgar V (king of Edessa) 40
abstract self 170–1
abstract time 170–1
Académie Francaise 190, 238
Accademia delle Arti del Disegno (Academy of the Art of Drawing) 83–4
Addison, Joseph 298–9
Adoration of Christ in the Forest (Lippi, Fra Filippo) 71
Adoration of the Magi (Leonardo da Vinci) 93
Adoration of the Magi, The (Botticelli, Sandro) 71, 72f, 74
Adoration of the Three Kings 70–1
Adrian I (Pope) 36
Aertsen, Pieter
  Christ and the Adulteress 101
Aesthetica (Baumgarten, Alexander) 301
aesthetics 300–1, 309–10, 356, 364 *see also* taste (preference)
  natural world 311, 329, 330
Alberti, Leon Battista 156
  De Pictura (*On Painting*) 62, 71, 81
Albrecht of Brandenburg 119
Albrecht of Brandenburg as St Jerome (Cranach, Lucas) 119, 121f
Altarpiece with scenes from the Life of the Virgin (Konrad, Meister) 192, 193f
altars 15f–16f
Alton Towers Triptych 38f, 54

Amaury of Bene 30
Amberger, Christoph
  Matthaus Schwarz 234–6f
Amorous Letters by Various Contemporary Authors (Scudéry, Madeleine de) 194, 195
Analysis of Beauty (Hogarth, William) 213, 307
analytical texts 114
Anatomie of Abuses (Stubbes, Philip) 235
Anatomy of Melancholy (Burton, Richard) 232
Angelico, Fra
  Annunciation, The 145
Angelus (Millet, Jean-François) 163, 164f
Annunciation (Crivelli, Carlo) 147
Annunciation, The (Angelico, Fra) 116f, 145
Annunciation, The (Campin, Robert) 145, 146f
Annunciation, The (Memling, Hans) 147, 148f
Antonello da Messina
  St Jerome in his Study 119, 120f
Apollo and Daphne (Bernini, Gian Lorenzo) 259–60
Arena Chapel fresco cycle (Giotto) 58–61, 62
Archduke Leopold Wilhelm in his Gallery (Teniers the Younger, David) 140f
architecture 22–5f, 26f, 27f *see also* studies
  in art 57, 58, 60f, 62
  demilitarisation 182
  Gothic 334
  picturesque, the 333–5
  ruins 333–5
  sensation 277–9

INDEX 393

sensuality 275–7, 279
Aretino, Pietro 264–5
  Ragionamenti ('Dialogues') 265
  Sonetti Lussuriosi ('Lustful Sonnets') 265
d'Argens, Marquis (Jean-Baptiste de Boyer)
  Thérèse Philosophe 269–71f
Ariosto, Ludovico
  Orlando Furioso 182
Arma Christi 46–7f
Arnolfini Portrait (Eyck, Jan van) 155
Ars Amatoria (*L'Art d'Aimer* [*The Art of Love*]) (Ovid) 273
Ars Poetica (Horace) 81
art 6–7, 8, 80–2, 360, 363, 365 see also imagery *and* portraits
  academies 83f–4
  appreciation 356, 364
  authenticity 341–2
  Chinese landscapes 315–16f
  Christian art 337
  classical mythology 255–63
  collecting 140–1, 343–4
  colour in 281–4
  composition 331–2, 354–5
  copper-plate engraving 86
  death of 365
  design in 281–4
  divine proportion, the 65
  drawing 281–4
  emotions 241–9, 284, 347–8
  eye contact 71–2, 73–9, 186, 367 n. 3
  frescos 58–61, 62–3f, 71, 111, 117–18f
  gallery paintings 140f–1
  Gilpin, William 333
  golden mean, the 64–5
  history painting 345–6
  intarsia 91–2f
  landscapes 163, 284, 315–16f, 321–2f, 333
  light 58, 59–61, 62, 63, 64f, 245f–6
  linseed oil 58
  mirrors 158–9
  natural world 88–93, 98
  nudity 158, 256, 258–61
  paragone 82
  patronage 70–1, 73, 242, 244, 246
  personal identity 69–70
  perspective. *See* perspective
  pictorial space 57–60f, 61–2
  poetry 81
  Pompeii 240
  purification 365
  radical thought 365
  realism 57–61, 62, 71, 88–91
  religion 349–51, 354, 355
  religious ecstasy 254–5, 269–70
  rinascita 82
  Rückenfigur (back-figure) 351–3, 354
  sanctity of 351, 353
  sculpture 80–2, 293–6f, 340–2, 357f–8
  self-portraits. *See* self-portraits
  shading 58, 59–61, 62, 63, 64f
  stained-glass windows 86, 87f
  status 107–8
  still life 100–4, 105, 106–7f
  subjectivity 363
  symbols 37, 88–9
  tapestries 87
  trompe l'oeil 105–8
  vanitas 102, 103f
  viewer, the. *See* viewer, the
L'Art du Menuisier ('Art of the Joiner') (Roubo, Andre-Jacob) 215
art for art's sake 365
art of memory 127–30, 136, 138
Artamène, ou Le Grand Cyrus (Scudéry, Madeleine de) 196
artists 70, 80–1, 344–5, 360–1
  archetype of 343–8, 353, 355
  classics, the 84
  difficultà 186
  eye contact 71–2, 73–9, 367 n. 3
  freedom of 360–1
  imagination 89
  phrenology 346–7, 348f, 349f
  preparatory sketches 89
  self-portraits 70–1, 72f, 73–9, 367 n. 3
  signatures 71
  status 82, 84–7
  studios 83f
  as subjects 345–6
  training 84
associationism 301–2
astrology 228–8f
atheism 336
Audley End House 337–8, 339f

Augustine, Saint 7–8, 113
  Confessions 7, 311–12
autonomy 364
Autun Cathedral 109, 110*f*

Bacci, Andrea
  Order of the Universe and the First Monuments of Human Knowledge, The 130–3
Back of a Painting (Gijsbrechts, Cornelius) 106
Baegert, Derick
  Crucifixion, The 45*f*, 71
balance-springs 168–70
Balzac, Jean-Louis Guez de 193
Bandinelli, Baccio 83*f*
Barbon, Nicholas 288
Barrin, Jean
  Venus dans le cloître 267–8
Bartolommeo, Fra 254
Bastide, Jean-François de
  Petite Maison, La (The Little House) 275–6
Bathsheba (wife of Uriah) 261, 319*f*–20
Baudouin, Pierre-Antoine 272
  Lecture, La (Reading) 272–3, 274*f*
Baumgarten, Alexander 300–1, 308–9
  Aesthetica 301
Baviero de' Carrocci 261–2
beauty 212–13, 309, 324, 356, 364 *see also* aesthetics *and* taste (preference)
  Gilpin, William 330–1
  line of beauty 212–3
  picturesque, the 322, 327–30, 332–5
  ugliness 328–9
Beauvais Cathedral 24–5*f*, 26*f*
Becket, Thomas 174
bedrooms 147–8*f*, 191 *see also* beds
beds 148*f*–50*f*
Beethoven, Ludwig van 347
bell towers 162–3
Bellini, Giovanni
  Young Woman at her Toilet 158, 159*f*
Bembo, Pietro 184
Benedict, Saint 111
  Rule 110–11, 113, 172–3, 174
Bergeret, Pierre-Nolasque
  Emperor Charles V picking up the paintbrush of Titian 345

Bernini, Gian Lorenzo
  Apollo and Daphne 259–60
  Blessed Ludovica Albertoni, The 254
  St Theresa in Ecstasy 254, 257*f*
Berruguete, Pedro
  Federico da Montefeltro and his son Guido 120–1, 122*f*
Berry, Jean duc de
  Tres Riches Heures 312*f*
bestiaries 89
Beuckelaer, Joachim
  Well-Stocked Kitchen, with Jesus in the House of Mary and Martha, The 101, 102*f*
Bhagavad Gita 336
Bible, the 31–2, 37, 96–8, 173, 261
  flood 313
  translation 118
Birth of Venus (Botticelli, Sandro) 255–6, 258*f*
Birth of Venus (Giotto) 62
Blacklock, Thomas 301
Blanchard, Louis Gabriel 283
Blessed Ludovica Albertoni, The (Bernini, Gian Lorenzo) 254
blindness 287, 288–9, 301
Blue Room, the 189. 191, 192
Boffrand, Germain 279
  Livre d'Architecture (Book of Architecture) 276–7
  'Salon de la Princesse', Hôtel de Soubise 212*f*, 277
Bonaventure, Saint
  On the Perfection of Life, Addressed to Sisters 48
Book of Hours of Catherine of Cleves 42, 43*f*
Book of the Courtier, The (Castiglione, Baldassare) 81, 183–6, 188
books 113–14, 129
books of hours 42, 43*f*, 161–2
Boothby, Brooke 326–7*f*
botanical treatises 98, 99*f*, 100*f*, 101*f*
Botticelli, Sandro 256
  Adoration of the Magi, The 71, 72*f*, 74
  Birth of Venus 255–6, 258*f*
  Calumny of Apelles 81, 84, 256, 258
Boucher, François 273*f*
  Leda and the Swan 272*f*

Marie-Louise O'Murphy 272
L'Odalisque 272
boudoirs 277
Boulainvilliers, Henri de 306
Essai de métaphysique 306
Boureau-Deslandes, Andre-François
Pigmalion, ou la Statue animée 294
Boyer, Jean-Baptiste de (d'Argens, Marquis)
Thérèse Philosophe 269–71f
Brancacci Chapel fresco cycle (Masaccio) 62–3f
brain, the 125, 126f, 131–3
Bray, Jan de
Regents of the Children's Almshouse in Haarlem 246f
Brescia, Moretto da
Portrait of a Young Scholar 232–4, 235f
Bridgeman, Charles 320, 321
Briullov, Karl
Last Day of Pompeii, The 340, 341f
Bronzino, Agnolo 186–8
Portrait of a Young Man 187f
Brown, Lancelot 'Capability' 323–4, 327
Bruce, Thomas (7th Earl of Elgin) 342
Brunelleschi, Filippo 62, 156
Brunfel, Otto 98
Herbarum vivae eicones (*Living Images of Plants*) 98, 99f
Buddhism 336
Buffon, Comte de (Georges-Louis Leclerc) 293–4
Naturelle Histoire 293
Bunyan, John
Pilgrim's Progress 318
Burghley House 218
Burke, Edmund 324, 329
Philosophical Enquiry into the Origin of Our Ideas into the Sublime and Beautiful 324, 329
Burnet, Thomas 313–15
Sacred Theory of the Earth, The 313–15
Burton, Richard
Anatomy of Melancholy 232
butteries 144

cabinet desks 216–18
cabinets 138–9f, 207–8

cabinets of curiosity 137f, 138–9
Caesarius of Heisterbach 49
Calumny of Apelles (Botticelli, Sandro) 81, 84, 256, 258
Cambridge Camden Society 339
Camillo, Giulio 138
L'Idea del Teatro 138
Campin, Robert
Annunciation, The 145, 146f
candles 145, 146
candlesticks 213
canon (church) law 11–12
canopies 148–9
Canova, Antonio 342
Cardano, Girolamo 229–30f
Carlyle, Thomas 358
On Heroes, Hero Worship and the Hero in History 358
Carpaccio, Vittore
Dead Christ 54
Dream of St Ursula, The 147, 148
carrels 114–15f
Carte de Tendre (Scudéry, Madeleine de) 195–6f, 318
Carthusian order 114
Carus, Carl Gustav 354
Nine Letters on Landscape Painting 354
Castel, Louis-Bertrand 285–6
Castell, Robert 316–17
Villas of the Ancients Illustrated 316–17f
Castiglione, Baldassare
Book of the Courtier, The 81, 183–6, 188
Catholicism 95, 253–4, 338
catoptromancy 156
cemeteries 357–8
cemetery of Père Lachaise, Paris 357
Cennini, Cennino
Craftsmen's Handbook 84, 89
Cesalpino, Andrea
De Plantis Libri XVI 99–100
chairs 208f–10, 213, 214–15f
chambers 144
Champaigne, Philippe de 282–3
Champs, Chateau de 211
Charlemagne I (Holy Roman Emperor) 36
Chateau de Champs 211
Chateau of Versailles 152f–3f, 210, 237

Chateaubriand, François-René de
    Génie du christianisme 337
Cheselden, William 288–9
chests 134*f*–7*f*
childbirth 149–50
Chimie de gout et d'odorat (Poncelet, Polycarp) 286
chimneys 144, 146–7
China 9
Chinese gardens 316–17
Chinese landscapes 315–16*f*
Chiswick House 321–2
chivalry 175, 177, 182
Christ
    Crucifixion 43–5*f*, 49, 51*f*
    horoscope of 229–30*f*
    identifying with 56, 77–8
    imagery 40–1, 43–7*f*, 52–4*f*, 77–8
    imitation of 48–9, 50*f*, 52*f*, 77–8
    Passion of 42–54
    pelicans 89
    Resurrection, the 54–6
    suffering of 42–56, 253–4
    Vision Dei 78
Christ and the Adulteress (Aertsen, Pieter) 101
Christian art 337
Christianity 7–8, 10–11, 336 *see also* Church, the
    art patrons 70–1
    Bible, the. *See* Bible, the
    Christian art 337
    classical narratives 255
    flagellation 49, 50*f*
    Gabriel (archangel) 178–9
    Gothic style 337–9
    history 31–2
    identification 48
    imagery. *See* imagery
    imagination 39, 41–2, 47–8, 54
    knighthood 176
    Locke, John 303
    Masaccio 62–3*f*
    mirrors 155–6
    naturalistic art 88–91
    New Testament 32, 37
    numerology 32, 33, 37
    Old Testament 31–2, 37, 97, 261
    original sin 288
    Passion, the 42–54
    passions, the 226–7
    patterns 37
    Piero della Francesca 64–5, 66
    possessions 133–4
    private meditation 42
    prophecy 32, 33
    revival 336–40
    Roman Empire 340
    stigmata 49, 50*f*
    Virgin, the 145, 147–8*f*
Church, the 10–20, 363 *see also* Christianity
    altars 15*f*–16*f*
    architecture 22–5*f*, 26*f*, 27*f*
    bell towers 162–3
    books of hours 42, 43*f*, 161–2
    canon (church) law 11–12
    Catholicism 95, 253–4, 338–9
    challenges to 93–4
    communion 10–19*f*
    Descartes, René 104
    emotions 254
    Eucharist, the 10–19*f*, 43, 94
    heresy 26–31, 33–4, 95
    imagery. *See* imagery
    individuality 30, 34
    light 22, 24
    mendicant orders 48
    monasticism. *See* monasticism
    morality 244, 253
    Orthodox 35–6, 42–3
    papal infallibility 11
    pilgrimages 18–19
    preaching orders 30
    Protestantism. *See* Protestantism
    Reformation, the 93–4
    relics 17–20*f*, 40, 94–5
    reliquaries 19–20*f*, 21*f*
    sacramentals 16
    sacraments 10–19*f*, 24
    sexuality 265–7
    subjectivity 363
    time-keeping 161–3
    transubstantiation 11–13, 17, 94
Cicero 127, 128
Civile Converzatione, La (Guazzo, Stefano) 188
civility 181–2, 205 *see also* manners
civility manuals 200 *see also* conduct books *and* courtesy books

INDEX

classical world 84, 127–8, 199, 236–8, 342
    Christianity 255
    Descartes, René 240
    gardens 316–17
    Greek mythology 155
    Greek philosophy 7
    Le Brun, Charles 241
    mythology 255–63, 271–2
    Pygmalion 294
    Quarrel between the Ancients and the Moderns 238–9
    Roman Empire 264, 339–42
    sexuality 255–63, 271–2
classification 98–100
    knowledge 133, 138
Claude glasses 331, 332*f*
Cleland, John
    Fanny Hill, or Memoirs of a Woman of Pleasure 269
Clélie (Scudéry, Madeleine de) 196, 197
clocks 164–70
closets 216, 218*f*
clothing 207, 235
coinage 264
Colbert, Jean-Baptiste 153–4
collections 133–41, 343–4
colour 285, 302
    in art 281–4
    science of 284
colourism 281–4
communal living 109–12, 142–3, 173
    beds 149
communication 3–5 *see also* conversations *and* letter-writing
communion 10–19*f*
Compagnia de' Magi 71
composition 331–2, 354–5
Concord of Discordant Canons (Gratian) 11
Concordance of the Old and New Testaments, A (Joachim of Fiore) 31, 32
Condillac, Etienne Bonnot de 289–93
    Treatise on the Sensations 289, 291
conditions 2
conduct books 203–4
Confessions (Augustine, Saint) 7, 311–12
conscience 28–30, 30
consciousness 2, 304,
    Descartes, René 104–5

Locke, John 305–6
contrapposto 187
Conversation on the Manner of Writing Letters (Scudéry, Madeleine de) 195
conversations
    art of 183–4, 188, 189–90
    Scudéry, Madeleine de 194–7
    with oneself 2–4
Conversations (Scudéry, Madeleine de) 195, 196
Conversations on Diverse Subjects (Scudéry, Madeleine de) 194–5
Cooper, Anthony Ashley (3rd Earl of Shaftesbury) 315
copper-plate engraving 86
Cornelis Cornelisz van Haarlem
    Monk and the Nun, The 266
Courbet, Gustave 346
    Painter's Studio, The 346, 347*f*
Courte of Civill Courtesie, The (Robson, Simon) 183
courtesy 172–5, 178, 181–3 *see also* manners
courtesy books 175, 178–86, 188–9 *see also* civility manuals *and* conduct books
courtiers 81, 183–9
courtly love 177–8, 182
Cousin, Louis
    St Catherine of Siena Drinking from the Wound in Christ's Side 254, 257*f*
Cousin, Victor 337
craftsmen 84–7, 338
    difficultà 186
Craftsmen's Handbook (Cennini, Cennino) 84, 89
Cranach, Lucas
    Albrecht of Brandenburg as St Jerome 119, 121*f*
Critique of Pure Reason (Kant, Immanuel) 309
Crivelli, Carlo
    Annunciation 147
Cross in the Mountains, The (Friedrich, Caspar David) 349, 351*f*
Crown of Thorns 20
Crucifixion, The (Baegert, Derick) 45*f*, 71
Crusades, the 175

culture 6, 7–8, 109, 364 *see also* art
  Europe 8
  Louis XIV (King of France) 210
  urban 181–2
cutlery 180–1

Danae 259
Daniel of Beccles 180
  Urbanus Magnus/Liber Urbani ('Book of the Civilised Man') 180
Dashwood, Francis 324
David (King of Israel) 261, 319*f*–20
David (Donatello) 258
David, Jacques-Louis
  Oath of the Horatii 345
Danae (Titian) 259*f*
De arca Noe pro arca sapientiae (*On Noah's Ark as an Ark of Wisdom*) (Hugh of St Victor) 129
De Civilitate Morum Puerilium ('On Civility in Boys') (Erasmus) 182–3
De Divina Proportione (Pacioli, Luca) 93
De Historia Stirpium (*On the History of Plants*) (Fuchs, Leonhart) 98, 100*f*, 101*f*
De Institutione Novitiorum (*On the Formation of Novices*) (Hugh of St Victor) 173
De Luce (*On Light*) (Grosseteste, Robert) 20, 22
De Modo Orandi ('On the Way to Pray') 117*f*
De Pictura (*On Painting*) (Alberti, Leon Battista) 62, 71, 81
De Plantis Libri XVI (Cesalpino, Andrea) 99–100
Dead Christ (Carpaccio, Vittore) 54
Dead Christ (Mantegna, Andrea) 54
Dead Christ in the Tomb, The (Holbein, Hans) 54*f*
Dead Christ with Plaintive Mourners 53
deafness 287
Death of Leonardo da Vinci in the arms of Francis I (Ménageot, François-Guillaume) 345, 346*f*
Decretals (Gratian) 11
Delacroix, Eugène 345
Delaroche, Paul
  Hemicycle 359
della Casa, Giovanni

Galateo, Il 188
Deposition from the Cross 53
Descartes, René 104–5, 251, 303, 363
  Passions of the Soul, The 239–41
Descent of Christ into Hell 54
Description of England, A (Harrison, William) 143–4
design 85–6
desks 215–20*f*
devotional texts 114
diabolic 38
Dialogue (Gilpin, William) 319
dialogues 3–4
Diana and Actaeon 260–1
Diana of Poitiers 236, 258
Diderot, Denis 287, 297
  Lettre sur les Aveugles a l'usage de ceux qui voient (*Letter on the Blind for the use of those who see*) 287
  Lettre sur les sourds et muets (*Letter on Deaf-mutes*) 287
difficultà 186
dignity of man 232
dining 135*f*, 142, 180–1 *see also* taste
diplomacy 182
divine proportion, the 65
Divine Right of Kings 152
domestic space 142, 207–8, 211–12
  bedrooms 147–8*f*, 191
  beds 148*f*–50*f*
  boudoirs 277
  butteries 144
  candles 145, 146
  candlesticks 213
  canopies 148–9
  chairs 208*f*–10, 213, 214–15*f*
  chambers 144
  chimneys 144, 146–7
  closets 216, 218*f*
  cutlery 180–1
  decoration 211–12
  desks 215–20*f*
  dining 135*f*, 142, 180–1 *see also* taste
  fireplaces 144–5
  furniture 134*f*–7*f*, 138–9*f*, 142, 207–10, 212–20, 223–4
  halls 142–4, 152–3*f*
  hearths 144, 146–7
  light 145–6, 191

long galleries 320
manners 173
mirrors 152–60f
noble 175
pantries 144
parlours 145
pleasure 274–5
privacy 143, 144, 145, 146, 211
Rambouillet, hôtel de 190–2
rococo style 211–13, 279
secrétaires 218–19f
sensuality 274–7, 279
solars 144, 146
status 207–8
studies (rooms) 119–20f, 121–7, 130, 133, 147
tables 223–4
time-keeping 166
toilet services 221–2f
toilette, the 220–2f
windows 145–7f, 191
Dominic, Saint 117
Dominican order 30, 115–18f
Donatello
 David 258
Dostoyevsky, Fyodor 54
drawers 136f, 137f
Dream of St Gregory, The (Giotto) 111f
Dream of St Ursula, The (Carpaccio, Vittore) 147, 148
Dubos, Jean-Baptiste 284–5
Duccio di Buoninsegna
 Maestà 54, 55f
Duchamp, Marcel 365
Ducornet, Louis-Joseph-César 347, 350f
Dürer, Albrecht 72, 74, 84, 93, 98
 Feast of the Rose Garlands, The 74–5f, 93
 Melencolia I 231f
 Self-Portrait 75–8, 79
Durham Cathedral 115

Eckhart 30–1, 56
Edict of Saint-Cloud 357
Elgin, 7th Earl of (Thomas Bruce) 342
Elgin Marbles 342
emotions 195–6, 201, 203, 204, 226 *see also* passions *and* sexuality
 architecture 277–9

 art 241–9, 284, 347–8
 Church, the 254
 Le Camus de Mézières, Nicolas 277–9
Emperor Charles V picking up the paintbrush of Titian (Bergeret, Pierre-Nolasque) 345
English Parnassus; or, A Help to English Poesie (Poole, Joshua) 313
Enlightenment, the 336, 339
epistolary novels 202–5
Erasmus 125, 127, 149
 De Civilitate Morum Puerilium ('On Civility in Boys') 182–3
Ermenonville 325, 326f
L'Escole des filles 267, 268f
Essai de métaphysique (Boulainvilliers, Henri de) 306
Essay Concerning Human Understanding (Locke, John) 288, 301–2, 303, 305–6
Essay on Prints containing Remarks upon the Principles of Picturesque Beauty (Gilpin, William) 332–3
Essays (Montaigne, Michel de) 127
Ethics (Abelard, Peter) 30
etiquette 177
Eucharist, the 10–19f, 43, 94
Europe 8–9
evolution, theory of 364
experiences (of the world) 1–2, 361–2
Exposition of the Apocalypse, An (Joachim of Fiore) 31
Eyck, Jan van
 Arnolfini Portrait 155

facial expressions 241–2f
Falconet, Etienne 295–6f, 297
Fame of the Antwerp School (Keyser, Nicaise de) 359
family 190 *see also* lineage
Fanny Hill, or Memoirs of a Woman of Pleasure (Cleland, John) 269
Farnese, Alessandro (Cardinal) 259
Fayette, Madame de la (Marie-Madeleine Pioche de la Vergne)
 Princess de Clèves, La 201
 Zayde 198
Feast in the House of Levi, The (Veronese, Paolo) 95, 180

Feast of Corpus Christi 17, 18*f*
Feast of the Rose Garlands (Dürer, Albrecht) 74–5*f*, 93
Federico da Montefeltro (Duke of Urbino) 120–5, 130
Federico da Montefeltro and his son Guido (Berruguete, Pedro) 120–1, 122*f*
Federico II of Gonzaga 261
feelings. *See* emotions
feudalism 175
Ficino, Marsilio 83, 231, 256
fiction 196–206
Fielding, Henry
    Shamela 205
fireplaces 144–5
Flagellated Christ Contemplated by a Christian Soul (Velázquez, Diego) 254, 255*f*
flagellation 49, 50*f*
Flagellation of Christ (Piero della Francesca) 64–5*f*
flood 313–14
Florence 357–8
Florence Cathedral 91–2*f*
Foscolo, Ugo
    Sepolcri, Dei (*The Sepulchres*) 357
France 189–90, 267, 304, 357
Francesco I of Tuscany (Duke) 138
Francis, Saint 49, 50*f*
Francis I (King of France) 236, 237*f*
Frederick II (Holy Roman Emperor) 33
Free Spirits 30, 33
free will 29
freedom 360–1
frescos 58–61, 62–3*f*, 71, 111, 117–18*f*
Friedrich, Caspar David 348–9
    Abbey in the Oak Forest 354
    Cross in the Mountains, The 349, 351*f*
    Monk by the Sea, The 355, 356*f*
    My Burial 354
    Wanderer above a Sea of Fog, The 352*f*–3
    Woman before the Setting Sun, The 352–3
friendship 195–6
Fuchs, Leonhart 98
    De Historia Stirpium (*On the History of Plants*) 98, 100*f*, 101*f*
furniture 134*f*–7*f*, 138–9*f*, 142, 207–10, 212–20, 223–4

Gabriel (archangel) 178–9
Galatea 294–7
Galateo, Il (della Casa, Giovanni) 188
gallery paintings 140*f*–1
gardens 315–25, 327, 340
genie de l'architecture; ou, L'analogie de cet art avec nos sensations, Le (*The Genius of Architecture; or, the Analogy of that Art with our Sensations*) (Le Camus de Mézières, Nicolas) 277–9
Génie du christianisme (Chateaubriand, François-René de) 337
genius, concept of 87, 345, 364
Gerard of Borgo San Donnino 34
Germany 357
Gian Gastone de' Medici in bed receiving the young Cosimo Riccardi (Pseudo-Marcuola) 150–1*f*
Gibbon, Edward
    History of the Decline and Fall of the Roman Empire 340, 342
Gijsbrechts, Cornelius
    Back of a Painting 106
Gilpin, William 330–3
    Dialogue 319
    Essay on Prints containing Remarks upon the Principles of Picturesque Beauty 332–3
    Observations 333
    On Picturesque Travel 329
    Tintern Abbey 331*f*
Giotto 58–61
    Arena Chapel fresco cycle 58–61, 62
    Birth of Venus 62
    Dream of St Gregory, The 111*f*
    Legend of St Francis fresco cycle 111
    Meeting of Joachim and Anna at the Golden Gate 58–61
    Pentecost 61
    realism 89
Girardin, Marquis René-Louise de 325
Giulio Romano
    Loves of the Gods 262–3*f*
    Modi, I (*The Ways/The Positions*) 261–4
    Palazzo Tè, Mantua 261
glass 154–5
    stained-glass windows 86, 87*f*
Gloucester Cathedral 115*f*

God
  man and 78–9
  rationality 313
  vision of 78–9
Goethe, Johann Wolfgang von
  Sorrows of Young Werther, The 205
golden mean, the 64–5
Gothic style 334, 337–9
Gozzoli, Benozzo
  Procession of the Magi 71, 74
grace 186
Great Man Theory 358
Greek mythology 155
Greek philosophy 7
Gregory I (the Great) (Pope) 35, 46*f*–7
Gregory IX (Pope) 111*f*
Greuze, Jean-Baptiste
  Lady Reading the Letters of Heloise and Abelard 273
Grosseteste, Robert 20, 24, 173
  De Luce (*On Light*) 20, 22
  Statutes for the Household 173
Guazzo, Stefano 189
  Civile Converzatione, La 188
Guidobaldo da Montefeltro (Duke of Urbino) 130
Gumpp, Johannes
  Self-Portrait 249–50*f*
gunpowder 182
Gutenberg, Johannes 155

ha-has 320*f*–1
Hall of Mirrors (Versailles) 152–3*f*, 237
halls 142–4, 152–3*f*
Ham House 218*f*
Hardwick Hall, Derbyshire 146, 147*f*
Harrison, John 170
Harrison, William 145
  Description of England, A 143–4
hearing 285–6, 287–8
hearths 144, 146–7
Hemicycle (Delaroche, Paul) 359
heraldry 175
herbals 89
Herbarum vivae eicones (*Living Images of Plants*) (Brunfel, Otto/ Weiditz, Hans) 98, 99*f*
Herculaneum 340
Hercules 188
heresy 26–31, 33-4, 95

heroes 357–9
heroic struggle 186–8
hierarchy 142, 144, 173, 175, 180, 181
  see also status
  communication 188–9
Hill, Aaron 318
Historia Calamitatum (*History of My Calamities*) (Abelard, Peter) 29
history 31–2, 78, 358
  writing 197
History of Modern Taste in Gardening (Walpole, Horace) 320
History of the Decline and Fall of the Roman Empire (Gibbon, Edward) 340, 342
history painting 345–6
Hogarth, William 307
  Analysis of Beauty 213, 307
Holbein, Hans
  Dead Christ, in the Tomb, The 54*f*
L'homme machine (*Man Machine*) (La Mettrie, Julian Offray de) 336
Honi Soit Qui Mal Y Pense (*Shame on Him who Thinks Evil of This*) (Hubert, François) 273, 275*f*
Hoogstraten, Samuel van 248, 249
  Introduction to the Academy of Painting 249
Horace
  Ars Poetica 81
Horologium Sapientiae (*The Clock of Wisdom*) (Suso, Henry) 166, 167*f*
Host von Romberch, Johannes 130, 131*f*
households. *See* domestic space
Houses of Parliament 339
Howell, James 312
Hubert, François
  Honi Soit Qui Mal Y Pense (*Shame on Him who Thinks Evil of This*) 273, 275*f*
Huert, Pierre Daniel
  Trait[t]é de l'origine des Romans 198–200
Hugh of St Victor
  De arca Noe pro arca sapientiae (*On Noah's Ark as an Ark of Wisdom*) 129
  De Institutione Novitiorum (*On the Formation of Novices*) 173

Hume, David 301, 306–8, 336, 364–5
  Treatise of Human Nature 306–7
humours, the 228–34
Hutcheson, Francis 299–300
  Inquiry into the Original of our Ideas of Beauty and Virtue 299–300

Iconoclastic Controversy 35–6, 54
icons 36
L'Idea del Teatro (Camillo, Giulio) 138
Ideal City, The (Piero della Francesca) 66f, 68, 74
identity 305 *see also* personal identity
Ignatius Loyola, Saint
  Spiritual Exercises 254
image (of a courtier) 185–6
imagery 35–40, 69–70, 129–30 *see also* art
  allegorical 236–7
  Catholicism 95
  Christ 40–1, 43–7f, 52–4f, 77–8
  classical mythology 255–61
  coinage 264
  defacing 94, 95f
  designed by maker 85–6
  Joachim of Fiore 33
  melancholy 232
  naturalism 57–61, 62, 71, 88–9
  Passion, the 42–7f, 52–3f
  patterns 37
  Protestantism 5, 95, 96–8
  Resurrection, the 54–6, 69
  sexuality 271f–4f
  symbols 37, 88–9
imagination 39–40, 41–2
  art 89
  novels 200–1
  Passion, the 47–8
  studies (rooms)s 125
imaginative selfhood 40
Imitation of Christ (Kempis, Thomas à) 78
Inclosure Acts 327
India 109
individuality 26, 29–30, 69, 210–11, 357–9
  Church, the 30, 34
  evolution, theory of 364
  heroes 357–9
  public, the 364

Ingres, Jean-Auguste-Dominique 345
inheritance 175
innate ideas 288, 289, 291
Inquiry into the Original of our Ideas of Beauty and Virtue (Hutcheson, Francis) 299–300
Inscriptiones vel tituli teatri amplissimi (*Inscriptions or labels for the most complete theatre*) (Quiccheberg, Samuel van) 136–8
intarsia 91–2f
internal dialogues 3–4
Introduction to the Academy of Painting (Hoogstraten, Samuel van) 249
Islam 35
Italy 181, 183, 189, 357–8

Jean duc de Berry 312
  Tres Riches Heures 312f
Jerome, Saint 28, 118–20f, 230
Jewish community 17, 19f
Joachim of Fiore 31–4
  Concordance of the Old and New Testaments, A 31, 32
  Exposition of the Apocalypse, An 31
  Liber Figerarum (*Book of Figures*) 31f
  Ten-Stringed Psaltery, The 31
Judgement of Paris 260
Judgement of Paris, The (Rubens, Peter Paul) 260
Julian of Norwich 49
Julie, ou La Nouvelle Héloise (Rousseau, Jean-Jacques) 204–5
Justice of Trajan (Weyden, Rogier van der) 78

Kant, Immanuel 171, 308–9, 363–4, 375 n. 17
  Critique of Pure Reason 309
Kempis, Thomas à
  Imitation of Christ 78
Kensington Valhalla 358–9
Kent, William 319, 321–1
Keyser, Nicaise de
  Fame of the Antwerp School 359
King Governs by Himself, The (Le Brun, Charles) 153
Kircher, Athanasius 285
knighthood 175–8, 182
knowledge 182–3, 289

shared 304
innate 288, 289, 291
organising 133, 138, 182
Boureau-Deslandes, Andre-François 294
Konrad, Meister
Altarpiece with scenes from the Life of the Virgin 192, 193f
Kramer, Simon de 94f

La Font Saint-Yenne, Etienne 212
La Mettrie, Julian Offray de 336
L'homme machine (*Man Machine*) 336
La Sainte Chapelle 20, 21f, 24
Lacan, Jacques 160
Laclos, Pierre Choderlos de
Liasons Dangereuses, Les 205
Lady Reading the Letters of Heloise and Abelard (Greuze, Jean-Baptiste) 273
Lamentation 53
landscape gardening 315–25, 327
landscapes 163, 284, 315–16f, 321–2f, 333
Langland, William
Vision of Piers Plowman 144
language 3–6, 189–90, 195, 238, 301, 303–5
capacity of 361
Last Day of Pompeii, The (Briullov, Karl) 340, 341f
Last Supper, The (Veronese, Paolo) 95
laughter 247
Le Brun, Charles 152, 241–2
design 283–4
King Governs by Himself, The 153
Le Camus de Mézières, Nicolas 279
genie de l'architecture; ou, L'analogie de cet art avec nos sensations, Le (*The Genius of Architecture; or, the Analogy of that Art with our Sensations*) 277–9
Leasowes, The 318, 324–5
Leclerc, Georges-Louis (Comte de Buffon). *See* Buffon, Comte de
Lecture, La (*Reading*) (Baudouin, Pierre-Antoine) 272–3, 274f
Leda and the Swan (Boucher, François) 272f
Legend of St Francis fresco cycle (Giotto) 111
Lely, Peter 244–5

Lentulus, Publius 41
Leonardo da Vinci 81, 93, 133
Adoration of the Magi 93
Salvator Mundi 367 n. 3
Trattato della pittura (*Treatise on Painting*) 81
Leopold II (Duke of Anhalt-Dessau) 340
Leopold Wilhelm (Archduke of Austria) 140–1
Letter of Lentulus 41f
letter-writing 192–4, 202, 215 *see also* communication
Balzac, Jean-Louis Guez de 193
epistolary novels 202–5
Scudéry, Madeleine de 194–5
Voiture, Vincent 193
writing chairs 215
writing desks 215–20
Lettre sur les Aveugles a l'usage de ceux qui voient (*Letter on the Blind for the use of those who see*) (Diderot, Denis) 287
Lettre sur les sourds et muets (*Letter on Deaf-mutes*) (Diderot, Denis) 287
Lettres Portugaises, Les 202
Liasons Dangereuses, Les (Laclos, Pierre Choderlos de) 205
Liber Figerarum (*Book of Figures*) (Joachim of Fiore) 31f
Liber Urbani ('Book of the Civilised Man') (Daniel of Beccles) 180
liberal arts 80, 85, 182–3
Libri Carolini (*Books of Charlemagne*) (Theodulf of Orleans) 36, 95
Life and Opinions of Tristram Shandy, Gentleman, The (Sterne, Laurence) 307, 308f
light 20, 22, 24
in art 58, 59–61, 62, 63, 64f, 245f–6
households 145–6, 191
science of 284
lineage 149, 175, 190
linseed oil 58
Lippi, Fra Filippo
Adoration of Christ in the Forest 71
literature 238–9 *see also* novels
erotic 265–71
Lives of the Most Excellent Painters, Sculptors and Architects (Vasari, Giorgio) 61, 82

Livre d'Architecture (Book of Architecture) (Boffrand, Germain) 276–7
Locke, John 288–9, 301–2, 303, 305–6, 363
  Essay Concerning Human Understanding 288, 301–2, 303, 305–6
Lombard, Peter 28
  Sentences 28
long galleries 320
longitude 170
Louis XIV (King of France) 151–3, 210, 236–7, 238*f*, 239*f*
Lovelace, Richard 245
Loves of the Gods (Giulio Romano) 262–3*f*
Luke, Saint 40
lunatic asylums 303
Luther, Martin 93
Lytylle Childrenes Lytil Boke, The 178

Madonna of the Goldfinch (Raphael) 90*f*–1
Maestà (Duccio di Buoninsegna) 54, 55*f*
Magi 70–1
man 78–9
  dignity of 232
  as microcosm 231–2
mannerism 186
manners 172–5, 181–3, 188, 199–200, 205 *see also* courtesy
Mantegna, Andrea
  Dead Christ 54
Manufacture royale de glaces de miroirs 153–4
Marie-Louise O'Murphy (Boucher, François) 272
Masaccio
  Brancacci Chapel fresco cycle 62–3*f*
  Peter cures a sick man with his shadow 63, 64*f*
  Tribute Money, The 63*f*
Mass of St Giles, The (Master of St Giles) 15–16*f*
Mass of St Gregory 46*f*–7
Master of St Giles
  Mass of St Giles, The 15–16*f*
masturbation 270
Matthaus Schwarz (Amberger, Christoph) 234–6*f*

Medici, Gian Gastone de' (Grand Duke of Tuscany) 150
Medici, Leopold de 250–1*f*
Medici, Marie de 189, 191
Medici family 71
medieval halls 142
Meeting of Joachim and Anna at the Golden Gate (Giotto) 58–61
Meister Eckhart 30–1, 56
melancholy 230–4
Melencolia I (Dürer, Albrecht) 231*f*
memento mori 232
Memling, Hans
  Annunciation, The 147, 148*f*
memoire, the 304
Memorial to Heroic Self-Sacrifice (Watts, George Frederic) 358*f*, 359
memory 125, 127–30, 136, 138, 183
  domestic space 144–5
Ménageot, François-Guillaume
  Death of Leonardo da Vinci in the arms of Francis I 345, 346*f*
mendicant orders 48
Metamorphoses (Ovid) 255, 294
Michelangelo 81, 232, 345, 348*f*
Mignard, Pierre, I 284
military prowess 175–7
Millet, Jean-François
  Angelus 163, 164*f*
mind, the 125, 127, 131–3, 138, 303
  indeterminacy of 307
mirror stage 160
mirrors 152–60*f*, 172, 363
  Claude glasses 331, 332*f*
modernists 239
Modi, I (The Ways/The Positions) (Giulio Romano) 261–4
Molyneux, William 288
momentariness 245*f*–9
monasticism 110–11, 113, 114
  books of hours 42, 43*f*, 161
  manners 174
  dissolution 144, 333
  monastic orders 30, 33, 48, 110–11, 113, 114–19
  memory 128
  monasteries 311
  ruins 333–5
  rules 172–3
  sexuality 265–6

Monk and the Nun, The (Cornelis Cornelisz van Haarlem) 266
Monk by the Sea, The (Friedrich, Caspar David) 355, 356f
Montaigne, Michel de 127
  Essays 127
monuments 357f–9
moral judgement 29
morality 244, 253
  gardens 318–19
mountains 311–13, 354
mnemonics 27, 127–8, 129–30, 138
Museo Chiaramonti 342
music 285–6, 287, 347
My Burial (Friedrich, Caspar David) 354

National Portrait Gallery, London 358
natural world 88–93, 98, 311
  Boothby, Brooke 326–7f
  Burnet, Thomas 313–15
  classification 98–100
  collections 133, 136, 137f
  danger 329–30, 340
  evolution, theory of 364
  exceptional aspects 327–30
  Friedrich, Caspar David 348–56f
  gardens 315–25, 327, 340
  Gilpin, William 319, 329, 330–3
  God 313–14
  mountains 311–13, 354
  picturesque, the 322, 327–30, 332–5
  Rousseau, Jean-Jacques 325–6
  Shaftesbury 3rd Earl of (Anthony Ashley Cooper) 315
  sublime, the 329–30, 340
  tourism 333
  ugliness 328–9
naturalism 57–61, 62, 71, 88–91 *see also* natural world
  studies (rooms) 123–4
Naturelle Histoire (Buffon, Comte de) 293
neo-classical history painting 345–6
neo-classical style 340
New Testament 32, 37 *see also* Bible, the
Newton, Isaac 284
  Opticks 284
Nicholas of Cusa 78–9
  On the Vision of God (De Visione Dei) 78

Nicolo dell'Arca 53
Nietzsche, Friedrich 365
Nine Letters on Landscape Painting (Carus, Carl Gustav) 354
nobility, the 173–5, 183–4
novels 196–206 *see also* literature
  erotic 265–71
nudity 158, 256, 258–61

Oath of the Horatii (David, Jacques-Louis) 345
objectivity 9, 281, 299–303, 355, 363–4
  Descartes, René 104–5
  Kant, Immanuel 309
  mirrors 157
Observations (Gilpin, William) 333
ocean navigation 170
ocular harpsichords 285–6f, 287–8
L'Odalisque (Boucher, François) 272
Old Testament 31–2, 37, 173, 261 *see also* Bible, the
On Heroes, Hero Worship and the Hero in History (Carlyle, Thomas) 358
On Perspective for Painting (Piero della Francesca) 67f, 68
On Picturesque Travel (Gilpin, William) 329
On the Perfection of Life, Addressed to Sisters (Bonaventure, Saint) 48
On the Vision of God (De Visione Dei) (Nicholas of Cusa) 78
oogenblikkig ('eye glancing') 249
optical communion 17, 19
optical realism 91
Opticks (Newton, Isaac) 284
Oration on the Dignity of Man (Pico della Mirandola, Giovanni) 232
Order of the Universe and the First Monuments of Human Knowledge, The (Bacci, Andrea) 130–3
Orlando Furioso (Ariosto, Ludovico) 182
d'Orleans, Duc (Philippe II) 210
Ovid
  Ars Amatoria (L'Art d'Aimer [The Art of Love]) 273
  Metamorphoses 255, 294
Oxford Movement 338–9

Pacioli, Luca 65
  De Divina Proportione 93

pain 293
Painter's Studio, The (Courbet, Gustave) 346, 347f
paintings 140–1
Palais de Luxembourg 191–2
Palazzo Tè, Mantua 261
Pallavicino, Ferrante
   Retorica della puttane (The Whore's Rhetoric) 266–7
Pamela, or Virtue Rewarded (Richardson, Samuel) 203f–5
pantries 144
papal infallibility 11
paragone 82
Parallel between Ancients and Moderns regarding the arts and sciences (Perrault, Charles) 239
Paris (prince of Troy) 260
parlours 145
Passion, the 42–54
Passion Plays 48
passions, the 188, 226–9 *see also* emotions *and* sexuality
   Descartes, René 239–41
   humours, the 228–34
Passions of the Minde, The (Wright, Thomas) 186, 240
Passions of the Soul, The (Descartes, René) 239–41
patronage 70–1, 73, 242, 244, 246
patterns 37
pelicans 89
pendula 168–70
Penshurst Place, Kent 142, 143f
Pentecost (Giotto) 61
Pepys, Samuel 267
perfume 286
Perrault, Charles 238
   Parallel between Ancients and Moderns regarding the arts and sciences 239
Perrot, Bernard 154
personal identity 1–4, 9, 295, 360, 362–3
   art 6–7, 69–70
   associationism 301
   Church, the 10, 13, 17
   Condillac, Etienne Bonnot de 291–3
   culture 6, 7–8
   evolution, theory of 364
   gardens 324
   Hume, David 307
   imagination 39–40
   Joachim of Fiore 32
   Kant, Immanuel 309
   language 3–6
   Locke, John 303, 305–6
   parameters 360–1
   Passion Plays 48
   psychological autonomy 364
   public, the 8, 364
   questioning 364–5
   reading 112–14
   religion 7–8
   rooms 125, 127
   self-consciousness 304–5
   solitude 109, 111–12
   subjectivity 363–4
perspective 57–8, 62, 88, 92–3
   Alberti, Leon Battista 81
   Brunelleschi, Filippo 62
   Dürer, Albrecht 93
   Giotto 58–61
   intarsia 91–2
   Leonardo da Vinci 93
   Masaccio 62–3f
   Piero della Francesca 63–5, 66f–8
   studies (rooms) 123–4
   Uccello, Paolo 91–2
   Vasari, Giorgio 92
Perugino, Pietro 89
Peter cures a sick man with his shadow (Masaccio) 63, 64f
Petite Maison, La (The Little House) (Bastide, Jean-François de) 275–6
Petrarch 120–1, 311–12
Philip the Chancellor
   Summa de Bono (*Treatise on Goodness*) 29
Philip II of Pomerania (Duke) 138, 139f
Philippe II (Duc d'Orleans) 210
Philosophical Enquiry into the Origin of Our Ideas into the Sublime and Beautiful (Burke, Edmund) 324, 329
Philosophie dans le boudoir, La (Sade, Marquis de) 277, 278f
philosophy 288–9, 294, 300
phrenology 346–7, 348f, 349f
Picasso, Pablo 361
Pico della Mirandola, Giovanni
   Oration on the Dignity of Man 232

picturesque, the 322, 327–30, 332–5
Pierantoni, Giovanni 341
Piero della Francesca 63–8
    Flagellation of Christ 64–5f
    Ideal City, The 66f, 68, 74
    On Perspective for Painting 67f, 68
    Resurrection 69
Piesse, Septimus 286
Pietà 53f
Pigmalion, ou la Statue animée (Boureau-Deslandes, Andre-François) 294
Piles, Roger de 284
pilgrim mirrors 155
pilgrimages 18–19, 48, 311
Pilgrim's Progress (Bunyan, John) 318
plants
    classification 98–100
    treatises 98, 99f, 100f, 101f
Plato 7, 80, 83
Platonic Academy 83
pleasure 252, 265–8, 281, 300 *see also* sensation *and* sexuality *and* taste (preference)
    Boureau-Deslandes, Andre-François 294
    Buffon, Comte de 293–4
    Condillac, Etienne Bonnot de 293
    gardens 324
    Hutcheson, Francis 299–300
    Pliny the Younger 316
poetry 81, 265
Pompeii 340
Poncelet, Polycarp
    Chimie de gout et d'odorat 286
Poole, Joshua
    English Parnassus; or, A Help to English Poesie 313
Pope, Alexander 315
pornography 265–71
Portrait of a Young Man (Bronzino, Agnolo) 187f
Portrait of a Young Scholar (Brescia, Moretto da) 232–4, 235f
portraits 70–3f, 186, 234, 244–5, 358 *see also* self-portraits
    emotions, portrayal of 241–7
    facial expressions 241–2f
    momentariness 245f–9
possessions 133–41
Poussin, Nicolas 283

Poussinistes 283
prayer 117
Price, Uvedale 328–9
Princess de Clèves, La (Fayette, Madame de la) 201
privacy 109, 111–12, 114–15 *see also* solitude
    beds 149
    closets 216, 218
    desks 215–20f
    domestic space 143, 144, 145, 146, 211
    letters 205
private meditation 42
Procession of the Magi (Gozzoli, Benozzo) 71, 74
prophecy 32, 33
Protestantism 232, 242, 244
    Bible, the 96–8
    Gothic style 339
    imagery 96, 97–8
    individuality 253
    melancholy 232
    momento mori 232
    mortality 232
    Reformation, the 93–8
Prudentius
    Psychomachia (The Battle of Souls) 217
Pseudo-Marcuola
    Gian Gastone de' Medici in bed receiving the young Cosimo Riccardi 150–1f
Psychologia Empirica (Wolff, Christian) 301
Psychologia Rationalis (Wolff, Christian) 301
psychological autonomy 364
psychological novels 201
psychology 301, 302–3, 307–9, 364, 365
Psychomachia (The Battle of Souls) (Prudentius) 217
public
    art appreciation 8, 340, 343–4, 360, 364
    domestic space 211, 220–2
    reading 112, 113
Pugin, A. W. N. 338, 339
Pygmalion 294–7

Quarrel between the Ancients and the Moderns 238–9

Quiccheberg, Samuel van
  Inscriptiones vel tituli teatri amplissimi (*Inscriptions or labels for the most complete theatre*) 136–8

Ragionamenti ('Dialogues') (Aretino, Pietro) 265
Raimondi, Marcantonio 261, 262, 265
Rambouillet, hôtel de 190–3
Rambouillet, Marquise de (Catherine de Vivonne-Savelli) 149–50, 189, 190–1
Raphael 87, 345, 346, 349f, 360–1
  Madonna of the Goldfinch 90f–1
  School of Athens, The 232, 234f
ratios 66
reading 112–14, 147, 197–202, 210
Reading from Molière (Troy, Jean-Françoise de) 210, 211f
realism 57–61, 62, 71, 88–91
Reformation, the 93–4
Regents of the Children's Almshouse in Haarlem (Bray, Jan de) 246f
Reid, Thomas 310
relationships 172–3, 177–80, 181, 189, 195–6
relics 17–20f, 40, 94–5
religion 7–8, 336 *see also* Christianity *and* Church, the
  art 349–51, 354, 355
  Buddhism 336
  conformity 205
  Descartes, René 104–5
  Islam 35
  sexuality 265–7
religious ecstasy 252–5, 269–70
reliquaries 19–20f, 21f
Rembrandt Harmenszoon van Rijn 247–8f
  Self-portrait with beret, wide eyed 248f
Renaissance, the 56, 360, 363
Republic of United Provinces 242, 244
Resurrection, the 54–6, 69
Resurrection (Piero della Francesca) 69
Retorica della puttane (The Whore's Rhetoric) (Pallavicino, Ferrante) 266–7
Reveries of the Solitary Walker (Rousseau, Jean-Jacques) 325–6
Rhetorica ad Herennium (*Rhetoric for Herennius*) 128

Richardson, Samuel 204
  Pamela, or Virtue Rewarded 203f–5
rinascita 82
Robson, Simon
  Courte of Civill Courtesie, The 183
rococo style 211–13, 279, 300, 307–8
Rochefoucauld, François de la 202
Roman Empire 264, 339–42
  coinage 264
romance 177–8, 182
  novels 198–201
Romano, Giulio. *See* Giulio Romano
Romberch, Johannes Host von 130, 131f
Roubo, Andre-Jacob
  L'Art du Menuisier ('Art of the Joiner') 215
Rousham 321–2
Rousseau, Jean-Jacques 297, 325–6f, 375 n. 17
  Julie, ou La Nouvelle Héloïse 204–5
  Reveries of the Solitary Walker 325–6
Rubenistes 283
Rubens, Peter Paul 283
  Judgement of Paris, The 260
Rückenfigur (back-figure) 351–3, 354
Rudolph II (Holy Roman Emperor) 138–9
ruelles 150
Rule (Benedict, Saint) 110–11, 113, 172–3, 174
Rupert of Deutz 29–30

sacramentals 16, 36
sacraments 10–19f, 24
Sacred Theory of the Earth, The (Burnet, Thomas) 313–15
Sade, Marquis de 205
  Philosophie dans le boudoir, La 277, 278f
'Salon de la Princess', Hôtel de Soubise (Boffrand, Germain) 212f, 277
salons 150, 189–92, 197, 212f, 277
Salvator Mundi (Leonardo da Vinci) 367 n. 3
San Marco, Florence 116
San Michele, Oleggio 22, 23f
San Nicolo, Treviso frescoes (Tommaso da Modena) 117–18f
Saunderson, Nicholas 287
Schalcken, Godfried 245
School of Athens, The (Raphael) 232, 234f

Scudéry, Madeleine de 194–7, 201
  Amorous Letters by Various Contemporary Authors 194, 195
  Artamène, ou Le Grand Cyrus 196
  Carte de Tendre 195–6f, 318
  Clélie 196, 197
  Conversation on the Manner of Writing Letters 195
  Conversations 195, 196
  Conversations on Diverse Subjects 194–5
sculpture 80–2, 293–6f, 340–2, 357f–8
seating 142
Sebastian, Saint 254, 256f
secrecy 218–20
secrétaires 218–19f
security 134f–5
self-assurance 186–8
self-awareness 79–80
  Descartes, René 104
  mirrors 157–8, 160
  self-portraits 249–51
self-consciousness 304–5
self-expression 344
self-perception 304, 306–7
Self-Portrait (Dürer, Albrecht) 75–8, 79
Self-Portrait (Gumpp, Johannes) 249–50f
Self-portrait with beret, wide eyed (Rembrandt Harmenszoon van Rijn) 248f
self-portraits 70–1, 72f, 73–9, 158
  Baegert, Derick 71
  Botticelli, Sandro 71, 74
  Dürer, Albrecht 74–8, 79
  emotions 247–8
  Gozzoli, Benozzo 71, 74
  Leonardo da Vinci 367 n. 3
  Medici, Leopold de 250–1f
  Nicholas of Cusa 79
  Rembrandt Harmenszoon van Rijn 247–8f
  self-awareness 249–51
  Vasari, Giorgio 84
  viewing 249–50
  Weyden, Rogier van der 78
self-reference 4, 8
  mirrors 157–8
self-reflexivity 7
self-sense 5–8, 225, 262, 364–5 *see also* personal identity

Kant, Immanuel 171, 308–9
  novels 200
sensation 281, 285, 286–7, 298 *see also* senses, the
  Addison, Joseph 299
  blushing 284
  Boureau-Deslandes, Andre-François 294
  Buffon, Comte de 293–4
  Condillac, Etienne Bonnot de 289–93
  Diderot, Denis 287–8
  Pygmalion 294–7
sensationism 288
senses, the 281, 285, 288, 361
  classification 281
  Diderot, Denis 287–8
  hearing 285–6, 287–8, 290
  pleasure 300
  smell 286, 289–90
  taste 284–5, 286, 298–9
  touch 291, 293
  vision. *See* vision
Sentences (Lombard, Peter) 28
Sepolcri, Dei (*The Sepulchres*) (Foscolo, Ugo) 357
Serenus of Marseilles 35
sexuality 252
  ambivalence 260–1
  architecture 275–7, 279
  Church, the 265–6
  classical mythology 255–63, 271–2
  coinage 264
  dramatisation 252–4
  Giulio Romano 261–4
  handkerchief 280f
  imagery 271f–4f
  interior design 274–7, 279
  masturbation 270
  narratives 252–5
  nudity 256, 258–61
  Old Testament imagery 261
  poetry 265
  pornography 265–71
  religious ecstasy 252–5, 269–70
Shaftesbury 3rd Earl of (Anthony Ashley Cooper) 315
Shakespeare, William
  Twelfth Night 261
Shamela (Fielding, Henry) 205

Sic et Non (Yes and No) (Abelard, Peter) 29, 129
silent reading 113
Simonides of Ceos 127–8
Sir Brooke Boothby (Wright, Joseph of Derby) 327*f*
smell 286, 289–90
smoothness 324
social conventions 172–3, 177
sociability 179–80, 189–95, 207, 210
  toilette, the 222*f*
solars 144, 146
solitude 109–12, 114
  boudoirs 277
  Dominican order 115–18*f*
  Federico da Montefeltro (Duke of Urbino) 120–5
  Jerome, Saint 28, 118–20*f*
  Montaigne, Michel de 127
  study and 114–16, 117–25
Sonetti Lussuriosi ('Lustful Sonnets') (Aretino, Pietro) 265
Sorrows of Young Werther, The (Goethe, Johann Wolfgang von) 205
soul, the 7, 30, 240–1, 303, 336
speculation 155
Spelt, Adriaen van der
  Still Life of Flowers with Curtain 106–7*f*
Spenser, Edmund 207
spiritual communion 17
Spiritual Exercises (Ignatius Loyola) 254
sprezzatura 185–6, 187
St Barbara, Kutna Hora 25, 27*f*
St Catherine of Siena Drinking from the Wound in Christ's Side (Cousin, Louis) 254, 257*f*
St Jerome in his Study (Antonello da Messina) 119, 120*f*
St Luke Painting the Virgin and Christ (Vasari, Giorgio) 84, 85*f*
St Peter's Island, Lake Bienne 325–6
St Theresa in Ecstasy (Bernini, Gian Lorenzo) 254, 257*f*
stained-glass windows 86, 87*f*
state beds 150–1*f*
status *see also* hierarchy
  art 107–8, 234–5
  artists 82, 84–7
  beds 149–50*f*

domestic interiors 207–8
gardens 324
knights 175–6
Louis XIV 152–3
Statutes for the Household (Grosseteste, Robert) 173
Sterne, Laurence
  Life and Opinions of Tristram Shandy, Gentleman, The 307, 308*f*
stigmata 49, 50*f*
Still Life of Flowers with Curtain (Spelt, Adriaen van der) 106–7*f*
still life painting 100–4, 105, 106–7*f*
Stoke Edith House 321*f*
storage 134*f*–7*f*, 138–9*f*
Stourhead 322
Stowe 319–20, 321–2, 323
Strawberry Hill 337, 338*f*
Stubbes, Philip
  Anatomie of Abuses 235
studies (rooms) 119–20*f*, 121–7, 130, 133, 147
study (activity) 114–16, 117–25
  Dominican order 115–18*f*
  Federico da Montefeltro (Duke of Urbino) 120–5
  Jerome, Saint 28, 118–20*f*
subjectivity 1, 9, 31, 299–303, 362–4
  Descartes, René 104–5
  Kant, Immanuel 309, 363–4
  Montaigne, Michel de 127
sublime, the 329–30, 340
Summa de Bono (Treatise on Goodness) (Philip the Chancellor) 29
sumptuary laws 134, 235
sundials 161
Suso, Henry 166
  Horologium Sapientiae (The Clock of Wisdom) 166, 167*f*
symbolon 37–8
symbols 37, 88–9, 124–5, 355
  memento mori 232
  mirrors as 158
  senses, the 281
  sexuality 252
synderesis 28–9

tables 223–4
tapestries 87

taste (preference) 298, 300, 319, 356 *see also* aesthetics
  Addison, Joseph 298–9
  aesthetics 300–1
  associationism 301–2
  Hutcheson, Francis 299–300
  Kant, Immanuel 309–10
  natural world 328–9
  subjectivity 302
taste (sense) 284–5, 286, 298–9
tazza 186
tea bowls 224–5
technology 9
Ten-Stringed Psaltery, The (Joachim of Fiore) 31*f*
Teniers the Younger, David 140–1
  Archduke Leopold Wilhelm in his Gallery 140*f*
texts 112*f*, 113–14
Theodulf of Orleans 36
  Libri Carolini (*Books of Charlemagne*) 36
theologians 114
Theresa of Avila, Saint 254–5, 271
Thérèse Philosophe (d'Argens, Marquis) 269–71*f*
Thomas Aquinas, Saint 88–9
thoughts 2–4
Three Maries at the Tomb 54
thresholds 354
time, abstract notion of 170–1
time-keeping 161
  art 249
  bell towers 162–3
  books of hours 161–2
  clocks 164–70
  Harrison, John 170
  longitude 170
  momentariness 245*f*–9
  sundials 161
  verge escapement 164–6
Tintern Abbey (Gilpin, William) 331*f*
Titian
  Danae 259*f*
  Virgin and Child with St John, The 282–3*f*
toilet services 221–2*f*
toilette, the 220–2*f*
Tommaso da Modena
  San Nicolo, Treviso frescoes 117–18*f*

touch 291, 293
Trait[t]é de l'origine des Romans (Huert, Pierre Daniel) 198–200
transubstantiation 11–13, 17, 94
Trattato della pittura (*Treatise on Painting*) (Leonardo da Vinci) 81
travel 135
Treatise of Human Nature (Hume, David) 306–7
Treatise on the Sensations (Condillac, Etienne Bonnot de) 289, 291
Tres Riches Heures 312*f*
Tribune of Galileo, Florence 357–8
Tribute Money, The (Masaccio) 63*f*
trompe l'oeil painting 105–8
Troy, Jean-Françoise de
  Reading from Molière 210, 211*f*
Turin Shroud 40
Twelfth Night (Shakespeare, William) 261

Uccello, Paolo 91–2
universal materialism 294
Upanishads 336
Urbanus Magnus ('Book of the Civilised Man') (Daniel of Beccles) 180
Urbino, Duke of (Federico da Montefeltro) 120–5, 130

vanitas paintings 102, 103*f*
Varchi, Benedetto 82
Vasari, Giorgio 92, 186, 282
  Lives of the Most Excellent Painters, Sculptors and Architects 61, 82
  St Luke Painting the Virgin and Christ 84, 85*f*
Vatican, the 342
Velázquez, Diego
  Flagellated Christ Contemplated by a Christian Soul 254, 255*f*
Venice 154
Venus dans le cloître (Barrin, Jean) 267–8
verbal language 5–6
verge escapement 164–6
Vergne, Gabriel-Joseph de La (comte de Guilleragues) 202
Vermeer, Johannes
  Woman Reading 192, 194*f*
Veronese, Paolo 95
  Feast in the House of Levi, The 95, 180
  Last Supper, The 95

Veronica, Saint 40
Versailles, Chateau of 152*f*–3*f,* 210, 237
Via Dolorosa 48
viewer, the 78, 108, 249–50, 260–1, 347
   see also perspective *and* vision
   Arena Chapel fresco cycle (Giotto) 59, 61, 62
   eye contact 71–2, 73–9, 186, 367 n. 3
   Monk by the Sea, The (Friedrich, Caspar David) 355, 356*f*
   Rückenfigur (back-figure) 352–3, 354
Villas of the Ancients Illustrated (Castell, Robert) 316–17*f*
Vimont, Joseph 346–7
Virgin, the 145, 147–8*f*
Virgin and Child with St John, The (Titian) 282–3*f*
virtues 227
vision 88, 281–5, 287, 288–9, 290, 291
   see also viewer, the
   God and 78–80
   line of beauty 213
Vision Dei 78
Vision of Piers Plowman (Langland, William) 144
Vivonne-Savelli, Catherine de (Marquise de Rambouillet) 149–50, 189, 190
Voiture, Vincent 193
volcanoes 340
voyeurism 261, 269
Vulgate, the 118

Walhalla Hall of Fame 357*f*
Walpole, Horace 320–1, 322, 337
   History of Modern Taste in Gardening 320
Wanderer above a Sea of Fog, The (Friedrich, Caspar David) 352*f*–3
Watteau, Antoine 300
Watts, George Frederic 358
   Memorial to Heroic Self-Sacrifice 358*f,* 359
Weiditz, Hans
   Herbarum vivae eicones (*Living Images of Plants*) 98, 99*f*
Well-Stocked Kitchen, with Jesus in the House of Mary and Martha, The (Beuckelaer, Joachim) 101, 102*f*
West Wycombe Park 324, 325*f*
Weyden, Rogier van der
   Justice of Trajan 78
Whately Thomas 323, 324
whore dialogues 265, 266
windows 145–7*f,* 191
   stained-glass windows 86, 87*f*
Wolff, Christian
   Psychologia Empirica 301
   Psychologia Rationalis 301
Woman before the Setting Sun, The (Friedrich, Caspar David) 352–3
Woman Reading (Vermeer, Johannes) 192, 194*f*
women 149–50, 158, 177–8
   letter-writing 192
   novels 199
   sexuality 265
   sociability 190
   toilette, the 220–2*f*
words 4–6
work ethic 244
Wright, Joseph of Derby 326
   Sir Brooke Boothby 327*f*
Wright, Thomas
   Passions of the Minde, The 186, 240
writing chairs 215
writing desks 215–20*f*

Young Woman at her Toilet (Bellini, Giovanni) 158, 159*f*

Zayde (Fayette, Madame de la) 198

www.ingramcontent.com/pod-product-compliance
Lightning Source LLC
Chambersburg PA
CBHW071236300426
44116CB00008B/1058